New Zealand Yearbook of International Law

New Zealand Yearbook of International Law

(this *Yearbook* covers the period 1 January 2017 to 31 December 2017)

General Editor

Róisín Burke (*University of Canterbury, New Zealand*)

Associate Editor

Christian Riffel (*University of Canterbury, New Zealand*)

Book Reviews Editor

Annick Masselot (*University of Canterbury, New Zealand*)

Editorial Assistant

George Wietzke (*University of Canterbury, New Zealand*)

VOLUME 15, 2017

The titles published in this series are listed at *brill.com/nzyb*

New Zealand Yearbook of International Law

Volume 15, 2017

Edited by

Róisín Burke
Christian Riffel

BRILL
NIJHOFF

LEIDEN | BOSTON

Typeface for the Latin, Greek, and Cyrillic scripts: "Brill". See and download: brill.com/brill-typeface.

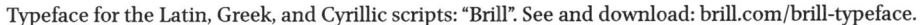

ISSN 1176-6417
ISBN 978-90-04-38791-1 (hardback)
ISBN 978-90-04-38793-5 (e-book)

Contents

The South Pacific

The Year in Review

New Zealand State Conduct

Book Reviews

Preface

The editors are pleased to publish this 15th volume of the *New Zealand Yearbook of International Law* covering the year 2017.

The first five articles in this volume are a series of papers developed following a symposium on increasing risks posed by transnational security threats, and the resultant growth in cross-border and multi-level integration in criminal law and co-operation mechanisms in state responses to these threats. This is particularly evident at a regional level, including in the Pacific and Europe. An insightful overview is provided by Hopkins and Boister on these series of papers and the complexity of legal issues covered by them, from corruption in Europe and the Pacific, Brexit and policing cooperation implications, the European Arrest Warrant, to the ever more topical issue of cybercrime.

This is followed by a paper by Murphy, who provides an important insight into recent developments in international criminal law on command responsibility and the impact of the International Criminal Court's Appeals Chamber decision in the *Bemba* case in June 2018. Command responsibility, which is set out in Article 28 of the *Rome Statute*, is a well-established mode for capturing individual criminal responsibility in international criminal law. In a simplified explanation, this mode of liability may arise, under certain circumstances, where commanders fail in their duty to exercise effective command and control over their subordinates or fail to hold them effectively to account when they commit atrocities under international criminal law. The recent Appeals Judgement by the International Criminal Court, which acquitted the Defendant in the *Bemba* case,[1] appears to have altered the threshold under international criminal law for conviction under the mode of command responsibility. Murphy's paper is timely in its critique and apt observations of the *Bemba* case and its potential implications for the concept of command responsibility as a mode of criminal liability in international criminal law.

This brings us to the next paper by Bartlett, whose article provides an interesting reflection on the power dynamics of private actors in shaping international law, illustrating this through global standard setting and the International Organisation for Standardisation ("ISO"). In essence, ISO standards are key to international trade law and in many ways, as the author demonstrates, impact on the global economy and the everyday lives of people. The author reflects on the operations of the ISO and their politicisation, which he

---

1   *Bemba Appeal* (International Criminal Court, Appeals Chamber, Case No ICC 01/05-01/08 A, 8 June 2018).

argues have a number of implications for international law. Firstly, he discusses how these mechanisms effect power dispersals, not least through increase in transaction cost, and marginalise weaker actors, often in the interests of wealthier states. Secondly, the author argues the ISO processes disempower citizens, including by blurring domestic and international contexts, and divert this power rather to a global private organisation. Ultimately, the author contends this process favours industry interests, and not those of states, NGOs, and citizens.

This volume includes a regular update by Angelo on the activities and developments with respect to the Pacific Island Forum. Yearly, the Yearbook encourages submissions on issues of international law affecting the South Pacific Region. The Year in Review section focuses inwardly and outwardly on New Zealand and its role in contemporary international law during the 2017 year. It covers international human rights law, indigenous peoples' rights under international law, international economic law, international environmental law, law of the sea and fisheries, the Antarctic treaty system, international criminal law and international humanitarian law, and international law and security. The commentators provide a brief overview and commentary on New Zealand's practice and developments with respect to each of these areas of international law during 2017. The Year in Review continues with a comprehensive report on New Zealand state conduct with respect to Treaty Action and Implementation in New Zealand for the period from July 2016 to June 2017. The Yearbook ends with a number of book reviews.

The views of the authors throughout are naturally their own.

The Editors wish to extend their gratitude to the Advisory Board, the academics who continue to provide annual contributions to the Yearbook, the authors contributing to this volume, and other academics, practitioners and government officials from New Zealand and globally who continue to support the development of this publication. A particular thanks to members of the Advisory Board and those taking the time to review contributions.

Finally, we would like to thank a number of individuals, without whom the publication of this Volume would not have been feasible. We would like to thank our Book Reviews Editor, Professor Annick Masselot, and our Editorial Assistant, George Wietzke, for their valuable contributions and hard work in producing the Yearbook.

Dr Róisín Burke
Editor

Dr Christian Riffel
Associate Editor

Articles and Commentaries

∵

Symposium
Multi-Level Responses to Security Threats: All in this Together?

Neil Boister and W. John Hopkins*

1   Trans-National Crime and the Regional Turn

The perception that there is an ever increasing risk from transnational security threats has led states in diverse parts of the globe to develop cross-border and multi-level integration (particularly at the regional level) most recently in the field of criminal law. The accepted view is that no individual state can achieve suppression of these criminal activities without cooperation from regional partners and thus such collaboration is required to address their growth. However, such functional regionalism in the field of criminal law creates a significant constitutional tension with the traditional state based approach to the field. This tension also leads to practical problems primarily through the continued dominance of the sovereign state model at the international level.

The aim of the symposium from which the following papers are drawn was to provide an opportunity for discussion of this risk identification and regional response in a Pacific context. The symposium presented a number of case studies that explore the kinds of criminal problems that can emerge at a regional level and different multi-level responses that have been developed to address, particularly in Europe, the incubator of the world's most advanced and innovative regional mechanisms.

2   Trans-National Crime in Europe and the Pacific

The first contribution, by Graham Hassall, deals with a delicate topic, "Corruption in Pacific Island Countries". It has two main elements: an examination of the magnitude of corruption in the South Pacific region in so far as this is actually discoverable, and an overview of the anti-corruption activities undertaken in the region. In regard to the assessment of the level of corruption, relying on a bewildering variety of existing sources, Hassall explores the types of corruption that are evident in the region, but also examines the premise of this exploration – what constitutes corruption – as well as the loaded issue

---

*   Professors, Law School, University of Canterbury.

© KONINKLIJKE BRILL NV, LEIDEN, 2019 | DOI:10.1163/9789004387935_002

of whether there is any room for cultural variations in the definition of acts of corruption. Hassall's assessment of the response provides a complete overview of the multi-level responses by identifying the anti-corruption measures in place domestically, regionally, and as a result of global commitments. He then goes on to assess how successful they are, and tries to answer the vexed question at the centre of much of the transposition like those developed against corruption. Can corruption be eradicated through the "external" imposition of global security agendas or is the internalisation of anti-corruption norms at "grass-roots" in the affected societies a necessary condition of success?

The contribution by Susanne Reindl-Krauskopf, "Anti-Corruption Measures from a European Perspective", provides a useful comparator to Hassall's piece as it provides a closer look at some of the regional mechanisms introduced to reduce corruption in Europe and their implementation at state level. Reindl-Krauskopf's piece takes corrupt activities as a given, and first provides an outline of the relevant European legal instruments before moving on to a closer look at the implementation of these regional measures in a European state, Austria. At the European level, she identifies not an EU instrument but rather the Council of Europe's *Convention on Corruption of 1999* (a standard intergovernmental regional treaty) as providing the crucial legal instrument for the European regional response. Reindl-Krauskopf highlights that this *Convention* was the precursor to many of the, now standard, substantive and procedural anti-corruption responses developed more recently in European and United Nations instruments. At the national level, she explores how Austria has responded to its international obligations by changing elements of its policing law and criminal procedure. In the Austrian case this led to institutional change including setting up specialized anti-corruption agencies as well as the introduction of an internet based "whistle-blower" system (under the ambit of the public prosecutor's office) in 2013.

Farsam Salimi provides a further piece on regional responses to a specific crime entitled "Cybercrime Threats, Offences and Special Investigation Measures from a European Perspective". This is a phenomenon against which the South Pacific region appears particularly unprepared and in regard to which its geographic isolation is irrelevant as a shield. Salimi points out that the intrinsically transnational nature of cybercrime renders borders and distance meaningless, and the growing connectedness of countries in the region to the rest of the globe simply increases the opportunity for criminal activities like hacking or denial of service attacks. Echoing the other contributors, he emphasises the necessity of multi-level responses, and explores various actions taken at a regional and national level to close legal loopholes and whether these provide adequate responses. He emphasises, however, that simply increasing the scope of substantive criminal offences will not have the desired effect, and that multi-national harmonization of the legal basis for transnational criminal investigations is necessary to act effectively against cybercrime. His discussion of these new measures includes the latest regional innovations such as the European Production and Preservation Order, which permits the authorities of a Member State to order Internet Service Providers that offer services in the EU to produce or preserve electronic evidence, wherever that data is physically held.

In his piece entitled "The European Arrest Warrant: Pitfalls and Promises", Harmen van der Wilt turns his attention to that archetype of closer, speedier, simpler regional cooperation in criminal matters, the European Arrest Warrant ("EAW"). Based on his own personal experience as a judge in the Dutch District Court on International Cooperation in Criminal Matters and a discussion of case law of the European Court of Human Rights, he first outlines the fundamental assumptions on which the EAW is predicated, namely, the principle of mutual recognition within an area of "freedom, justice and security" and the manifestations of those assumptions in the EAW itself, such as dispensing with double criminality for a range of crimes. He then takes a critical view of the idea that the EAW has rendered interstate differences in criminal law and procedure on the surrender of fugitives irrelevant and ensured that domestic courts do not scrutinize the case behind EAW requests. Instead he argues that practice has shown that these aspirations have not been met and that Courts still find ways to interpose dual criminality and question the quality of the criminal justice systems in the Member States issuing these warrants. In addition, differences between state approaches and a lack of understanding of unfamiliar "foreign" processes means that elements of requests are often "lost in translation".

The final piece raises a different type of predicament, namely what happens when states become very reliant on regional support against transnational organised crime but then for political reasons the state in question decides to withdraw from the regional structures as a whole. What Liz Campbell illustrates in her aptly entitled "Brexit and the policing of transnational organised crime in Europe" is that the United Kingdom has committed heavily to and now relies upon many of the EU's regional innovations against transnational crime. She signals out Europol (the European Police Office), Eurojust (the EU's judicial cooperation unit), the EU's version of joint investigation teams ("JITS"), the EAW and the European Investigation Order ("EIO" – an order issued in one member state for the gathering of evidence in another) as among the principal legal and institutional mechanisms to which the UK wants to retain access in a post-Brexit world. But she notes that this desire to retain the status quo is likely to come at a highly uncomfortable price for Brexiteers, namely continued supervision by the Court of Justice of the EU.

3   The Limits of Regional Criminal Co-operation

The papers in this section provide clear evidence both that regional co-operation in the field of transnational crime (as a sub-set of the security co-operation) is possible and that such developments should come with a health warning. Criminal lawyers and particularly those who practice the prosecutorial arts often divorce their subject from the social and political context in which it operates. Crimes are "essentialised" as a global or regional norm applicable across states and jurisdictions. However, even the most normative of criminal activities can raise political issues when placed in the context of other states. As Hassall notes in the Pacific context, "corruption" in the western sense is embedded in the cultural and political practices of many Pacific Island states and while some of these practices would also draw criticism from Pacific Island communities many are regarded as acceptable. By contrast many countries may engage in corrupt practices that are not defined as corruption under this definition (for example, the favouring of a friend network, sometimes referred to as "mateship" in Australia and New Zealand). These practices may be equally or more corrosive to the Rule of Law than financial corruption but will escape opprobrium as such behaviour falls outside the "international" norms which apply.

Even in Europe where a degree of cultural commonality and norm acceptance applies, differences in approach between the Common and Civil traditions leads to significant issues. As van der Wilt explores, the procedural focus of the Common Law creates frustration and confusion amongst civilian prosecutors while the civilian traditions of non-extradition of citizens leads to similar frustrations amongst Common law colleagues. However, the legal differences tend to obscure deeper concerns about the operation of criminal law in different European states. As van der Wilt also makes clear in his article, societal interests continue to play a role.

Recent attempts by Spanish prosecutors to use the EAW to extradite the exiled former leaders of the Catalan government have exposed this very clearly and put further strain on regional criminal co-operation. The use of EAWs in these cases, particularly as they were used selectively and in certain EU jurisdictions (where one assumes that the Spanish prosecutors felt they had a greater chance of success), threatened to expose the political and constitutional elements of the EAW in a way which may make its continued use untenable. In essence, the reluctance of several European state courts (Germany and Scotland being the most notable) to extradite the Catalan leaders (ostensibly on procedural grounds) reflects deep seated concerns that the politicians concerned should not be being tried for "rebellion". The decision by the current Spanish authorities to row back from such aggressive and political use of the EAW may prove to be crucial to the survival of the model.

If Europe suffers from these political problems with the application of the EAW, in a region where common cultural norms are relatively strong, it should be no surprise that developing such regional responses in a region as diverse as the Pacific, raises far more fundamental questions. In the South Pacific, democracy may be the norm, but significant problems remain around the application of the Rule of Law (e.g., Fiji, Nauru) and the operation of one party states (e.g., Samoa). The level of trust that exists across European criminal justice systems is simply not shared in the South Pacific. This is particularly true when one draws the Pacific lens wider. Criminal co-operation with many states in the wider Pacific and ASEAN regions, for example, requires dealing with states where the conception of the Rule of Law is fundamentally different and at times at odds with western norms. The idea that criminal co-operation with China, for example, can be undertaken without reference to political and constitutional norms, is fanciful. The nature of the Chinese system (the formal role of political bodies in the judicial process and the prevalence of closed trials are merely two examples) make co-operation difficult at best and constitutionally fraught at worst.

4 Trans-National Criminal Law and Constitutionalism

The inescapable and inconvenient truth is that criminal co-operation cannot be separated from the wider constitutional, cultural and political contexts in which it operates. Criminal law is public law, recognised by and reflective of its communities and the institutional frameworks that support it at the domestic level. Establishing co-operative frameworks in the field without the accompanying constitutional scaffolding that accompanies it in domestic contexts will always raise questions around legitimacy and accountability. In a region like Europe where there is a high level of mutual trust and a degree of institutional scaffolding to support it then such co-operation will be possible, if still fraught with difficulty at the controversial edges. In regions which lack either cultural affinity or mutually compatible approaches to criminal law, such co-operation becomes fraught with problems. The areas of effective and legitimate co-operation are reduced to those in which norms are shared by the systems concerned. In the South Pacific region this is further complicated as perceived universal regional or global norms (in corruption for example) are often externally imposed by an international order which has little relevance to the specific South Pacific island context. In this context, effective and legitimate transnational criminal co-operation becomes even more difficult. To resolve these difficulties requires a recognition of the public nature of the criminal law and the development of international and regional institutions to hold such public decisions accountable. Without it, such co-operation is likely to remain at the margins, to the detriment of both the states concerned and their citizens.

Taken together these pieces suggest some fundamental insights particularly about regional alignment against a security threat like transnational crime. First, the "real" alignment of different states in a region is very difficult to achieve and there are a number of preconditions. These may include a shared commitment to basic standards of due process and treatment (that level of commitment may be relatively low so long as all states share it, although for obvious reasons this is undesirable). Second, alignment can be achieved at a "paper" level in part by a rhetorical commitment to the same values. However, once enforcement agencies in cooperating states begin to realise the instrumental value of this alignment, in a Weberian response their level of commitment can rise steeply, leaving that of the general populace far behind. Finally, the ideal of a strong and authentic internal commitment to these norms by the community of individuals within a region in a Durkheimian sense appears extremely difficult to realise.[1] Although models of technical regionalism have proved successful, particularly in Europe, perhaps deep trans-national criminal co-operation is a step too far for technically advanced but un-constitutionalised regionalism.

---

1   R. Cotterrell, "The Concept of Crime and Transnational Netowrks of Community" in V Mitsilegas, P Alldridge and L Cheliotis (eds), *Globalisation, Criminal Law and Criminal Justice* (Hart, 2015) 7, 10 et seq.

Law, Culture, and Corruption in the Pacific Islands

Graham Hassall[*]

1 The Pacific Islands: Corruption and Context

This paper surveys the challenge of corruption in the context of the small island developing states of the Pacific Islands. It is part of a wider study that seeks to not merely document instances of corruption in the region,[1] but to understand their socio-legal circumstances, and the policy and legal remedies capable of strengthening their integrity systems. Being an overview of the region, the paper does not seek to review all 22 populated Pacific Island territories.

There are many sensitivities associated with discussion of the topic of corruption in the Pacific Islands.[2] Whereas a legal text analysis focuses on questions of law, the cultural and political context is also important.[3] Who is speaking of corruption in the Pacific? And for what purposes? What definitions are applied, and who developed them? Exposing corruption affects the reputation of countries, governments, business communities, investors, and individual leaders. One might say all this is merely a matter of law and its application, but in small states that feel vulnerable under the relentless forces of globalization, national pride and reputation are valued highly, and preference may be given to addressing corruption internally rather than through international scrutiny.

---

[*] School of Government, Victoria University of Wellington. This paper was presented at the CIAR annual symposium: "Multi-Level Responses to Transnational Security Threats: are we really all in this together?" *Victoria University Wellington, Faculty of Law,* 2 October 2017.

1 *Transnational Security – Regional Integration in the Suppression of Transnational Crimes,* European Union Centres Network <https://jeanmonnet.nz/european-union-centres-network/>.

2 The term "Pacific" is invariably used to denote the states and peoples of the Pacific Ocean. But one must be careful when addressing specific social, historical, political, legal, or economic issues across the region, for these comprise diversity as well as commonality. The region is home to approximately 10 million inhabitants, spread across thousands of islands, which in modern times have evolved into 12 sovereign states and eight additional non-sovereign states. In the colonial period, traditional law was largely superseded by introduced law of colonial powers: *Anglo-English* (Tonga, Solomon Islands, Pitcairn, Fiji, and Vanuatu); *Anglo-Australian* (Papua New Guinea, Nauru); *Anglo-New Zealand* (Cook Islands, Western Samoa and Niue); *French* (Marquesas, Tahiti, Wallis & Futuna, New Caledonia and Vanuatu); *Spanish-Japanese-American* (Marshall Islands, Guam, Northern Marianas, Truk, Yap, Kosrae, Ponape); and *American* (American Samoa, Hawaii).

3 See Grant W Walton and Jon ST Quah, "Silent Screams and Muffled Cries" (2016) 5(2) *Asian Education and Development Studies* 211.

Furthermore, whereas some Pacific Island Countries have been tagged in the literature as "failed states", Pacific Island commentators generally prefer the alternative term "fragile", provided that the analysis is sufficiently nuanced: corruption is best understood – in this line of argument – in specific historical and cultural contexts.[4]

So, is corruption best understood as a problem of law, culture, or ethics? The cultural argument suggests that there are practices that were traditionally acceptable which modern law has failed to appreciate or accommodate. Traditions of "gift-giving", for instance, have been put forward as traditional "reciprocity relationships"[5] which do not include or imply an intent to corrupt.[6] Electoral candidates, when interacting with communities during campaign periods, are said to face traditional obligations to "bear gifts" which are signs of hospitality rather than inducements for votes. In Gilbertese culture, for instance, a gift was traditionally used to introduce a person to the spirit of a place. *Bubuti*, a traditionally accepted method of distributing resources within the extended family (in which a request for specific assistance or gift could not be refused), has spread in contemporary times into exchange relationships in contemporary politics. Gift-giving is integral to Samoa's traditional chiefly (*matai*) system, although Tuimaleali'ifano has documented the "corruption" of these processes under the pressures of the cash economy.[7]

In the Melanesian cultures of the South-West Pacific, the "big man" was traditionally expected to not only possess wealth, but to distribute it for the benefit of all; this value system has transferred over to expectations of Members of Parliament and even senior public servants. Huffer argues that until Pacific indigenous concepts of ethics and law are better understood, efforts to "combat" corruption that rely on formal laws and Western notions of "good governance" are destined for continued failure.[8]

---

4   Resina Katafono, "The Commonwealth Pacific Small States: The Future in the Mirror of the Past" in Resina Katafono (ed), *A Sustainable Future for Small States* (Commonwealth Secretariat, 2017).

5   Maxine Pitts, *Crime, Corruption and Capacity in Papua New Guinea* (Asia Pacific Press, 2002). Sefulu I. Ioane, "Turmoil in Paradise: A View of the Sociopolitical Upheavals in Western Samoa, Consequent on the Marriage-of-Convenience between the Fa'a-Samoa and Western-Oriented Democratic Ideaologies" (1983) 92(4) *The Journal of the Polynesian Society* 521.

6   Peter Larmour, "Culture and Corrruption in the Pacific Islands: Some Conceptual Issues and findings from Studies of National Integrity Systems" in *Asia Pacific School of Economics and Government. Discussion Papers* (Australian National University, 2006).

7   A Morgan Tuimaleali'ifano, "Matai Titles and Modern Corruption in Samoa: Costs, Expectations and Consequences for Families and Society" in Stewart Firth (ed), *Globalisation and Governance in the Pacific Islands* (ANU ePress, 2006).

8   Elise Huffer, "Governance, Corruption, and Ethics in the Pacific" (2005) 17(1) *The Contemporary Pacific* 118.

The challenge of ensuring integrity in government is, of course, a global one. The United Nations ("UN") estimates that corruption, bribery, theft and tax evasion cost some US$1.26 trillion for developing countries per year. The UN's "human development" perspective counts the cost of corruption not only in economic terms, but in terms of "...eroded opportunities, increased marginalization of the disadvantaged and feelings of injustice...".[9] The UN has included targets for promoting the rule of law, and substantially reducing corruption and bribery in all their forms in Goal 16 of its "2030 Agenda for Sustainable Development Sustainable Development", namely "Peace, justice and Strong Institutions".[10]

The size and nature of corruption in Pacific Island countries has been assessed through several regional projects, and by governmental, intergovernmental, and non-governmental bodies. Transparency International ("TI") oversaw "National Integrity System" ("NIS") surveys of 12 Pacific Countries,[11] and reported evidence of:

– Abuse of ministerial and official travel, and unnecessary travel;
– Suspicions of ministerial favouritism towards relatives in appointments, contracts, and scholarships;
– Budget processes distorted by pet projects and what is called (in the case of the Federated States of Micronesia) "pitch and catch" where legislators benefit from expenditure they authorise.[12]

These NIS surveys found, furthermore, that sectors more susceptible to corruption than others included:

– Police and customs;
– Land and titles administration;
– Forestry and fisheries;
– Ports;
– Health and education;
– Retirement funds;
– Tendering;
– Trade in the tokens of sovereignty (Passports, internet domain names);
– Offshore banking (but not offshore trust funds).[13]

---

9   United Nations Development Programme, *Tackling Corruption, Transforming Lives: Accelerating Human Development in Asia and the Pacific* (MacMillan, 2008) vii.

10   *Goal 16: Promote just, peaceful and inclusive societies*, United Nations Sustainable Development Goals <http://www.un.org/sustainabledevelopment/peace-justice/>.

11   A Mellam and D Aloi, "National Integrity Systems Ti Country Study Report: Papua New Guinea 2003" (Report, Papua New Guinea Institute of National Affairs, January 2003).

12   Peter Larmour and Manuhuia Barcham, *National Integrity Systems Pacific Islands* (Overview Report, Transparency International, 2004) 5.

13   Ibid 6.

Just as the scope of corruption has increased in the contemporary period, so too has its visibility, due to the emergence of mass media such as radio and newspapers, the advocacy of non-governmental organisations ("NGOs") and development agencies, and more recently, internet-based social media. These are replete with accusations about corruption and in the case of the social media, much of this is anonymously leaked evidence.

Transparency International's *Corruptions Perceptions Index* only covers two Pacific countries at present: Papua New Guinea and Solomon Islands. However, TI also monitors social media for reports on corruption in 19 Pacific Island countries and territories.[14] Global Integrity, another global NGO, has used a score-card method to survey five Pacific Island Countries (Fiji, Papua New Guinea, Solomon Islands, Tonga, and Vanuatu),[15] in a more rigorous manner than is possible through a "perceptions" index.

The United Nations Development Programme's ("UNDP") Pacific Centre produced a survey in 2007,[16] and the UN's Asia Pacific Human Development Report for 2008 *Tackling Corruption, Transforming Lives: Accelerating Human Development in Asia and the Pacific,*[17] provides a range of case studies from the region, and seeks to systematize an understanding of the phenomenon.

In addition to dedicated anti-corruption sites,[18] the *Facebook* platform carries many pages focused on governance and integrity in individual Pacific Island Countries. Claims not brought before courts for adjudication, however, remain accusations rather than proven facts, and must thus be treated cautiously. Legislation is appearing which allows government to prosecute individuals for online comments. However, this significant increase in public access to information about the activities of governments has not been uniform across countries, and reflects the realities of the "digital divide": the urban Pacific has online "public spaces" in ways the "rural Pacific" does not; but since urban publics to not yet constitute the majority in most countries, their concerns are not felt at constituency-level nation-wide.

---

14   Transparency International <https://www.transparency.org/>.

15   *Countries & Territories covered,* Global Integrity <https://www.globalintegrity.org/research /countries/>.

16   Manuhuia Barcham, *Corruption in Pacific Island Countries* (UNDP Pacific Centre, 2007). See also Manuhuia Barcham "Cleaning up the Pacific: Anti-Corruption Initiatives" (2009) 63(2) *Australian Journal of International Affairs* 249.

17   United Nations Development Programme, *Tackling Corruption, Transforming Lives: Accelerating Human Development in Asia and the Pacific* (MacMillan, 2008).

18   Significant sites include PNG exposed <https://pngexposed.wordpress.com>; and ACT-NOWPNG <http://actnowpng.org/>; See *Stop the Stealing,* Act Now for a Better Papua New Guinea <http://actnowpng.org/campaign/stop%20the%20stealing>.

2   The Political Economy of Corruption

Peiffer has identified clientelism, collusion, and high levels of mistrust as the main features of state-business relations in the Pacific Islands.[19] However, attempts to separate analysis of corruption into distinct spheres such as "public sector" and "private sector" may lose sight of the interrelations between government and non-government actors in such activities – although it is certainly the case that members of the executive and the legislature, as well as senior public servants, are perceived as being the major practitioners of embezzlement, fraud, unsanctioned procurement, collusion, and nepotism.[20] Their transactions include laundering through law firms, either as commissions for services rendered or as compensation claimed from state agencies. Ministers and public servants have been accused of corrupt practices in relation to the allocation of land and housing, awarding of scholarships, and the granting of licences and work permits. In general, those agencies or individuals exercising "gatekeeper" functions, whether for big business or for the humble citizen, are those most open to abuse. Hence, methods for issuing licenses and permits for matters pertaining to land ownership and use, customs, immigration and employment, scholarships, labour, and commerce, are amongst those that require high levels of transparency and integrity.

In the case of Papua New Guinea ("PNG"), high profile instances of corruption by politicians and public servants date from soon after independence, and have generated considerable academic study and commentary.[21] An enquiry into the Forestry Industries Council which commenced in 1987 found corruption entrenched from village level to the National Executive Council, but inadequacies in the legal system prevented the successful prosecution of several

---

19   Caryn Peiffer, *The Politics of State Business Relations in the Pacific What Is Already Documented and What Do We Need to Know?*, Background Paper 13 (2012) *Developmental Leadership Programme* <http://www.dlprog.org/publications/the-politics-of-state -business-relations-in-the-pacific-what-is-already-documented-and-what-do-we-need -to-know.php>.

20   Ron Duncan and Graham Hassall, "How Pervasive is Clientelist Politics in the Pacific?", in Ron Duncan (ed), *The Political Economy of Economic Reform in the Pacific* (Asian Development Bank, 2011) 265–75.

21   Barcham R DeVere, "What Should Be Done About Corruption and Bribery?" (Working Paper, Law Reform Commission of Papua New Guinea, 1982); Bui Mana, "An Anti-Corruption Stategy for Provincial Government in Papua New Guinea" (Working Paper, Asia Pacific School of Economics and Management – Australian National University, 1999); Albert Ayius, "Corruption in Papua New Guinea" in *National Research Institute. Bibliography No. 11* (National Research Institute, 2007); M Pitts, "Crime and Corruption – Does Papua New Guinea Have the Capacity to Control It?" (2001) (16)2 *Pacific Economic Bulletin*.

well-known political figures that the report identified as corrupt. In concluding his enquiry Justice Barnett described the condition of the logging industry
in Papua New Guinea as "a mixture of meandering intellectual neglect, bu-
reaucratic inefficiency and lack of honest political commitment to the vision-
ary ideals of the Constitution", and found that there was no national forestry
policy, no clear management plan, and that control over the industry rested
with a Minister who was not required to place decisions before Cabinet.[22] Accusations concerning corruption in PNG's Forestry Industry have not abated.[23]
Inadequacies of laws concerning bribery and corruption, and proposed legislation to correct them, were documented in the *Papua New Guinea Law Reform
Commission's report No 13 of November 1988, "Bribery and Corruption"*. In subsequent years a great number of national and regional politicians and public
servants have figured in corruption scandals, some of which have resulted in
prosecution and imprisonment. The nation's "founding father" Prime Minister
Sir Michael Somare was referred to the Leadership Code overseen by the Ombudsman Commission and found guilty of failing to provide accurate financial
statements for a period of 20 years.

Reports by Papua New Guinea's Auditor-General ("AGO") and Parliament's
Permanent Committee on Public Accounts ("PAC") have for more than two
decades highlighted the extent of government departments' noncompliance
with their own rules and regulations – with little impact on behaviour. The
Auditor-General has reported concerns about district-level government procurement processes, and about time delays with providing audit reports. Both
statutory bodies and government departments have used "lack of funds" as an
excuse for delays in preparation of their financial reports for inspection by the
AGO which has, in an effort to improve the situation, introduced an internal
control framework and conducted workshops for government departments
and agencies on internal controls, risk, informed communications, and monitoring. In summary, the reports of the AGO reflect the culture of disregard that
exists around public sector finances and diminish any expectation that public
sector ethics will experience rapid rejuvenation. To illustrate the condition of
public sector practices in 2006, for instance, the Public Accounts committee
reported in 2010:

> To the end of 2006, service delivery had faltered and, in some areas failed,
> in large measure the result of fiscal mischief and/or incompetence on

22   Kevin Murphy, "The Rape of PNG" *The Bulletin* (29 August 1989) 32.
23   Jennifer Gabriel and Michael Wood, "The Rimbunan Hijau Group in the Forests of Papua
       New Guinea" (2015) 50(3) *The Journal of Pacific History* 322.

a huge scale by the very persons responsible for properly and lawfully applying public monies–our Public Service at all levels of Government and administration. The results are clear to see in any social indicator of health and education and we believe this situation continues currently.[24]

Despite such feedback senior public servants whose inappropriate actions were highlighted by the PAC had their contracts renewed just weeks afterward; improper use of funds continues to occur; vehicles purchased with public funds are not always placed on a government asset register; and vendors are sometimes paid in a manner that fails basic standards of documentation. There is also a widespread practice of diverting funds from designated purposes, generally in the name of expediency, as well as the practice of diverting funds to trust accounts rather than to consolidated revenue. Up to 2008 the PAC had identified more than 50 public servants for prosecution, not a single one of whom had been brought to trial.[25]

Papua New Guinea is not alone in facing corruption at the highest levels of public office. The story of Nauru's descent from wealth to poverty through the actions of its leaders is well known.[26] Profligate and/or unwise public expenditure, and corruption, reduced one of the world's smallest sovereign states, an independent republic worth AUD 3 billion, to the verge of bankruptcy and potential loss of national sovereign status.[27]

The Solomon Islands, too, has faced considerable problems with corruption in public office. Numerous Prime Ministers have either been accused of corruption or convicted for it. In 2017 the Permanent Secretary in the Ministry of Infrastructure Development was arrested for misuse of funds.[28] Until recently, Vanuatu's most noted episode of corruption in public office had been Minister Barak Sope's effort to defraud the state, which resulted in imprisonment,

---

24   Public Accounts Committee, Parilament of Papua New Guinea, *Inquiry into the Part 1 Report of the Office of the Auditor General for the Financial Year 2006* (2010).

25   R Repe Rambe, "Work of Parliamentary Accounts Committee and the Report of 2007" in Institute of National Affairs (ed), *National Development Forum on Improving the Budget Spending Process: Ensuring Transparency and Accountability at All Levels. Vol. 2: Papers and Discussion* (Institute of National Affairs, 2008).

26   Meibitobure Gaunibwe "The Selling of Nauru" (2004) 68 *Australian Rationalist.*

27   John Connell "Nauru: The First Failed Pacific State?" (2006) 95(383) *The Round Table* 47.

28   *Solomons Permanent Secretary Of The Ministry Of Infrastructure Development Arrested On Multiple Counts Of Corruption* (18 August 2017) Pacific Islands Report <http://www.pireport.org/articles/2017/08/18/solomons-permanent-secretary-ministry-infrastructure-development-arrested>.

followed by a presidential pardon.[29] However, this may now be eclipsed by the 2015 conviction and imprisonment of fourteen Members of Parliament ("MPs") for accepting bribes from former Prime Minister Moana Carcasses to vote Prime Minister Joe Natuman out of office.[30] In Tonga, allegations have been made that a loan provided to the Government by the Exim Bank of China, and overseen by the Nuku'alofa Development Corporation, were not used for projects as set out in the contract.[31] Elsewhere in the Pacific, leaders have been sanctioned for corrupt practices from French Polynesia to the Commonwealth of the Northern Mariana Islands.

A major area of corrupt practice has been obtaining and holding elected office. Although this has often involved some form of inducement offered by candidates to voters (cash, or food, or other goods), it has also at times involved payments between candidates (such as to encourage retirement from a contest, or to switch allegiances), and has even involved payments by candidates for the Office of Head of State. A change from *first-past-the-post* to *limited preferential voting* in Papua New Guinea was justified in part as an effort to curb corruption, since in the *first-past-the-post* system seats could be, in some instances, won with just 5–10% of the vote, making vote-buying somewhat feasible.[32] The shift to *limited preferential voting*, which requires a 50% threshold for success, renders such vote-buying less possible.[33] In countries allied to the Republic of China (Taiwan), incumbent members of parliament have used

---

29   Patrick Keyzer, "The Executive Pardon of Barak Sope The Struggle for Constitutional Standards in the Republic of Vanuatu" (2004) *LAWASIA Journal*; Michael Morgan, "Converging on the Arc of Instability? The Fall of Barak Sope and the Spectre of a Coup in Vanuatu" in Ron May (ed), *"Arc of Instability"? Melanesia in the Early 2000s*, (State, Society and Governance in Melanesia Project, 2002).

30   A good summary is provided in Kelly Buchanan, *Vanuatu: Fourteen Politicians Sentenced to Prison for Corruption* (26 October 2015) Library of Congress < http://www.loc.gov/ law/foreign-news/article/vanuatu-fourteen-politicians-sentenced-to-prison-for-corruption/>. See also Howard van Trease, "Vanuatu" (2017) 29(2) *The Contemporary Pacific* 361.

31   Matthew Dornan and Philippa Brant, "Chinese Assistance in the Pacific: Agency, Effectiveness and the Role of Pacific Island Governments" (2014) 2(1) *Asia and the Pacific Policy Studies* 349–63.

32   Kelly D Edmiston "Fostering Subnational Autonomy and Accountability in Decentralized Developing Countries: Lessons from the Papua New Guinea Experience" (2002) 22(3) *Public Administration and Development* 221, 229.

33   *Limited Preferential Voting*, Electoral Commission of Papua New Guinea <http://www .pngec.gov.pg/docs/default-source/default-document-library/limited_preferential_ voting_.pdf?sfvrsn=0>.

constituency funds to purchase electoral support.[34] There has not been much documented corruption on the part of electoral officials.

Corrupt practices occur at local as much as at national level. Theoretically, devolution of government services to lower levels of government is intended to foster greater accountability and democracy at sub-national levels. In certain circumstances, however, it also increases opportunities for expenditure of public money with minimal oversight, and is thus regarded as a catalyst to increased corruption.[35] This resulted in corruption increasing in local-level governments, as the reforms actually handed over an unprecedented amount of autonomy to MPs, who were assigned to positions at the provincial and local-level, which was previously held by the provinces.

Papua New Guinea's capital district has struggled to establish and maintain a corruption-free administration. When Prime Minister Morauta suspended the National Capital District government in 1999 for "widespread corruption in the administration of the NCDC, gross mismanagement of the commission's financial affairs, a breakdown in administration of the NCD and a pattern by the NCDC of persistently exceeding its powers and disobeying applicable laws",[36] an editorial in one of the national papers expressed despair at the gap between official response, and commonly known transgressions of the law:

> The rorts have been legendary, and many observers believe that the capital's urban government has stayed afloat for years on the basis of massive bribes. There have been persistent rumours of bribes for land allocation and bribes to approve the erection of poorly designed and cheaply constructed buildings. Then there are the bribes to deliver nonsense contracts to stationery and equipment suppliers, the ghost employment of youth and women's groups, and massive unofficial and illegal grants to privileged sporting clubs and cultural groups. At the same time, the NCDC has provided a sheltered and powerful base to aspiring politicians in the NCDC electorates, and the funds and influence to make the leadership of the Commission a highly desirable prize. What is amazing is that all these facts are well-known on the streets, and have long ago

---

34   Matthew Allen, "Politics of Disorder: The Social Unrest in Honiara", in Sinclair Dinnen and Stewart Firth (eds), *Politics and Statebbuilding in Solomon Islands* (Asia Pacific Press, 2008); John Breaithwaite et al., *Pillars and Shadows: Statebuilding as Peacebuilding in Solomon Islands* (ANU E Press, 2010).

35   Mana, above n 21; Edmiston, above n 33.

36   "PNG's National Capital District Government Suspended for Corruption", *The National* (*PNG*), 7 September 1999.

ceased to titillate even the most gossip-starved citizen. Yet action has been time and again thwarted, or findings and enquiries have been so slow to reach a conclusion, that people have long since lost interest in the outcome when it is finally delivered. Port Moresby city needs an entirely new and revolutionary system of civic government, one in which politics can and will play no part whatsoever.[37]

3   Initiatives by Pacific Island Countries

In the face of extensive corruption from local to national levels in Pacific Island countries, legal clarity as to what constitutes corruption within a jurisdiction is gradually emerging through both legislation and case law. Pacific Island countries have been guided by global and regional initiatives, but the establishment of effective anti-corruption law and institutions remains a domestic responsibility. This can include the effective resourcing of the police, special anti-corruption units, the auditor-general, ombudsman, and public prosecutor.[38] Parliaments have been legislating for anti-money laundering and counter-terrorism, and for a range of financial crimes. Leadership codes and commissions handle subtler activities such as lobbying; party registration, membership and financing; and integrity in appointments to public offices. Within public administration, the goal is to reduce concentrations of power, increase transparency in decision-making, remove "gate-keeper" roles wherever possible, and increase accountability measures which are sustainable.

In the case of Papua New Guinea, a 1982 Law Reform Commission study, *What Should be Done about Corruption and Bribery?*, provided impetus for strengthening anti-corruption laws and policies.[39] However, the challenge is not related to an absence of law, as the country has numerous institutions with a strong focus on strengthening integrity (Parliamentary Public Accounts Committee; Public Prosecutor's Office; Auditor General's Office; Police; Police Fraud Squad; the Ombudsman Commission; and the Finance Intelligence Unit) in addition to a plethora of laws providing for equity, efficiency, and openness when hiring officials; assuring proper use of resources; preventing bribery; and promoting private sector accountability, etc. Nonetheless, Parliament enacted

---

37   "PNG Government Should Reinstate Fired Auditor", *The National* (PNG), 11 February 2004.
38   Although Ombudsman Commissions exist across the region, most are considerably under-resourced.
39   T Deklin, "Bribery and Corruption" (Report, Papua New Guinea Law Reform Commission, 1989).

a suite of anti-money laundering and counter-terrorist financing laws in 2015,[40] and in 2017 the O'Neil government agreed to work with the Constitutional and Law Reform Commission on additional anti-corruption laws, including development of a whistle-blower protection law in time for a November sitting of Parliament; removal of existing protections of public servants who need to be disciplined; and establishment of a Sovereign Wealth Fund.[41] This range of institutions and laws not-withstanding, studies suggest that funding for key anti-corruption agencies has declined over the past decade,[42] and that one of the real challenges is lack of capacity in law enforcement.

Some countries have responded to the on-going challenge of corruption by establishing Independent Commissions Against Corruption. The Solomon Islands, Kiribati, Tuvalu and Palau have all considered establishing such commissions or leadership code commissions. Fiji established the Fiji Independent Commission Against Corruption ("FICAC") as part of a "clean-up campaign" after the Military's coup of December 2006.[43] PNG took steps toward implementation of an Anti-Corruption Commission in 2017, whilst in neighbouring Solomon Islands an anti-corruption bill introduced to Parliament in 2016 was withdrawn in 2017, with promises of re-introduction in 2018. This delay drew accusations from opposition MPs that the government has little interest in establishing an Independent Commission Against Corruption ("SIICAC") in which it might itself become ensnared.[44]

Several Pacific Island countries have conducted official inquiries into corruption. There have been three significant Commissions of Inquiry in Papua New Guinea in recent times. Transcripts of a Commission of Inquiry into

40   *Anti-Money Laundering and Counter Terrorist Financing Act 2015* (Papua New Guinea), established a Financial Analysis and Supervision Unit ("FASU") with in the Bank of PNG.

41   An organic law concerning the Sovereign Wealth Fund exists but has not yet been implemented. Revenues from a large liquid natural gas project are a currently paying off government debt and have not yet contributed to its consolidated revenue.

42   Grant Walton and Husnia Hushang, "Promises, Promises: A Dcade of Allocations for and Spending on Anti-Corruption in Papua New Guinea", *Development Policy Centre Discussion Paper* (Crawford School of Public Polic, Australian National University, 2017).

43   Peter Larmour, "From Clean up to Ficac: Anti-Corruption in Fiji's Post Coup Politics" (2009) 53 *Crime, Law and Social Change* 55.

44   *Solomons' PM Says Revised Anti-Corruption Bill Will Be Tabled In 2018* (30 August 2017) Pacific Islands Report <http://pireport.us10.list-manage.com/track/click?u=d27dd3dc8 b2d121b9fb9fe556&id=7840ef11bd&e=fc8e6d271a>; Solomons CSOs Petitioning PM Regarding Withdrawal Of Anti-Corruption Bill (13 September 2017) Pacific Islands Report <http://www.pireport.org/articles/2017/09/13/solomons-csos-petitioning-pm-regarding -withdrawal-anti-corruption-bill>.

the Department of Finance and the final report are online[45] but a 2010 court
order sought by Paraka Layers restricting implementation of the commission's findings remains in effect. A Commission of Inquiry into the Special
Agriculture and Business Leases, of 2011, issued an interim report in 2013. A
third Commission of Inquiry, into the sinking of MV Rabaul Queen, is also
online.[46]

In the Solomon Islands, the report of a Commission of Inquiry into riots
in Honiara was presented to government in April 2008, which has been made
available online in redacted form.[47] The sections naming the perpetrators of
the riot were withheld by the government of Prime Minister Sikua. The Commission's transcripts appear to be online in full.[48]

Tonga's most significant Royal Commission of recent times investigated the
causes of the sinking of the ferry Princess Ashika in August 2009 with the loss
of 74 lives.[49] The Commission found that the Tongan government failed to have
independent due diligence conducted at the time of the ferry's purchase, and
that the former Minister of Transport had made inaccurate and unsubstanti-
ated statements to a number of authorities. Unlike inquiries in PNG and the
Solomon Islands, the Tongan inquiry resulted in the laying of charges, although
these did not result in prosecution, which the government attributed to lack of
funds, and others interpreted as obstruction of justice.

Civil society organizations have been established to promote integrity in
Pacific Island Countries. In Papua New Guinea the NGO "Community Coalition Against Corruption" paved the way for building societal awareness of
the issues. Other significant groups are Transparency International and the
business-sponsored think tank, the Institute of National Affairs.[50] Transparency

---

45   *Transcripts*, Commission of Inquiry <http://www.coi.gov.pg/transcripts.html>; *The Com-
      mission of Inquiry generally into the Department of Finance: Final Report* <http://www.coi
      .gov.pg/documents/COI%20Finance/COI%20Finance%20Final%20Report.pdf>.

46   The Honourable Peter O'Neill, *The Commission of Inquiry into the Sinking of the Rabaul
      Queen* (28 June 2012) <http://www.coi.gov.pg/documents/COI%20MV%20RABAUL%20
      QUEEN/Rabaul%20Queen%20COI%20final%20report%20June%202012.pdf>.

47   *Recommendations, Conclusions and Findings,* Commission of Inquiry into the April 2006
      Honiara Civil Unrest <http://www.parliament.gov.sb/files/library%20and%20informa-
      tion/commision_of_inquiry/Commission_of_Inquiry.pdf>.

48   *Transcripts*, Office of the Commission of Inquiry into the April 2006 Honiara Civil Unrest
      <http://www.comofinquiry.gov.sb/april_riots/myweb3/Archives.htm>.

49   *Tonga: Royal Commission Report on Princess Ashika Ferry Disaster* (19 April 2010) Library of
      Congress <http://www.loc.gov/law/foreign-news/article/tonga-royal-commission-report
      -on-princess-ashika-ferry-disaster/>.

50   PNG Institute of National Affairs <http://www.inapng.com/>.

International has established chapters in Fiji, Papua New Guinea, the Solomon Islands, and Vanuatu. Transparency International's PNG chapter plays a leading role in building public awareness of corruption issues and in building alliances. It has a core team through which it multiplies its capabilities through coalition building and smart use of new communications technologies. The Business Against Corruption Alliance is using the internet to communicate its messages.[51] Faith-based organizations also play a significant role in civil society, fostering links between urban and rural consciousness. Christian churches are participating in anti-corruption activities, and the Catholic Bishops' Conference has continuously spoken out on issues of concern.[52]

3.1   Regional Initiatives

Anti-corruption activities at regional level and international levels have long been integral to the work of development assistance programmes, whether badged as anti-corruption, "good governance", leadership, or something else.[53] Major international counter-corruption initiatives include: the *UN Anti-Corruption Convention*; the *UN Transnational Organised Crime Convention*; the *ADB-OECD Asia Pacific Anti-Corruption Action Plan*; and the *Financial Action Task Force: Asia-Pacific Group on Money Laundering*.[54] The 2005 *Paris Declaration on Aid Effectiveness* is another international instrument that includes a commitment to publishing timely, transparent and reliable financial reports.

At regional level, the Pacific Islands Forum initiated a number of projects in the early 2000s to promote integrity amongst Pacific leaders: a draft leadership code, Forum Principles of Good Leadership, and Forum Principles of Accountability. At its inaugural meeting in 2001 the regional meeting of speakers of Pacific island legislatures declared a set of guiding principles for

---

51   Act Now For a Better Papua New Guinea <http://actnowpng.org/>

52   Volker Hauck, Angela Mandie-Filer and Joe Bolger, *Ringing the Church Bell: The Role of Churches in Governance and Public Performance*, Discussion Paper No.57E (European Centre for Development, 2005) <https://ecdpm.org/wp-content/uploads/2013/11/DP-57E-Role-of-Churches-Governance-and-Public-Performance-Papua-New-Guinea.pdf>.

53   AusAID, "Approaches to Anti-Corruption through the Australian Aid Program: Lessons from Papua New Guinea, Indonesia and Solomon Islands" (AusAID, 2007).

54   Barcham, "Clean up the Pacific", above n 16. Secretariat, "Anti-Corruption Policies in the Pacific Islands and Asia – Cook Islands" (Self-Assessment Report, Anti-Corruption Initiative for Asia and the Pacific, 2003).

legislatures and in 2003 Pacific leaders endorsed the "Forum Principles of Good Leadership":

> Key principles of good governance which we hold to be fundamental to good leadership:
> 1. RESPECT FOR THE LAW AND SYSTEM OF GOVERNMENT
> 2. RESPECT FOR CULTURAL VALUES, CUSTOMS AND TRADITIONS
> 3. RESPECT FOR FREEDOM OF RELIGION
> 4. RESPECT FOR PEOPLE ON WHOSE BEHALF LEADERS EXERCISE POWER
> 5. RESPECT FOR MEMBERS OF THE PUBLIC
> 6. ECONOMY AND EFFICIENCY
> 7. DILIGENCE
> 8. NATIONAL PEACE AND SECURITY
> 9. RESPECT FOR OFFICE[55]

In 2002 the Pacific Islands Forum concluded the "Forum Model Provisions on Counter Terrorism and Transnational Organised Crime", and this was revised in 2016 in response to such developments in international counter terrorism and transnational criminal obligations of States as periodic mutual evaluations by the Financial Action Task Force ("FATF") and the Asia Pacific Group on Money Laundering as well as obligations relating to foreign terrorist fighters.

An additional framework, the "Forum Principles of Accountability" issued in 2003 drew on standards developed by the International Monetary Fund ("IMF"), to provide the basis for a biennial stock-take of implementation of leadership codes and principles of accountability presented to meetings of the Forum Economic Ministers ("FEMM").

1   Budget processes, including multi-year frameworks, to ensure Parliament/Congress is sufficiently informed to understand the longer-term implications of appropriation decisions.

2   The accounts of governments, state-owned enterprises and statutory corporations to be promptly and fully audited.

3   Loan agreements or guarantees entered into by governments to be presented to Parliament/Congress.

---

55   *Governance*, Pacific Island Forum Secretariat <https://www.forumsec.org/governance/ #1509851988864-ecf5c4a7-37e2>. These remain visible on the Forum Secretariat's website, but the results of a survey conducted in 2008 to check country-specific practices against the regional standards have been removed (the report for Fiji was never made public).

4   All government and public sector contracts to be competitively awarded, and publicly reported.

5   Contravention of financial regulations to be promptly disciplined.

6   Public Accounts Committees of the legislature to be empowered to require disclosure.

7   Auditor General and Ombudsman to be provided with adequate fiscal resources and independent reporting rights to Parliament/Congress.

8   Central bank with statutory responsibility for non-partisan monitoring and advice, and regular and independent publication of informative reports.

In 2005 Forum leaders approved Pacific Plan Initiatives 12.1, Pacific Regional Audit Initiative ("PRAI"), which the Asian Development Bank ("ADB") subsequently supported through the provision of technical assistance to Pacific member countries. In addition, the Pacific Islands Forum partnered with UNDP to promote Freedom of Information in Pacific states as one strategy to reduce corruption by strengthening open government.[56]

Other Pacific regional organizations with mandates to establish or promote anti-corruption measures include the Oceanic Customs Organization, the Pacific Islands Chiefs of Police, the Pacific Islands Law Officers Network, and the Pacific Association of Supreme Audit Institutions.

In addition to these Pacific Islands-wide organizations are several Asia Pacific Initiatives. The 41-member Asia/Pacific Group on Money Laundering, for instance, is an inter-governmental organisation, which focuses on '... ensuring that its members effectively implement the international standards against money laundering, terrorist financing and proliferation financing related to weapons of mass destruction'.[57] A second initiative, which has been in existence for longer but which has had only nominal impact to date, is the ADB/OECD Anti-Corruption Initiative for Asia Pacific, which includes seven Pacific Island countries. As part of this programme, the ADB conducted a "Governance and Anticorruption Action plan 2000–2004", followed by a second GACAP II, 2006–2008. Although the initiative still exists, only two countries (Cook Islands and Vanuatu) appear to have submitted voluntary reports on progress with the work program during the period 2011–2016.

---

56   Charmaine Rodrigues, Isikeli Valemei and Henry Ivarature, "Freedom of Information for Pacific Policy Makers" (Paper persented at 2008 Regional Workshop, Honiara, Solomon Islands, 30 June–2 July 2008)

57   Asia / Pacific Group on Money Laundering <http://www.apgml.org/>.

Region/country or territory	Date joined	Country report 2016[a]	Country Report 2015[b]	Country Report 2014[c]	Country Report 2013[d]	Country Report 2011[e]
MELANESIA /						
1. Fiji	2001					
2. Papua New Guinea	2001					
3. Solomon Islands	2012					
4. Vanuatu	2001				√	
MICRONESIA /						
5. Palau	2004					
POLYNESIA /						
6. Cook Islands	2001	√				
7. Samoa	2001					

a   *Compilation of Written Reports by Steering Group Members on Recent Developments and Activities* (8 November 2016) ADB/OECD Anti-Corruption Initiative for Asia and the Pacific <http://www.oecd.org/site/adboecdanti-corruptioninitiative/ADB-OECD-21st-Steering-Group-Meeting-Compilation-Written-Reports.pdf>.

b   *Compilation of Written Reports by Steering Group Members on Recent Developments and Activities* (18 November 2015) ADB/OECD Anti-Corruption Initiative for Asia and the Pacific <http://www.oecd.org/site/adboecdanti-corruptioninitiative/ADB-OECD-20th-Steering-Group-Meeting-Compilation-Written-Reports.pdf>.

c   *Compilation of Written Reports of Steering Group Members on UNCAC Implementation and Other Specific Topics in the Anti-Corruption Field* (2 September 2014) ADB/OECD Anti-Corruption Initiative for Asia and the Pacific and Kingdom of Cambodia <http://www.oecd.org/site/adboecdanti-corruptioninitiative/19th-StG-Compilation-Written-Reports.pdf>.

d   *Compilation of Written Reports of Steering and Advisory Group Members and Observer Countries on UNCAC Implementation and Other Specific Topics in the Anti-Corruption Field* (24 July 2013) ADB/OECD Anti-Corruption Initiative for Asia and the Pacific and the Anti-Corruption Commission of Timor-Leste <http://www.oecd.org/site/adboecdanti-corruptioninitiative/18thSteeringGroupMeeting_CountryReportingCompilation.pdf>.

e   *Recent steps taken to implement the ADB/OECD Anti-Corruption Action Plan and United Nations Convention against Corruption (UNCAC)* (27 September 2011) ADB/OECD Anti-Corruption Initiative for Asia and the Pacific <http://www.oecd.org/site/adboecdanti-corruptioninitiative/CountryReporting2012.pdf>.

3.2   *International Initiatives*

In addition to the national and regional anti-corruption programmes noted in the sections above, are several international initiatives, which appear to have had generated more commitment from Pacific Island countries. These include the International Criminal Police Organization ("INTERPOL"),[58] the IMF's Pacific Financial Technical Assistance Centre ("PFTAC"),[59] and a number of United Nations initiatives, notably the *United Nations Convention Against Corruption* ("*UNCAC*").[60] PFTAC assists 16 Pacific Island countries promote macro-financial stability through a focused program of technical assistance and training. Whilst not expressed as an anti-corruption organization, its focus on competent public financial management must be viewed as an important contribution to strengthening public finances against the threat of corruption.

The *United Nations Convention Against Corruption* establishes an international treaty setting global standards for preventive measures, criminalization and law enforcement, international cooperation, asset recovery, and technical assistance and information exchange. A majority of the sovereign Pacific Island countries have acceded to the treaty, and participated in COP sessions and peer review processes. In 2016 the UN announced that all Pacific Island countries have completed the peer review process, and the commencement of a US$4.3 million four-year second phase of a regional anti-corruption project to mainstream its initiatives.[61] Also in 2016, Vanuatu announced the establishment of an 18-member Anti-Corruption committee (Order No. 166 of 2016), comprising government and non-government members, to oversee the implementation of the recommendations made in *UNCAC*'s Review Report for Vanuatu, and to assist in the development and oversight of a National Anti-Corruption Strategic Framework.

---

58   Pacific Island country members of Interpol are Fiji, Marshall Islands, Nauru, Papua New Guinea, Samoa, Solomon Islands, and Tonga.

59   Pacific Technical Assistance Center (PFTAC) <https://www.imfconnect.org/content/PFTAC/en1.html>.

60   *United Nations Convention Against Corruption*, opened for Signature 31 October 2003, UN Doc A/58/422 (entered into force 14 December 2005).

61   *Country* profiles: *Fiji*, United Nations Office on Drugs and Crime <https://www.unodc.org/unodc/treaties/CAC/country-profile/CountryProfile.html?code=FJI>; *Country* profiles: *Kiribati*, United Nations Office on Drugs and Crime <https://www.unodc.org/unodc/treaties/CAC/country-profile/CountryProfile.html?code=KIR>.

Region/country or territory	Political Status	Sign	Ratification, Acceptance (A), Approval (AA), Accession (a), Succession (d)[a]	Participation in 6th Session (2015)[b]	Participation in 5th session (2013)[c]	Reports
MELANESIA						
1. Fiji	independent		14 May 2008 a	√	√	ES 2012
2. New Caledonia	French territory	9 Dec 2003	11 Jul 2005			
3. Papua New Guinea	independent	22 Dec 2004	16 Jul 2007		√	ES 2013
4. Solomon Islands	independent		6 Jan 2012 a	√	√	ES 2014
5. Vanuatu	independent		12 Jul 2011 a	√	√	ES 2013CR
MICRONESIA						
6. Federated States of Micronesia	independent		21 Mar 2012 a	√	√	
7. Guam	United States Island Territory	9 Dec 2003	30 Oct 2006			
8. Kiribati			27 Sep 2013 a		√	
9. Marshall Islands	independent		17 Nov 2011	√	√	
10. Nauru	independent		12 Jul 2012 a	√	√	
11. Northern Mariana Islands	United States Commonwealth	9 Dec 2003	30 Oct 2006			
12. Palau	independent		24 Mar 2009 a	√	√	
POLYNESIA						
13. American Samoa	United States Territory	9 Dec 2003	30 Oct 2006			
14. Cook Islands	Free Association with New Zealand		17 Oct 2011	√	√	2015[d]
15. French Polynesia	French territory	9 Dec 2003	11 Jul 2005			
16. Niue	Free Association with New Zealand	10 Dec 2003	1 Dec 2015			
17. Pitcairn Islands	British Overseas Territory	9 Dec 2003	9 Feb 2006			

Region/country or territory	Political Status	Sign	Ratification, Acceptance (A), Approval (AA), Accession (a), Succession (d)[a]	Participation in 6th Session (2015)[b]	Participation in 5th session (2013)[c]	Reports
18. Samoa	Independent	?				
19. Tokelau	Associated State, part of "realm of New Zealand"	10 Dec 2003	1 Dec 2015			
20. Tonga	Independent	?				
21. Tuvalu	Independent		04 Sep 2015 a	√		
22. Wallis and Futuna	French territory	9 Dec 2003	11 Jul 2005			

a   *Signature and Ratification Status*, United Nations Office on Drugs and Crime <https://www.unodc.org/unodc/en/treaties/CAC/signatories.html>.

b   Conference of the States Parties to the United Nations Convention against Corruption, *Final List of Participants*, 6th sess, UN Doc CAC/COSP/2015/INF.2 (6 November 2015).

c   Conference of the States Parties to the United Nations Convention against Corruption, *Final List of Participants*, 5th sess, UN Doc CAC/COSP/2013/INF.2/Rev.1 (20 December 2013).

d   *Country Review Report of the Cook Islands* (12 August 2015) United Nations Office on Drugs and Crime <http://www.unodc.org/documents/treaties/UNCAC/CountryVisit FinalReports/2015_12_08_Cook_Islands_Final_Review_Report.pdf>.

UNDP is assisting Pacific countries to implement anti-corruption initiatives related to *UNCAC*.[62] In 2017, for instance, the Solomon Islands government agreed to co-fund, with UNDP, the project "Transparency and Accountability for the people of Solomon Islands", to support its National Anti-Corruption Strategy ("NACS") Action Plan (2017–2019). The project will also be provided with technical support from the United Nations Office for Drugs and Corruption ("UNODC").

---

62   *Anti-Corruption for Development Effectiveness*, UNDP <http://www.pg.undp.org/content/papua_new_guinea/en/home/operations/projects/democratic_governance/anti-corruption-for-development-effectiveness.html>; *Tackling integrity risks in government contracts*, UNDP <http://www.pg.undp.org/content/papua_new_guinea/en/home/library/SDGacceleration_offer.html>; *Anti-Corruption Workshop For Regional Prosecutors, Law Enforcement Convenes* (13 June 2017) Pacific Islands Report <http://www.pireport.org/articles/2017/06/13/anti-corruption-workshop-regional-prosecutors-law-enforcement-convenes>.

4   Conclusions

This paper has surveyed the extensive global, regional and national initiatives underway to strengthen anti-corruption measures in Pacific Island countries. The presence of corrupt practices in Pacific Island countries from petty to grand is well-documented. Yet notwithstanding the considerable resources provided by development partners for the development of integrity laws and law enforcement institutions, the problem persists. The challenge is thus ongoing, and requires a suite of remedies, which include not only legal remedies, but those aimed at achieving political, normative, and societal change. Legal and institutional aspects of this suite currently under construction include: (1) comprehensive legal frameworks, together with laws that explicitly proscribe corrupt practices; increased transparency, freedom of and access to information, freedom of speech; and protection for whistle-blowers; (2) adequately resourced institutions, with strengthened abilities in standard setting, monitoring, information gathering, and prosecution. But these legal remedies remain insufficient if not accompanied by: (3) political will, evidenced by Members of Parliament and other political actors abiding by codes of conduct and codes of ethics, and providing leadership and impetus to the anti-corruption initiatives their countries have committed to; and (4) public endorsement and support, in the form of vigilant monitoring of officials' conduct, fair use of mass media and social media, and endorsement at elections of candidates and parties who demonstrate adherence to corruption-free values and practices.

Anti-corruption Measures from a European and Austrian Perspective

Concepts – Control – Concerns

*S. Reindl-Krauskopf**

1 Introduction

This article explores developments surrounding the criminalisation of corruption in Europe, beginning with early notions of corruption and extending across multiple European legal instruments since the 1990s. Furthermore, it aims to investigate how the Austrian legislator fulfilled the obligations arising from these instruments to create specialised investigative bodies within the police force and public prosecution authorities. Highlighting the Austrian situation as a European example, the article further focuses on how these control measures were implemented and raises concerns whether statutory exemptions and third party contributions to public authorities are blurring the demarcation line between admissible sponsorships and criminally punishable corrupt practices.

2 Concepts of Corruption and Corresponding Legal Instruments in Europe

2.1 First Steps

When discussing corruption and criminal law in Europe, one has to first consider the concept of corruption. The initial understanding of criminal corruption was limited to so-called "passive bribery" in the public sector, where a public official accepted a bribe in order to act or refrain from acting in breach of his or her official duties only. The public official was supposed to be criminally liable in such a scenario; for example, a national public official illegally granting a visa in exchange for a bribe should be sentenced. This very limited understanding of corruption was quickly widened, now also comprising

* University of Vienna, Department of Criminal Law and Criminology, ALES – Austrian Center for Law Enforcement Sciences.

active bribery where not only the official but also the offeror of the bribe is criminalised.

Given that corruption not only undermines public trust in the fairness and impartiality of national public administrations, but also undermines good governance in international relations, especially economic relations, the scope of application of the core corruption offences has been extended to bribery of foreign public officials, public officials in international organisations such as UN officials, and European Community officials in the context of EU regulations.

This development is mirrored by European legal instruments that oblige the member states to criminalise certain corrupt practices in their national laws: the first relevant legal instrument on the European level addressing bribery was the *Protocol to the Convention on the Protection of the European Communities' Financial Interests* (*"EC Protocol"*).[1] It was adopted in 1996 within the – at that time – European Community ("EC"). According to this protocol, the EC member states were obliged to criminalise passive as well as active bribery.[2] These European regulations on corruption, however, had a crucial limit, as the member states' criminalisation obligation was placed under the condition that bribery was effectuated in order to damage the EC's financial interests. As long as corruption had no effects on such financial interests, criminalisation of corruption was not compulsory.

This narrow scope of the *EC Protocol* was due to the extremely restricted legislative power of the EC in criminal law matters.[3] On one hand, the EC was not

---

1   *Council Act of 27 Sept 1996 drawing up a Protocol to the Convention on the Protection of the European Communities' Financial Interests*, [1996] OJ C 313/1 (entered into force 17 October 2002) (*"The Protocol"*); Gerhard Dannecker, "Strafrechtlicher Schutz der Finanzinteressen der Europäischen Gemeinschaft gegen Täuschung" (1996) 8 *ZStW Zeitschrift für die gesamte Strafrechtswissenschaft* 577, 594–608; Laura Garcia Marques and Robert Kert, "Strafrechtsänderungsgesetz 1998: Umsetzung des EU-Betrugs-Übereinkommens in Österreich" (1999) 6 *ÖJZ Österreichische Juristenzeitung* 213; Florian Singer, "Korruptionstatbestände neu im Europarecht" (2009) 14 *Zivilrecht aktuell* 267; Fritz Zeder, "Die Rolle des Strafrechts beim Schutz der finanziellen Interessen der Europäischen Union", in Federal Ministry of Justice (ed) *Schriftenreihe des BMJ* (1996) Vol 82, 183.

2   *The Protocol* art 2 (Passive corruption) and art 3 (Active Corruption).

3   The development of the ECs' and EU's legislative power in criminal law matters concerning the protection of financial interests is reflected in the *Treaty on the European Union*, opened for signature on 7 February 1992, Official Journal of the European Communities C 325/5 (entered into force 1 November 1993) art 209(a) (*"Maastricht Treaty"*), which was changed into art 280 by the *Treaty of Amsterdam amending the Treaty on European Union, the Treaties establishing the European Communities and certain related acts*, opened for signature on 2 October 1997, [1992] C191/01 (entered into force 1 May 1999) (*"Treaty of Amsterdam"*), amending the *Maastricht Treaty*, the *Treaties establishing the European Communities* and certain related acts. Finally, this article was transformed by the *Treaty of Lisbon amending the Treaty on*

as equally harmonised and as "supranational" as today's European Union. On the other hand, criminal law was still seen as a traditional and sacrosanct element of state sovereignty. Therefore, criminal law legislation could and should only be centralised when the matter of concern was at the heart of the EC, i.e. economy-related. And, even in these areas, criminal law legislation was only considered to be an annex to other mechanisms governing the EC's policies. That explains why the *EC Protocol* on corruption stipulated the potential damage of the EC's financial interests as a threshold for the criminalisation of corrupt behaviour. Seen from the anti-corruption perspective, such a limited legal instrument seems rather disappointing.

As early as 1997, the EC made an attempt to broaden the range of anti-corruption measures. The so-called *Convention on the Fight against Corruption involving Officials of the European Communities or of Officials of Member States of the European Union ("Convention")*[4] waived the limitation to corruption cases damaging the ECs' financial interests and penalised active and passive bribery in the public sector in any conceivable scenario of breach of duties.[5]

As an intermediate result of the development in the mid-1990s, the member states of the EC reached a consensus that active and passive bribery should be penalised in cases where corruption aimed at the breach of official duties by the bribed public official.

At about the same time, namely on 21 November 1997, the member states of the Organisation for Economic Co-operation and Development ("OECD") adopted the *Convention on Combating Bribery of Foreign Public Officials in*

European Union and the Treaty establishing the European Community, opened for signature 13 December 2007, [2007] OJ C 306/01 (entered into force 1 December 2009) (*"Treaty of Lisbon"*), into art 325 of the *Treaty on the Functioning of the European Union*, opened for signature 25 March 1957 (entered into force 1 January 1958) (*"FEU"*), which allows the European Union to counter fraud and any other illegal activities affecting its financial interests. Furthermore, Ch. 4 of the *FEU* (arts 82–86) provides comprehensive rules on judicial cooperation in criminal matters, which also comprises the legislative power to establish minimum rules concerning the definition of criminal offences and sanctions in the areas of particularly serious crime with a cross-border dimension resulting from the nature or impact of such offences or from a special need to combat them on a common basis. Such areas of crime are: terrorism, trafficking in human beings and sexual exploitation of women and children, and corruption.

4 *Council Act of 26 May 1997 drawing up, on the basis of Article K.3 (2) (c) of the Treaty on European Union, the Convention on the Fight against Corruption Involving Officials of the European Communities or Officials of Member States of the European Union* [1997] OJ C 195/1; Singer, above n 1; Zeder, above n 1.

5 *Council Act of 26 May 1997 drawing up, on the basis of Article K.3 (2) (c) of the Treaty on European Union, the Convention on the Fight against Corruption Involving Officials of the European Communities or Officials of Member States of the European Union*, above n 4, art 2 and art 3.

International Business Transactions ("OECD Convention").[6] This convention only covers active bribery of foreign public officials in the context of international business. This thematic limitation is to be attributed to the fact that the OECD aims to foster international cooperation and economic development. Therefore, the OECD *Convention* limits itself to tackling those aspects of corruption that hinder cooperation and development the most in international business. As the OECD *Convention* is not an exclusively European approach (for example, Australia is also a party to the convention, and more recent European instruments cover the scenarios addressed by the OECD *Convention* as well), the OECD *Convention* will not be further explored in this article.[7]

2.2   The Council of Europe Criminal Law Convention on Corruption

Legal development regarding public sector corruption only expanded from adoption of the *Council of Europe Criminal Law Convention on Corruption*. As previously outlined, corruption was originally required to be punishable only if the public official was bribed in order to breach his or her official duties. More recent concepts do not require this element any longer. Consequently, public officials shall be criminally liable even if they accept the bribe for acting or for refraining from action without breaching any of their official duties. If, for example, an official accepts a bribe after having correctly issued a passport, this will constitute a criminal offence even though the public official did not breach any duties when issuing the passport. Such behaviour is often not called passive bribery but merely accepting undue advantages.[8]

---

6   *Convention on Combating Bribery of Foreign Public Officials in International Business Transactions* opened for signature 17 December 1997, (entered into force 15 February 1999).

7   For further information concerning the OECD *Convention* see, for example, OECD *Convention on Combating Bribery of Foreign Public Officials in International Business Transactions*, OECD <http://www.oecd.org/corruption/oecdantibriberyconvention.htm>; Mark Pieth, Lucinda A Low and Peter J Cullen (eds), *The OECD Convention on Bribery: A Commentary* (Cambridge University Press, 2nd ed, 2014); Michael P Van Alstine, "Treaty Double Jeopardy: The OECD Anti-Bribery Convention and the FCPA" (2012) 73 *Ohio State Law Journal* 1321; Indira Carr and Opi Outhwaite, "The OECD Anti-Bribery Convention Ten Years On" (2008) 5 *Manchester Journal of International Economic Law* 3; Gertraud Eppich, "Korruptionsbekämpfung: Internationale Vorgaben und deren Einhaltung durch Österreich" in Gerhard Dannecker, Roman Leitner (eds), *Handbuch Korruption* (Linde, 2011) 143; Pilar Koukol, "Die Instrumente der OECD zur Korruptionsbekämpfung: Hypertrophie der Compliance?" in Peter Lewisch (ed), *Zauberwort Compliance* (MANZ, 2012) 35; Martijn Wilder and Michael Ahrens, "Australia's Implementation of the OECD Convention on Combating Bribery of Foreign Public Officials in International Business Transactions" (2001) 2 *Melbourne Journal of International Law* 569.

8   See *Criminal Code* (Austria) s 305.

This altered approach can be found in the Council of Europe *Criminal Law Convention on Corruption of 1999* (*"Council of Europe Convention"*) for the first time.[9] This convention is a landmark in the European anti-corruption criminal law development. This is not only due to the waiver of the breach of official duties as a definitional element of the corruption offence. It is also true because the *Council of Europe Convention* aims at the co-ordinated criminalisation of a large number of corrupt practices and, furthermore, it obliges a greater number of states to combat corruption as the Council of Europe has more member states than the EC and the EU respectively.[10]

The *Council of Europe Convention* contributed greatly to the broadening of the concepts of corruption within criminal law as this convention extended the scope of possible perpetrators: according to the terms of the *Council of Europe Convention*, it is not only the domestic public official who incurs criminal liability when requesting or receiving an undue advantage in order to act, or refrain from acting, in the exercise of his or her functions.[11] Criminal liability further extends to foreign public officials,[12] members of a domestic as well as of a foreign public assembly,[13] officials of international and supranational organisations,[14] members of international parliamentary assemblies,[15] as well as national and international judges.[16]

In all these scenarios, both the recipient as well as the briber is punishable.[17] This extremely ambitious scope in the public sector was, in a sense, revolutionary. Some members of parliament, for instance, still tend to show a certain reluctance when it comes to their liability in relation to advantages they request or receive for the exercise of their legislative tasks. The respective Austrian

---

9   *Criminal Law Convention on Corruption*, opened for signature 27 January 1999, ETS No 173 (entered into force 1 July 2002) (*"Council of Europe Convention"*).
10   Currently, 47 States are members of the Council of Europe. Canada, the Holy See, Israel, Japan, Mexico, and the United States of America are observer states.
11   *Explanatory Report to the Criminal Law Convention on Corruption* ETS 173 "Article 3 – Passive Bribery of Domestic Public Officials" [40]–[43] (*"Explanatory Report on the Convention"*).
12   Ibid [47]–[50]: "Article 5 – Bribery of Foreign Public Officials".
13   Ibid [44]–[46]: "Article 4 – Bribery of Members of Domestic Public Assemblies"; [51]: "Article 6 – Bribery of Members of Foreign Public Assemblies".
14   Ibid [57]–[61]: "Article 9 – Bribery of Officials in International Organizations".
15   Ibid [62]: "Article 10 – Bribery of Members of International Parliamentary Assemblies".
16   Ibid [63]: "Article 11 Bribery of Judges and Officials in International Courts".
17   Ibid. Article 2 of the *Council of Europe Convention* penalises active bribery of domestic public officials and art 3–5, 9–11 make reference to this article.

regulation only entered into force as recently as 2013.[18] Previously, only the buying of votes could lead to criminal sanctions.[19]

For the first time in the history of European anti-corruption criminal law instruments, the *Council of Europe Convention* addresses corruption in the private sector, thus corruption relating to business conducted in the free market. Therefore, this convention also provides for criminal offences in this field.[20] In light of the existing European anti-corruption laws of the time, this approach must appear as a pioneering step, as none of the other instruments comprised respective rules. Establishing a criminalisation obligation regarding active and passive bribery in the private sector became necessary without any doubt.[21] Firstly, because corruption undermines values like trust, confidence and loyalty, which are also necessary for the maintenance and development of social and economic relations. Secondly, corruption in this field also touches on the guarantee of fair competition in the free market. Fair and free competition is a legal interest of high importance, not only for those competing in the same market, but also for consumers who rely on fair competition in so far as they expect correct pricing policies and undistorted offers of goods and services. Thirdly, one also has to take the privatisation process into account. In the 1990s, the states had already started to increase the transfer of public functions such as transport, health and telecommunications to the private sector. Such transfers typically also entail a transfer of substantial budgetary allocations and regulatory powers. Therefore, with regards to the great social importance of these functions, it is not only logical and proper, but also compelling, to protect the public from the damaging effects of corruption in the private sector as well.

There is still a considerable difference as to the constituting elements of the offences concerning corruption in the public and private sectors. Whereas corruption offences addressing the public sector waive the element of breach of duties, a breach of duties is still stipulated as a threshold for criminal

---

18   *Korruptionsstrafrechtsänderungsgesetz 2012 – KorrStrÄG 2012* [*Corruption Criminal Law Amendment Act 2012 – KorrStrÄG 2012*] 28 June 2012, BGBl I 2012/61.

19   Criticising the long-lasting reluctance to comply with the respective international criminalisation obligations in this field e.g., Hubert Hinterhofer, "Eingeschränktes Korruptionsstrafrecht für Abgeordnete österreichischer Vertretungskörper" (2009) 9 *ecolex – Fachzeitschrift für Wirtschaftsrecht* 250; Susanne Reindl-Krauskopf, "Neues Antikorruptionsstrafrecht: Alles neu – alles gut?" in Clemens Jabloner and others (eds), *FS Heinz Mayer – Vom praktischen Wert der Methode* (MANZ, 2011) 613, 616–7.

20   *Explanatory Report on the Convention* [52]–[56]: "Article 7 – Active Bribery in the Private Sector", and "Article 8 – Passive Bribery in the Private Sector".

21   Ibid [52].

liability in the private sector.[22] This divergence probably stems from the different legal interests protected by these regulations. In the public sector, trust of the citizens in public authorities, in particular that public officials carry out their duties in an independent, impartial and non-discriminatory manner, is the prevailing issue. Even the mere semblance of partiality must be prevented if state authorities want to remain trusted and keep their powers in order to ensure the functioning of society. Therefore, this trust and confidence is to be protected no matter whether an official breaches any duties or not.

In the private sector, on the other hand, the primary interest threatened by corrupt acts is usually property. Employees are typically bribed to act in a way which would result in damage to their employer's property. As a rule, such damage is only caused if the employee breaches special duties he or she personally has towards his or her employer. For example, the manager of a company might be bribed in order to conclude a contract on the purchase of overpriced goods on behalf of the company, whereas they could have concluded a contract on better terms with another competitor. The manager has the duty to preserve the economic interests of their company in the best way possible. And, in the present case, he or she acted in breach of this duty which resulted in damage to the company's property. Therefore, it seems rather logical to mirror the difference between the protected legal interests in the definitional elements of the various offences.

In addition to the core corruption offences, the *Council of Europe Convention* also contains a criminalisation obligation for related or subsequent forms of crime which typically go hand in hand with corruption, such as trading in influence, money laundering of proceeds from corruption offences and on accounting offences.[23] In all these fields, the *Council of Europe Convention* requires the state's parties to provide for effective and dissuasive sanctions and measures, including deprivation of liberty that can lead to extradition.[24] Furthermore, the *Council of Europe Convention* incorporates provisions concerning aiding and abetting, immunity, criteria for determining the jurisdiction of states, liability of legal persons, the setting up of specialised anti-corruption bodies, protection of persons collaborating with investigating or prosecuting authorities, gathering of evidence, and confiscation of proceeds.[25] It also addresses matters of international cooperation such as mutual assistance and extradition.[26]

---

22   Ibid art 7: '... to act, or refrain from acting, in breach of their duties'.
23   *Council of Europe Convention* art 12–14; *Explanatory Report on the Convention* [64]–[75].
24   *Council of Europe Convention* art 19: "Sanctions and Measures".
25   *Council of Europe Convention* art 15–23; *Explanatory Report on the Convention* [76]–[115].
26   *Council of Europe Convention* Ch. IV; *Explanatory Report on the Convention* [119]–[135].

Even without going into further details, the picture drawn so far clearly shows that this convention is a comprehensive legal instrument touching on a great variety of aspects related to the criminalisation and persecution of corrupt practices. That is why the *Council of Europe Convention* may rightly be called a milestone and a rather successful instrument. The fact that it set up a monitoring system certainly fostered its implementation to an enormous extent.[27] The Group of States against Corruption ("GRECO")[28] started operating in May 1999 and is supposed to monitor the implementation of the *Council of Europe Convention*. Ever since GRECO started, the states' parties have regularly been monitored. GRECO issues progress reports on the respective state as to the implementation of the provisions and gives recommendations if need be.[29] These publicly available reports are a rather effective instrument to assure that member states fulfil their obligations under the *Council of Europe Convention* and that, if necessary, national laws are adjusted to new challenges.

2.3   Further Developments

Despite the adoption of additional international legal instruments on corruption and criminal law in subsequent years, these did not further develop the criminal law concepts of corruption and the respective offences. The Council of Europe adopted an *Additional Protocol to the Criminal Law Convention on Corruption on the Bribery of Arbitrators* in 2003, but this protocol has not reached any practical importance so far.[30]

The *European Union's Framework Decision on Combating Corruption in the Private Sector of 2003* ("*Framework Decision*")[31] builds on a concept of bribery

---

27   *Council of Europe Convention* Ch. III (Monitoring of Implementation); *Explanatory Report on the Convention* [116]–[118].

28   Council of Europe, Group of States against Corruption <https://www.coe.int/en/web/greco>.

29   Detailed information on the evaluation by round, as well by country, including evaluation and progress reports is available under *Evaluations* Council of Europe <https://www.coe.int/en/web/greco/evaluations>.

30   *Additional Protocol to the Council of Europe Criminal Law Convention on Corruption,* opened for signature 15 May 2003, ETS 191 (entered into force 1 February 2005).

31   *Council Framework Decision 2003/568/JHA of 22 July 2003 on Combating Corruption in the Private Sector* [2003] OJ L 192/54; See also *Report from the Commission to the Council based on Article 9 of this Council Framework Decision* (SEC/2007/808 final and COM/2011/0309 final); *Communication from the Commission to the European Parliament, The Council and the European Economic and Social Committee: Fighting Corruption in the EU* (COM/2011/0308 final); *Report from the Commission to the Council and the European Parliament: EU Anti-Corruption Report* (COM/2014/038 final); *European Parliament Resolution of 23 October 2013 on organized crime, corruption and money laundering: recommendations on action and initiatives to be taken* [2016] OJ NC 208/89; Eppich, above n 7.

in the private sector identical to the *Council of Europe Convention*.[32] The only difference lies in the required penalties. Whereas the *Council of Europe Convention* merely asks for effective and dissuasive sanctions enabling extradition, the *Framework Decision* requires EU member states to ensure a maximum penalty of at least one to three years of imprisonment.[33]

Likewise, the *United Nations Convention Against Corruption of 2003* (*"UNCAC"*)[34] copies the concepts and structures of the criminal law corruption offences,[35] as laid down in the *Council of Europe Convention*. Nevertheless, *UNCAC* may be seen as a further step in anti-corruption work as this convention stipulates new standards in other fields such as corruption prevention.[36]

In fact, since 1999, corruption has been tackled by concepts constituted by the following elements:

In the public sector, the potential perpetrator of passive bribery may be:
– a domestic or foreign official or an official of an international organisation;
– a member of a domestic, foreign or international assembly; or
– a national or international judge.

The punishable act is the intentional request or receipt of any undue advantage, or the acceptance of an offer, or a promise of such an advantage, in order to act or refrain from acting in the exercise of official functions.

In the private sector, passive bribery means that an employee or director of a private entity requests or receives any undue advantage, or accepts an offer, or a promise of such an advantage, in order to act or refrain from acting in breach of his or her duties.

And in both sectors criminal sanctions are stipulated to punish the person promising, offering or giving the bribe.

---

32   *Council of Europe Convention* art 2 – "Active and Passive Corruption in the Private Sector".

33   Ibid art 4 "Penalties and Sanctions"; see sub-para 2.2.

34   *United Nations Convention against Corruption*, opened for signature 9 December 2003, 2349 UNTS 41 (entered into force 14 December 2005) (*"UNCAC"*). For further information, see e.g. Eppich, above n 7; Rainer Hofmann and Christina Pfaff (eds), *Die Konvention der Vereinten Nationen zur Bekämpfung der Korruption* (Nomos, 2007); Dirk Monsau, "Vereinte Nationen und Korruptionsbekämpfung" in Sabine von Schorlemer (ed), *Dresden Papers on Law and Policy of the United Nations* (Peter Lang, 2010) Vol 12; Philippa Webb, "The United Nations Convention Against Corruption. Global Achievement or Missed Opportunity?" (2005) 8 *Journal of International Economic Law* 191; A Katharina Weilert, "United Nations Convention against Corruption (*'UNCAC'*) – After Ten Years of Being in Force" (2016) 19 *Max Planck Yearbook of United Nations Law Online* 216–40.

35   UNCAC art 15 "Bribery of National Public Officials"; art 16 "Bribery of Foreign Public Officials and Officials of Public International Organizations"; art 21 "Bribery in the Private Sector".

36   UNCAC Ch. II.

3   Control: The Implementation of International Requirements for
        Specialised Investigative Bodies in Austria

3.1   *Specialised Police Authorities in Austria*
The international instruments previously highlighted also require that specialised and independent authorities should investigate corruption cases.[37] Austria has made great efforts to fulfil this obligation.

As early as 2001, the Minister of the Interior established the Austrian Federal Bureau of Internal Affairs ("BIA") for the purpose of investigating corruption in the public sector. The BIA was a special police department under direct
responsibility of the Minister. The Bureau was set up outside the traditional
ministerial hierarchy, nevertheless, it was integrated in the ministerial chain of
command which, in fact, still contradicted the independence of such a body as
required by the international instruments.[38]

Subsequently, the BIA was transformed into the Bundesamt zur Korruption-
sprävention und Korruptionsbekämpfung [Federal Anti-Corruption Bureau]
in 2010.[39] This Bureau still acts under direct responsibility of the Minster but
forms a special organisational unit and, therefore, acts independently. The Bureau is not only authorised to conduct criminal investigations in corruption
matters,[40] but is also the central national contact point in international police
cooperation in the field of corruption, for example, for Interpol.[41] Additionally,
the Bureau fulfils preventive tasks according to art 5 and 6 *UNCAC*, it analyses
corrupt practices and develops appropriate preventive measures.[42]

Unlike in ordinary police work, all commands given to the Bureau on how
to carry out a specific investigation must be in writing, spelling out the reasons
for the order. Only in the case of an emergency may commands be given orally,
but they must still be furnished in writing with reasons as soon as possible.[43]

Compared to ordinary police forces, the Bureau has a second particularity.
The legislator aimed to foster transparency and control within this field. Therefore, in addition to the legal remedies which are generally available to have a

---

37   See e.g. *The Council of Europe Convention* art 20.
38   *Sicherheitsbericht 2006* [Safety Report] (Austria), 111-114 der Beilagen XXIII. GP – Bericht –
      Hauptdokument Teil 1, 336.
39   *Bundesgesetz über die Einrichtung und Organisation des Bundesamts zur Korruption-
      sprävention und Korruptionsbekämpfung (BAK-Statute)* [Federal Act on the Federal Office
      for the Prevention of Corruption and Corruption] (Austria), BGBl 1 2009/72.
40   Ibid s 4(1).
41   Ibid s 4(2).
42   Ibid s 4(3).
43   Ibid s 7.

specific police conduct reviewed, the legislator installed an independent commission with the power to examine violations of law allegedly committed by members of the Bureau.[44]

3.2   The Austrian Public Prosecutor's Office for Economic Crime and Corruption

3.2.1   The Office

A specialised Public Prosecutor's Office against Corruption started its nationwide work in Vienna, with only five prosecutors, in 2009.[45] In 2012, the Office was changed into the Public Prosecutor's Office for Economic Crime and Corruption.[46] As its competencies grew, so did the number of staff. Nowadays, 35 public prosecutors[47] and 13 additional experts[48] on finance, economic and IT matters work in the Office. These experts are permanent staff and can be consulted by the prosecutors unbureaucratically during the whole investigation. This is something unique in the Austrian system. Other public prosecutors may also need the support of experts, but they still have to appoint the expert for a particular case, assign him or her a specific task and are not continuously supported by the expert.[49] The possibility of working hand in hand with the experts has proved to be of great benefit to the quality, expediency, and promptness of investigation proceedings conducted by the Office.

3.2.2   The Whistle-Blower-System

Since 2013, the Office has been using an internet-based whistle-blower system.[50] Through this platform, reports of suspicions can be submitted

---

44   Ibid s 8.

45   *Strafrechtsänderungsgesetz 2007* [Amendment Act] (Austria) BGBl I 2007/109.

46   *Strafrechtliches Kompetenzpaket 2010* [Reform Act] (Austria) BGBl I 2010/108.

47   There are a total of approximately 420 public prosecutors currently acting nationwide in Austria (see the *Regulation on the Distribution of Functions and Organisation of Staff in the Ministry of Justice*; <https://www.justiz.gv.at/web2013/home/ministerium/organisation~8 ab4a8a422985de30122a91a6504629f.de.html>).

48   *Staatsanwaltschaftsgesetz* [Public Prosecution Act] (Austria) s 2a(5).

49   For details, see *Strafprozessordnung* [Code of Criminal Procedure] (Austria) ("*Strafprozessordnung*") ss 126, 127; Eugen Fabrizy, *StPO und wichtige Nebengesetze* (MANZ, 13th ed, 2017) 350; Hubert Hinterhofer and Alexander Tipold, "ss 126, 127 StPO" in Helmut Fuchs, Eckart Ratz (eds), *Wiener Kommentar zur Strafprozessordnung* (MANZ, 2nd ed, 2011) 18.

50   The whistle-blower report form of the Office of Prosecution for Economic Crime and Corruption is available at: <https://www.bkms-system.net/bkwebanon/report/clientInfo?cin=1at21>; Originally the system was based on *Ministerial Decree BMJ-S585.000/0009-IV 3/2013 of 17 March 2013*; since 2015, the system has been operational based on *Staatsanwaltschaftsgesetz* s 2a(6).

anonymously and without being traceable. After reporting, the whistle-blower can set up a secured online dropbox. This way the Office, unlike in the case of other anonymous reports, has the possibility to directly communicate with the informer to verify or complete the information already given and to take appropriate and successful investigative measures on this basis. The anonymity of the whistle-blower is maintained by using encryption and other special technical security procedures. Besides this, the informer is reminded several times during the reporting procedure not to reveal any personal details if he or she wishes to stay anonymous.

If the whistle-blower sets up an online dropbox, the Office will give feedback regarding the state of investigations. As a result, the whistle-blower will be informed on whether his or her report led to the opening of investigations or contributed to current proceedings, whether the information was forwarded to another authority, for example, the tax authorities, or whether the information given was not substantial enough to take any further steps. If the report indeed leads to a criminal investigation, the information will also be part of the official case file.

The Office has authority to deal with corruption and money laundering, as well as some types of serious economic crime. For this purpose, the legislator considers embezzlement, fraud, social security fraud, accounting fraud and capital market crimes causing financial loss of more than €5 million as serious economic crimes.[51] Between 2013 and 1 September 2017, 5970 reports were given via the whistle-blower-platform.[52] Approximately 27 per cent of these reports concerned tax crime, 23 per cent related to corruption, 21 per cent to economic crime, 15 per cent referred to social security fraud, 2 per cent related to money laundering, 1.1 per cent to accounting fraud and capital market crimes, and in about 11 per cent of the reports other matters were communicated to the Office.

From this high number of reports, 304 were void of any substantial information, and 2567 reports did not lead to any initial suspicion, not even after communication with the whistle-blower. In these cases, no investigations were opened.

For competence reasons, 1741 reports were forwarded to the tax authorities. There were 124 reports that concerned cases which the Office had already been investigating and 582 reports lead to the opening of criminal investigations by

---

51   *Strafprozessordnung* s 20a.
52   I dedicate my thanks to Ilse-Maria Vrabl-Sanda, Head of the Public Prosecutor's Office for Economic Crime and Corruption who provided the cited data on the whistle-blower system.

the Office. In 41 cases, suspects were charged by the Office, 18 charges resulted in convictions, six in acquittals and 12 cases were terminated by diversion measures (deferred prosecution agreements). The remaining reports are still under examination.

4   Concerns: Sponsorships and Austrian Anti-corruption Criminal Law

Several concerns have arisen in Austria regarding the separation between punishable corruption and third party contributions to public authorities, so-called "sponsoring" or sponsorships. Two typical examples highlight the current debate:

(1)   Andrew is a victim of burglary. The local police manage to quickly find the perpetrator and the stolen goods. Grateful for this speedy and successful solving of the crime, Andrew wants to thank the police and support their future work, especially in the area of crime prevention. Therefore, he gives money to the head of the local police unit in order to finance a so-called "Präventionsbus". This bus, eventually owned by a club supporting the police in crime prevention work, is supposed to tour around areas highly affected by burglaries and similar crime and offer advice and counselling on crime prevention to the interested public. The head of the local police unit is cooperating with the club, but he himself or she herself is not a member.

(2)   Each year, official photos are taken in a public school. The director of the school received several offers from photographers and assigned the job to the photographer who promised to give five new laptops to the school in addition to taking the photos. The director is authorised to make this decision and is not personally enriched by this deal. Had the particular photographer not paid for the laptops, these would have had to be financed either by additional payments made by parents or – if possible at all – from the school budget allocated by the state. The photographer made this offer hoping to get the contract.

Such scenarios have in common the fact that third parties financially support public institutions so that these authorities are able to save public money as they can finance some expenditures by the third party contributions. In all such cases, the official or authority concerned may enter into, or already be in, a situation to officially decide on a matter concerning the sponsor, may it come to fining someone for speeding, allocating a contract, granting or denying administrative permissions. In such cases, the benefit drawn from the support of public budgets directly contravenes the maxim that public institutions have to avoid any semblance of partiality. And, of course, the public will be inclined to think that authorities act more favourably towards their sponsor than towards any other "ordinary" citizen. Therefore, third-party contributions to public authorities have corruption "written all over them".

4.1   *Statutory Exemptions from Punishment*

Considering the ever-increasing pressure on public budgets, a solution to the problem must be found. Regarding the first example, the *Criminal Code* itself provides a solution: as a rule, the giving, as well as the receipt, of an undue advantage in exchange for an official act is punishable even if no official duties were violated (s 305 (1);[53] s 307a[54]). Therefore, even if a gift is merely supposed to express one's gratitude towards the official in relation to the exercise of functions, this could result in criminal sanctions. The *Criminal Code* expressly states four exemptions from criminal liability where there is no breach of duties (s 305 (4)). In short, advantages (gifts and other contributions) do not touch on criminal law if they can lawfully be accepted,[55] if they are provided in the context of events in which there is an official interest to participate,[56] if the advantage serves charitable causes and the official has no particular influence

---

53   *Criminal Code* (Austria) s 305: "Accepting Undue Advantages"; for details, see Christoph Aichinger, "s 305 StGB" in Christoph Aichinger and others (eds), *StGB Strafgesetzbuch Kommentar* (Linde, 4th ed, 2017) 1761; Eugen Fabrizy, *StGB und ausgewählte Nebengesetze* (MANZ, 12th ed, 2016) 922; Eva Marek and Robert Jerabek, *Korruption und Amtsmissbrauch* (MANZ, 10th ed, 2017) 73; Florian Messner, "s 305 StGB" in Alois Birklbauer and others (eds), *StGB Strafgesetzbuch Praxiskommentar* (Facultas, 2017) 1591.

54   *Criminal Code* (Austria) s 307a: "Giving Undue Advantages"; for details, see Christoph Aichinger, "s 307a StGB" in Christoph Aichinger et al. (eds), *StGB Strafgesetzbuch Kommentar* (Linde, 4th ed, 2017) 1776; Fabrizy, above n 53, 927; Günther Hauss and Peter Komenda, "s 307a StGB", in Hubert Hinterhofer, Christian Rosbaud (eds), *Salzburger Kommentar zum Strafgesetzbuch* (LexisNexis, 2014) 1; Marek and Jerabek, above n 53, 105; Messner, above n 53, 1617.

55   First alternative *Criminal Code* (Austria) s 305(4)1; Aichinger, "s 305 StGB", above n 53, 1764 [10]; Fabrizy, above n 53, 923 [5]; Günther Hauss and Peter Komenda, "s 305 StGB", in Hubert Hinterhofer, Christian Rosbaud (eds), *Salzburger Kommentar zum Strafgesetzbuch* (LexisNexis, 2014) 14–6 [38]–[41]; Marek and Jerabek, above n 53, 95 [43a]; Messner, above n 53, 1594–5 [6]–[7]; Susanne Reindl-Krauskopf and Stefan Huber, *Korruptionsstrafrecht in Fällen* (Verlag Österreich, 2014) 22–3.

56   Second alternative *Criminal Code* (Austria) s 305(4)1; Aichinger, "s 305 StGB", above n 53, 1765–1766 [15]; Fabrizy, above n 53, 923–4 [6]; Hauss and Komenda, above n 55, 23–6 [57]–[65]; Marek and Jerabek, above n 53, 95–7 [43b]; Messner, above n 53, 1596–7 [8]–[9]; Reindl-Krauskopf and Huber, above n 55, 23–5.

on its use,[57] and, if the advantage is a local or customary courtesy of small value (less than €100).[58]

In the first example, Andrew gives money, therefore an advantage,[59] to the head of the police unit (a public official),[60] in the context of the exercise of official functions, namely the successful solving of the crime and restoration of stolen goods. However, the granted advantage is supposed to be used in crime prevention work for the public's benefit. This qualifies as a benefit serving charitable causes.[61] Therefore, the first requirement of the exemption from punishment is fulfilled. As to the second precondition, the head of the local police unit receiving the money must not have a particular influence on its use.[62] Even though this influence may be a legal as well as a factual one, the cooperation between the official and the private club is not sufficient per se to assume that the official has a particular influence and, consequently, to deny the exemption from punishment. Rather, there is no indication of such an influence whatsoever in that example. Therefore, Andrew, as well as the head of the local police unit, does not incur criminal liability in the present case.

---

57   *Criminal Code* (Austria) s 305 (4) 2; Aichinger, above n 53, 1766–7 [16]–[18]; Fabrizy, above n 53, 924 [7]; Hauss and Komenda, above n 55, 24–9 [66]–[73]; Marek and Jerabek, above n 53, 97–8 [43c]; Messner, above n 53, 1597–9 [10]–[11]; Reindl-Krauskopf and Huber, above n 55, 25–6.

58   *Criminal Code* (Austria) s 305 (4); EBIA 1950/A 24. GP 6; Aichinger, "s 305 StGB", above n 53, 1764–5 [11]–[13]; Fabrizy, above n 53, 924 [8]; Hauss and Komenda, above n 55, 16–22 [42]–[56]; Marek and Jerabek, above n 53, 98–9 [43d]; Messner, above n 53, 1599–1605 [12]–[17]; Reindl-Krauskopf and Huber, above n 55, 26–9.

59   An advantage is a benefit to which the official is not entitled and that places him in a better position than he was before the receipt of this (material or immaterial) benefit: Christoph Aichinger, "s 304 StGB", in Christoph Aichinger et al. (eds), *StGB Strafgesetzbuch Kommentar* (Linde, 4th ed, 2017) 1756 [11]; Fabrizy, above n 53, 920 [4]; Günther Hauss and Peter Komenda, "s 304 StGB", in Hubert Hinterhofer, Christian Rosbaud (eds), *Salzburger Kommentar zum Strafgesetzbuch* (LexisNexis, 2014) 20–7 [60]–[84]; Marek and Jerabek, above n 53, 84–9 [19]–[23]; Reindl-Krauskopf and Huber, above n 55, 8–11.

60   According to s 74 (1) 4a lit b *Criminal Code*, this is any person who exercises legislative, administrative, or judicial functions as an organ or employee of the Federal Government, a State Government, a municipalities association, a municipality, or a public corporation, not including churches and religious groups, another country or an international organisation.

61   Susanne Reindl-Krauskopf, "Verwaltungssponsoring aus strafrechtlicher Sicht" in Federal Ministry of the Interior and Federal Bureau of Anti-Corruption (eds), *Lobbying und Sponsoring* (BMLVS Heersdruckzentrum, 2012) 9, 19; René Wenk, *Korruption im öffentlichen Bereich* (Pro Libris, 2nd ed, 2013) 116.

62   Aichinger, "s 305 StGB", above n 53, 1766–7 [17]–[18]; Hauss and Komenda, above n 55, 28–9 [70]–[73]; Marek and Jerabek, above n 53, 98 [43c]; Messner, above n 53, 1598–9 [11]; Reindl-Krauskopf and Huber, above n 55, 26.

Nevertheless, this exemption for charitable causes is highly debated because, first of all, it does not limit the value of the granted benefit. Therefore,
it would even be possible to offer millions of euros for the exercise of official
functions, as long as there is no breach of duties and the requesting or receiving official has no particular influence on the use of the granted means. Furthermore, the notion of "particular influence" is problematic where a certain
closeness can be detected between the person receiving the advantage and
the one deciding on its use. A slight variation of the initial example may illustrate the problem: if the public official was married to the president of the club
deciding on the use of the money granted by Andrew, the official's influence
on the decision-making could, obviously, not be considered to be a forbidden
particular influence due solely to him or her being married to the club's president.[63] Therefore, from a criminal law perspective, such a scenario will typically not give rise to sanctions. Still, such a behaviour might be perceived as
corrupt, or at least unethical, by the public knowing that similar structures and
procedures have been used to circumvent anti-corruption rules in the past.[64]

4.2 Third Party Contributions and Non-sovereign Administration

In other cases, such as the second example above, the Criminal Code does not
provide for any explicit exemption from punishment. The example illustrating the problem was recently dealt with by the Austrian Supreme Court.[65] The
Court came to the conclusion that third party contributions are not admissible
in the field of sovereign tasks.[66] This finding is appropriate: citizens depend
on the impartial execution of these tasks as, in this field, the citizen is subject
to state powers and no egalitarian partner as in civil law relations. If one cannot rely on independence when state power is applied (this may concern the
granting of an administrative permission, the giving of a judgment or the exercise of police powers), one might easily lose trust in public administration and
this has the potential to harm, or even destroy, society.

But, even outside sovereign tasks, sponsoring is contentious: firstly, citizens pay taxes and it is for the state to finance its tasks by responsibly having
recourse to these resources; secondly, it is often difficult to strictly separate

---

63   Reindl-Krauskopf and Huber, above n 55, 26.
64   The vast scope of this and other exemptions has therefore been criticised, see e.g. Markus
      Brandstetter, Florian Singer, „Gedanken zum KorrStRÄG 2012 – aller guten Dinge sind
      drei" (2012) 6 Journal für Strafrecht 209, 213; Markus Höcher, Peter Komenda, "Spezialfra-
      gen des KorrStRÄG 2012" (2012) ecolex Fachzeitschrift für Wirtschaftsrecht, 688, 689; Robert
      Jerabek, "Neuerungen im Korruptionsstrafrecht – KorrStRÄG 2012" (2013) 3 SIAK Journal
      36, 40; Reindl-Krauskopf and Huber, above n 55, 25.
65   Austrian Supreme Court 17 Os 8/16d, 6 June 2016.
66   Ibid [10].

sovereign from non-sovereign administration. The Supreme Court decided this question in a different manner and held that third-party contributions may be negotiated as part of the contract if state authorities act in the free market. Therefore, providing laptops to the school in this example is only part of the photographer's contractual duties. As long as the contract is not invalid according to the principles of private law,[67] i.e. as long as it is not a bogus contract, the scenario does not give rise to corruption matters in the criminal law sense.[68] Rather, if the school director intentionally accepted an offer disadvantageous to his school, he might even be liable for embezzlement.[69] As, in this specific case, the director had accepted the best offer for the school, and the contract was correct from the civil law perspective, the director would not be criminally liable nor would the photographer.

This judgment might solve some practical problems. Unfortunately, the Supreme Court merely stated that third party contributions are forbidden only in relation to sovereign tasks, without spelling out any criteria for precisely demarcating this area. Therefore, and as pressure on public budgets will inevitably increase, the discussions on third party contributions and sponsoring will surely go on. However, the need for relieving public budgets must not validate a decline of those standards in the fight against corruption that have been established in the past.

5   Conclusion

The development of criminal law instruments against corruption has indeed been successful in Europe, and Austria has effectively implemented the

---

67   For further details concerning the relevant private law regulations see inter alia Martin Binder and Wolfgang Kolmasch, "s 916 ABGB" in Michael Schwimann and Georg Kodek (eds), *ABGB Praxiskommentar* (LexsNexis, 4th ed, 2014); Raimung Bollenberger, "s 867, s 879 and s 916 ABGB" in Helmut Koziol et al. (eds), *ABGB Kurzkommentar* (Verlag Österreich, 5th ed, 2017); Georg Graf, "Section 879 ABGB" in Andreas Kletecka, Martin Schauer (eds), *ABGB-ON* (MANZ, ed 1.03, 2017); Helmut Heiss, "s 916 ABGB" in Andreas Kletecka, Martin Schauer (eds), *ABGB-ON* (MANZ, ed 1.01, 2017); Heinz Krejci, "s 879 ABGB" in Peter Rummel, Meinard Lukas (eds), *Kommentar zum Allgemeinen Bürgerlichen Gesetzbuch* (MANZ, 4th ed, 2017); Stefan Perner, "s 867 ABGB" in Andreas Kletecka, Martin Schauer (eds), *ABGB-ON* (MANZ, ed 1.02); Andreas Riedler, "s 867 and s 879 ABGB" in Michael Schwimann, Georg Kodek (eds), *ABGB Praxiskommentar* (LexisNexis, 4th ed, 2014); Peter Rummel, "s 867 and s 916 ABGB" in Peter Rummel, Meinard Lukas (eds), *Kommentar zum Allgemeinen Bürgerlichen Gesetzbuch* (MANZ, 4th ed, 2017); Andreas Vonkilch, "s 916 ABGB" in Attila Fenyves et al. (eds), *Klang-Kommentar* (Verlag Österreich, 3rd ed, 2011).

68   Austrian Supreme Court 17 Os 8/16d [9].

69   Ibid [11].

obligations deriving from the relevant European legal instruments, despite the concerns described above. However, the European Union and the Council of Europe, as well as the respective member states, have to take the next step, namely starting effective prevention work. The developments on the European, as well as the national, level have greatly contributed to raising awareness to corrupt practices and their consequences in politics and everyday life. The big challenge in the future is to create an effective corruption prevention system. It is probable that corruption will never be totally extinguished, but pursuing a twofold approach that combines preventive measures and criminal persecution will, surely, help reduce corruption. In the end, corruption prevention is not a task to be addressed only by state authorities. Rather, it concerns all members of our societies who must stay alert and refrain from closing their eyes to corruption whenever experienced.

Cybercrime Threats, Offences and Special Investigation Measures from a European Perspective

*Farsam Salimi**

1   Introduction

Cybercrime is a prototype for a transnational threat. Cybercriminals do not act within national borders, the effects of their actions can occur around the world and they act in an increasingly aggressive and confrontational way. According to reports by Europol, there has been a shift from hidden intrusions towards direct confrontation between criminals and victims. The reason for this is that traditional organised criminal groups have turned to cybercrime for its high profits.[1] In the future, this development might increase the amount of media reports and put public pressure on politicians. The fight against cybercrime may thus feature more prominently in public and political debate.

This article focuses on some of the most urgent threats caused by cybercriminals and on the responses on part of the European Union and international organisations. Both substantial law, as well as investigation measures related to information and communication technologies ("ICT"), will be the subject of examination. First, the article gives an overview of new manifestations of cybercrime by examining whether Austrian and similar European legal frameworks adequately cover these threats and how supranational and international treaties try to target them. The article then turns to investigative measures currently hotly debated in Austria and Germany and analyses whether these are reflected in the legal frameworks mentioned above. After giving an impression of the status quo, the article finally takes a look at possible future developments and explores the question of whether there is a need for more multinational responses to these threats.

---

*   Assistant Professor, Department of Criminal Law and Criminology, University of Vienna.
1   *IOCTA 2015* (2015) Europol <https://www.europol.europa.eu/iocta/2015/>; *UNODC Comprehensive Study on Cybercrime, Draft* (February 2013) United Nations Office on Drugs and Crime, xvii   <https://www.unodc.org/documents/organized-crime/UNODC_CCPCJ_EG.4_2013/CYBERCRIME_STUDY_210213.pdf>.

2   The Status Quo: Threats and Responses

2.1   *Hacking Smart Systems*

Ten years ago, the only way to become a victim of cybercrime was by intentionally using the internet via a modem, providing access to the world wide
web. Modern life without using internet devices was still possible. This has dra-
matically changed in recent years. More and more items of daily use are connected to the internet, such as smartphones, smart TVs, smart cars and even
– as a whole – smart homes. With an increasing number of parts of daily life
connected to the internet, the threat of cybercrime has become ever-present,
particularly the danger of the system being hacked i.e. accessed illegally. For
example, a cybercriminal could hack a smart home system that automatically
regulates the air-conditioning and the heating of an apartment or hack into
a smart TV and use the integrated camera to spy on the owner.[2] Even a smart
car can be hacked so that the driver loses control and suffers an accident.[3]
These attacks can be planned and carried out within national borders or from
abroad.

If the attack affects the property or causes physical damage, traditional
criminal offences such as property damage or assault are applicable. They do
not cover the aspect of gaining illegal access to the computer system though.
Article 2 of the *Convention on Cybercrime* (or *Budapest Convention*) (*"Cybercrime Convention"*) obliges the States Parties to establish as criminal offences
under their domestic laws,[4] when committed intentionally, illegal access to the
whole or any part of a computer system. Contracting states may also require
that the offence be committed by infringing security measures, with the intent
of obtaining computer data or other dishonest intent, or in relation to a computer system that is connected to another computer system. Effectively, the
contracting states enjoy a wide discretion in implementing the provision into
national law.

Austria introduced the criminal offence of illegal access to a computer system in s 118a of the *Criminal Code* (Austria) in 2002. Nevertheless, this section
was rarely applied until 2016 because of the strict *mens rea* requirements set

---

2   Cara McGoogan, "Why Your Smart TV is the Perfect Way to Spy On You", *The Telegraph* (on-
      line), 19 February 2018 <http://www.telegraph.co.uk/technology/2017/03/08/smart-tv-perfect
      -way-spy/>.
3   Olivia Solon, "Team of Hackers Take Remote Control of Tesla Model S from 12 Miles Away",
      The Guardian (online), 19 February 2018 <https://www.theguardian.com/technology/2016/
      sep/20/tesla-model-s-chinese-hack-remote-control-brakes>.
4   *Convention on Cybercrime*, opened for signature 23 November 2001, ETS 185 (entered into
      force 1 July 2004).

forth in the provision.[5] The perpetrator had to act with the direct intention (purpose) to acquire knowledge of the data processed in the attacked system. Furthermore, he or she had to intend to personally use that data, make it available to other unauthorised persons or to publish it and, as a result, create a financial benefit or cause damage to another person.[6] In contrast, the corresponding offence in s 202a of the German *Criminal Code* does not require any comparable legal prerequisites.[7] Both concepts, the strict Austrian *mens rea* criteria, as well as the lack of such criteria in the German *Criminal Code*, were regarded as compatible with the standards of art 2 of the *Cybercrime Convention*. This example illustrates the wide national legislative discretion.

The European Union's ("EU") responses to the illegal access to computer systems are very similar: according to art 2 of the *EU Directive on attacks against information systems* ("*Cybercrime Directive*"),[8] member states shall ensure that the intentional access without right to the whole or any part of an information system is punishable as a criminal offence, at least for cases "which are not minor". The similarities to art 2 of the *Cybercrime Convention* are obvious. In fact, the *Directive* is generally based on the *Convention* and, in addition, only introduces aggravating circumstances. Regarding the Austrian provision, the European Commission expressed serious reservations about its compliance with the European standards in 2012 because of the additional *mens rea* elements.[9]

In 2015, the Austrian legislature decided to amend s 118a of the *Criminal Code*. The intent to commit data espionage and to use the data obtained in order to make a profit or to cause damage was fundamentally revised.[10] Surprisingly,

5   Susanne Reindl-Krauskopf, "s 118a StGB" in Frank Höpfel and Eckart Ratz (eds), *Wiener Kommentar zum Strafgesetzbuch* (MANZ, 2nd ed, 2017) 16 [4/3]; Farsam Salimi, "Zahnloses Cyberstrafrecht?" (2012) 22 *Österreichische Juristenzeitung*, 998, 999–1000.

6   Reindl-Krauskopf, "s 118a StGB", above n 5, 16 [4/3]; Clemens Thiele, "s 118a StGB" in Otto Triffterer et al. (eds) *Salzburger Kommentar zum Strafgesetzbuch* (LexisNexis, 2007) 16–9, [57]–[69].

7   Theodor Lenckner and Jörg Eisele, "s 202a StGB" in Albin Eser et al. (eds) *Schönke/Schröder Strafgesetzbuch Kommentar* (CH Beck, 29th ed, 2014) 1948 [27]; Jürgen Peter Graf, "s 202a StGB" in Wolfgang Joecks and Klaus Miebach (eds) *Münchener Kommentar zum Strafgesetzbuch* (CH Beck, 3rd ed, 2017) [80]; Walter Kargl, "s 202a StGB" in Urs Kindhäuser et al. (eds) *Strafgesetzbuch* (Nomos, 5th ed, 2017) [15].

8   *Directive 2013/40/EU of the European Parliament and of the Council of 12 August 2013 on Attacks Against Information Systems and Replacing Council Framework Decision 2005/222/JH* [2013] OJ L 218/8.

9   *Report from the Commission to the Council, based on Article 12 of the Council Framework Decision of 24th February 2005 on attacks against information systems*, 14 July 2008, COM/ (2008)/448/final; Susanne Reindl-Krauskopf, "s 118a StGB", above n 5, 15 [4/2].

10   Austrian Parliament, *Explanatory report to the draft proposal* (8 April 2018) <https://www .parlament.gv.at/PAKT/VHG/XXV/I/I_00689/fname_423854.pdf> 20 f; Reindl-Krauskopf,

the reason for the amendment was not the Commission's review, but the recommendations made by a working group of various academics and state representatives in the Ministry of Justice.[11] Since 1 January 2016, s 118a of Austrian
Criminal Code applies if the illegal access is conducted with the purpose either
to acquire knowledge of personal data, knowledge of which would violate con-
fidential interests worthy of protection. Alternatively, the section requires the
purpose to cause a detriment to another person by using the information or
the computer system itself. This new design of *Criminal Code* s 118a now probably complies with the standards of the EU Directive.

As far as the *actus reus*, or physical elements, are concerned, the unlawful
access is punishable only if committed by infringing security measures.[12] In
practice, the question whether the system was protected by special security
tools such as firewalls or passwords is crucial and lies at the nexus of cyber
security measures and criminal liability.

Section 118a of the *Criminal Code* (Austria) in its new form is now applicable
when somebody hacks a smart home system with the intent of causing harm
by interfering with the heating system, a smart TV with the purpose of spying
on the owner or a smart car with the intent of causing an accident. In all three
cases, the perpetrator either intends to obtain personal data (smart TV) or to
use the system in order to afflict damage on another person. If the person has
to overcome special security settings, the provision applies. This new form of
the offence, covering all these acts, is not the result of European standards but
of efforts on the national level. In other words, national responses to transnational threats.

2.2   DDoS Attacks – DRDOS Attacks and Botnets

Computer systems can also be threatened by denial-of-service attacks. If these
attacks are conducted not by a single computer system but by a person using a large number of infected computer systems, in particular their computing capacity, they are called distributed denial-of-service attacks ("DDoS").[13]

"s 118a StGB", above n 5, 15–7 [4/2]–[4/5]; Diana Maria Carina Bernreiter, "Zum 'StRÄG
2015' und den Änderungen im Bereich des Computerstrafrechts" (2015) 4 *Zeitschrift für
IT-Recht, Rechtsinformation und Datenschutz* 128–9.

11   Austrian Parliament, above n 10, 20 f.
12   Reindl-Krauskopf, "s 118a StGB", above n 5, 22–6, [22]–[29].
13   Johannes Öhlböck and Balaszs Esztegar, "Rechtliche Qualifikation von Denial of Service
Attacken" (2011) 4 *Journal für Strafrecht* 126, 126; Martin Daxecker, "s 126b StGB" in Otto
Triffterer et al. (eds) *Salzburger Kommentar zum Strafgesetzbuch* (LexisNexis, 2012) 8 [24];
Christian Bergauer, "Viren, Würmer, Trojanische Pferde – Computerstrafrecht auf dem

Therefore, criminals often use so-called "botnets", a network of computer systems that have been infected by malware and used to perform specific illegal actions without the owner's knowledge.[14] There is now a third category: cyber criminals often use "amplifier" tools, available on the internet, which amplify the power of the attack, so that the criminal's system sends a small amount of data, but the amount of data influencing the target system is much higher. These attacks are called distributed reflection denial-of-service attacks ("DRDoS").[15]

Denial-of-service attacks are generally covered by art 5 of the *Cybercrime Convention* ("system interference", especially by inputting or transmitting computer data) and by art 4 of the EU *Cybercrime Directive*, which is very similar to the provision in the *Cybercrime Convention*. But it is doubtful whether the special new threats caused by botnets and amplifiers are covered.

First, the creation of a bot-net requires access to the system, which can constitute the criminal offence of hacking, in Austrian law: *Criminal Code* s 118a. The EU *Cybercrime Directive* has also recognised the threat by botnets and therefore provides aggravating circumstances in case the attack affects a significant number of computer systems.[16] These aggravating circumstances have also been implemented in Austrian law. The use of a botnet in order to affect

Prüfstand" in Federal Ministry of the Interior (ed), *35, Ottensteiner Fortbildungsseminar* (2007) 37–8; *Christian Bergauer*, "Das materielle Computerstrafrecht" (Jan Sramek Verlag, 2016) 287–96; Stephan Beukelmann, "Cyberattacken – Erscheinungsformen, Strafbarkeit und Prävention" (2017) 12 *Neue juristische Wochenschrift Spezial* 376, 376.

14   *Directive 2013/40/EU* [2013] OJ L 218/8 recital 5;, *Botnets: Detection, Measurement, Disinfection & Defence* (2011) ENISA (European Network and Information Security Agency) <www.enisa .europa.eu/activities/Resilience-and-CIIP/critical-applications/botnets/botnets -measurement-detection-disinfection-and-defence>; Whitepaper MacAfee, "Das neue Zeitalter der Botnets" (2010) <http://doczz.nl/doc/705008/das-neue-zeitalter-der-botnets>;
Austrian Federal Criminal Police Office, *Cybercrime-Report of the Austrian Federal Criminal Police Office* (2012) 13; Federal Criminal Police Office (Germany) *Bundeslagebild Cybercrime 2011* (2011) 16 f; Philipp Roos and Philipp Schumacher, "Botnetze als Herausforderung für Recht und Gesellschaft" (2014) 6 *MMR Multimedia und Recht* 353, 377; Susanne Reindl-Krauskopf, "Cyberstrafrecht im Wandel" (2015) 3 *Österreichische Juristenzeitung* 112, 113 f; Farsam Salimi, "Kampf gegen Cyberkriminalität: Das österreichische Strafrecht rüstet auf" (2016) 10 *Die Polizei* 286, 289.

15   Stephanie Vogelsang, Frederik Möllers and Karin Potel, "Strafrechtliche Bewertung von 'Honeypots' bei DoS-Angriffen, Strafbarkeit bei der digitalen Spurensuche" (2017) 5 *Multimedia und Recht* 291; Markus Schmidt, "s 3 Technische Grundlagen des Internets", in: Astrid Auer-Reinsdorff and Isabell Conrad (eds) *Handbuch IT- und Datenschutzrecht* (CH Beck, 2nd ed, 2016) [234].

16   *Directive 2013/40/EU* [2013] OJ L 218/8, recital 5, 6 and 13; art 9 [3].

one single system, though, is not specifically mentioned in the *Directive*.[17] The only time the *Directive* does mention botnet attacks on one single system is in the context of attacks against an information system which is part of critical infrastructure. Critical infrastructure is defined as facilities, assets, systems and their components, that are of critical significance for maintaining special public services, for example, public security, national defence or public information and communication technology.[18] In this case, the penalties are higher. These standards concerning the special protection of critical infrastructure and the threats by botnets in general led to an expansion of cybercrime law in Austria – transnational standards modifying national law.

The use of amplifiers makes attacks much more effective.[19] Nevertheless, this threat is not explicitly covered in the EU directive nor – at least as far as Austrian and German criminal laws are concerned – by national law. The significant risks of DDoS and DRDoS attacks and the absence of provisions covering all forms of these attacks confirm the need for international and national law to stay ahead of technological developments in cybercrime.

2.3   *Cyber Terrorism – The Internet as a Weapon*

Attacks on critical infrastructure build a bridge to the next threat: the differences between cybercrime and cyber terrorism are becoming more and more unclear. The European Council Cyber Convention Committee states that the "substantive crimes in the *Convention* may be carried out as acts of terrorism, to facilitate terrorism, to support terrorism, including financially, or as preparatory acts".[20]

For example, the attack on a computer system of public healthcare services is considered an act of cybercrime if conducted with the purpose of extortion. In many cases, the system is infected by malware, which encrypts the data stored in the system and afterwards the user – in this case, say, a public

---

17   Farsam Salimi, "Kampf gegen Cyberkriminalität: Das österreichische Strafrecht rüstet auf" (2016) 10 *Die Polizei* 286, 289–90.

18   Section 74 (1) 1 Austrian Criminal Code; Robert Jerabek, Richard Ropper, "s 74 StGB" in Frank Höpfel and Eckart Ratz (eds), *Wiener Kommentar zum Strafgesetzbuch* (MANZ, 2nd ed, 2017) 81–3 [60/20]–[60/31].

19   "1,35 Terabit pro Sekunde: Weltgrößte DDoS-Attacke gegen Github", *Der Standard* (online), 2 March 2018, <https://derstandard.at/2000075316595/1-35-Terabit-pro-Sekunde -Weltgroesste-DDoS-Attacke-gegen-Github>; Stephanie Vogelsang, Frederik Möllers, Potel, above n 15, 291, 292.

20   Cybercrime Prevention Committee (T-CY) *T-CY Guidance Note #11 (Aspects of Terrorism Covered by the Budapest Convention)*, adopted by the 16th Plenary of the T-CY (14–15 November 2016) <https://rm.coe.int/16806bd640>.

hospital – is requested to pay a certain amount of money, often by using bit-coin or another internet currency.[21]

If this attack is conducted without intent to gain a financial benefit, it might be an act of cyber terrorism. In Ukraine, a massive cyberattack on the power supply system recently caused an extensive blackout, affecting hundreds of thousands of people.[22] After a couple of hours, the power supply was restored. Nevertheless, such blackouts can have dramatic impacts on modern informa-tion societies.[23] Even the central water supply in modern societies does not work without electricity. In Austria, such an attack would probably have more severe effects: due to the excellent water quality of our tap water, hardly any-body now keeps supplies of bottled water.[24]

Attacks on systems of critical infrastructure incur more severe penalties due to the *EU Cybercrime Directive*.[25] One could say that real cyberterrorists might not be deterred by higher penalties and that effective cyber security measures and intelligence services are crucial. Nevertheless, new threats have to be re-flected in our criminal offences. And, considering the fact that cyber terrorist attacks are not necessarily committed by terrorists themselves, but by criminal organisations being paid for their activities, more severe penalties may not be futile.

---

21   Franziska Boehm and Paulina Pesch, "Bitcoins: Rechtliche Herausforderungen einer vir-tuellen Währung, Eine erste juristische Einordnung" (2014) 2 *Multimedia und Recht* 75, 77; Christian Rückert, "Vermögensabschöpfung und Sicherstellung bei Bitcoins, neue jurist-ische Herausforderungen durch die ungeklärte Rechtsnatur von virtuellen Währungsein-heiten" (2016) 5 *MMR Multimedia und Recht* 295; 295; Christoph Safferling, Christian Rückert, "Telekommunikationsüberwachung bei Bitcoins – Heimliche Datenauswertung bei virtuellen Währungen gem. s 100a StPO?" (2015) 12 *Multimedia und Recht* 788, 789.

22   Pavel Polityuk, Oleg Vukmanovic and Stephen Jewkes "Ukraine's power outage was a cyber attack: Ukrenergo", *Reuters* (online) 19 January 2017, <https://www.reuters.com/ar-ticle/us-ukraine-cyber-attack-energy/ukraines-power-outage-was-a-cyber-attack-ukren-ergo-idUSKBN1521BA>; "Ukraine power cut 'was cyber-attack'", BBC (online), 11 January 2017 <http://www.bbc.com/news/technology-38573074>.

23   Stefan Altenschmidt, "Die Versorgungssicherheit im Lichte des Verfassungsrechts" (2015) 9 *Neue Zeitschrift für Verwaltungsrecht* 560; Ralf Krauter, *Blackout – ohne Strom geht nichts* (27 March 2013) Deutschlandfunk, <http://www.deutschlandfunk.de/technik -gegen-terror-blackout-ohne-strom-geht-nichts.676.de.html?dram:article_id=380001>; Laura Gaida and Vanessa Valkovic, *Experten: Flächendeckender Stromausfall wäre nationale Katastrophe mit vielen Toten* Online Focus (24 August 2016) <https://www.focus.de/poli tik/deutschland/zivilverteidigungskonzept-experten-flaechendeckender-stromausfall-waere-nationale-katastrophe-mit-vielen-toten_id_5856252.html>.

24   Fabian Schmid, "Blackout durch Hacker wird real – ist Österreich vorbereitet?", *Der Stan-dard* (online), 6 August 2017, <http://derstandard.at/2000061032966/Blackout-durch-Hac ker-wird-real-ist-Oesterreich-vorbereitet>.

25   *Directive 2013/40/EU* OJ L 218/12, art 9(4)(c).

3   Combatting these Threats: Effective Investigative Measures

Criminal offences are of little use without efficient investigative measures enabling police authorities to investigate crime within a reasonable period of time. The next part outlines two investigative measures that are essential but create many problems.

3.1   *Transborder Access to Data*
Data storing methods have fundamentally changed in recent years. Data is not primarily stored on local devices but, far more often, on external servers such as cloud services.[26] In many cases, this data is stored outside national borders.

Traditional provisions, such as search and seizure, cannot be applied without infringement of sovereign rights of the state in which the data is physically stored, not to mention the difficulty in detecting the country where the data is physically stored in this time of cloud-computing, where data is stored on servers all around the world. The need to access data which is stored outside national borders has become the rule rather than the exception. From a mere national perspective, national law could provide the access without taking into consideration the national sovereignty of the state where the seizure actually takes place. In fact, the Austrian *Code of Criminal Procedure* does not explicitly mention access to external data but, in practice, access to data is, according to prevailing opinion, considered legitimate.[27] In German law, there is an explicit provision in art 110 (3) of the *Code of Criminal Procedure* (Germany) about access to externally stored data. Neither Austrian nor German law deal with transborder access.

The international treaties do not respond to these problems either. Article 32 of the *Cybercrime Convention* and the *Guidance Note No 3 of the Cyber Convention Committee*[28] deal with transnational access to data. The *Cybercrime*

---

26   Ingeborg Zerbes and Mohamad El-Ghazi, "Zugriff auf Computer: Von der gegenständlichen zur virtuellen Durchsuchung" (2015) 8 *Neue Zeitschrift für Strafrecht* 425, 428; Sonja Dürager, "Outsourcing in die Cloud, Ein (un-)beherrschbares Risiko aus datenschutzrechtlicher Sicht?" (2017) *ipCompetence* 36; Andreas Popp, "IT-Outsourcing und Cloud Computing – zwei neue Herausforderungen für die Criminal Compliance" (2012) 1 *Journal für Strafrecht* 30; Christian Schröder and Christian Haag, "Neue Anforderungen an Cloud Computing für die Praxis – Zusammenfassung und erste Bewertung der 'Orientierungshilfe – Cloud Computing'" (2011) 4 *Zeitschrift für Datenschutz* 147.

27   Alexander Tipold and Ingeborg Zerbes, "s 111 StPO" in Helmut Fuchs and Eckart Ratz (eds), *Wiener Kommentar zur Strafprozessordnung* (MANZ, 2015) 59 [14].

28   Cybercrime Convention Committee (T-CY) *Guidance Note # 3 Transborder access to data (Article 32)* Adopted by the 12th Plenary of the T-CY (2–3 December 2014) <https://www.coe.int/en/web/cybercrime/guidance-notes>.

Convention and the *Guidance Note* are very clear: the *Convention* only covers access to publicly available data or access with consent of the user of the system. Access to data stored in another country without the suspect's consent is not covered by this article. There is another provision in art 29 of the *Convention*, providing that one party may request another party to order the expeditious preservation of data stored by means of a computer system, located within the territory of that other party. After this preservation, the requesting party has to submit a regular request for mutual assistance. This article does not include direct access for law enforcement authorities of one state on data stored on the territory of another either. To conclude: one can either accept that the principle of sovereignty of states is not effective anymore when it comes to computer systems or find new answers to transborder access. The existing national laws cannot solve the problems of state sovereignty.

A significant change is emerging at the level of the European Union: in April 2018, the European Commission presented a proposal for a regulation on *"European Production and Preservation Orders for electronic evidence in criminal matters"*.[29] Article 1 of the regulation empowers an authority of a member state to order a service provider offering services in the Union, to produce or preserve electronic evidence, regardless of the location of data. The proposal distinguishes between orders to produce transactional[30] or content data and orders to produce subscriber data[31] or access data.[32] Access to content data, which would probably be the most important category of data for evidence purposes, is limited to special types of criminal offences. However, if this regulation enters into force, it might solve the most urgent problems in relation to transborder access to data – merely from a European perspective, of course. However, the European legislative process has just been initiated and might take a long time.

---

29   *Proposal for a regulation of the European Parliament and of the Council on European Production and Preservation Orders for electronic evidence in criminal matters*, Strasbourg, 17 April 2018 COM (2018) 225 final.
30   Ibid. Article 2(9) defines transactional data as data related to the provision of a service offered by a service provider that serves to provide context or additional information about such service and is generated or processed by an information system of the service provider, such as the source and destination of a message or another type of interaction, data on the location of the device, date, time, duration, size, route, format, the protocol used and the type of compression, unless such data constitutes access data ...
31   Ibid art 2(7).
32   Ibid art 2(8).

3.2   Data Retention

Cybercriminals usually act anonymously. In many cases, traffic data of their electronic communication is the only way to identify the subscriber or registered user. The *Data Retention Directive* of the EU obliged member states to retain data for at least six months and to ensure that data retained in accordance with this directive is forwarded only to the competent national authorities in specific cases and in accordance with national law.[33] After very heated discussions, this directive was implemented in Austria, making it compulsory for telecommunication companies and internet providers to retain data for a period of six months.[34] Prior to the implementation of the *Data Retention Directive*, traffic data was also retained by the providers, but not because they were obliged to do so. On the contrary, they were required to delete personal traffic data unless they needed this data for internal technical or billing reasons.[35] This situation caused uncertainty among the police and prosecution services, as it was uncertain for how long the data was actually stored by the different providers.[36]

The *Data Retention Directive* was suspended in April 2014. The European Court of Justice declared the *Data Retention Directive* invalid, for violating fundamental rights.[37] Afterwards, the Austrian Constitutional Court repealed the national provisions.[38] Now, the Austrian law enforcement authorities face the same situation as before: the prosecution service and the police can obtain traffic data from providers under court authorisation but there remains lack of clarity regarding its duration. Meanwhile, the EU Court of Justice declared that some national systems of data retention do indeed violate fundamental human rights of the *European Charter of Fundamental Rights*[39] and has

---

33   *Directive 2006/24/EC of the European Parliament and of the Council of 15 March 2006 on the retention of data generated or processed in connection with the provision of publicly available electronic communications services or of public communications networks and amending Directive 2002/58/EC* [2006] OJ L 105/54.

34   Lisa Pühringer, "Vorratsdatenspeicherung, Zugriffsmöglichkeiten durch Sicherheits – und Strafverfolgungsbehörden" (2012/2013) 2 *Juristische Ausbildung und Praxis* 80; Christoph Tschohl, "Vorratsdatenspeicherung – Aufstieg und Fall in Österreich" in Dietmar Jahnel (ed), *Jahrbuch Datenschutzrecht* (NWV Verlag, 2014) 31; Lukas Feiler and Ana Stahov, "Die Einführung der Vorratsdatenspeicherung in Österreich" (2011) 3 *Medien und Recht* 111.

35   *Telecommunication Act 2003* (Austria), s 99(2); Pühringer, above n 34.

36   Pühringer, above n 34.

37   *Digital Rights Ireland Ltd v Minister for Communications, Marine and Natural Resources* (Court of Justice of the European Union, C-293/12 and C-594/12, 8 April 2014).

38   *Government of the Province of Carinthia* (Austrian Constitutional Court, G47/2012, 27 June 2014).

39   *Charter of the Fundamental Rights of the European Union* [2000] OJ C 364/1.

established even higher barriers to a general data retention system.[40] The current German data retention system is very likely to be incompatible with the standards of the European Court of Justice.[41] In Austria, a replacement regulation of data retention, called "quick freeze", has recently been introduced.[42] Quick freeze means that, only in the case of a prosecution service order must a suspect's data be stored by the private providers.[43] It differs from real data retention systems where the traffic data of every user is stored in advance without the requirement of suspicion and without a formal order by a court or the prosecution service.

4   The Future: Need for More Multinational Responses?

This part examines whether there is a need for further international instruments in the fight against cybercrime. First of all, there is still no international instrument at the UN level. In recent years, however, there have been substantial efforts to develop such instruments. In 2010, the UN General Assembly, in its 71st Plenary Meeting, recommended that the Commission on Crime Prevention and Criminal Justice ("CCPCJ") should establish an Intergovernmental Expert Group with the task to conduct a comprehensive study on cybercrime. In 2013, a draft study (*Comprehensive Study on Cybercrime*) was published.[44]

In summary the "key findings" of the study are:

– There is an insufficient harmonisation. "Core" cybercrime offences, investigative powers, and the rules on admissibility of electronic evidence have to be harmonised.

– The existence of multiple instruments with different thematic and geographic scope may lead to the emergence of country cooperation "clusters"

---

40   *Tele2 Sverige AB v Post- och telestyrelsen* and *Secretary of State for the Home Department v Watson* (Court of Justice of the European Union, C-203/15 and C-698/15, 26 December 2016).

41   Alexander Roßnagel, "Vorratsdatenspeicherung vor dem Aus?" (2017) 10 *Neue Juristische Wochenschrift* 696; Aqilah Sandhu, "Die Tele2-Entscheidung des EuGH zur Vorratsdatenspeicherung in den Mitgliedstatten und ihre Auswirkungen auf die Rechtslage in Deutschland" (2017) 3 *Europarecht* 453.

42   Section 134(3)(b) *Code of Criminal Procedure* (Austria).

43   Jens Eckhardt, "s 113 TKG" in Martin Geppert and Raimund Schütz (eds) *Beck'scher Kommentar TKG* (CH Beck, 4th ed, 2013) [34]; Marian Arning and Flemming Moos, "Quickfreeze als Alternative zur Vorratsdatenspeicherung? – Auseinandersetzung mit dem Diskussionsentwurf des BMJ und der Stellungnahme des DAV" (2012) 4 *Zeitschrift für Datenschutz* 154.

44   United Nations Office on Drugs and Crime, above n 1.

that are not suited to the global nature of cybercrime; within these clusters the mutual support may work but this is not enough.

- In a world of cloud computing and data centres, the role of evidence "location" needs to be reconceptualised, including direct access to extraterritorial data by law enforcement authorities.
- Developing countries require long-term, sustainable, comprehensive technical support and assistance for the investigation and combating of cybercrime.[45]

On the basis of the key findings the study frames so-called "options"; in fact these are more recommendations to the member states. These options include:

- development of international model provisions;
- development of a comprehensive multilateral instrument on cybercrime;
- development of a multilateral instrument on international cooperation regarding electronic evidence in criminal matters; and
- delivery of enhanced technical assistance for the prevention and combating of cybercrime in developing countries.[46]

Referring to the study, there is an urgent need for new international tools and harmonisation of cybercrime laws.[47] But, looking at the comments on the draft study made by some member states, one will come to the conclusion that it is very unlikely that there will be a new instrument in the near future. Some comments are generally in favour of the efforts towards harmonisation, such as the comments made by China[48] and Brazil.[49] But major Western powers such as the United States,[50] Germany[51] and also Australia[52] strongly oppose

---

45   Ibid xi–xii.

46   Ibid xii.

47   Ibid 56.

48   China, *Comments to the Comprehensive Study on Cybercrime* (2016) <https://www.unodc .org/documents/organized-crime/Cybercrime_Comments/Contributions_received/ China.pdf>.

49   The Permanent Mission of the Federative Republic of Brazil to International Organizations in Vienna, *Comments to the Comprehensive Study on Cybercrime* (2016) <https:// www.unodc.org/documents/organized-crime/Cybercrime_Comments/Contributions_ received/Brazil_updated.pdf>.

50   *Comments of the United States of America to the Comprehensive Study on Cybercrime* (2016) <https://www.unodc.org/documents/organized-crime/Cybercrime_Comments/Contributions_received/United_States_of_America.pdf>.

51   *German Comments on the Comprehensive Study on Cybercrime* (*Draft – February 2013*) (2016) <https://www.unodc.org/documents/organized-crime/Cybercrime_Comments/ Contributions_received/Germany.pdf>.

52   *Australia – Comments on the Draft Comprehensive Study on Cybercrime* (2016) <https:// www.unodc.org/documents/organized-crime/Cybercrime_Comments/Contributions_ received/Australia.pdf>.

some of the key findings and solutions proposed by the study. Germany, for example, emphasises the importance of the *Cybercrime Convention*, already ratified by 49 States around the world, together with the efforts of the Cybercrime Convention Committee and the *EU Cybercrime Directive*. Germany is of the view that new model provisions would inevitably lead to a lowering of already achieved standards.[53] The US and Australia point out that a sufficient range of multilateral instruments already exist, thus a debate on a new convention would take time and divert attention and resources from the more pressing need for practical capacity building and technical support.[54] The US further asserts that the problem appears to be the absence of knowledge and technical skills, not an absence of law.

It is questionable whether these concerns are justified, for example, whether it is true that there is no absence of law. Instruments such as the *Cybercrime Convention* already exist. But they are not ready for current threats. For example, they do not cover the increased danger of attacks conducted by using botnets. The Cyber Convention Committee has announced a *Guidance Note* specifically dealing with botnets.[55] However, reading the note is rather disillusioning: it is just a list of articles of the 2002 *Cybercrime Convention* that – in some way – can be applied on the creation and use of botnets. Nevertheless, it is obvious that no article of the *Cybercrime Convention* in particular deals with botnets. Transborder access to data stored in clouds is not covered either. Article 32 and art 29 of the *Convention* and the *Guidance Note No 2* address the transborder access to data, as mentioned before, a very important issue in times of cloud computing. But the *Cybercrime Convention* and the *Guidance Note* do not cover the direct access to data stored in another country without the suspect's consent.

This shows that the *Cybercrime Convention* is still at the level of 2002, not dealing with major current cybercrime threats. The EU *Directive* has more relevance regarding these threats but is only effective within the EU and merely deals with substantial law. The regulation on *European Production and Preservation Orders for Electronic Evidence in Criminal Matters* which is being discussed would only solve the problem between member states of the European Union. Therefore, an updated version of the *Cybercrime Convention* is necessary to cover all new manifestations of cybercrime and create a minimum

---

53   Germany, above n 51.
54   United States of America, above n 50; Australia, above n 52.
55   T-*CY Guidance Note #2 Provisions of the Budapest Convention Covering Botnets* (2013) <https://rm.coe.int/CoERMPublicCommonSearchServices/DisplayDCTMContent?docu mentId=09000016802e7094>.

consensus of core cybercrime offences in order to avoid safe havens. Even within the EU, among countries which have ratified the *Cybercrime Convention*, there are differences regarding the scope of criminal responsibility. Without a binding framework, the differences between countries with differing legal backgrounds and traditions will always lead to safe havens for transborder cybercriminals. Such a framework could possibly be based on the *Cybercrime Convention*, including answers to new threats. And it is doubtful that such a framework would inevitably lead to a lowering of already achieved standards. A new treaty could indeed foresee obligatory minimum standards for the ratifying states, as well as provisions that are not mandatory, going beyond the standards of the current *Cybercrime Convention*.

What about a further major concern – difficult negotiations distracting from more urgent issues, such as capacity building and technical support? The debate on new minimum standards and a UN-framework on cybercrime could easily be accompanied by practical efforts to strengthen the capacities and the knowledge of law enforcement authorities – especially in developing countries. One could get the impression that these are hypocritical reasons. Maybe industrialised countries are rather satisfied with their standards and domestic law and do not want any changes, as long as the extradition of suspects from developing countries works well.

5   Conclusion

Cybercrime is not limited to national boundaries. Although amendments to national criminal law are essential to close legal loopholes, the mere increase of the national level of punishment without harmonisation of the standards with other countries is hardly useful in fighting transnational criminality. Transnational criminal investigations, such as transborder data access, need multinational harmonisation to guarantee the successful fight against cybercrime. Yet is not an either/or question. The fight against cybercrime needs national efforts combined with minimum standards and harmonisation on a multinational level.

The European Arrest Warrant: A Blueprint for International Cooperation in Criminal Matters in Other Regions?

*Harmen van der Wilt**

1 Introduction

On 13 June 2002, the Council of Ministers of the European Union adopted the *Framework Decision on the European Arrest Warrant and the Surrender Procedures between Member States ("Framework Decision").*[1] The establishment of this instrument can only be understood against the backdrop of the lifting of inner frontiers within Europe, a process that started with the creation of the Schengen Area in 1985 and gradually extended, involving other states, concurrent with the expansion of the European Union. Obviously, the intention of this measure was to facilitate the free movement of persons within "an area of freedom, security and justice"[2] but it had its flipside as well. Within the realm of criminal law enforcement, the abolition of customs checks was conducive to an inversion of the natural order (to put it with a sense of drama): criminal offenders could henceforth freely roam in this paradise of golden opportunities, whereas law enforcement officials were the inmates of their own states. This inconvenient situation was partially alleviated by art 41 of the *Schengen Convention* which allowed officers of one of the contracting parties to enter the territory of another party in pursuit of a person caught in the act of committing a crime, without the prior authorisation of the latter state.[3] However, the pursuing officers had no right to apprehend the fugitive, let alone be allowed to take him to their home country. Custody over the offender for the purpose of criminal proceedings could only be accomplished by means of cumbersome extradition proceedings which, in the words of John Spencer, were "slow,

---

* Professor of International Criminal Law, University of Amsterdam.

1 *Framework Decision on the European Arrest Warrant and the Surrender Procedures between Member States* [2002] OJL 190/1 (*"Framework Decision"*).

2 Compare art 3(2) of the *Consolidated Version of the Treaty on the European Union* [2012] OJ C 326, 1.

3 *Convention of 19 June 1990, applying the Schengen Agreement of 14 June 1985 between the Governments of the States of the Benelux Economic Union, the Federal Republic of Germany and the French Republic, on the Gradual Abolition of Checks at their Common Borders*, opened for signature 19 June 1990, 30 ILM 84 (entered into force 1 September 1993).

---

costly and uncertain".[4] In other words: extradition had to be adapted to modern times.

The path was paved by the European Council's endorsement of the principle of "mutual recognition" as the "cornerstone of judicial co-operation in both civil and criminal matters within the Union" during the summit of the European Council at Tampere, Finland, in October 1999.[5] The wording of the conclusions prefigures the establishment of the European Arrest Warrant ("EAW"):

> With respect to criminal matters, the European Council ... considers that the formal extradition procedure should be abolished among the Member States as far as persons are concerned who are fleeing from justice after having been finally sentenced, and replaced by a simple transfer of such persons, in compliance with Article 6 of the *Treaty on the European Union*. Consideration should also be given to fast track extradition procedures, without prejudice to the principle of a fair trial.[6]

And indeed, the 2002 *Framework Decision* was the first fruit of the concept of mutual recognition.

The aim of this contribution is to shed some light on the legal nature of the EAW, how the system works out in practice and to explore whether (parts of) it can be transplanted to the context of international cooperation in criminal matters in other regions, like, for instance, Oceania. To that purpose, I will first give a bird's eye view of the objectives that the *Framework Decision* seeks to accomplish and how they have materialised in the envisaged procedure on the mutual surrender of suspects and convicts between member states of the European Union (Section 2). In Section 3, I will address three topics that, in my view, cause the most controversy in the execution of EAWs and frequently come up before the (Dutch) Chamber for International Cooperation in legal matters of the Amsterdam District Court (hereafter "IRC", according to the Dutch acronym).[7] Then I will discuss who may qualify as a "resident of the

---

4 John R. Spencer, "The European Arrest Warrant" (2004) 6 *Cambridge Yearbook of European Legal Studies*, 202.

5 European Union: Council of the European Union, "Presidency Conclusions", *Tampere European Council, 15–16 October 1999* (1999), (15/16 October 1999) s 33 <http://www.europarl.europa.eu/summits/tam_en.htm>.

6 Ibid s 35.

7 I would like to acknowledge that, as a part-time judge in the IRC, I have some experience with the assessment of EAWs. It should be stressed that all opinions are expressed in my personal capacity as a scholar in international criminal law and do not necessarily reflect the view of the IRC.

executing member state", with a view to being entitled to return to that state in order to serve there the custodial sentence imposed by the issuing member state (Section 3.1).[8] Next, I will explore the technically difficult issue of decisions rendered in absentia that often leaves judges literally "lost in translation" (Section 3.2). In Section 3.3, I will revisit the well-known problem of (potential) conflicts between the obligation to surrender fugitives from justice and the duty to respect human rights, whenever the requested person runs a risk of being maltreated or of being exposed to an unfair trial in the issuing state. Any suggestions on the adoption of certain features of the EAW in other geographical regions – Section 4 – can only be very tentative, in view of my lack of in-depth knowledge of extradition law and practice in other parts of the world. Therefore, I propose to consider these contexts as *terra incognita* and simply investigate to what extent the EAW can be detached from the specific institutional architecture of the European Union. Section 5 closes with some final reflections.

2 The Legal Nature of the European Arrest Warrant, as Envisaged by the EU Council *Framework Decision*

The primordial objective of the *Framework Decision* has been to expedite the procedure on the surrender of fugitives from justice and to make the outcome certain and predictable. Article 17 stipulates that – if the requested person does not consent to his surrender – the final decision on the execution of the EAW must be taken within a period of 60 days after the arrest of that person. Subsequently, the person requested must be surrendered no later than 10 days after the final decision on the execution of the EAW.[9] Although the *Framework Decision* does not explicitly preclude appellate proceedings, the timeframe will usually be too tight to procure this. Moreover – and importantly – the Minister of Justice or Home Secretary, who traditionally has the final say in extradition proceedings, is completely side-lined.[10]

Obviously, such a severe curtailment of the procedure can only be accomplished if the decision-making process is simplified as well. Article 3 of the *Framework Decision* comprises a rigid system of grounds for refusal, limiting them to:

---

8   Compare art 5(3) of the *Framework Decision*.

9   *Framework Decision* art 23.

10   Spencer, above n 4, 207, observes that "the transfer of suspects and convicted persons between the UK and the rest of Europe is 'depoliticised'".

- An amnesty in the executing state, where that state had jurisdiction to prosecute the offence under its own law (s 1).
- A final judgment by a member state in respect of the same acts provided that, where the person has been convicted, the sentence has been served or is currently being served or may no longer be executed according to the law of the executing State (s 2).
- Lack of criminal responsibility, due to the age of the requested person, under the law of the executing state (s 3).

The most salient element of the *Framework Decision* is the partial abolition of the dual criminality requirement. Article 2 delimits the scope of the EAW, providing that an arrest warrant can be issued for acts punishable by the law of the issuing member state by a custodial sentence (or detention order) for a maximum period of at least 12 months or, where a sentence has been passed (or a detention order has been made), for sentences of at least 4 months. The crime must reach a threshold of seriousness, because otherwise it would be futile to make all the fuss.[11] But it is the perspective of the issuing member state that counts, as s 2 contains a list of 32 offences for which surrender is mandatory, provided that they are punishable in the issuing member state by a custodial sentence (or detention order) of at least three years and without verification of the double criminality of the act. In other words: in these circumstances the requested state has to comply, even if the act is not a criminal offence under its own law. The list comprises transnational crimes, like terrorism and trafficking in human beings, but also home-grown offences like murder and swindling.[12] Many of these offences have been the subject matter of European legal instruments (framework decisions or directives) that aim at the harmonisation of (substantive) criminal law of the member states, so it is fair to wonder whether the abolition of double criminality is not redundant. However that may be, the arrangement leaves the requested state very little room for discretion. In principle, it has to accept the judgment of the issuing state that certain conduct qualifies as a listed offence, because any assessment on the basis of its own standards would imply a disguised attempt to reintroduce double criminality.[13] If the offence incurs less than three years' imprisonment in the

---

11   In practice, however, the threshold is meaningless, because it allows the issue of an EAW for scratching a car, shoplifting and simple possession of marijuana.

12   For an extensive discussion of these categories, see Nico Keijzer, "The Double Criminality Requirement" in Rob Blekxtoon and Wouter van Ballegooij (eds), *Handbook on the European Arrest Warrant* (TMC Asser Press, 2005) 138.

13   See on the (non) assessment of dual criminality the acute observations of Elies van Sliedregt, "The Dual Criminality Requirement" in Nico Keijzer and Elies van Sliedregt (eds), *The European Arrest Warrant in Practice* (TMC Asser Press, 2009) 51, 64–7.

requesting state, or does not feature on the list, the executing judicial authority is allowed to refuse surrender if the dual criminality test is not met (art 2(4) and art 4(1), *Framework Decision*). Other optional grounds for refusal include pending criminal proceedings in the requested or another member state and foreign *res judicata* in non-member states.[14] Of special interest is the so called territoriality exception in art 4(7)(a) that allows the executing judicial authority to refuse surrender when the offence, according to the law of the executing state, is committed in whole or in part in the territory of that state.[15] It serves as a compensation for the (partial) abolition of the dual criminality and accommodates states harbouring a liberal policy towards – for instance – drug use, abortion and euthanasia. After all, in the absence of this facility, the executing state would probably be obliged to comply with requests of less broad-minded states, whereas it now has the option to safeguard its sovereign sphere from foreign intrusion.

It is clear that the *Framework Decision* exhibits a logically coherent system. Compared to extradition, the number and scope of grounds for refusal have reduced. Time-honoured exceptions, like the political, military and fiscal offence exception and the right to refuse the extradition of nationals, have disappeared or have been severely curtailed. The line of reasoning has been that the decision on the execution of the EAW could be entrusted to a single judicial authority that could reach a judgment within a short time.[16] Appellate proceedings were considered redundant, as the decision-making process would be relatively straightforward and no intricate legal issues were likely to arise. Underpinning the entire system is a "high level of confidence between member states", as the Preamble explicitly propounds.[17] The executing judicial authority should trust that the requesting state has sufficient evidence to pursue criminal prosecution and should take the quality of the issuing state's administration of justice for granted.

Within the concise scope of this contribution, it is impossible to indicate whether legal practice has met the high expectations. A general impression should suffice. In the early years, the European Court of Justice ("ECJ") was often seized to elucidate specific legal concepts in the new *Framework of the*

---

14   Respectively art 4(2) and art 4(5) of the *Framework Decision*.

15   The territoriality exception is also incorporated in art 7 of the *European Convention on Extradition*, opened for signature 13 December 1957, ETS No 24 (entered into force 18 April 1960), and has apparently survived the transition from extradition to surrender.

16   It is interesting to note that some countries, like Germany and the Netherlands, have indeed concentrated the consideration of EAWs in a specialised Chamber on international cooperation in criminal matters.

17   *Framework Decision*, preamble (10).

European Arrest Warrant.[18] In *Advocaten voor de Wereld,* the ECJ rejected the view, as presented by plaintiffs, that the abolition of dual criminality implied a violation of the legality principle.[19] Other preliminary decisions concerned the double jeopardy (or *ne bis in idem*) principle as ground for refusal and addressed the question which judicial decisions triggered *non bis in idem* or what should be understood by "the same acts".[20] In respect of the latter issue, the Court clarified that the relevant criterion is "identity of the material acts, understood as the existence of a set of facts which are inextricably linked together, irrespective of the legal classification given to them or the legal interest protected".[21] That approach makes sense in view of the fact that fully-fledged harmonisation of substantive law within the European Union is not intended and that protection by the *non bis in idem* rule would be reduced to zero if the assessment of "the same fact" were to be governed by diverging legal classifications.

Gradually, domestic courts have found their way in the application of the law on the EAW, supported by the ECJ's finding that implementing legislation should be interpreted in light of the wording and purpose of the EAW *Framework Decision.*[22] However, many decisions on the execution of an EAW involve a balancing of societal interest in effective law enforcement and the interests of the requested person, especially if the latter's fundamental rights are at stake. It is in this area that tensions between the issuing and executing state often arise. Such delicate decision-making is the topic of the next section.

3   **Controversial Issues in the Execution of European Arrest Warrants**

3.1   *Nationals, Residents and Persons Staying in the Requested State*
Whereas nationals are no longer protected against extradition/surrender, they still enjoy a privileged position. For one thing, member states are not under

---

18   According to art 267 of the *Treaty on the Functioning of the European Union,* the ECJ has
       jurisdiction, by way of a preliminary ruling, to give an interpretation of the Treaties and
       the (legislative) acts of the organs and institutions of the European Union. *Treaty on the
       Functioning of the European Union,* opened for signature 7 February 1992 (OJ C 326/164, 26
       October 2012) entered into force 1 November 1993,
19   *Advocaten voor de Wereld VZW v Leden van de Ministerraad* (C-303/05) [2007] ECR I-5305,
       s 53.
20   *Gözütok and Brügge* (joined cases C-187/01 and C-385/01) [2003] ECR I-01345; *Gasparini*
       (C-467/04) [2006] ECR I-09199; *Mantello* (C-261/09) [2010] ECR I-11477.
21   *Van Esbroeck v Openbaar Ministerie* (C 436/04) [2006] ECR I-02333, s 42.
22   *Pupino v Italy* (C-105/03) [2005] ECR I-05285.

an obligation to surrender their nationals for the purposes of the execution of a custodial sentence or detention order, provided they undertake to execute the (foreign) sentence in accordance with their own law.[23] This arrangement meets the objections of states belonging to the civil law tradition that are usually adamant to surrender their nationals, reasoning that detention in foreign countries does not promote resocialisation and rehabilitation. Secondly, and in line with this consideration, the surrender of a national may be conditioned on the guarantee that he is allowed to return to the executing member state in order to serve there the custodial sentence or detention order passed against him in the issuing member state.[24] These privileges are not confined to nationals, but are also attributed to "residents" (art 5(3) *Framework Decision*) or to "residents and persons staying in the executing State" (art 4(6) *Framework Decision*). The introduction of "residency" and "staying in" raised questions as to the content of these concepts and whether Member States had discretion to determine the definitions. In the case of *Kozlowski*, a Polish national who claimed "residency" in Germany and invoked art 4(6) of the *Framework Decision*, the ECJ shed some light on the matter.[25] The Court effectively lumped "residency" and "staying" together by holding that:

> A requested person is "resident" in the executing Member State when he has established his actual place of residence there and he is "staying" there when, following a stable period of residence in that State, he has acquired connections with that State which are of a similar degree to those resulting from residence.[26]

In elaborating on the concept of "staying", within the meaning of art 4(6), the Court allowed the executing member state a wide measure of discretion, pointing at:

> ...various objective factors characterising the situation of that person, including, in particular, the length, nature and conditions of his presence and the family and economic connections which that person has with the executing State.[27]

---

23   *Framework Decision* art 4(6).
24   Ibid art 5(3).
25   *Kozlowski* (C-66/08) [2008] ECR I-06041.
26   Ibid s 54.
27   Ibid.

Objective as these factors may be, they obviously require an assessment on a case by case basis. The use of the plural – objective *factors* – implies that one single factor, such as the length of time, would not suffice to conclude that the requested person had acquired strong links with his state of residence. In *Wolzenburg*, the ECJ turned it the other way around by accepting that a member state could condition the privileges attached to residency in the realm of the execution of a sentence on the person having lawfully resided for a period of five years in that member state.[28] In other words, length of stay only served as a minimum requirement that would have to be sustained by other indicators of connection. Referring to the special position of nationals of other member states who enjoy Union citizenship, the Court indicated, however, that supplementary administrative requirements, such as a residence permit of indefinite duration, were not allowed.[29]

Whereas the ECJ has provided guidelines as to the interpretation of the concept of "residency" and has corroborated the discretion of the executing member state, the assessment of the question whether foreign residents should be considered on the same par as nationals is fraught with difficulties. Article 6 Section 5 of the Dutch *Surrender Act* stipulates that a foreigner with a residence permit of unlimited duration is allowed to return to the Netherlands in order to serve a prison sentence, imposed by the issuing State, provided that it can be reasonably expected that this person will not forfeit his residence permit on account of the punishment that will be imposed after the surrender. The precondition makes sense, because execution of the sentence in the Netherlands will serve no rehabilitative purposes if the foreign resident has to leave the country afterwards. However, the provision saddles the Court with the difficult task of predicting the outcome of a trial. The Amsterdam IRC relies on the assessment of the Immigration and Naturalisation Service ("IND") which enables it to reach a "provisional" opinion. In a fairly recent case, in which Belgium requested the surrender of a national from Morocco who was born in the Netherlands, on the suspicion of him being implicated in drugs trafficking, the IND had indicated that the requested person would possibly lose his residence permit. The Prosecutor's Office had estimated that he would incur a custodial sentence of six years and the Court concluded that the requested person was not entitled to the guarantee that he could return to the Netherlands in order to serve his sentence there.[30]

---

28   *Wolzenburg* (C-123/08) [2009] ECR I-09621 s 74.
29   Ibid s 53.
30   District Court Amsterdam, 3 January 2017, ECLI:NL:RBAMS:2017:66.

In this particular case, the assessment was rather straightforward, but decisions that are predicated on prognoses are by definition precarious, especially if the stakes are high. In a similar vein, the calculation of the "five-year term" and the assessment of the objective factors, as identified by the ECJ in *Wolzenburg*, is often arduous. The onus of proving a "real connection" with the executing state is on the requested person and, to that end, defence counsel often submits exhibits of health insurance or employment contracts. Quibbling over gaps in employment that would negate a real connection is not unusual and small margins may decide the fate of the requested person.[31]

3.2   *Trials in Absentia*

Trials in the absence of the accused are anathema in countries that adhere to the adversarial system of criminal procedure and are not very popular in civil law countries, although the inquisitorial procedure allows such trials and they are not rare. The distaste for such trials is not hard to understand. The accused has the right to be heard and confront witnesses for the prosecution, he or she is the prime source of information on the full facts of the case and prison sentences cannot be executed if he or she is not in custody. In *Colozza*, one of the landmark cases on the topic, the European Court of Human Rights ("ECtHR") confirmed that "although not explicitly mentioned in paragraph 1 of Article 6 [of the *European Convention of Human Rights*], the object and purpose of the article taken as a whole show that the person 'charged with a criminal offence' is entitled to take part in the hearing".

The Court suggested, however, that the right of the defendant to be present is not absolute and has to be balanced again the public interest.[32]

In the context of surrender proceedings, trials in absentia are of special relevance, because there is a reasonable presumption that the fugitive has absconded precisely in order to avoid the criminal trial. In order to reconcile the interests of law enforcement with the rights of the defendant, art 4bis of the *Framework Decision* has introduced an elaborate and balanced system which allows the executing state to refuse the request if the judgment is rendered in absentia, unless the EAW indicates that certain guarantees have been satisfied.[33] First of all, the person concerned must have been summoned in person and thereby been informed on the scheduled place and time of the trial that

---

31   For a good example, see District Court Amsterdam, 16 March 2017, ECLI:NL:RBAMS:2017: 3612. In this specific case the District Court suspended its judgment, awaiting the outcome of a preliminary ruling in *Poplawski* of the ECJ.

32   *Colozza v Italy* (1985) 89 Eur Court HR (ser A) [27], [29].

33   Article 4 bis was inserted by an amendment of the initial *Framework Decision* of 2002, *Council Framework Decision 2009/299/JHA of 26 February 2009* [2009] OJ L 81/24.

has resulted in the decision or have been officially apprised in another way, so that it is unambiguously clear that the person was privy to knowledge of the imminent trial. Moreover, he or she must have been informed that a decision in his or her absence could be taken. In other words, the official authorities must have made every effort in their power to properly inform the suspect. In a preliminary ruling in *Dworzecki*, the ECJ held that "summoning in person" should be taken literally. The handing over of the summons to an adult person, belonging to the suspect's household, would not suffice if it could not be ascertained from the EAW whether, and, if so, when, that person had actually passed that summons on to the person concerned.[34]

If the requested person has been properly informed of the impending trial and has not appeared in person, the EAW should, in any case, be executed if the requested person has given power of attorney to an appointed lawyer or counsel of his own choice to defend him and that counsel actually conducted the defence during the trial (art 4bis s 1(b)). And finally, the EAW should not be refused if the issuing state provides for a retrial or appellate proceedings where the requested state is entitled to be present and during which trial the facts will be ascertained, new evidence can be adduced and a revision can be obtained. Such a guarantee can still be given during surrender proceedings, reassuring the executing state that the requested person will be adequately and timeously informed of his rights to a re-assessment of his case by another court (art 4bis s 1(d)). In *Melloni*, the ECJ clarified that member states are not allowed to amplify the scope of refusal in case of trials in absentia, by invoking – as in the case at hand – a domestic constitutional provision that guarantees a full review (*recurso de amparo*) in case of trials in absentia.[35] In other words, if one of the circumstances mentioned in art 4bis applies, the executing member state has no discretion to refuse the EAW.

The IRC tends to investigate whether the requested person was present at the trial during which the merits of the case were discussed. In a recent decision on an EAW from Poland, the Court noticed that the requested person had been present at a *pro forma* hearing, had pleaded guilty and had made propositions as to the punishment. As the Prosecutor did not agree with the proposals, the Polish District Court had conducted the trial in the absence of the requested person, heard five witnesses, disclosed the remaining evidence and issued the judgment. The Dutch Court concluded that the requested person had not been present at the *moment supreme* and that the execution of the

---

34   *Openbaar Ministerie v Dworzecki* (European Court of Justice, C-108/16, 24 May 2016) s [54].
35   *Melloni v Ministerio Fiscal* (Tribunal Constitucional, Madrid (Spain), C-399/11, 26 February 2013) [64].

EAW had to be refused, as Poland had not offered any guarantee that a revision could be obtained. While there might be terms to wonder whether the absence of the requested person could perhaps be attributed to the requested person's own behaviour, the Dutch *Surrender Act* does not leave room for taking such negligence into consideration.[36]

Sometimes, domestic courts have a difficult time finding out what procedural steps have been taken, because the information is incomplete or guarantees are drawn up in ambiguous language. The decision of the IRC on an EAW from Romania provides a good example.[37] In spite of several queries for clarification, the Romanian authorities had persisted in reassuring the Dutch Court that the requested person "may request" a revision, which, according to the Court, did not equal an unconditional guarantee. Therefore, the surrender was refused. Often, such incidents can be attributed to procedural differences or language difficulties.

3.3 *Surrender and Human Rights*

The right to be present at and be heard during the trial is an aspect of the right to a fair trial, as the ECJ has elucidated in *Colozza*.[38] Formally, a past or prospective infringement of a fair trial in the requesting state is not an obstacle to surrender. At least, it does not feature in the grounds for refusal in the *Framework Decision*. In *Soering*, the EctHR has acknowledged, however, that the requested state may be found in violation of art 6, which guarantees the right to a fair trial, of the *European Convention* by extraditing the requested person to a state where the risk of a violation of due process rights is considerable. However, the threshold is extremely high.[39]

---

36   District Court Amsterdam, 27 March 2018, ECLI:NL:RBAMS:2018:2130. Interestingly, the ECJ allows member states to take the conduct of the requested person into account, as emerged in *Dworzecki* (European Court of Justice, C-108/16, 24 May 2016) s 51:

> In the context of such an assessment of the optional ground for non-recognition, the executing judicial authority may thus have regard to the conduct of the person concerned. It is at this stage of the surrender procedure that particular attention might be paid to any manifest lack of diligence on the part of the person concerned, notably where it transpires that he sought to avoid service of the information addressed to him.

37   District Court Amsterdam, 12 September 2017, ECLI:NL:RBAMS:2017:7139.

38   *Colozza* (1985) 89 Eur Court HR (ser A).

39   *Soering v United Kingdom* (1989) 161 Eur Court HR (ser A) [113]: "... it cannot be ruled out that an issue might exceptionally arise under Article 6 of the Convention by an extradition decision in circumstances where the fugitive has suffered or risks suffering a flagrant denial of a fair trial in the requesting country". See *Al Moayad v Germany* (European Court of Human Rights, Chamber V, Application No 35865/03, 20 February 2007) [101] for an elaboration of the concept of "flagrant denial".

The acknowledgement of a (potential) serious breach of human rights in another member state is a delicate affair in a political constellation that postulates a high level of mutual trust. *The Preamble* reflects this ambiguity. *The Preamble*, in [12], explicitly declares that the *Framework Decision* respects fundamental rights and complies with the principles that are incorporated in the *Charter of the European Union*. It is not immediately clear what this entails. One might surmise that the establishment of a simplified procedure as such does not impinge on fundamental rights, but one could also argue that an obligation to surrender must yield to human rights concerns. Such an implied hierarchy is corroborated in the *Preamble* under [13] which provides that no one is to be expelled or surrendered to a state in which he runs a serious risk that he will be exposed to capital punishment, torture or other inhuman or degrading treatment or punishment. All member states of the European Union have abolished the death penalty and the prohibition of torture is a peremptory norm of international law that prevails over any other obligation.[40] So, one may be inclined to wonder whether this honourable principle offers anything new. The EctHR has put degrading and inhuman treatment on a par with torture and has held that the *European Convention* prohibits such practices in any circumstances, including those of the fight against terrorism and organised crime.[41]

The risk of inhuman or degrading treatment is often invoked in relation to dismal detention conditions which are caused by overcrowded prison facilities. The recurring question is how domestic courts are to obtain proof that the detention conditions are below the standard of art 3 of the *European Convention of Human Rights ("ECHR")*,[42] prohibiting torture and inhuman or degrading treatment,[43] and what the consequences of a positive finding should be. On both issues, the ECJ has shed light in the *Aranyosi and Căldăraru* cases.[44] The Court starts by pointing out that the executing judicial authority must rely on information that is objective, reliable, specific and properly updated,

---

40   Compare also the *UN Convention against Torture and other Inhuman or Degrading Treatment or Punishment*, 10 December 1984, 1465 UNTS 85, art 3 s 1: "No State shall expel, return ('refouler'), or extradite a person to another State where there are substantial grounds for believing that he will be subjected to torture".

41   *Bouyid v Belgium* (European Court of Human Rights, Grand Chamber, Application No 23380/09, 28 September 2015) [81].

42   *European Convention on Human Rights*, opened for signature 5 November 1950, ETS 5 (entered into force 1 June 2010).

43   Article 4 of the EU Charter of Fundamental Rights (7 December 2000, [2000] OJ C 364) reads exactly the same as art 3 ECtHR. For the ECJ the Charter is the normative framework.

44   *Aranyosi v Hungary* and *Căldăraru v Romania* (European Court of Justice, Grand Chamber, C-404/15 and C-659/155, 5 April 2016).

indicating that there are deficiencies in the detention conditions prevailing in the requesting member state which may be specific or generic, affect certain groups of people or certain places of detention.[45] However, a finding that there is a real risk of inhuman or degrading treatment in general does not suffice for a refusal; there must be a substantial ground to presume that the individual in question is exposed to such a danger.[46] And, even if such a real risk may be assumed, the execution must only be postponed, until sufficient guarantees have been obtained from the requesting state that the fear is unfounded or that the situation can be mitigated; it should not be abandoned.[47] In the meantime, the requested person's provisional detention may be suspended, but in that case the executing state must take all measures to prevent him from absconding. Only if it appears to be impossible to obtain, within a reasonable time, the supplementary information that allows the state of execution to discount the existence of the risk, it must decide whether the surrender proceeding should be brought to an end.[48]

The *Aranyosi and Căldăraru* case is important, because it demonstrates that the ECJ makes every attempt to reconcile the obligations stemming from human rights treaties with the smooth functioning of the EAW system, emphasising the relevance of diplomacy and assurances. The decision to refuse the execution of an EAW should not be taken light-heartedly, but if, at the end of the day, it is impossible to obtain reassuring information that the requested person will be spared from inhuman or degrading treatment, the surrender procedure must stop, which effectively boils down to a refusal.

While the ECJ in *Aranyosi* developed a procedural framework, the ECtHR in the case of *Muršić* addressed in detail the substance of a violation of art 3 *ECHR* in relation to detention conditions.[49] In many cases the Court has held that the allocation of less than three square meters to an individual prisoner in a multi-occupancy accommodation would serve as a red light that a violation of art 3 was occurring.[50] In *Muršić*, the Court corroborated earlier case law that

---

45   Ibid. The Court adds that such information may be obtained from judgments of international courts (like the European Court of Human Rights), judgments of courts of the requesting State and decisions, reports and so on produced by bodies of the Council of Europe or the United Nations.

46   Ibid [91], [92].

47   Ibid [98].

48   Ibid [104].

49   *Muršić v Croatia* (European Court of Human Rights, Grand Chamber, Application No 7334/13, 20 October 2016).

50   See *Ananyev v Russia* (European Court of Human Rights, Application No 42525/07, 10 January 2012) [145] with a survey of previous case law.

such a circumstance only created a "strong presumption" that could be rebutted by other factors.[51] Subsequently, the Court summarised the circumstances that should be cumulatively met in order to rebut the "strong presumption":

(a)   the reductions in the required minimum space are short, occasional and minor;

(b)   these reductions are accompanied by sufficient freedom of movement outside the cell and adequate out-of-cell activities; and

(c)   the applicant is confined in an appropriate detention facility and there are no other aggravating aspects of the conditions of detention.[52]

Meticulously checking the particular situation of Muršić against these parameters, the Court concluded that the relatively favourable conditions together compensated for his lack of personal space and that art 3 of the ECHR had not been violated.[53]

The judgments in *Aranyosi and Căldăraru* and in *Muršić* have served domestic courts as a true normative framework. Often, they have succeeded in refining the criteria. In a decision on a French EAW, the IRC held that *Muršić* also had implications for the available personal space during the night, which, according to the French authorities, could amount to a maximum of 12 hours. As detention conditions in this respect were below standards in the prison of the French town Nîmes, the Court was only prepared to allow the surrender after guarantees had been obtained that the requested person would "under no circumstances be incarcerated in Nîmes".[54] Interestingly, domestic courts have followed their own course in the interpretation of the standards supplied by the European courts. A reference by the Prosecutor to a judgment of the German *Hanseatisches Oberlandesgericht Hamburg* which allowed the surrender to Romania, in spite of defence counsel's claim that dismal detention conditions amounted to inhuman or degrading treatment, was ignored by the IRC with the argument that the German courts apparently did not hold a steady course, in view of earlier refusals of Romanian requests by other courts. In the same decision the Dutch Chamber elucidated that the *Muršić* criteria were applicable in both open and semi-open regimes of detention.[55]

While the standards expounded in *Muršić* are quite detailed and specific, national courts will still render their own interpretation, not only because each case is different, but also because it reflects their own sense of justice. The

---

51   *Muršić* (European Court of Human Rights, Grand Chamber, Application No 7334/13, 20 October 2016) [125].

52   Ibid [138].

53   Ibid [169].

54   District Court Amsterdam, 14 December 2017, ECLI:NL:RBAMS:2017:9757.

55   District Court Amsterdam, 18 April 2017, ECLI:NL:RBAMS:2017:2079.

European courts can issue guidelines, but they do not mimic a constitutional or supreme court in a national system. The disparity in decisions on EAW's in view of the risk of degrading or inhuman treatment bears testimony to the limitations of harmonisation. Whereas the EAW system is generally predicated on the assumption that the member-states of the European Union share similar values in respect of their criminal justice being in conformity with human rights obligations, the preamble clarifies that each member state is still responsible for checking whether surrender of the requested person would be admissible in view of the requesting state's observance of these human rights. The preamble equally conveys the message that the requested state will not be considered as a deal-breaker, whenever it decides to refuse surrender, because such a decision is implicit in a shared commitment of upholding human rights.

4   The EAW System as a Role Model for Other Regions?

The answer to the question whether the EAW system serves as a model that might be (partially) adopted by other states or in other regions depends, in my view, on the extent in which political, social and economic conditions resemble those in Europe. As indicated above, two elements stand out in the explanation of the establishment of the EAW. First, the *Framework Decision* was triggered by the lifting of inner borders as the outcome of a process of advanced economic and political integration. Secondly, the principle of mutual recognition that underpins the EAW system can only be introduced if states have sufficient mutual confidence in the quality of law enforcement. These aspects are inter-related: only kindred states that trust each other's political and legal systems are inclined to abolish border control.

While trade liberation has made headway in several regions in the world, no regional organisation so far has followed the example of the European Union by lifting border controls. Physical and geographical peculiarities may account for the fact that there are no or less economic benefits to be reaped by such a measure. If you are living on an island, like New Zealand, I imagine that there is not much to be gained by sending home the coastal guards, except a reduction in public expenditure. Most visitors to New Zealand come and leave by air and it is inconceivable that the authorities will dispense with passenger checks at the airport.[56] In short, as there are no strong economic and political incentives

---

[56]   EU-citizens enjoy the privilege of being allowed to join a smaller queue at customs control when they travel within the Union, but they are exposed to the same anti-terrorism measures as everyone else.

to abolish border control, there is no urgent need to introduce an expedited surrender procedure along the lines of the EAW, in order to counter the uninhibited influx of criminal suspects either. This does not imply, however, that there may not be good reasons for simplification of extradition with a view of the improvement of transnational law enforcement. Such a quest brings the second prong – mutual trust in the legal system – to the fore. Obviously, the degree of confidence depends on the partner one is dealing with, but it is also informed by the specific topic under consideration. In view of the limited size of this contribution, I must confine myself to a couple of observations.

4.1 Bi-lateral versus Multi-Lateral Extradition Treaties and the Dual Criminality Rule

Although multi-lateral extradition treaties are on the rise, especially in respect of the repression of specific crime categories, bi-lateral relationships still prevail. At first blush, bi-lateral treaties appear to be more suitable for the introduction of legal short-cuts, as state parties could tailor the content of the treaty to the specific counterpart. That conclusion would, however, be too quick, as it disregards power differences. The relationship between Canada and the United States provides an example in kind. It transpires that the vast majority of US extradition requests to Canada involve the suspicion of (thwarted) conspiracies that emanate from Canadian territory.[57] The net result reveals a glaring asymmetry in performances, as Botting notes: "The targets of such alleged conspiracies are usually residents of the requesting country [i.e. the United States]. And there's the rub. It is almost always one way. Canada rarely if ever prosecutes cross-border scams originating in the United States".[58]

Canada could benefit from the introduction of a territoriality exception, as envisaged in art 4 s 7(a) of the *Framework Decision on the European Arrest Warrant*, in order to fence off its sovereign realm against intrusion by the United States. However, it is the personal experience of this author that claims on this optional ground for refusal are rarely sanctioned.

Multi-lateral conventions that aim to suppress specific crime categories, like illicit drug trade, terrorism or organised crime, have proliferated during the past decennia. One of the drawbacks of these legal devices is that, in principle,

---

57   It is a matter of controversy whether the United States, in case of thwarted conspiracies, would have jurisdiction on the basis of the objective territoriality principle, as it would arguably strain the limits of that principle (the effects do not actually occur on US territory). See for a discussion Christopher L Blakesley, "Extraterritorial Jurisdiction" in M Cherif Bassiouni (ed), *International Criminal Law, Volume II: Procedure* (Transnational, 1986) 17, 18, who suggests application of the protective principle instead.

58   Gary Botting, *Canadian Extradition Law and Practice* (Lexis Nexis, 5th ed, 2015) 9.

all states, including those with a notorious reputation in respect of observance of human rights, can ratify and become a party, forcing human rights' observant states to invigorate, rather than to relax their scrutiny of extradition requests. Whatever their shortcomings, these conventions at least effectively address one of the time-honoured topics of extradition law, to wit, the dual criminality rule. By enjoining states' parties to incorporate the elements of the crime in their national legislation, these conventions actually obliterate the rule. Beyond the scope of such piecemeal solutions, dual criminality remains a thorny issue. One of the strongest arguments against abolition of the rule is that it seems counterintuitive, if not unjust, for a state to apply its criminal law system in respect of conduct it does not consider punishable itself. Neil Boister quotes with approval the famous sociologist of law, Roger Cotterrell, who argues that the punishability of conduct should, in a Durkheimian sense, resonate in the collective conscience of the people of the requested state.[59] I tend to agree with these observations. There is something untoward in surrendering a person accused of small trade in cannabis to a state where he faces a considerable prison sentence, when the scent of weed saturates the Amsterdam air and the quality of party drugs is openly discussed in the Dutch media.

While such principled discussions on the pros and cons of dual criminality are highly relevant, the assessment of the condition hardly ever presents problems in practice. That is, however, not an argument in favour of adopting the EAW system in this respect. It is the impression of this author that the outcome would not have been much different, if the rule of dual criminality had been conserved. It confirms the paradox of the abolition of dual criminality: it is most effective when it is unwarranted, while it is senseless when the penal codes of the cooperating parties are nearly similar. To put it differently: if the penal laws of states have approximated to the degree that it is warranted to relax the assessment of dual criminality, the (partial) abolition of the rule is actually redundant.

4.2 Human Rights

In Section 3, I have discussed the topics that primarily engage domestic courts of the requested state. It is no coincidence that such topics encompass the

---

59 Roger Cotterrell, "The Concept of Crime and Transnational Networks of Community" in Valsamis Mitsilegas, Peter Alldridge and Leonidas Cheliotis (eds), *Globalisation, Criminal Law and Criminal Justice* (Hart, 2015) 22, quoted in Neil Boister, "Global Trends towards the Simplification of Extradition Procedures: From the Substantive to the Procedural without a Universal Framework of Reference" in Tiyanjana Maluwa, Max du Plessis and Dire Tladi (eds), *The Pursuit of a Brave New World in International Law: Essays in Honour of John Dugard* (Brill/Nijhoff, 2017) 544–5.

question of which residents deserve equal treatment as nationals. After all, the promotion of the interests of its citizens should be the core business of every state and it is crucial to determine who is to benefit from this heightened attention. In a similar vein, the increased frequency of surrenders under the aegis of the EAW system aggravates the responsibility of the requesting state if due process rights are subsequently flouted in the requesting state or the requested person is exposed to inhuman or degrading treatment. Understandably, courts are keen on preventing such responsibility and attentive to serious risks. Political and cultural affinity do not guarantee that awkward, but necessary, inquiries into human rights situations are not conducted.[60] In this context, it is remarkable – but perhaps not surprising – that the scrutiny of detention conditions by courts of the requested state has intensified. In its turn, this has given impetus to an increased attention to the improvement of prison facilities and this is unquestionably a beneficial side-effect of the introduction of the EAW.

It is doubtful whether this would have been accomplished without the pioneering work of the ECJ and the ECtHR which have set the standards by scrupulously indicating what detention conditions would amount to an inhuman or degrading treatment. As noticed earlier, domestic courts have found some leeway in interpreting these standards and applying them to the case at hand, but the normative importance of the European Courts' guidelines should not be underestimated.[61] States that consider establishing a network of international cooperation in criminal matters that borrows from the European system are therefore well advised to embed this network in a parallel system of protection of human rights under the supervision of a supra-national court.

4.3   The Trimming of the Procedure

One of the most striking features of the EAW system is that it has succeeded in considerably simplifying and expediting surrender proceedings. This accomplishment is by no means self-evident, because the number of grounds for refusal has hardly diminished and some of them require a searching examination. There is no doubt that the *Framework Decision* has paved the way by encouraging member states to appoint a central authority that might assist the courts and to envisage a simple procedure of direct contacts between

---

60   It is telling that the Dutch courts have refused the execution of European Arrest Warrants that had been issued by Belgium and France, countries with whom they maintain cordial relations.

61   I am grateful to my colleague, Dr. Denis Abels, for drawing my attention to this aspect.

the judicial authorities of the issuing and executing state.[62] But that arrangement was predicated on the assumption that the executive who in common extradition proceedings ultimately decides on the surrender could easily be dispensed with. Practice has proved that assumption to be correct.

In my view, there are two explanations for this phenomenon. First, extradition has traditionally always been considered as a matter of foreign policy which could not be delegated to the courts. The rapprochement between states within the context of the European Union obviates such concerns with sovereignty. Secondly, and perhaps more importantly, practice has demonstrated that courts are very capable of settling issues that were previously considered to be the domain of the executive, because they involved politically sensitive questions. Courts have assessed, for example, whether residents have developed sufficiently close connections with the state to be eligible for "repatriation" after having been sentenced abroad and have requested assurances that the fugitive will be incarcerated in decent prison facilities. The shift of the assessment of such issues away from the executive to the courts corroborates their legal nature. It proves that like-minded states can establish a system of international cooperation in criminal matters that can do without the pomp and circumstances of extradition proceedings.

5   Some Final Reflections

The objective of this paper has been twofold. First, I have tried to give an impression of the law and practice of the EAW to those who are a stranger to the device. But this analysis has served as a prelude to an inquiry whether parts of the EAW system could be adopted in other geographical regions. The law of the EAW has been refined in preliminary rulings of the ECJ which has canvassed the interpretation of time honoured concepts like dual criminality and double jeopardy in a new institutional context. The daily practice of the EAW has been exemplified by means of a brief discussion of some decisions of the IRC in criminal matters with which I am most familiar. Obviously, such a perfunctory survey can only produce a rough impression.

It transpired that the run-of-the-mill cases of domestic courts of the executing state concern two legal issues. The first one is the question of whether residents are eligible to be considered on the same par as nationals in view of the transfer of the execution of a foreign sentence. Secondly, courts are often seized to assess compensatory measures for default procedures and detention

---

62   Compare, respectively, art 7 and art 9 of the *Framework Decision*.

conditions in the requesting state. It has been concluded that (contemplated) prison reforms have been an unexpected but salutary side-effect of the introduction of the EAW.

Despite the fact that surrender proceedings are by no means a formality and domestic courts often have to address difficult issues of law and fact, the procedure has been curtailed considerably and that is arguably the most conspicuous achievement of the introduction of the EAW. States on other continents are well advised to reconsider whether protracted extradition proceedings, involving executive powers, are always necessary, if courts are perfectly capable of resolving certain issues inter se. Like-minded states that adhere to democratic principles and the rule of law and share broadly similar views on what conduct constitutes a criminal offence can expedite surrender proceedings, because intricate questions of dual criminality or political offences will rarely arise. The legal practice of the execution of EAWs has demonstrated that even kindred states cannot ignore the responsibilities that touch on the fundamental rights of the requested person. However, it has also proved that the dynamic interaction between courts and prosecutors, informed by the normative guidance of the ECJ can address these issues, rendering any diplomatic intervention by the executive redundant.

A prerequisite for a successful operation of such a system is that states and their citizens indeed share common opinions on what constitutes a decent society. Cotterrell has emphasised that "there has to be a degree of solidarity among the transnational networks of community that enforce these offences".[63] Apart from a basic trust between the states involved, there is another aspect that deserves brief discussion. The EAW system has been established within a multi-lateral context, between states that can boast a long tradition of economic, political and judicial cooperation on (more or less) equal terms. There is a risk in transposing aspects of such a system to a bilateral configuration between unequal treaty parties. In Part 4.1, I alluded to the asymmetric performances in the extradition practice between the United States and Canada. Any intention to copy parts of the system, by – for example – abolishing the dual criminality rule – should take such disparities in political power into due consideration.

---

63   Cotterrell, above n 59, 16.

Brexit and the Policing of Transnational Organised Crime in Europe

Liz Campbell*

1   Introduction

The United Kingdom's forthcoming withdrawal from the European Union ("EU") in 2019 poses many, as yet unresolved, challenges for the policing, investigation, and prosecution of transnational organised crime ("TOC"), which is responded to increasingly on a regional rather than purely domestic level. The preferred option of most commentators is retention of the status quo, in terms of maintenance of access to key regional policing structures and tools. This paper sets out some significant mechanisms that facilitate police cooperation currently between the UK and the EU in respect of TOC. It considers these in turn, sketching out the purposes of existing structures and mechanisms; the potential legislative, process or political barriers to the UK's ongoing participation in these; and the options available to the UK Government post-Brexit.

Currently the UK enjoys a "special status" in relation to EU cooperation on Justice and Home Affairs matters, insofar as it has negotiated the right to "opt in" to provisions rather than being automatically bound. At the expiry in 2014 of the transitional protocols after the Lisbon Treaty, the UK opted out of all pre-Lisbon instruments, then opted back into 35 of these measures. When the UK leaves the EU in 2019, it will also leave these 35 measures. The UK's "varied" participation in some areas of EU criminal law has led to an increase in cross-border cooperation in terms of extradition and the exchange of police information, all of which is of considerable benefit to the UK.[1] As outlined below, Brexit will lead inevitably to a diminution in the level and nature of cooperation between the UK and remaining EU member states, for structural, legal, political and practical reasons.

The issues of policing and security in the context of Brexit and the challenges posed have been explored in a number of fora, and numerous expert practitioners and academics have expressed views on this. Strikingly, the House of Lords EU Committee noted considerable consensus among UK law

*   Francine McNiff Chair of Criminal Jurisprudence, Monash University.
1   See Valsamis Mitsilegas, "The Uneasy Relationship between the UK and European Criminal Law: From Opt-Outs to Brexit?" (2016) 24(2) *Criminal Legal Review* 517, 522.

enforcement agencies on the EU tools and capabilities that should be retained or replaced after Brexit, including Europol, Eurojust, the European Arrest Warrant ("EAW"), the Second Generation Schengen Information System ("SIS II"), and the European Criminal Records Information System ("ECRIS").[2] Moreover, the UK government has emphasised its "ambition ... to construct a model that establishes mechanisms to maintain operational capabilities between the UK and the EU and its Member States".[3]

The significance of TOC, the distinct challenges it poses, and the necessity for regional cooperation lie in its durability, gravity and complexity, as well as the crossing of borders in its enterprise. It involves numerous markets and actions, ranging from the trafficking of drugs, weapons and people, through to cybercrime and corruption, and it varies in scope and complexity. Though organised crime sometimes is local or "homegrown", TOC involves the crossing of borders, as part of transporting and selling illicit goods or services. Moreover, organised crime groups exploit legal and policing differences between jurisdictions to develop criminal markets and to evade justice. All of this underlines the importance of mutual legal assistance and cooperation in investigating and addressing it adequately.

Joining and participating in a regional organisation such as the EU increases cooperation against TOC because it entails a shift from formal inter-state cooperation against crime to more regionally integrated systems. Conversely, exiting the EU presents a risk factor as it has the potential at least to decrease cooperation, which should serve as a warning to other regions on the path towards increased collaboration strategically and operationally against TOC. Brexit, with its process of disentangling the UK from numerous legal measures, as well as the reconstruction of comparable schemes of criminal justice cooperation, is a reminder of the extent to which cooperation is contingent on on-going buy-in, and of the precarity of some of these structures.

This paper is cognisant of the fact that current and potential future mechanisms for investigating and policing organised crime operate across international, state, devolved, and bilateral planes. In addition, the protections for the individual that apply in this context, whether as suspect, victim or witness, also operate on these dimensions.

---

2   House of Lords European Union Committee, *Brexit: future UK-EU security and police cooperation*, House of Lords Paper No 77, Session 2016–2017 (2016) [25].

3   Department for Exiting the European Union and the Home Office, *A Future Partnership Paper: Security, law enforcement and criminal justice*, Policy Paper (2017) [39] <https://as sets.publishing.service.gov.uk/government/uploads/system/uploads/attachment_data/ file/645416/Security__law_enforcement_and_criminal_justice_-_a_future_partnership_pa per.PDF>.

It is important also to recall that the legal responses to transnational organised crime in the UK are sometimes reserved matters for the Westminster
Parliament, such as regarding money laundering, illicit drugs or firearms, say,
and in other instances devolved, such as in relation to substantive organised
crime legislation and court proceedings.[4] This interwoven and intersecting legal landscape underlines the significance of Brexit for the distinct systems in
Scotland and Northern Ireland, not least given that the nature of the threat
from TOC, as well as the responses, differ in the constituent jurisdictions of
the UK. The cooperation that is required to investigate and police TOC sometimes is sought and steered by the prosecution authorities in the constituent
jurisdictions.

And, of course, Brexit holds significant implications for other jurisdictions,
in particular Ireland, due to the shared land border with part of the UK.[5] These
consequences are pronounced in relation to TOC, which exploits differences in
taxation on both sides of the border, for instance, to dump illegally and to sell
laundered fuel.[6]

If the UK wishes to continue cooperating with EU member states, which
it will in fact need to do in respect of the investigation and policing of TOC,
the likelihood is that it will need to comply with the substance of EU law as a
whole. This need for consistency inside and outside the EU in order to permit
data sharing, for instance, and cooperation overall, appears to be overlooked
in much of the political debate. Adherence to schemes of cooperation will require the UK to recognise the jurisprudence of the Court of Justice of the EU
("CJEU"), and this will trigger a strong scrutiny of UK domestic law, including jurisprudence, from the EU. Though oversight by the CJEU is anathema
to "Brexiteers", it is likely to occur if the UK wishes to maintain its current
scheme of cooperation and access in this context, though the UK Government
notes as "the UK will no longer be subject to direct jurisdiction of the CJEU ...
consideration will need to be given to dispute resolution as part of the new
relationship".[7]

Throughout this paper, various cross-cutting themes emerge, relating to the
timing and speed of negotiations and the related role of interim provisions, the

---

4   *Scotland Act 1998* (UK) sch 5.

5   See Brian Doherty et al., "Northern Ireland and "Brexit": The European Economic Area Op-
     tion" (2017) 2018(1) *Queen's University Belfast Law Research Paper* <https://papers.ssrn.com/
     sol3/papers.cfm?abstract_id=2933715>.

6   See Organised Crime Task Force, *OCTF Annual Report and Threat Assessment 2017*, Depart-
     ment of Justice of Northern Ireland, 32 <https://www.justice-ni.gov.uk/sites/default/files/
     publications/justice/annual-report-threat%20Assessment-2017.PDF>.

7   Department for Exiting the European Union and the Home Office, above n 3, [39].

need for consistency and continuity in law and practice, and the importance of due process protections. While Brexit could be re-framed as an opportunity for revision and for reflection on continued involvement in certain measures, the reality is that the UK will want to maintain a structure as close to the status quo as possible. The irony is that Brexit means that the UK will be required to adhere to EU law in this context without retaining its negotiating power and capacity.

Europol, Eurojust, Joint Investigation Teams, and the European Arrest Warrant and European Investigation Order are now considered in turn.

2   Europol

Europol (the European Police Office) supports law enforcement agencies of the EU member states through the provision of operational analysis and support, the exchange of information with liaison officers who are seconded to Europol as representatives of their national law enforcement agencies, and the generation of strategic reports and analysis on the basis of intelligence.[8]

Europol provides a multi-lateral cooperation platform and involves liaison bureaux from member states and third countries, representing the interests of their own state. Usually, around 20 UK staff work in Europol, including officers from Her Majesty's Revenue and Customs, the Metropolitan Police and Police Scotland. The UK comprises the second largest bureau, the biggest being the United States of America as a third country. Currently, the UK benefits considerably from Europol and also has a strong impact in respect of its involvement.[9] Such multi-lateral engagement and cooperation are crucial in tackling fast-moving crime, especially cyber-crime and TOC.

One consequence of Brexit is that the UK will not influence the strategic direction and priorities of Europol, as it will not maintain involvement in Europol's Management Board. At present, there is considerable strategic benefit from the UK's role in the Board, which comprises officials from each member state; third countries are not involved other than as observers. The Board identifies and sets out crime priorities based on threat assessments and crime

---

8   *Convention Drawn up on the Basis of Article K.3 of Treaty on European Union, on the Establishment of a European Police Office*, opened for signature 26 July 1995, [1995] OJ C 316/01 (entered into force 1 October 1998).

9   Department for Exiting the European Union, *Technical Note: Security, Law Enforcement and Criminal Justice* (May 2018) [17]–[18] <https://assets.publishing.service.gov.uk/government/uploads/system/uploads/attachment_data/file/710802/FINAL_INTERNAL_SECURITY_COMBINED.pdf>.

analysis, and these steer Europol's four-year policy cycle. The priorities are sorted into threats and sub-threats, which are significant in terms of staffing allocation for many member states. The UK has been able to drive the policy agenda towards crimes like people-trafficking, whereas post-Brexit other member states may place a stronger emphasis on other crime to the detriment of UK priorities. Currently, the UK chairs four out of 13 European multidisciplinary platform against criminal threats ("EMPACT") groups, and co-chairs another five, which is more than any other EU state. This will not continue past 2019. In addition, the UK will also no longer be able to have Seconded National Experts in Europol. Another consequence lies in the fact that the UK will not be able to join Europol Focal Points without unanimous invitation from other member states. A "focal point" is an area within Europol's information processing system which focuses on a certain phenomenon from a particular theme or angle. For instance, there is a focal point on firearms, focusing on Slovakia and Lithuania; access to which will be lost post-Brexit. A further consequence is that the UK will not be able to check and rely on the Second Generation Schengen Information System ("SIS II"), which allows competent national authorities to issue and consult alerts on persons who may have been involved in a serious crime, as well as information on certain property like banknotes, firearms and identity documents.[10] The only option in this respect appears to be the acceptance of observer status in the Board. There is no precedent for another role, and it is highly unlikely that anything else would be sanctioned.

In terms of the legal framework, the UK's involvement in Europol currently is predicated on an operational agreement as a member state, but Brexit will mean the UK must get agreement as a third country. If the objective is to retain as much operational engagement and effectiveness as possible, a standard third country arrangement is unlikely to match the operational desires and needs of the UK. While there is precedent for the third country involvement, this does not occur on a bilateral basis. Moreover, though bilateral agreements can sometimes be useful, they are less effective and costlier, and, in respect of certain offences like child sexual exploitation and cyber-crime, a multi-lateral response is needed. UK would have to be invited in by Europol, with the agreement of the other member states.

As for potential obstacles, according to art 218 of the *Treaty on the Functioning of the European Union* ("*TFEU*"),[11] the consent of the European Parliament is required for the conclusion of international agreements by the EU with third

---

10   Although the UK is not a Schengen country it is a member of the SIS II.

11   *Consolidated version of the Treaty on the Functioning of the European Union* [2008] OJ C 115/47 (entered into force 1 December 2009) ("*FEU*").

countries that cover fields to which ordinary legislative procedure applies. The negotiation will be carried out by the Commission and made by the Council on behalf of the European Union. This has significant implications in terms of timing. It often takes three to four years to get third country agreements, and there should be no assumption that it will be easy for the UK to replicate the existing structures. This underlines the need for urgency. In addition, it is difficult to ascertain other member states' priorities or likely objections. Furthermore, it is unclear whether approval from the Standing Committee on Operational Cooperation on Internal Security will be required.[12]

Switzerland, Norway and the USA are third countries involved in Europol so there is a precedent for comparable participation by the UK. It also is instructive to recall the situation of Denmark, which has negotiated an agreement with Europol, but it was lengthy and costly, notwithstanding being an EU member state.

UK negotiators will emphasise the UK's historical and on-going provision of intelligence to Europol, in particular in respect of trafficking and cyber-crime. British intelligence on smuggling and trafficking is valuable as a result of the UK's footprint in Africa and the strong presence of liaison officers worldwide. In return, the intelligence held by Europol helps the UK to cross-reference and check its own information. The present task is for the UK to present itself as a vital partner for other member states and Europol, thereby increasing the likelihood of the negotiation of a preferential arrangement. The US has been strategically shrewd in its offering of good intelligence to justify their presence.

A further obstacle may lie in the shifting terrain of data protection. In 2016, the CJEU ruled in *Watson*, in relation to the UK's Government Communications Headquarters' bulk interception of call records and online messages under the *Data Retention and Investigatory Powers Act 2014*, that only targeted interception of traffic and location data in order to combat serious crime is justified.[13] In addition, any data sharing is predicated on a positive data protection adequacy assessment of the UK from the European Commission.[14]

---

12   The Committee on Operational Cooperation on Internal Security ("COSI") consists of high-level officials from each EU member state's Ministry of Interior/Justice, as well as Commission and European External Action Service representatives. Europol, Eurojust and other relevant bodies may attend COSI meetings as observers. COSI facilitates, promotes and strengthens coordination of EU member states' operational actions related to the EU's internal security.

13   *Secretary of State for the Home Department v Watson* (Joined Cases C-203/15 and C-698/15) [2016] OJ C53/11.

14   The Council and the European Parliament have given the Commission the power to determine, on the basis of art 25(6) of *Directive 95/46/EC*, whether a third country ensures

Further, the General Data Protection Regulation has just been implemented,[15] strengthening and unifying data protection for individuals within the EU, and addressing the export of data beyond the EU.

In addition, a regulation updating Europol's governance structure, objectives and tasks, took effect from 1 May 2017.[16] The UK gave notice to opt in to this, which speaks volumes as to its intentions and aspirations.

3 Eurojust

Eurojust was established in 2002 as a "body of the Union" with legal personality,[17] in an effort "to reinforce the fight against serious organised crime".[18] Its mission is "to support and strengthen coordination and cooperation between national investigating and prosecuting authorities in relation to serious crime affecting two or more Member States".[19] Within two years of its creation, the House of Lords EU Committee noted that "[i]n a remarkably short time it has established itself as a highly effective means of facilitating cooperation between investigating and prosecuting authorities in Member States in serious criminal cases".[20]

The Crown Prosecution Service of England and Wales is a "heavy" user of Eurojust, listing it among its top priorities for forthcoming negotiations on Brexit, and Eurojust's value was similarly endorsed by Crown Office and Procurator

---

an adequate level of protection by reason of its domestic law or through its international commitments.

15 *Regulation (EU) 2016/679 of the European Parliament and of the Council of 27 April 2016 on the protection of natural persons with regard to the processing of personal data and on the free movement of such data, and repealing Directive 95/46/EC (General Data Protection Regulation)* [2016] OJ L 119/01.

16 *Regulation (EU) 2016/794 of the European Parliament and of the Council of 11 May 2016 on the European Union Agency for Law Enforcement Cooperation (Europol) and replacing and repealing Council Decisions 2009/371/JHA, 2009/934/JHA, 2009/935/JHA, 2009/936/JHA and 2009/968/JHA* (Europol) [2016] OJ L 135/53.

17 *Council Decision of 28 February 2002 Setting up Eurojust with a View to Reinforcing the Fight Against Serious Crime 2002/187/JHA* [2002] OJ L63/01.

18 European Union: Council of the European Union, "Presidency Conclusions", *Tampere European Council, 15–16 October 1999* (1999).

19 *Treaty on European Union*, opened for signature 7 February 1992 [1992] OJ C 191/1 (entered into force 1 November 1993), as amended by the *Treaty of Lisbon Amending the Treaty on European Union and the Treaty Establishing the European Community*, opened for signature 13 December 2007 [2007] OJ C 306/1 (entered into force 1 December 2009) ch 4 art 85.

20 House of Lords European Union Committee, *Judicial Co-Operation in the EU* House of Lords Paper No 138 Session 2003–2004 (2004) 6.

Fiscal Service in Scotland.[21] The benefits of Eurojust lie in the ability to work multilaterally rather than bilaterally in real time with partners in the EU, the access to the Eurojust Case Management System, as well as the neutral physical space. Eurojust mediates jurisdictional conflicts of law and serves as a vehicle for problem-solving. Just as the use, value and experience of Eurojust are becoming embedded, prosecutors are faced with the likelihood of leaving.

The UK will aim to retain access to Eurojust to the greatest extent possible, ideally with a closer relationship than would normally be envisaged by third country agreements. Such agreements have been concluded with Norway, Iceland, the USA, Switzerland, and the former Yugoslav Republic of Macedonia, and liaison prosecutors from Norway, Switzerland, and the USA are based at Eurojust.

It is unquestionable that future arrangements regarding Eurojust will be "suboptimal" to the current situation.[22] Post-Brexit, the UK is unlikely to have access to the Case Management System, which is a valuable resource as well as serving a cross-checking purpose in respect of case files and details.

An obstacle lies in the extent to which agreements may be negotiated for the exchange of judicial information and personal data outside the EU. As noted in relation to Europol, the European Parliament needs to consent to this. It is questionable how politically acceptable this will be to other member states. Another obstacle lies in the fact that continued involvement will also entail oversight from the supranational EU institutions. According to art 85 of the *TFEU*, the European Parliament and national parliaments shall be involved in the evaluation of Eurojust's activities, though no specific arrangements have yet been adopted. The CJEU retains ultimate oversight. Though it is questionable whether this will be palatable from the UK-side, these dimensions cannot be circumvented.

One option is the use of liaison prosecutors situated in different member states as a potential alternative to the status quo. Precedents already exist for third country agreement with Eurojust involving a liaison prosecutor, but these cannot replicate Eurojust's capacity to facilitate multi-national co-ordination. In addition, any liaison prosecutors will not be part of the Eurojust management board, and therefore cannot influence its strategic direction. This implies that in the longer term, continental influence will grow, with implications for Ireland especially, as the other common law/adversarial justice system in the

---

21   House of Lords European Union Committee, above n 2, [74].
22   United Kingdom, *Parliamentary Debates*, House of Lords, 7 February 2017, vol 778, col 1669 (Baroness Prashar).

EU. There are issues of logistics and resources also, in terms of replacing prosecutors in all other member states.

4 Joint Investigation Teams

A joint investigation team ("JIT") is a team consisting of prosecutors and law enforcement authorities of two or more states, established for a fixed period and a specific purpose by way of a written agreement, to carry out criminal investigations in one or more of the involved states.[23] There is a direct link to the response to TOC, as it was the *Decree of the Council Plan of Action* for combating organised crime that had prompted the setting up of "joint teams".[24]

JITs enable the direct gathering and exchange of information and evidence without the need to use traditional channels of mutual legal assistance. In addition, "seconded members" of the team (i.e. those originating from another state than the one on the territory of which the JIT operates) are entitled to be present and to take part in investigative measures outside of their state of origin. JITs are an efficient and effective cooperation tool, facilitating coordination of investigation and prosecution conducted in parallel in several countries. They help to increase operational capacity in dealing with serious and organised transnational crimes.

While some concerns have been raised about the bureaucracy and lack of speed of JITs,[25] the alternative in terms of the use of parallel investigations would not be any different, and so it is not suggested that they be replaced or reconsidered.

It is conceivable that the UK could opt for a bilateral or ad hoc arrangement with Eurojust, and/or with individual states. There are no legal obstacles to the continued used of JITs involving the UK post-Brexit. Indeed, JITs can be set up with and between competent authorities of States outside the European

---

23 *Council Act of 29 May 2000 Establishing in Accordance with Article 34 of the Treaty on European Union the Convention on Mutual Assistance in Criminal Matters between the Member States of the European Union* [2000] OJ C197/1; and in the *Council Framework Decision of 13 June 2002 on joint investigation teams (2002/465/JHA)* [2002] OJ L 162/1.

24 *Action Plan to Combat Organized Crime* (adopted by the Council 28 April 1997) [1997] OJ C 251/01.

25 Directorate-General for Migration and Home Affairs, *Study on paving the way for future policy initiatives in the field of fight against organised crime* (2015) European Commission <https://ec.europa.eu/home-affairs/sites/homeaffairs/files/e-library/docs/20150312_1_amoc_report_020315_0_220_part_2_en.pdf>.

Union.[26] Thus, Brexit will not prevent the UK from participating in JITs. It appears that the UK remaining a party to the *Council of Europe Mutual Legal Assistance Convention 1959* will permit it to continue benefiting from involvement in JITs.[27]

Under the existing framework, a JIT can only be launched by a request from a member state, so the UK's future role in these will be initiated elsewhere. Currently, the UK is party to 31 JITs, whereas there were just 12 applications for JITs involving non-EU member states in 2014.[28] That said, the UK may be distinguished from other non-members in that it has been heavily involved in JITs historically. This may be cited in the negotiations to carve out a special role for UK.

The Network of National Experts on Joint Investigation Teams observed in 2014 that there is limited practical experience in JITs involving non-EU member states.[29] Nonetheless, the threats caused by organised crime represents a strong incentive for using swift and flexible cooperation tools with countries located outside the EU. This would suggest that the UK's involvement in JITs will continue, albeit in a different form.

5   European Arrest Warrants and European Investigation Orders

The European Arrest Warrant ("EAW") allows for the extradition of individuals between EU member states to face prosecution for a crime of which they have been accused, or to serve an outstanding prison sentence.[30] It is based on the principle of mutual recognition of criminal decisions and enforcement of

---

26   See e.g. *Agreement between the European Union and the Republic of Iceland and the Kingdom of Norway on the Application of Certain Provisions of the Convention of 29 May 2000 on Mutual Assistance in Criminal Matters between the Member States of the European Union and the 2001 Protocol thereto; Agreement on Mutual Legal Assistance between the European Union and the United States of America* 2003 [2003] OJ L26/3 art 5; *Police Cooperation Convention for South-East Europe (PCC-SEE), Applicable Between Several Member States (Austria, Bulgaria, Hungary, Romania, Slovenia) and Countries of the Balkans (Albania, Bosnia and Herzegovina, fYROM, Moldova, Montenegro, Serbia)* [2003] art 27.

27   *European Convention on Mutual Assistance in Criminal Matters*, opened for signature 20 April 1959, ETS 030 (entered into force 12 June 1962)

28   House of Lords European Union Committee, above n 2, [75].

29   *Conclusion of the Tenth Annual Meeting of National Experts on Joint Investigation Teams (JITs)*, (June 2014) <https://www.europol.europa.eu/sites/default/files/documents/2526 june.pdf>.

30   *Council Framework Decision 2002/584/JHA, 13 June 2002 on the European Arrest Warrant and the Surrender Procedures between Member States* [2002] OJ L 190.

arrest warrants, and represented a move away from the conventional refusal of extradition on the grounds of nationality. In addition, the dual criminality requirement is not applicable to a list of offences, based on mutual trust between the judicial authorities of the member states.[31]

Once issued, EAWs are circulated on the EU-wide Second Generation Schengen Information System ("SIS II") as an art 26 alert,[32] via the National Crime Agency, which acts as a conduit for information/subsequent questions relating to the UK. Once the individual is arrested, the process is purely judicial with no involvement of political authorities/executive. There is also a speedy return of the requested person: ten days if the defendant consents to their return, and up to 60 days otherwise.[33]

Future cooperation lies in the form of the European Investigation Order ("EIO").[34] The EIO aims to supersede existing letters of request ("LORS") for the gathering of evidence from another member state, with a single comprehensive regime based on the principle of mutual recognition of judicial orders/decisions and use of a common template recognised by all. Its objective is "to create a single, efficient and flexible instrument for obtaining evidence in another Member State in the framework of criminal proceedings".[35] The EIO is an order, not a "request", and is either issued or validated by a "judicial authority" (court, judge or public prosecutor). As with the EAW, the dual criminality requirement does not apply to a given list of offences.[36] There are limited grounds to refuse to recognise or execute an EIO, and the executing state must try to execute the order in compliance with its own legislation.

The Directive came into force on 21 May 2014, and participating member states (all except Denmark and Ireland) had three years to transpose and implement it into domestic law. As from 22 May 2017, this directive replaced most of the existing rules on mutual legal assistance between member states. It was implemented into UK law by means of the *Criminal Justice (European Investigation Order) Regulations 2017*.

If the UK withdraws from these schemes it would revert to relying on mutual legal assistance, which continues to be used to obtain material that cannot

---

31   Ibid art 2.2.

32   *Council Decision 2007/533/JHA* [2007] OJ L 205/63, art 26.

33   Ibid art 17.

34   *Directive 2014/41/EU of the European Parliament and the Council Regarding the European Investigation Order in Criminal Matters* [2014] OJ L 130/1.

35   *Proposal for a Directive of the European Parliament and the Council Regarding the European Investigation Order in Criminal Matters – Explanatory Memorandum* [2017] COM/2017/0386 final – 2017/0165, 1.

36   Ibid art 11.

be obtained on a police cooperation basis, particularly enquiries that require coercive means. The *European Convention on Extradition 1957* would apply. One critical difference is that there is no extradition of nationals, but rather an undertaking to try the offence(s) in his/her own country. Under this scheme a request is sent via diplomatic channels by means of a formal international Letter of Request ("LOR"), unless other arrangements exist,[37] and except in urgent applications regarding provisional arrest. This is a political decision followed by a judicial decision, and there are no time constraints. All LORs on criminal matters from the UK are sent via the Home Office's UK Central Authority or the Crown Office in Edinburgh. The problem with such a process is that the execution of LORs can be inconsistent and protracted.

One possible resolution is the conclusion of an agreement between the UK and the EU, as well as EU agencies, whereby the UK would be a third country, to maintain the existing situation. This would be preferable to bilateral arrangements. There are precedents for this, in that there are now arrangements with Norway and Iceland regarding surrender, for instance, but these countries are full Schengen members, and have strong cooperation with EU members such as Denmark and Sweden through the Nordic arrest warrant. That said, the UK may not be in the same position as those countries as it is already an EU member. It is important to recall that it took Norway and Iceland eight years to negotiate their admission to an extradition scheme, which has yet to be implemented, and with this comes the need for them to recognise the ECJ jurisprudence. There remains a "capability gap" for these countries relative to the EAW.[38] Oversight by the CJEU applies, given that an EU *acquis* must be interpreted in accordance with CJEU decisions.

6   Conclusion

The UK's membership of the EU has enabled and strengthened regional cooperation against TOC. The EU's structures facilitated a shift from inter-state cooperation against crime to stronger regional integration, while the UK's involvement in turn contributed pragmatism, intelligence, and operational capabilities. Thus, the UK's likely exit from the EU has serious implications for the policing, investigation and prosecution of TOC, in terms of procedural matters and cooperation. Despite stakeholder and political desire to ensure maintenance of the status quo, there are legal and political obstacles to this.

---

37   Ibid art 12.
38   Department for Exiting the European Union, above n 9, [12]–[14].

While historical contributions and operational pragmatism may be cards for the UK to play, the nature and nuances of the negotiations do not give much cause for optimism, not least given the fast-approaching departure date of 30 March 2019.

There are wider implications of and lessons to draw from the UK's process of leaving the EU. Joining and participating in a regional organisation such as the EU increases and eases cooperation against TOC and other social problems. Conversely, exiting such an organisation is likely to hinder cooperation, at least temporarily, which sounds a note of caution to other regions that are seeking to augment regional collaboration. Cognisance of the consequences of withdrawal, as well as clarity as to the process of withdrawal from any regional organisations' collaboration, is vital in this respect.

Command Responsibility after Bemba

Ray Murphy *

1   Introduction

Command responsibility is a subject that has generated significant controversy since its adoption in the post-World War II trials. It took a long time for omission liability to evolve under international criminal law.[1] However, today it is a well established principal that superiors are criminally responsible for the actions of subordinates under their effective command or authority.[2] According to Schabas, the topic has generated "more heat than light".[3] This seems an apt description of how this doctrine is interpreted and applied by international tribunals and courts. Command responsibility is a complex form of criminal responsibility and its most recent iteration is Article 28 of the *Rome Statute* ("*ICC Statute*"), governing responsibility of commanders and other superiors. This contains a lengthy and complex definition of what is a long established modality dealing with individual criminal responsibility under international law.[4] For an act or omission to constitute the physical element of a crime, it is not sufficient that a commander be under a mere duty to act; he or she must

---

* Professor, Irish Centre for Human Rights, School of Law, National University of Ireland Galway
1 Antonio Cassese and Paola Gaeta, *Cassese's International Criminal Law* (Oxford University Press, 3rd ed, 2013) 180.
2 Otto Triffterer and Kai Ambos (eds), *Rome Statute of the International Criminal Court – A Commentary* (Beck Hart Nomos, 3rd ed, 2016) 1059; UK Ministry of Defence, *The Manual of the Law of Armed Conflict* (Oxford University Press, 2004) 436–8.
3 William Schabas, *The International Criminal Court* (Oxford University Press, 2010) 455.
4 *Rome Statute of the International Criminal Court*, opened for signature 14 July 1998, 2187 UNTS 90 (entered into force 1 July 2002) Article 28 ("*Rome Statute*"):
    Responsibility of commanders and other superiors:
    In addition to other grounds of criminal responsibility under this Statute for crimes within the jurisdiction of the Court:
        (a) A military commander or person effectively acting as a military commander shall be criminally responsible for crimes within the jurisdiction of the Court committed by forces under his or her effective command and control, or effective authority and control as the case may be, as a result of his or her failure to exercise control properly over such forces, where: (i) That military commander or person either knew or, owing to the circumstances at the time, should have known that the forces were committing or about to commit such crimes; and (ii) That military

also have the material ability to do so.[5] This was an important factor in the *Bemba* decision before the International Criminal Court ("ICC").[6]

It has long been recognised that perpetrators of war crimes, crimes against humanity and genocide seldom carry out such atrocities on their own initiative. While such acts may not be formally approved by superiors, lack of oversight or tacit approval may implicate those in command or superior positions. Where crimes such a rape and murder are widespread, there is a greater onus on the commander of forces perpetrating such crimes to respond appropriately.[7] The jurisprudence in relation to command responsibility remains "highly disputed" and sometimes inconsistent.[8] The controversy of applying this mode of liability was particularly evident in the aftermath of the ICC Appeal Chamber's decision in the *Bemba* case.[9] The ICC did at least confirm that the Rome Statute does not endorse the concept of strict liability. However, the Appeals Chamber's decision seems, inter alia, to have raised the burden of proof threshold to establish command responsibility to a degree that may be almost impossible to meet in future cases. This article examines the doctrine of command or superior responsibility as defined by Article 28 of the ICC Statute and interpreted by the ICC Trial Chamber and Appeals Chamber. It outlines the background to the Bemba case and analyses the reasoning and inconsistencies

---

   commander or person failed to take all necessary and reasonable measures within his or her power to prevent or repress their commission or to submit the matter to the competent authorities for investigation and prosecution.

   (b) With respect to superior and subordinate relationships not described in paragraph (a), a superior shall be criminally responsible for crimes within the jurisdiction of the Court committed by subordinates under his or her effective authority and control, as a result of his or her failure to exercise control properly over such subordinates, where: (i) The superior either knew, or consciously disregarded information which clearly indicated, that the subordinates were committing or about to commit such crimes; (ii) The crimes concerned activities that were within the effective responsibility and control of the superior; and (iii) The superior failed to take all necessary and reasonable measures within his or her power to prevent or repress their commission or to submit the matter to the competent authorities for investigation and prosecution.

   Trifftterer and Ambos, above n 2.

5 *Prosecutor v Lubanga (Decision on the Confirmation of Charges)* (International Criminal Court, Pre-Trial Chamber I, Case No ICC 01/40-01/06-803, 29 January 2007) [152], [351]–[352].

6 *Prosecutor v Bemba (Judgment on the appeal of Mr Jean-Pierre Bemba Gombo against Trial Chamber III's "Judgment pursuant to Article 74 of the Statute")* (International Criminal Court, Appeals Chamber, Case No ICC 01/05-01/08 A, 8 June 2018) ("*Bemba Appeal*").

7 *United States of America v Yamashita* (1948) 4 LRTWC 1, 35.

8 Trifftterer and Ambos, above n 2, 1060.

9 *Bemba Appeal* (International Criminal Court, Appeals Chamber, Case No ICC 01/05-01/08 A, 8 June 2018).

between the decisions of each chamber in order to understand the implications for applying the doctrine in future cases.

2   Background to the Bemba Case

The events and crimes that gave rise to Bemba's conviction and appeal took place in the Central African Republic ("CAR") from October 2002 to March 2003. Despite finding that Bemba was President of the Mouvement de libération du Congo ("MLC"), a political party founded by him and based in the northwest of the Democratic Republic of the Congo ("DRC"), and Commander-in-Chief of its military branch, the Armée de libération du Congo ("ALC"), the ICC Appeals Chamber exonerated Bemba for the alleged crimes that occurred during a MLC intervention to support the then-President of the CAR to suppress a rebellion.[10] It is evident that the Appeals Chamber was significantly divided on the issue.[11] The majority appeared to dismiss the 2016 trial judgment's reasoning and conclusions. The Appeals Chamber then went on to evaluate the case *de novo* and overturn the Trial Chamber's convictions.

The Trial Chamber had relied on Article 28(a) as the basis for convicting Bemba. However, a majority of the Appeals Chamber overturned that result in a decision that was based on a restrictive interpretation of Article 28(a)(ii), requiring a military commander to take *all necessary and reasonable measures* (emphasis added) within his or her power to prevent or repress the commission of crimes or to submit the matter to the competent authorities for investigation and prosecution. The Appeals Chamber interpreted what might be construed as "necessary" and "reasonable" in a manner most favourable to the defendant. It appeared to have attached little significance to the word "all".

An insight into the reasoning and approach can be gleaned from the statement by the Appeals Chamber, without referring to any authorities; that "Commanders are allowed to make a cost/benefit analysis when deciding which measures to take, bearing in mind their overall responsibility to prevent and repress crimes committed by their subordinates".[12] This seems to provide any

---

10   Ibid [13]. Bemba was acquitted of crimes against humanity and war crimes, but remained detained because of his conviction in another ICC case for offenses against the administration of justice.

11   Judges Sanji Mmasenono Monageng and Piotr Hofmański wrote an almost three hundred page dissent. Two members of the majority, Judges Christine Van den Wyngaert and Howard Morrison, wrote a thirty four page separate opinion.

12   *Bemba Appeal* (International Criminal Court, Appeals Chamber, Case No ICC 01/05-01/08 A, 8 June 2018) [170].

defendant with the equivalent of a "get out of jail" card that effectively allows him or her to evade criminal responsibility. As such, it represents a potentially retrograde step in linking remote perpetrators to particular crimes on the basis of command responsibility.

The Trial Chamber listed a range of measures it considered necessary and reasonable which should have been taken, to assist in determining whether the defendant had done all within his power to prevent atrocities by the troops under his command.[13] The Appeals Chamber rejected this formulation and found the scope of duty to take "all necessary and reasonable measures" to be intrinsically connected to the extent of the commander's material ability to prevent or repress the commission of crimes or to submit the matter to competent authorities for investigation and prosecution.[14] The Chamber was not convinced that Bemba had the power to take such measures as outlined, and therefore found that he should not be blamed for his inability.[15] It also found that the assessment of whether a commander such as Bemba took all "necessary and reasonable measures" must be based on considerations of what crimes he knew or should have known about and at what point in time.[16] The Appeals Chamber considered such a listing of measures as unfair without giving notice to the defendant that they would be taken into account. The Trial Chamber's juxtaposition of certain crimes committed by subordinates with a list of measures which their commander could have hypothetically taken did not, in and of itself, show that the commander acted unreasonably at the time.[17] Instead, the Appeals Chamber found that the Trial Chamber must specifically identify what a commander should have done *in concreto*.[18] This seems to turn on its head the practical implementation of command responsibility as a mode of liability and dilute greatly the responsibilities and duties of commanders in these circumstances.

3   Command Responsibility

As Bemba was the Commander-in-Chief of the relevant forces, the focus of this discussion is responsibility of military superiors. The International

---

13   *Prosecutor v Bemba (Judgment pursuant to Article 74 of the Statute)* (International Criminal Court, Trial Chamber III, Case No ICC-01/05-01/08, 21 March 2016) [203] (*"Bemba Trial"*).

14   *Bemba Appeal* (International Criminal Court, Appeals Chamber, Case No ICC 01/05-01/08 A, 8 June 2018) [5].

15   Ibid.

16   Ibid [6].

17   Ibid [7].

18   Ibid.

Criminal Tribunal for the former Yugoslavia ("ICTY") Appeals Chamber in *Hadžihasanović* found that there cannot be an organized military force except on the basis of responsible command.[19] Wherever international law recognizes that crimes can be committed by an organized military force, it also recognizes that a commander can be penally sanctioned for such conduct. In this way the concept of command responsibility is inextricably linked to that of responsible command. The ICTY Appeals Chamber distinguished between both concepts. It declared that the difference was due to the fact that the concept of responsible command looks to the duties comprised in the idea of command, whereas that of command responsibility looks at liability flowing from breach of those duties.[20]

It is also important at the outset not to place unreasonable demands on commanders or superiors. For this reason, it is imperative to distinguish between moral and legal obligations, the latter being matters of concern to a court or tribunal. Command implies some form of hierarchy which will comprise personnel of different ranks with varying responsibilities. Some command structures will be more rigid than others and it may be that a commander will be unable to prevent or punish because his or her superiors are directly implicated in the crimes.[21] A commander is not expected to do the impossible, but rank brings responsibilities when it is accompanied by effective control. In this way the doctrine of command responsibility is based on the notion of guarantor position of a superior, which is limited to his or her sphere of influence or competence at the time the crimes occurred.[22] It is not a form of strict liability or collective responsibility.

A commander or superior will only be liable for activities that were within his or her effective responsibility and control.[23] The essential elements of command responsibility, based on the jurisprudence of the international tribunals, are: the existence of a superior-subordinate relationship involving effective control of subordinates; actual or constructive knowledge by a superior that subordinates have or are about to commit serious crimes; and failure to adopt reasonable and necessary measures to prevent, punish or report the offences in

---

19 *Prosecutor v Hadžihasanović (Decision on Interlocutory Appeal Challenging Jurisdiction in Relation to Command Responsibility)* (International Criminal Tribunal for the Former Yugoslavia, Appeals Chamber, Case No IT-01-47-AR72, 16 July 2003) [16]–[18].

20 Ibid [22].

21 *Prosecutor v Kristić (Appeal Judgment)* (International Criminal Tribunal for the Former Yugoslavia, Appeals Chamber, Case No IT-98-33-A, 19 April 2004) [143] n 250.

22 Trifftterer and Ambos, above n 2, 1103.

23 Ibid.

question.[24] This may appear a relatively straight forward principle to apply in practice. The reality of investigating and prosecuting cases in the expectation of invoking this mode of liability has been very different and it has led to relatively few convictions before the ad hoc tribunals.[25] As most cases before international tribunals involve senior level perpetrators, command responsibility is a key concept in the armoury of any prosecution team. It has the potential to link remote perpetrators to particular crimes. Its apparent failure in the *Bemba* case is significant and it is important to ascertain what went wrong and why. Only then may lessons be learned for future investigations and prosecutions.

4   Article 28 of the ICC Statute

In its analysis of Article 28 of the Rome Statute, the Trial Chamber in *Bemba* found that Article 28(a) codifies the responsibility of military commanders and persons effectively acting as such.[26] For an accused to be found guilty and convicted as a military commander or person effectively acting as a military commander under Article 28(a), the following elements must be fulfilled:

a.   crimes within the jurisdiction of the Court must have been committed by forces;

b.   the accused must have been either a military commander or a person effectively acting as a military commander;

c.   the accused must have had effective command and control, or effective authority and control, over the forces that committed the crimes;

d.   the accused either knew or, owing to the circumstances at the time, should have known that the forces were committing or about to commit such crimes;

e.   the accused must have failed to take all necessary and reasonable measures within his power to prevent or repress the commission of such crimes or to submit the matter to the competent authorities for investigation and prosecution; and

f.   the crimes committed by the forces must have been a result of the failure of the accused to exercise control properly over them.[27]

---

24   *Prosecutor v Delalić (Judgment)* (International Criminal Tribunal for the Former Yugoslavia, Trial Chamber, Case No IT-96-21-T, 16 November 1998) ("*Celebici Case*").

25   Schabas, *The International Criminal Court*, above n 3, 455.

26   *Bemba Trial* (International Criminal Court, Trial Chamber III, Case No ICC-01/05-01/08, 21 March 2016) [170].

27   Ibid.

It is essential that the crimes in question were actually committed by the relevant forces.[28] It is not necessary that the specific identity of those directly responsible be known to the commander; it is sufficient to identify the relevant group responsible, over which effective control was exercised.[29] It is also necessary to establish a superior-subordinate relationship, either *de jure* or *de facto*,[30] and a chain of command.[31] Proof of a superior-subordinate relationship ultimately depends on the existence of effective control.[32] The Pre-Trial Chamber in *Bemba* cited the factors indicative of effective control adopted by the ICTY.[33] The key question is: has the superior the material ability to prevent or punish the perpetrator(s)? The Trial Chamber concluded that establishing effective control was case-specific and is more a matter of evidence than of substantive law.[34]

---

28   *Bemba Trial* (International Criminal Court, Trial Chamber III, Case No ICC-01/05-01/08, 21 March 2016) [175]; *Prosecutor v Orić (Appeal Judgment)* (International Criminal Tribunal for the Former Yugoslavia, Appeals Chamber, Case No IT-03-68-A) [35] (*"Orić Appeal"*). The Appeals Chamber in *Orić* held that the existence of culpable subordinates, who would have taken part in the commission of the crimes for which the accused superior is found responsible, must be established. This incorporates modes of liability beyond "commission" in the strict sense, such as, planning, instigating, or aiding and abetting in the commission by some other person. See *Orić Appeal* (International Criminal Tribunal for the Former Yugoslavia, Appeals Chamber, Case No IT-03-68-A) [21]; *Prosecutor v Blagojević and Jokić (Appeal Judgment)* (International Criminal Tribunal for the Former Yugoslavia, Appeals Chamber, Case No IT-02-60-A) [280]–[282]; *Prosecutor v Nahimana (Appeal Judgment)* (International Criminal Tribunal for Rwanda, Appeals Chamber, Case No ICTR-99-52-A) [485]–[486].

29   *Prosecutor v Hadžihasanović (Judgment)* (International Criminal Tribunal for the Former Yugoslavia, Trial Chamber, Case No IT-01-47-T, 15 March 2006) [90]; *Bemba Appeal* (International Criminal Court, Appeals Chamber, Case No ICC 01/05-01/08 A, 8 June 2018) [194].

30   *Prosecutor v Popović (Judgment)* (International Criminal Tribunal for the Former Yugoslavia, Trial Chamber II, Case No IT-05-88-T, 10 June 2010); *Celebici Case* (International Criminal Tribunal for the Former Yugoslavia, Trial Chamber, Case No IT-96-21-T, 16 November 1998) [193].

31   *Celebici Case* (International Criminal Tribunal for the Former Yugoslavia, Trial Chamber, Case No IT-96-21-T, 16 November 1998) [354].

32   *Prosecutor v Halilović (Judgment)* (International Criminal Tribunal for the Former Yugoslavia, Trial Chamber, Case No IT-01-48-T, 16 November 2005) [311].

33   *Prosecutor v Bemba (Decision Pursuant to Article 61(7)(a) and (b) of the Rome Statute on the Charges of the Prosecutor Against Jean-Pierre Bemba Gombo)* (International Criminal Court, Pre-Trial Chamber II, Case No ICC-01/05-01/08, 15 June 2009) [417] (*"Bemba Pre-Trial"*).

34   *Bemba Trial* (International Criminal Court, Trial Chamber III, Case No ICC-01/05-01/08, 21 March 2016) [188]; *Orić Appeal* (International Criminal Tribunal for the Former Yugoslavia, Appeals Chamber, Case No IT-03-68-A) [20].

Knowledge has always been a central issue in proving command responsibility. According to the ICTY, there can be no doubt that a superior who simply ignores information within his possession compelling the conclusion that criminal acts occurred commits a most serious dereliction of duty.[35] More importantly, according to the jurisprudence from the immediate aftermath of World War II, commanders have a duty to remain informed of the activities of their subordinates and if some specific information is available, he or she must act.[36] It is sufficient if the superior was put on inquiry by the information, i.e. if it indicated a need to investigate further.[37] There is no requirement for specific information relating to offences.[38] A commander must exercise due diligence in the discharge of his or her duties. In this way, some general information which would put a commander on notice of some possible criminality by his subordinates would be sufficient to prove he or she "had reason to know".[39]

The standard under Article 28(a) of the ICC Statute is "should have known" and this was interpreted by the ICC Pre-Trial Chamber II as a type of negligence requiring a more active and stringent duty on the part of the superior to take necessary measures to secure knowledge of the conduct of his or her troops.[40] Actual knowledge cannot be presumed and must be established on the basis of evidence.[41] Nevertheless, the ICC Statute appears to have adopted a significantly looser standard of liability for military commanders than that required by customary international law.[42] The Pre-Trial Chamber found that the "should have known standard" requires the commander to have "merely been negligent" in failing to acquire the relevant knowledge of his or her subordinates criminal behaviour.[43] It is important to stress that the crime is

---

35   *Celebici Case* (International Criminal Tribunal for the Former Yugoslavia, Trial Chamber, Case No IT-96-21-T, 16 November 1998) [387]–[393].

36   Ibid [388].

37   Ibid [393].

38   *Prosecutor v Blaškić (Judgment)* (International Criminal Tribunal for the Former Yugoslavia, Trial Chamber, Case No IT-95-14-T, 3 March 2000) [324].

39   *Celebici Case* (International Criminal Tribunal for the Former Yugoslavia, Trial Chamber, Case No IT-96-21-T, 16 November 1998) [238]. See also *Prosecutor v Taylor (Judgment)* (Special Court for Sierra Leone, Trial Chamber II, Case No SCSL-03-01-T, 18 May 2012) [498].

40   *Bemba Pre-Trial* (International Criminal Court, Pre-Trial Chamber II, Case No ICC-01/05-01/08, 15 June 2009) [432]–[433].

41   Ibid [429].

42   Guenael Mettraux, *The Law of Command Responsibility* (Oxford University Press, 2009) 26.

43   *Bemba Pre-Trial* (International Criminal Court, Pre-Trial Chamber II, Case No ICC-01/05-01/08, 15 June 2009) [432]. William Schabas, *An Introduction to the International Criminal Court* (Cambridge University Press, 4th ed, 2011) 232.

not negligence per se or negligent supervision of troops under military law. The commander is prosecuted for the crime committed by his or her subordinate due to negligent performance of the commander's duty. For civilian superiors, the threshold of proof is somewhat higher. However, according to Mettraux, the "consciously disregarding information" standard for civilian superiors set out in article 28(b)(i) "does not diverge in any significant manner from the standard of mens rea applicable to all superiors under customary international law".[44] Despite differences with the "had reason to know" criterion provided for in the statutes of earlier tribunals, the criteria or indicia adopted by the tribunals may be useful to consider.[45]

The failure to adopt the necessary and reasonable measures to prevent and punish his subordinates was a key element in the *Bemba* trial. The Trial Chamber found that under Article 28(a)(ii) a commander was required to prevent, repress or submit the matter to appropriate authorities for investigation and prosecution. The scope of the duty to prevent depends on the material power of the commander to intervene in a specific situation. What are reasonable and necessary measures to fulfil a commander's duty is a matter of evidence in each case and not substantive law.[46] This means that in practice there is no objective standard with regard to what measures a superior can or must take. This gives a commander discretion with regard to the choice of measures he or she considers appropriate to adopt in each case and these will vary depending on the circumstances.[47] While it is then for a tribunal or court to assess if the action taken meets the necessary and reasonable test, the role of the court is not to substitute its judgment for that of the commander. At a minimum however, when crimes within the jurisdiction of the ICC are in issue, a commander should initiate an investigation or report the matter up the chain of command for appropriate action. Article 28 also differs from the practice of the ad hoc tribunals in so far as it requires an element of causation. It provides that the subordinate's crimes must have occurred "as a result of" the superior's failure to exercise control properly over his or her subordinates.[48] According to the Trial Chamber, this does not require a direct causal link; rather it must

---

44   Mettraux, above n 42, 195.
45   *Bemba Pre-Trial* (International Criminal Court, Pre-Trial Chamber II, Case No ICC-01/05-01/08, 15 June 2009) [434].
46   *Prosecutor v Halilović* (*Judgment*) (International Criminal Tribunal for the Former Yugoslavia, Appeals Chamber, Case No IT-01-48-A, 16 October 2007) [63].
47   *Prosecutor v Halilović* (*Judgment*) (International Criminal Tribunal for the Former Yugoslavia, Trial Chamber, Case No IT-01-48-T, 16 November 2005) [74].
48   *Rome Statute*, Article 28(a).

be shown that the superior's omission increased the risk of the commission of the crimes.[49]

It is noteworthy that the ICTY established guidelines for determining whether necessary and reasonable measures have been taken. The degree of effective control and the commander's material ability to take action may guide the Trial Chamber in deciding if appropriate steps were taken.[50] According to the ICTY Trial Chamber, the relevant factors to be considered include: whether specific orders prohibiting or stopping the criminal activities were issued; what measures to secure the implementation of these orders were taken; what other measures were taken to ensure that the unlawful acts were interrupted and whether these measures were reasonably sufficient in the specific circumstances, and, after the commission of the crime, what steps were taken to secure an adequate investigation and to bring the perpetrators to justice.[51]

Owing to the central importance of what was expected of Bemba, it is worth stating some of the measures that he should have taken according to the ICC Trial Chamber. It referred to what the Pre-Trial Chamber had identified as:

> relevant measures which include: (i) ensuring that the forces are adequately trained in international humanitarian law; (ii) securing reports that military actions were carried out in accordance with international law; (iii) issuing orders aiming at bringing the relevant practices into accord with the rules of war; and (iv) taking disciplinary measures to prevent the commission of atrocities by the forces under the commander's command ...[52]

The Trial Chamber then went on to list additional measures which should be taken under Article 28(a)(ii).[53] These may include:

---

49 *Bemba Pre-Trial* (International Criminal Court, Pre-Trial Chamber II, Case No ICC-01/05-01/08, 15 June 2009) [425].

50 *Prosecutor v Blaškić (Judgment)* (International Criminal Tribunal for the Former Yugoslavia, Appeals Chamber, Case No IT-95-14-A, 29 July 2004) [70]–[72]; See *Prosecutor v. Blaškić (Judgment)* (International Criminal Tribunal for the Former Yugoslavia, Trial Chamber, Case No IT-95-14-T, 3 March 2000) [335].

51 *Prosecutor v Strugar (Judgment)* (International Criminal Tribunal for the Former Yugoslavia, Trial Chamber, Case No IT-01-42-T, 31 January 2005) [254], [378]; *Prosecutor v Halilović (Judgment)* (International Criminal Tribunal for the Former Yugoslavia, Trial Chamber, Case No IT-01-48-T, 16 November 2005) [74].

52 *Bemba Trial* (International Criminal Court, Trial Chamber III, Case No ICC-01/05-01/08, 21 March 2016) [203]. See also Triffterer and Ambos, above n 2, 1083.

53 *Rome Statute*, Article 28 (a)(ii): "That military commander or person failed to take all necessary and reasonable measures within his or her power to prevent or repress their

may include: (i) issuing orders specifically meant to prevent the crimes, as opposed to merely issuing routine orders; (ii) protesting against or criticising criminal conduct; (iii) insisting before a superior authority that immediate action be taken; (iv) postponing military operations; (v) suspending, excluding, or redeploying violent subordinates; and (vi) conducting military operations in such a way as to lower the risk of specific crimes or to remove opportunities for their commission...[54]

It also referred to what the *ad hoc* tribunals established as meeting the "minimum standard" for measures that may fulfil the duty to punish, directing that a Trial Chamber "must look at what steps were taken to secure an adequate investigation capable of leading to the criminal prosecution of the perpetrators".[55] The duty to punish includes, at least, the obligation to investigate possible crimes in order to establish the facts.

5   Judgment on the Appeal of Jean-Pierre Bemba Gombo

The Appeals Chamber reversed the Trial Chamber's judgment which had found Bemba criminally responsible for the crimes against humanity of murder and rape, and the war crimes of murder, rape, and pillaging committed by the MLC forces during the 2002–3 CAR Operation.[56] The majority of the Appeals Chamber judges found that the Trial Chamber erred when it found him responsible as a commander pursuant to Article 28(a). In particular, that the Trial Chamber erred when it found that Bemba did not take all necessary reasonable measures to prevent or repress the commission of crimes and these

---

commission or to submit the matter to the competent authorities for investigation and prosecution". See Triffterer and Ambos, above n 2, 1063–73.

54   *Bemba Trial* (International Criminal Court, Trial Chamber III, Case No ICC-01/05-01/08, 21 March 2016) [204].

55   Ibid [207]; *Prosecutor v Popović* (*Appeal Judgment*) (International Criminal Tribunal for the Former Yugoslavia, Appeals Chamber, Case No IT-08-88-A, 30 January 2015) [1932].

56   In its Conviction Decision, the Trial Chamber stated that Bemba was guilty, under Article 28(a) of the Statute, as a person effectively acting as a military commander, of the crimes of: (a) Murder as a crime against humanity under Article 7(1)(a) of the Statute; (b) Murder as a war crime under Article 8(2)(c)(i) of the Statute; (c) Rape as a crime against humanity under Article 7(1)(g) of the Statute; (d) Rape as a war crime under Article 8(2)(e)(vi) of the Statute; and (e) Pillaging as a war crime under Article 8(2)(e)(v) of the Statute. *Prosecutor v. Bemba* (*Conviction Decision*) (International Criminal Court, Trial Chamber III, Case No ICC-01/05-01/08, 21 March 2016) [752].

were determinative in the outcome of the appeal.[57] Beyond reversing the Trial Chamber's *Judgment pursuant to Article 74 of the Statute*, the Appeals Chamber identified crimes that were not within the facts and circumstances described in the charges and upon which the Trial Chamber should not have entered a verdict.[58] It declared the proceedings as to those charges discontinued and Bemba was "acquitted of all remaining charges brought against him" in this case.[59]

5.1   *Key Findings by the Appeals Chamber*

Among its key findings, the Appeals Chamber noted its responsibility to assess whether or not the Trial Chamber applied the standard of proof correctly.[60] It explained that an accused may identify sources of doubt about the accuracy of the Trial Chamber's finding in order to oblige the Appeals Chamber to independently review the Trial Chamber's reasoning on the basis of the evidence available to it.[61] Since the Appeals Chamber must be satisfied that the factual findings made beyond a reasonable doubt are clear and unassailable in terms of evidence and rationale, the Appeals Chamber must overturn findings that can be reasonably called into doubt.[62] The Appeals Chamber found that it was not sufficient under Regulation 52(b)[63] for the Trial Chamber to simply list categories of crimes with which a person is to be charged or stating, in broad

---

57   Bemba raised six grounds of appeal: (1) that this was a mistrial; (2) that the conviction exceeded the charges; (3) that Bemba is not liable as a superior and the Trial Chamber erred when it found him responsible as a commander pursuant to Article 28(a); (4) that the contextual elements were not established; (5) that the Trial Chamber erred in its approach to identification evidence; and (6) that other procedural errors invalidated the conviction. The Appeals Chamber addressed the second ground and part of the third ground of appeal. *Bemba Appeal* (International Criminal Court, Appeals Chamber, Case No ICC 01/05-01/08 A, 8 June 2018) [29], [32].

58   Ibid [4].

59   The Appeals Chamber also dismissed the *Defence application to present additional evidence in the appeal against the Judgement pursuant to Article 74 of the Statute* and rejected the *Prosecution's Request for Leave to Present Additional Authority* (ICC-01/05-01/08-3343). Ibid.

60   Ibid [2].

61   Ibid.

62   Ibid [3].

63   International Criminal Court, *Regulations of the Court*, Doc No ICC-BD/01-01-04 (adopted 26 May 2004) r 52: "The document containing the charges referred to in article 61 shall include: ... (b) a statement of the facts, including the time and place of the alleged crimes, which provides a sufficient legal and factual basis to bring the person or persons to trial, including relevant facts for the exercise of jurisdiction by the Court".

general terms, the temporal and geographical parameters of the charge.[64] Such broad terms and categories do not allow for meaningful application of Article 74(2) of the Statute.[65]

The Appeals Chamber found the scope of duty to take "all necessary and reasonable measures" to be intrinsically connected to the extent of the commander's material ability to prevent or repress the commission of crimes or to submit the matter to competent authorities for investigation and prosecution.[66] It was not convinced that Bemba had the power to do so, and therefore found that he should not be blamed for his inability.[67] It also found that the assessment of whether a commander such as Bemba took all "necessary and reasonable measures" must be based on considerations of what crimes he knew or should have known about and at what point in time.[68] The Trial Chamber's juxtaposition of certain crimes committed by subordinates with a list of measures which their commander could have hypothetically taken did not, in and of itself, show that the commander acted unreasonably at the time.[69] Instead, the Appeals Chamber found that the Trial Chamber must specifically identify what a commander should have done *in concreto*.[70]

Article 28 of the Statute requires commanders to do what is necessary and reasonable under the circumstances,[71] but does not require them to employ every single conceivable measure within his or her arsenal, irrespective of considerations of proportionality and feasibility.[72] A commander is obliged to act in good faith when adopting "necessary and reasonable measures"; the reasonableness of these adopted measures is not automatically negated by that commander's motivating desire to preserve the reputation of his or her troops.[73] The Appeals Chamber noted that just because a commander's deployed measures

---

64   *Bemba Appeal* (International Criminal Court, Appeals Chamber, Case No ICC 01/05-01/08 A, 8 June 2018) [4].

65   Article 74: The Trial Chamber's decision shall be based on its evaluation of the evidence and the entire proceedings. The decision shall not exceed the facts and circumstances described in the charges and any amendments to the charges. The Court may base its decision only on evidence submitted and discussed before it at the trial.
      Schabas, *The International Criminal Court*, above n 3, 872–7.

66   *Bemba Appeal* (International Criminal Court, Appeals Chamber, Case No ICC 01/05-01/08 A, 8 June 2018) [5].

67   Ibid.

68   Ibid [6].

69   Ibid [7].

70   Ibid.

71   *Rome Statute*, Article 28.

72   *Bemba Appeal* (International Criminal Court, Appeals Chamber, Case No ICC 01/05-01/08 A, 8 June 2018) [8].

73   Ibid [9].

were insufficient to prevent or repress an extended crime wave does not mean that those measures were also insufficient to prevent or repress the limited number of specific crimes for which he was ultimately convicted.[74]

Finally, the Appeal Chamber explained that an accused person must be informed of the factual allegations on the basis of which the Prosecutor seeks to establish that the accused failed, as a commander, to take all necessary and reasonable measures within his or her power to prevent or repress the commission or crimes or to submit the matter to the competent authorities for investigation and prosecution.[75]

5.1.1   Command Responsibility: Necessary and Reasonable Measures

Bemba argued that the Trial Court erred when it found he was responsible as a commander pursuant to Article 28(a) for crimes that MLC troops had committed during the CAR Operation.[76] According to the Trial Court, what constitutes "all necessary and reasonable measures" is to be established on a case-by-case basis, by focusing on the commander's material power.[77] The Trial Chamber found that Bemba took measures which were all limited in mandate, execution, and/or results in response to allegations of crimes committed by MLC troops in the CAR.[78] In particular, the Trial Chamber noted that the Mondonga Inquiry did not address a number of issues adequately.[79]

---

74   Ibid [10].
75   Ibid [11].
76   Ibid [29]–[30].
77   Ibid [121]; *Prosecutor v Bemba* (*Conviction Decision*) (International Criminal Court, Trial Chamber III, Case No ICC-01/05-01/08, 21 March 2016) [197]–[198].
78   *Bemba Appeal* (International Criminal Court, Appeals Chamber, Case No ICC 01/05-01/08 A, 8 June 2018) [122]. These measures included: (1) The Mondonga Inquiry which led to Colonel Mondonga forwarding on 27 Nov 2002 the case file containing information on the proceedings against Lt Bomengo and other soldiers, arrested only on charges of pillaging on 30 Oct 2002, to MLC Chief of Staff and Bemba; (2) Bemba's visit to the CAR on or around 2 Nov 2002 to meet with the UN representative and President Patassé; (3) a speech given by Bemba in the CAR sometime in November 2002; (4) the trial of Lt Bomengo and others at the Gbadolite court-martial commencing on 5 Dec 2002 and the report of conviction transmitted to Bemba on 12 Dec 2002; (5) the Zongo Commission which questioned witnesses between 25 and 28 Dec. 2002, with the head of the commission sending a report on 17 Jan 2003 to MLC Secretary General and Bemba; (6) a letter by Bemba to UN representative General Cissé on 4 Jan 2003; (7) correspondence responding to the FIDH Report on its investigative mission in Bangui, namely Bemba's letter to President of the FIDH on 20 Feb 2003 and the latter's reply on 26 Feb 2003 offering to bring the contents to the attention of the UN Secretary General and conduct investigation; and (8) the establishment of the Sibut Mission at the end of Feb 2003.
79   Ibid [128].

The Trial Chamber found the measures taken by Bemba to be minimal and inadequate in the circumstances.[80] Furthermore, this inadequacy was aggravated by indications that the actions were not genuine, but rather were primarily motivated by Bemba's desire to counter public allegations and rehabilitate the public image of the MLC.[81] It found that his primary intention was not to genuinely take all necessary and reasonable measures within his material ability to prevent or repress the commission of crimes.[82]

Instead of, or in addition to the insufficient measures taken by Bemba, the Trial Chamber suggested a list of measures within his power and ability that he could have taken (e.g. ensuring that MLC troops were properly trained and supervised; initiating genuine investigations, trials and punishments for the commission of crimes; issuing orders to stop violations; and redeploying forces and replacing commanders where appropriate).[83] It is noteworthy that the Pre-Trial Chamber found that Article 28 of the Statute does not define the specific measures required by the duty to prevent crimes.[84] In this context, the Chamber considered it appropriate to be guided by relevant factors such as measures: (i) to ensure that the superior's forces are adequately trained in international humanitarian law; (ii) to secure reports that military actions were carried out in accordance with international law; (iii) to issue orders aiming at bringing the relevant practices into accord with the rules of war; (iv) to take disciplinary measures to prevent the commission of atrocities by the troops under the superior's command.[85]

Bemba could and did create commissions and missions in reaction to allegations of crimes, both in and outside of the CAR territory, at the height of the 2002–3 military operation.[86] Nevertheless, the Trial Chamber found that he failed to take all necessary and reasonable measures within his power to prevent or repress the commission of crimes by his subordinates or to submit the matter to the competent authorities. However, the Appeals Chamber noted that it did not link his putative failure to take adequate measures to any of the

---

80   Ibid [131].
81   Ibid.
82   Ibid; *Prosecutor v Bemba* (*Conviction Decision*) (International Criminal Court, Trial Chamber III, Case No ICC-01/05-01/08, 21 March 2016) [728].
83   *Bemba Appeal* (International Criminal Court, Appeals Chamber, Case No ICC 01/05-01/08 A, 8 June 2018) [133]; *Prosecutor v Bemba* (*Conviction Decision*) (International Criminal Court, Trial Chamber III, Case No ICC-01/05-01/08, 21 March 2016) [729].
84   *Bemba Pre-Trial* (International Criminal Court, Pre-Trial Chamber II, Case No ICC-01/05-01/08, 15 June 2009) [438].
85   *Bemba Appeal* (International Criminal Court, Appeals Chamber, Case No ICC 01/05-01/08 A, 8 June 2018) [133].
86   Ibid [135].

specific criminal acts of which he was ultimately convicted.[87] In this way the Appeals Chamber found that the Trial Chamber's finding was unreasonable because it was tainted with serious errors.[88]

5.1.2   Assessing Bemba's Conduct against the Correct Legal Standard

The Appeals Chamber noted that the scope of duty to take all necessary and reasonable measures is intrinsically connected to the extent of the commander's material ability to prevent or repress the commissions of crimes or to submit the matters to the competent authorities for investigation and prosecution; he cannot be blamed for not doing something that he lacked the power to do.[89] According to the Appeals Chamber, international jurisprudence suggests that such an assessment requires consideration of what measures were at the commander's disposal in the circumstances at the time and what crimes he knew or should have known about and at what point in time.[90] A commander is not required to take each and every conceivable measure at their disposal, irrespective of considerations of proportionality and feasibility.[91]

To assess reasonableness, pursuant to Article 28, other parameters must be considered, such as the operational realities on the ground at the time.[92] The Appeals Chamber noted that Article 28 is not a form of strict liability; commanders may make cost-benefit analyses as to which measures to take, under their responsibility to prevent and repress crimes committed by subordinates, in order to choose the least disruptive measure which is expected to be effective.[93]

The Prosecutor argued that Bemba was required to take *all* necessary and reasonable measures within his power, pursuant to Article 28, to prevent or repress crimes committed by MLC troops, or to refer the matter to competent authorities. However, the Appeals Chamber agreed with Bemba that a

---

87   Ibid [136].

88   Ibid [166].

89   Ibid [167].

90   Ibid [168]; *Prosecutor v Strugar (Judgment)* (International Criminal Tribunal for the Former Yugoslavia, Trial Chamber, Case No IT-01-42-T, 31 January 2005) [374]–[378]; *Prosecutor Halilović (Judgment)* (International Criminal Tribunal for the Former Yugoslavia, Trial Chamber, Case No IT-01-48-T, 16 November 2005) [74]; *Prosecutor v Renzaho (Judgment)* (International Criminal Tribunal for Rwanda, Trial Chamber I, Case No ICTR-97-31-T, 14 July 2009) [755]; *Prosecutor v Karadžić (Public Redacted Version of Judgment)* (International Criminal Tribunal for the Former Yugoslavia, Trial Chamber, Case No IT-95-5/18-T, 24 March 2016) [588].

91   *Bemba Appeal* (International Criminal Court, Appeals Chamber, Case No ICC 01/05-01/08 A, 8 June 2018) [169].

92   Ibid [170].

93   Ibid.

commander must not be required to take every possible measure conceived in hindsight by jurists, and that the Trial Chamber erred by comparing his conduct and the certain crimes committed by subordinates to a list of hypothetical measures he could have taken instead.[94] Abstract findings of what the commander may theoretically have done was unhelpful and difficult to disprove. Bemba argued that the Trial Chamber deprived him of the opportunity to present evidence as to why these hypothetical measures were not practicable, appropriate, or possible.[95]

The Prosecutor pointed out that four of the hypothetical measures set out by the Trial Chamber are, in fact, inherent in the duties of a commander and always apply: (1) ensuring proper international humanitarian law training and adequate supervision; (2) conducting investigations and prosecutions and punishments as necessary; (3) issuing proper orders; and (4) replacing, dismissing, and removing subordinates.[96] However, the Appeals Chamber determined that the Trial Chamber must specifically identify what a commander should have done *in concreto* and must demonstrate in its reasoning that the commander did not take specific and concrete measures that were available to him and which a reasonable diligent commander in comparable circumstances would have taken.[97]

The Appeals Chamber determined that, although the unique conditions that Bemba asserted that he was limited by did not completely impede his ability to investigate crimes committed by MLC troops, the Trial Chamber failed to properly assess whether the range of measures taken by Bemba were necessary and reasonable based on his material abilities.[98] As to the extensiveness of Bemba's control over MLC forces, the Appeals Chamber found that the Trial Chamber paid insufficient attention to the fact that MLC troops were operating in a foreign country and Bemba faced attendant difficulties in taking measures as a remote commander.[99] This is one of the weakest reasons given for overturning the conviction. They were in the CAR under Bemba's orders and he remained their commander at all relevant times.

5.1.3   Limitations of MLC's Jurisdiction and Competence to Investigate
The Prosecutor argued that the Trial Chamber reasonably and carefully analysed Bemba's concrete powers to discipline his forces, including any relevant

---

94   Ibid [138].
95   Ibid [170].
96   Ibid [142].
97   Ibid [170].
98   Ibid [171].
99   Ibid.

limitations, when arriving at the conclusion that he had ultimate disciplinary authority over MLC troops in the CAR and was the competent authority to investigate crimes and establish court-martials.[100] Bemba did exercise disciplinary powers at various times in the CAR, including the establishment of the Mondonga Inquiry, dispatching a MLC delegation to Sibut, and the court-martials of several soldiers detained under his authority.[101] There were also broader findings of his authority over MLC military operations in the CAR.[102] In turn, Bemba argued that the Trial Chamber ignored the testimony of a witness which demonstrated that the MLC's investigative efforts were dependent on the cooperation of the CAR authorities, and thus the Trial Chamber erred in not taking into account the limitations on his ability to conduct investigations in the CAR territory.[103]

The Appeals Chamber determined that the witness' testimony did not support the broad proposition that Bemba's material ability to initiate investigations in the CAR was completely impeded, but the testimony did demonstrate logistical difficulties faced by the MLC in conducting investigations.[104] The investigations that did take place by the MLC in the CAR[105] were in fact limited and required the assistance of CAR authorities, according to Bemba.[106] He argued that the Trial Chamber failed to address evidence of these difficulties as well as the realities on the ground in a foreign war zone, with unfamiliar terrain and enemies.[107] The Appeals Chamber determined that the Trial Chamber ought to have given weight in its assessment to the measures that were taken by Bemba, noting that even if he had ultimate disciplinary authority in the CAR, it does not mean that this authority was not subject to limitations.[108] It noted in particular that the Trial Chamber did not address Bemba's statement written to the CAR Prime Minister, requesting the establishment of an international commission of inquiry.[109]

---

100   Ibid [147].
101   Ibid.
102   Ibid.
103   Ibid [172].
104   Ibid.
105   Namely, the Mondonga Inquiry, the Sibut Mission, and the court-martialling of seven MLC troops in Bangui.
106   *Bemba Appeal* (International Criminal Court, Appeals Chamber, Case No ICC 01/05-01/08 A, 8 June 2018) [146].
107   Ibid [146], [173].
108   Ibid [173].
109   Ibid [174]. The Trial Chamber also did not address witness testimony regarding this correspondence.

5.1.4   Taking into Account Irrelevant Considerations

The Appeals Chamber rejected Bemba's submission that the motives of an accused commander are never relevant to the assessment of necessary and reasonable measures, noting that a commander is required to act in good faith and must show that he genuinely tried to prevent or repress the crimes in question or submit the matter to the competent authorities.[110] However, it found that the Trial Chamber took an unreasonably strict approach when assessing Bemba's motives.[111] The Prosecutor asserted that Bemba took minimal, limited, and insufficient measures which required the Trial Chamber to investigate his motives in order to illuminate the genuineness of the measures taken, and to determine whether he took all necessary and reasonable measures within his material possibilities. The Appeals Chamber agreed with Bemba's argument that measures taken by a commander motivated by preserving the reputation of his troops do not intrinsically render those measures any less necessary or reasonable in preventing or repressing the commission of crimes, and ensuring proper investigation and prosecution.

While the Trial Chamber stated that the motives in question were an aggravating factor in his failure to exercise his duties, the Appeals Chambers determined that these motives were treated as determinative in and of themselves, of the adequacy or otherwise of the measures.[112] However, even Bemba contended that the Trial Chamber did not rely solely on his motivations when finding that he failed to take proper measures.[113]

The Appeals Chamber determined that Bemba's motivations were not intrinsically negative and did not necessarily conflict with the taking of genuine and effective measures.[114] Furthermore, a commander may have multiple motives for his or her actions.[115] Thus the Appeals Chamber found the Trial Chamber erred because it took into consideration an irrelevant factor, by considering Bemba's motivation to protect the MLC's image, and also failed to

---

110   Ibid [176].

111   Ibid.

112   The Appeals Chamber noted Bemba's motivations in establishing the Mondonga Inquiry, used to assess the genuineness of his establishing the inquiry: countering media allegations, demonstrating the taking of action, vindicating MLC leadership, and generally rehabilitating MLC's image. Additionally, the Trial Chamber considered his motives regarding his correspondence with the UN representative in the CAR and his withdrawal from the CAR: demonstrating good faith and maintaining the MLC's image, and external pressure directly related to the negotiation of the Sun City agreements, respectively.

113   *Bemba Appeal* (International Criminal Court, Appeals Chamber, Case No ICC 01/05-01/08 A, 8 June 2018) [156].

114   Ibid [179].

115   Ibid.

make an assessment as to how *in concreto* such motives ultimately affected the necessity or reasonableness of the measures which were taken by Bemba.[116]

5.1.5 Reasonableness of Trial Chamber's Findings on the Measures Taken

The Appeals Chamber criticised the Trial Chamber for "los[ing] sight of the fact that the measures taken by a commander cannot be faulty merely because of shortfalls in their execution"; the Trial Chamber had stated that these measures were limited in mandate, execution, and/or results.[117] The Appeals Chamber noted that limitations in the results of an inquiry, such as the Mondonga Inquiry, is not always attributable to the manner of its establishment.[118] In order to determine whether Bemba's establishment of the Inquiry was the cause of such limitations, the Trial Chamber should have conducted a proper assessment:

   (i)   that the shortcomings of the inquiry were sufficiently serious;
   (ii)   that the commander was aware of the shortcomings;
   (iii) that it was materially possible to correct the shortcomings; and
   (iv) that the shortcomings fell within his authority to remedy.[119]

According to the Appeals Chamber, without undertaking this assessment, the Trial Chamber made no finding as to the sham nature of the measures, or whether Bemba purposively limited the mandates of the commissions and inquiries.[120]

The Trial Chamber cited no evidence to support its finding that Bemba failed to empower MLC officials to fully and adequately investigate and prosecute allegations of crimes.[121] The Appeals Chamber found this to be inconsistent with the finding that certain MLC commanders also had some disciplinary authority in the field.[122] It also noted that the Trial Chamber failed to explain what more Bemba should have done to empower other MLC officials to fully and adequately investigate and prosecute allegations of crimes.[123]

The assessment of the measures taken by a commander also depends on the number of crimes that were committed; the Appeals Chamber noted that the actual number of crimes established beyond reasonable doubt was "comparatively

---

116   Ibid.
117   Ibid [180].
118   Ibid.
119   Ibid.
120   Ibid [181].
121   Ibid [182].
122   Ibid.
123   Ibid.

low".[124] It also stated that the Trial Chamber failed to give an indication of the approximate number of crimes committed in the specific locations established by reliable evidence.[125] There was also difficulties determining how widespread the criminality of MLC troops was and assessing the proportionality of the measures taken.[126] The Appeals Chamber found a discrepancy between the limited number of crimes for which Bemba was held responsible under Article 28 and the Trial Chamber's assessment of measures he should have taken, which was based on a broader and more general finding concerning widespread MLC criminality in the CAR.[127] It also noted that most of the criminal incidents to which the Prosecutor presented evidence occurred at the beginning of the operation, implying that the measures taken by Bemba may have actually had a deterrent effect and the Trial Chamber should have taken this into consideration.[128]

An accused person must be informed promptly and in detail of the nature, cause, and content of a charge prior to the start of trial.[129] Such detail would include the factual allegations on the basis of which the Prosecutor seeks to establish the element of command responsibility pursuant to Article 28(a).[130] The Appeals Chamber found that Bemba was not sufficiently notified of factual allegations, such as the redeployment of troops, and that he suffered prejudice as the result of the lack of proper notice.[131]

In summary, the Appeals Chamber identified multiple serious errors in the Trial Chamber's assessment of whether Bemba took all necessary and reasonable measures to prevent or repress the commission of crimes by his subordinates or to submit the matter to the competent authorities for investigation and prosecution:

(i)   the Trial Chamber erred by failing to properly appreciate the limitations that Bemba would have faced in investigating and prosecuting crimes as a remote commander sending troops to a foreign country;

---

124   Ibid [183].
125   Ibid. The Appeals Chamber noted that this "reliable evidence" appeared, for the most part, very weak and often consisting of media reports including anonymous hearsay.
126   Ibid.
127   Ibid.
128   Ibid.
129   Ibid [186]; *Rome Statute*, Article 61(1)(a); *Prosecutor v Lubanga* (*Judgement*) (International Criminal Court, Trial Chamber I, Case No 01/04-01/06-2842, March 2012) [118]–[130].
130   *Bemba Appeal* (International Criminal Court, Appeals Chamber, Case No ICC 01/05-01/08 A, 8 June 2018) [186].
131   Ibid [187].

(ii)   erred by failing to address Bemba's argument that he sent a letter to the CAR authorities before concluding that he had not referred allegations of crimes to the CAR authorities for investigation;

(iii)   erred in considering that the motivations that it attributed to Bemba were indicative of a lack of genuineness in adopting measures to prevent and repress the commission of crimes;

(iv)   erred in attributing to Bemba any limitations it found in the mandate, execution, and/or results of the measures taken;

(v)   erred in finding that Bemba failed to empower other MLC officials to fully and adequately investigate and prosecute crimes;

(vi)   erred in failing to give any indication of the approximate number of the crimes committed and to assess the impact of this on the determination of whether Bemba took all necessary and reasonable measures; and

(vii)   erred by taking into account the redeployment of MLC troops for example to avoid contact with the civilian population as a measure available to Bemba.[132]

These errors, according to the Appeals Chamber, materially affected the Trial Chamber's conclusion that Bemba failed to take all necessary and reasonable measures in response to MLC crimes.[133] Because of this, the Appeals Chamber found that this element of command responsibility was not properly established pursuant to Article 28(a).[134] Thus, it found that Bemba could not be held criminally liable under Article 28(a) for crimes committed by MLC troops during the 2002–3 CAR Operation.

6   Conclusion

Recalling the Preamble and Article 1 of the ICC Statute that the "most serious crimes of concern to the international community should not go unpunished" and "determined to put an end to impunity", an "International Criminal Court is hereby established … and shall have jurisdiction over persons for the most serious crimes".[135] Ensuring accountability is important as an objective of international criminal law in itself, but it is also important because facilitating impunity for what are often termed atrocity crimes can have serious adverse consequences for international peace and justice. The judgment of

---

132   Ibid [189].
133   Ibid [194].
134   Ibid.
135   *Rome Statute*, Preamble, Article 1.

the Nuremberg Tribunal famously declared, "Crimes against international law are committed by men, not by abstract entities, and only by punishing individuals who commit such crimes can the provisions of international law be enforced".[136]

Rank brings both privileges and responsibility, and military commanders are aware of this. It was acknowledged that Bemba was Commander-in-Chief of the troops at the time they carried out the murders, rapes and pillage. While the issues surrounding superior responsibility are complex, the *Bemba* Appeal decision marks a disturbing development in terms of its potential impact on accountability. Many cases in the past have been controversial, most notably the famous *Yamashita* case heard by an American military commission in the aftermath of World War II.[137] General Yamashita had commanded Japanese forces in the Philippines at a time when he had lost almost all command, control and communications. He was found guilty of not exercising "effective control" when soldiers under his command committed atrocities. Some critics, including two US Supreme Court judges, considered this to be an extraordinarily high standard of responsibility for the actions of his subordinates.[138] In practice, command or superior responsibility is not extended as far up the chain of command as might logically be implied to include a commander-in-chief such as the president of the USA. It is generally applied to superiors who play some meaningful role where effective control is more evident.[139]

Co-perpetration was more often adopted by the ad hoc criminal tribunals than superior responsibility as a mode of liability.[140] In fact joint criminal enterprise as a mode of liability was extensively used by the prosecutor at the ICTY in successfully pursuing a range of high level officials and commanders.[141] This was appropriate, given the nature of the offences and the direct role played by senior level perpetrators in the commission of specific crimes. Joint criminal enterprise has since fallen out of favour,[142] making superior responsibility as a mode of liability, at least up until the appeal decision in *Bemba*, all the more important in cases before the ICC.

---

136   *United States of America v Göring (Judgment in The Trial of German Major War Criminals)* (International Military Tribunal (Nuremberg), 1 October 1946) 55.
137   *Yamashita*, above n 7.
138   Ibid.
139   Roy Gutman, David Rieff and Anthony Dworkin, *Crimes of War* (Norton, 2007) 118.
140   Schabas, *The International Criminal Court*, above n 3, 455.
141   See generally Selma Kafedžić, "Determining Modes of Liability in International Criminal Law: Why the Common Purpose Doctrine is the Strongest Legal Response to Mass Atrocity Crimes" (2016) 14 *New Zealand Yearbook of International Law* 134–79.
142   Ibid 156–7.

Superior responsibility is not a form of co-perpetration, nor is it liability based on aiding or abetting. Instead, it is grounded on a commander's own negligence in failing to exercise control properly when he or she knew or should have known of criminal behaviour by subordinates. The assessment of what measures are necessary and reasonable must be based on a full consideration of the circumstances in which the commander found him or herself at the relevant time. The Pre-Trial Chamber found that the "should have known standard" under Article 28(a) requires the commander to have "merely been negligent" in failing to acquire the relevant knowledge of his or her subordinates criminal behaviour.[143] This imposed a more active and stringent duty on the part of the superior to take necessary measures to secure knowledge of the conduct of troops under his or her effective control. This is not negligence per se or negligent supervision of troops. The commander is prosecuted for the crime committed by his or her subordinate due to negligent performance of the commander's duty. This also addresses the issue of causation. The Trial Chamber went to great lengths to outline what was necessary and reasonable and it is regrettable that reasoning and conclusions by the Trial Chamber were not accepted by the Appeals Chamber.

There were a number of procedural issues in *Bemba* that are also a matter of concern. The Appeals Chamber overruled the Trial Chamber and at the same time appeared to bestow a much more significant role to the Pre-Trial Chamber in the proceedings. The Pre-Trial Chamber will now be required to do much more than confirm the charges before trial. Previously, it was required to find "substantial grounds to believe" that the defendant committed the alleged crimes. This innovative safeguard to protect an accused was never intended to resemble a "mini-trial" of the issues. The Appeals Chamber reviewed the findings of fact after a lengthy trial. In so doing, it departed from the standard of review for factual errors used consistently in previous cases before international tribunals. This is all the more alarming given the evidence of witness tampering by Bemba.[144]

Contemporary conflicts are characterised by widespread and systematic forms of violence deliberately targeted at civilians, especially sexual and gender based violence. Such crimes often involve planning and coordination at senior political and military levels. If these crimes do not involve some form of

---

143   *Bemba Pre-Trial* (International Criminal Court, Pre-Trial Chamber II, Case No ICC-01/05-01/ 08, 15 June 2009) [432].

144   *Prosecutor v Bemba (Decision pursuant to Article 61(7)(a) and (b) of the Rome Statute)* (International Criminal Court, Pre-Trial Chamber II, Case No ICC-01/05-01/13-749, 15 November 2014).

direct participation by those in authority, at the very least there is a degree of acquiescence. Either way, they should not go unpunished. This is why superior responsibility remains a critical mode of liability in international criminal law.

The Appeals Chamber's departure from the standard of review for factual errors used consistently in previous trials presents particular difficulties in cases involving sexual and gender based violence crimes. There is reluctance to hold remote perpetrators such as commanders responsible for rape and other sexual crimes.[145] Nevertheless, the ICTY has recognized that leaders can be held accountable for sexual crimes when they neither were present nor ordered their commission.[146] Recognizing this will often require the court to take into consideration all the evidence holistically and then make common sense inferences based on that evidence. In this way, sexual crimes will most often require a comprehensive analysis of the context in which they are committed in order to gain insights into how and why sexual violence happens in times of conflict.[147] Initially such violence may be perpetrated because the chaotic situation created by an armed conflict facilitates criminality. This situation will deteriorate quickly if commanders do not respond appropriately and try to prevent it.

The appeal reasoning marks a dilution of a well-established principle of international criminal law and in so doing it bestows a level of discretion on commanders that will be hard to challenge in the courtroom. Few if any judges have military experience, let alone first hand knowledge of operating in an armed conflict situation. The doctrine of command responsibility has evolved from bitter experience in attempting to plug the accountability gap among senior military and political figures. These leaders are most often charismatic and intelligent people. They will learn from the *Bemba* case how to manipulate the law and evade responsibility.

---

145   Kelly Dawn Askin, "Holding Leaders Accountable in the International Criminal Court (ICC) for Gender Crimes Committed in Darfur" (2006) 1 *Genocide Studies and Prevention* 13, 24.

146   *Prosecutor v Plavšić (Sentencing Judgment)* (International Criminal Tribunal for the Former Yugoslavia, Trial Chamber, Case No IT-00-39 & IT-00-40/1, 27 February 2003) [27], [29], [34], [120], [126]; *Prosecutor v Kvočka (Judgment)*, (International Criminal Tribunal for the Former Yugoslavia, Trial Chamber, Case No IT-98-30/1-T, 2 November 2001) [318].

147   Askin, above n 145, 24.

Standard Deviation: Global Standardisation and Implications for International Law

*Matt Bartlett**

1   Introduction

On 25 April 2006, the BBC celebrated the anniversary of one of the world's "most significant inventions" with little fanfare and much surprise from the wider viewing audience.[1] The subject of the feature was the humble shipping container box. Business correspondent Toby Poston acknowledged the circumstances:

> there is perhaps no obvious reason to get excited about the fiftieth anniversary of a large metal box. Such containers are an everyday sight, hauled by trucks, trains and ships all over the world. But without them, it is very unlikely we would all be buying Japanese TVs, Costa Rican bananas, Chinese underwear or New Zealand lamb. In fact, globalisation would probably not exist and the World Trade Organisation would have a lot less to talk about.[2]

The source of the miraculous development of standard container boxes? The similarly unheralded International Organisation for Standardisation ("ISO"). The ISO did not just gather agreement on what the standard size for those boxes should be; but also set standards for the ships and trains that carried the containers, the specifications of the docks and centres where they were loaded and unloaded, the design of the cranes that lifted them and the training of the crane's operators.[3] In this way, the ISO oversees much of the physical infrastructure that props up the global economy. But the ISO also provides the standards needed for the technical infrastructure of the new modern economy:

---

*   LLB(Hons)/BA from the University of Auckland. I would like to thank Caroline Foster for her feedback and patience with my many haphazard ideas. I also wouldn't have completed this work (or much else) without unfailing support from Mum.

1   Toby Poston, *Thinking inside the box* (25 April 2006) BBC <http://news.bbc.co.uk/2/hi/business/4943382.stm>.

2   Ibid.

3   Craig N Murphy and Joanne Yates, *The International Organization for Standardisation (ISO)* (Routledge, 2009) 47.

standard documents for the transit of goods, standard barcodes to summarise and allow efficient checking of those documents, and standardised bank cards with secure codes that enabled the economic interactions to begin with.[4]

This article makes three contributions to the legal literature of international law and global standard-setting. The first is an understanding of the unique way in which the ISO "disperses" power. The ISO is structured so that standard-setting discussions and decisions occur across hundreds of autonomous technical committees. This dispersal increases the transaction costs and logistical barriers for smaller and weaker actors, and entrenches the ability of wealthier industry representatives to advance their own interests. The second contribution is an assessment of the shift in contemporary standard-setting from states to a global private institution that disempowers citizens. The blurring of domestic and international contexts risks the critical loss of input from domestic constituencies as to new standards that affect their work and life. Lastly, contemporary standard-setting represents an empowerment of industry. The internal mechanics of the ISO as an organisation favour the interests of industry, to the exclusion of states and non-governmental organisations; and this entrenches the position of wealthier actors from more developed economies.

These arguments are grounded on an analysis of the power dynamics in the ISO itself. It is not the case that individual standards are themselves causing shifts in international law. Rather, the *cumulative* impact of the way each standard is shaped reflects a shift from states to the ISO as the key producer of global standards. Given that context, the first three sections set out important fundamentals about the ISO: how it sets standards, and the role it plays in global standardisation. This article first looks at the structure of the ISO, and establishes the basic tenets of the organisation. These include the nature of the ISO as a federation of national standards bodies, and the decentralised way standards are created. Then the ISO is situated in the context of global standardisation, looking at how and why the ISO came to possess such regulatory authority in global standard-setting and international trade law. The next section focuses on the ISO technical committees, the heart of the organisation, and specifically the way in which standards are created through those committees. This article's arguments about change in international law stem from the power dynamics at play in the ISO technical committee process. The article then addresses the implications for international law, arguing that the ISO *disperses* power uniquely, *disempowers* citizens, and *empowers* industry.

---

4   Nils Brunnsson and Bendt Jacobsson, *A World of Standards* (Oxford University Press, 2000) 1.

2   The International Organisation for Standardisation

A brief overview of the International Organisation for Standardisation in terms of its structure and organisation will ground the legal analysis to follow. Simply put, the ISO is a body set up to create and promote a range of global standards. A "standard" can be understood as a particular technical specification. A "global standard" attempts to overcome technical barriers in international commerce that are caused when technical specifications are developed independently.[5] To date, the ISO has produced over 20 000 global standards.[6] There are significant advantages to having different standards for a particular technical specification "harmonised", or brought into line, with a single global standard. Having a single global standard reduces transaction costs, helps facilitate international trade and improves the everyday lives of consumers and citizens.[7] The irritation of needing adaptors for different kinds of electrical sockets, for instance, is brought about by a lack of a global standard. With standardisation offering such important benefits, particularly economically, most objects today comply with some kind of global standard.[8] The organisations that set these standards consequently possess significant power in the world economy.

The ISO is the largest standard-setting organisation.[9] The first key to understanding the structure of the organisation is by understanding the character of the ISO as a federation of national standards bodies.[10] In this way, the ISO is an "organisation of organisations", rather than a collection of representatives from national governments.[11] These groups differ hugely in how they themselves are structured. The majority, like the British Standard Association ("BSA") or American National Standards Institute ("ANSI"), are private organisations made up of private members and industry representatives.[12] The Japan Industrial Standards Committee, for instance, has 11,000 members who include trade associations, large corporation and other industry interests – many being groups who had set standards themselves in the past.[13] The varying structure

---

5   Murphy, above n 3, 2.
6   ISO, *Economic benefits of Standards: International Case Studies* (Geneva, International Standards Organisation, 2011).
7   Ibid 3.
8   Murphy, above n 3, 28.
9   ISO, *Economic benefits of Standards: International Case Studies*, above n 6.
10   ISO "Navigating the World in Transition" (Annual Report, International Standards Organisation, 2016).
11   Murphy, above n 3, 28.
12   Murphy, above n 3, 29.
13   Ibid 30.

of the ISO's national standards bodies has repercussions for the representation of government and non-governmental organisations ("NGOs") in the ISO.
Because the ISO is structured as a federation of different national standards
bodies, governments and NGOs can only directly participate in ISO processes
if they are part of their national standards body.[14] Given that most national
bodies are composed of industry and corporate representatives, ISO processes
are accordingly dominated by private interests.[15]

The other distinctive characteristic of the ISO is how it delegates decision-
making autonomy. The ISO is extremely decentralised.[16] While there is a central secretariat, based in Geneva, it consists of a relatively small number of
bureaucrats who solely assist with administration and coordination.[17] The ISO
does have a centralised decision-making body in the form of the ISO council,
composed of eighteen national standards bodies that rotate in and out.[18] The
decision-making of that council, however, is confined to agenda-setting for areas of future standardisation.[19] The council does not actually legislate or influence the content of ISO standards. All the standard-setting power of the ISO
is held by technical committees: small groups formed around functionally defined areas with full autonomy and decision-making authority to decide standards in their particular area.[20] "Machine tools" is an example of one technical
committee, and "laboratory equipment" is another – in all, there are more than
three hundred technical committees. The committees themselves are made up
of a small number of national standards bodies, usually those with industry
interests in the particular area.[21] Those national standards bodies then usually
submit individuals as "experts" to different working groups that deliver recommendations to the particular technical committee.[22]

The importance of national standards bodies to the standard-setting
process of the ISO cannot be overstated. The ISO is not operationally independent or self-sufficient. Instead, the ISO functions through the national standards bodies of each of its member states, who provide logistical and technical

---

14   ISO, *Economic benefits of Standards: International Case Studies*, above n 6.
15   Tim Buthe and Walter Mattli, *The New Global Rulers* (Princeton, 2011) 12.
16   ISO, "Navigating the World in Transition", above n 10.
17   Ibid.
18   Ibid.
19   Murphy, above n 3, 29.
20   ISO, *Economic benefits of Standards: International Case Studies*, above n 6.
21   Stavros Gadinis, "Three Pathways to Global Standards: Private, Regulator and Ministry
      Networks" (2015) 109 *The American Journal of International Law* 1.
22   Ibid.

support.[23] The ISO is also reliant on national standards bodies for financing.[24] In this respect, the ISO differs from other international regulatory organisations.[25] The International Accounting Standards Committee, for instance, has a wide range of financiers and funds itself not just through membership fees but with external contributions from other international organisations.[26] The IASC also discloses all financial sources on an annual basis.[27] By comparison, the ISO limits its financing to standards fees, membership fees and the participants' self-financing, and does not disclose these numbers at all.[28] The ISO is a private organisation, with little information from technical committees made public.[29] This is vital groundwork for understanding the ISO's unique position in international law.

3   The Role of the ISO in Global Standard-Setting

This section sets out the role that standards play in the modern world, and analyses the role of the ISO as the main arbiter of those standards. While there are some other bodies with small niches of the global standard-setting project, like the ISO's sibling body, the International Electro-technical Commission ("IEC"), which looks at electro-technical standards, the ISO is by far the biggest and oldest.[30] It is therefore no surprise that many writers have already attempted to answer the difficult questions posed by the quiet omnipresence of the ISO. ISO standards are not legally binding, but many states around the world have incorporated them wholesale into domestic law. Why have states done so, and how has the ISO come to dominate the process of setting global standards?

Understanding an abridged history of the ISO is necessary for exploring both questions. The organisation was born in 1947, after the end of World War II. That war highlighted the need for greater international standardisation.[31]

---

23   ISO, *Economic benefits of Standards: International Case Studies*, above n 6.
24   Gadinis, above n 21, 10.
25   Buthe, above n 15, 50.
26   Ibid 51.
27   Kristina Tamm Hallstrom, *Organising International Standardisation: ISO and the IASC in the Quest of Authority* (Edward Elgar Publishing, 2004) 173.
28   Ann Rhodes, "ISO enters the Public Sector through the United States Forest Service" (2007) 18 *Colorado Journal of International Environmental Law and Policy,* 422.
29   Ibid.
30   Murphy, above n 3, 17.
31   Ibid.

The Economist, for instance, estimated that differences between American and British standards for screw threads alone added over 25 million pounds to the cost of the war.[32] For at least the first three decades of the ISO's existence, it was largely a European organisation.[33] In 1964, every major participant in the standard-setting processes was European, other than the United States and members of the Commonwealth like Australia and Canada.[34] That the British and French standards associations provided almost half the lead staff for the organisation in 1964–92 of 227 total – underscores this idea.[35] In the post-war period, the ISO was primarily focused on standardising the physical infrastructure of the global economy.[36] States to that point had set their own standards, usually distinct from the standards of other states because of differing processes and differing industrial concerns. The ISO began to harmonise those national standards. As it built a larger sphere of influence through more and more influential decisions, it began to seek a broader mandate.[37] One simple but illustrative change that the organisation underwent was to rename its decisions – previously known as "recommendations" – to the now-prevalent "global standards".[38]

This broader mandate became more pronounced in the 1970s and 1980s, where the ISO developed close relations with the United Nations and the *General Agreement on Tariffs and Trade* ("GATT", later becoming the World Trade Organisation ("WTO")).[39] This began in 1979 where the parties to the GATT, in an effort to reduce non-tariff barriers to trade, adopted the *Agreement on Technical Barriers to Trade* ("*TBT Agreement*") supporting the standardisation of technical specifications globally.[40] The alignment of the ISO with the GATT would prove to have profound consequences for the authority of the ISO's standardisation. Normatively, the endorsement of the parties to the GATT helped drive widespread expectation that the ISO was indeed the obvious forum for global regulation – the institution that *should* be setting global standards for

---

32   Ibid 19.
33   Winton Higgins, *Engine of Change: Standards Australia since 1922* (Brandl & Schlesigner, 2005) 14.
34   Murphy, above n 3, 21.
35   Ibid 18.
36   Gadinis, above n 21, 6.
37   Ibid 7.
38   Murphy, above n 3, 21.
39   Gadinis, above n 21, 6.
40   *Agreement on Technical Barriers to Trade*, opened for signature 15 April 1994, 1186 UNTS 120 (entered into force 1 January 1995) preamble ("*TBT Agreement*").

the world.[41] Many individual governments lacked the requisite technical expertise, financial resources, and flexibility to deal with complex and increasingly sophisticated regulatory tasks.[42] Firms and other private actors also pushed for the delegation of regulatory governance, likely because they perceive the ISO to set more corporate-friendly and cost-effective standards than government regulators.[43] As the *GATT* became the WTO and gained more and more members, the ISO accordingly became more ingrained in international trade law.

Given the implications of global devolution of standard-setting power to the ISO, it is worth drawing out at length how exactly this process has occurred in the WTO context. Take the *TBT Agreement* as an example. Article 2(3) of the *Agreement* requires members to use "relevant international standards as a basis" for their technical regulations.[44] This provision is designed to be read alongside Article 2(5), which reads that "whenever a technical regulation is in accordance with relevant international standards, it shall be rebuttably presumed to not create an unnecessary obstacle to international trade".[45] Essentially, this means that states who adopt standards that are different to the applicable global standard may face challenges through WTO dispute settlement mechanisms. Consider the significance of this in light of the fact that the *TBT Agreement* is binding for all members of the WTO, numbering 164 member states and every single large economy in the world. International trade law now provides a powerful incentive to *not* create their own standards or technical regulations, whatever the particular merits are in the circumstances.[46]

The shift from particular national standards to global standards offers substantial gains to multinational and internationally competitive firms; particularly where commercial operations were previously handicapped by international differences in standards.[47] About a third of global trade in goods is harmed by standards that differ across countries; the boost in trade from a *complete* international alignment of those standards would be equivalent to a huge reduction in tariffs.[48] Consumers should also benefit from this process, through having access to a broader range of goods and services, and be able

---

41   Filippo Fontanelli, "ISO and Codex Standards and International Trade Law: What Gets Said Is Not What's Heard" (2011) 60 *International and Comparative Law Quarterly* 908.
42   Gadinis, above n 21, 6.
43   Murphy, above n 3, 21.
44   *TBT Agreement* Art 2 (3).
45   *TBT Agreement* Art 2 (5).
46   Fontanelli, above 41, 908.
47   ISO, *Economic benefits of Standards: International Case Studies*, above n 7, 3.
48   Nils Brunsson and Bendt Jacobsson, *A World of Standards* (Oxford University Press, 2000) 6.

to buy them more cheaply.[49] However, the shift to global standards entails a new set of costs for a wide range of actors. To comply with new international standards, many firms have to redesign their products, retool their production methods or pay licensing fees to the firms whose proprietary technology is required for implementation of a global standard.[50] While the convergence of international standards may bring overall gain for the world, these gains differ in terms of states and especially in terms of firms.[51]

ISO's web of global standards shape the global economy in a variety of ways. On the one hand, the technical infrastructure provided by a web of ISO standards allows for linkages where they are badly needed: good examples of this are communication and transport, where products have a very literal need to be able to work together.[52] On the other hand, even where standards are not essential to link systems, they are still integral for shaping competition and innovation. Gadinis argues that effective industrial standards spur socially desirable innovation.[53] Because regulation is so closely linked with competition, and competition is so closely linked with innovation, a swap to global standards can carry important consequences for the ongoing production of new ideas.[54] This idea can be seen playing out in the competition between mobile phone providers. In the 1990s, advertisements from mobile phone providers, particularly in the United States, predominantly emphasised the size of their networks in order to entice consumers to sign up to their services.[55] This was viable because the providers limited communications with a mobile phone to people on the same network, meaning a bigger network was a selling point for reaching more friends and prospective contacts.[56] Once communication networks were standardised, however, this barrier dropped entirely and people were able to talk between networks and providers.[57] This has forced the same mobile phone providers to compete on price and innovation instead.[58]

ISO officials, to some extent, recognise and acknowledge the enormous power the organisation now wields in the global economy.[59] The ISO council,

---

49   Gadinis, above n 21, 6.
50   Murphy, above n 3, 17.
51   ISO, *Economic benefits of Standards: International Case Studies*, above n 6, 3.
52   Ibid.
53   Gadinis, above n 21, 5.
54   Ibid 9.
55   Ibid 8.
56   Ibid.
57   Ibid.
58   Ibid 9.
59   Murphy, above n 3, 47.

according to Murphy, see the organisation as "creating and maintaining the infrastructure of contemporary economic globalisation".[60] The omnipresent position of ISO standards in the global economy is partly due to how historic ISO standards underpin the global logistical and physical infrastructures, and partly due to the new empowerment of those global standards in international trade law by the WTO. This elevation of global standards into international legal norms by the *TBT Agreement* is critical for understanding why the ISO now wields the power that it does. This new paradigm is important not just for different states, but for corporations and industries who stand to be impacted by the imposition of a particular standard. It unsurprisingly follows that a detailed look at the way in which the ISO sets standards reveals a high degree of industrial lobbying. The next section explores these standard-setting processes and what they mean for the allocation of power in the global economy.

4 Power Allocation in ISO Technical Committees

Given the dominant position of the ISO in the setting of standards, the actual process of how those standards are set is of pivotal importance. This makes the closed, secretive nature of the ISO processes troubling, and a hurdle for this analysis.[61] Empirical answers to questions in the ISO, particularly those relating to who has power, are hard to come by as the ISO is an intensely private organisation. However, it is possible to make a range of observations based on available information.

As a starting point, the very structure of the ISO carries implications in itself for who has power. As this article has discussed, the organisation is composed entirely of national standards bodies; themselves composed of a variety of industry interests.[62] Technical committees are then composed of a small number of these national standards bodies.[63] Unlike other international rulemaking groups like the World Health Organisation, where international non-government, non-economic groups ("NGOs") can often exert significant influence, the very way the ISO is structured renders such groups almost powerless. The ISO lacks a central legislature or similar body, instead operating through hundreds of individual and autonomous technical committees.[64]

---

60   Ibid.
61   Buthe, above n 15, 10.
62   ISO, *Economic benefits of Standards: International Case Studies*, above n 6.
63   ISO, "Taking Standards Forward" (Annual Report, International Standards Organisation, 2014).
64   Rhodes, above n 28, 423.

Logistically, this constrains NGOs to only being able to focus on a few areas of standardisation at a time should they wish to lobby the ISO.[65] Even then, as the ISO makes no allowance for actors outside a national standards body, the participation of an NGO is contingent on the willingness of a technical committee to include that particular voice.

Another aspect about the ISO structure illustrates an aspect of power in the organisation: the prominence of technical committees.[66] The ISO places great emphasis on their national standards bodies coming to consensus around the technically correct standard in each case.[67] The ISO characterises this process as the apolitical, scientific process of developing or identifying the "technically optimal solution" to a regulatory or technical challenge.[68] In this view, consensus and standard-setting is easy because "scientific technological knowledge is the same everywhere".[69] In this way, the authority of the standard-setting process stems from the technical expertise and industrial "consensus" of the ISO technical committees. The power of standards set by ISO, and standard-setting bodies generally relies on their presentation as politically neutral, but scientifically unarguable.

However, this idea that standards embody some objective truth or scientific consensus in each case has been attacked and broken down by a series of scholars, who show how national standards bodies are hardly disinterested or neutral aides to the ISO.[70] The evidence points towards national standards bodies promoting and defending the regulatory preferences of their domestic stakeholders in ISO processes. This is unsurprising in light of the importance of standards to the global economy.[71] According to Murphy, consensus "usually means the acquiescence of those who care about a particular decision, supported by the apathy of those who don't".[72] Even empirically, the rhetoric of scientific expertise has been debunked by participants. One standards authority in Japan admitted that "there is no right or wrong answer ... it's like religion".[73] Participants in the ISO technical committees "usually" struggle to come to a compromise on what a particular standard should be.[74] Almost

---

65   Ibid.
66   ISO, "Navigating the World in Transition", above n 10.
67   ISO, "Taking Standards Forward", above n 63.
68   Buthe, above n 15, 11.
69   Ibid 10.
70   Murphy, above n 3, 10.
71   Rhodes, above n 28, 422.
72   Murphy, above n 3, 30.
73   Buthe, above n 15, 11.
74   Ibid 12.

always, ISO standard reflects the standard used by one or many of its member bodies already.[75] It follows that standard-setting process should be understood as intensely political, even if the politics are shrouded under layers of technical rhetoric.[76]

The politicisation of the ISO's technical committees occurs across a number of levels. In the broadest sense, standard-setting processes are political as there are a number of different interests represented in the technical committee process, which inevitably have to conflict in some manner. Hallstrom refers to the ISO as an "arena", where a huge variety of organisations try to achieve their standards-related aims in the complex interplay provided for in the "voluntary consensus" process.[77] Not only do technical committees consist of different national bodies, which often have differing aims and desired outcomes from each other, but those national bodies themselves can often struggle to achieve a consensus themselves.[78] This makes the process of voluntary consensus fraught with difficulty. The ISO cheerfully refers to this "arena" in their official documents as a "multi stakeholder environment which ensures that a wide range of technical views are represented".[79] The ISO goes on to assert this "multi stakeholder" process as a key strength, ensuring that "the standards therefore already have the buy-in of a wide range of stakeholders".[80] This may be true, but it obscures the more accurate picture – in this case, that the "multi stakeholder" process is a divided and political one.

Further undermining this idea of standard-setting as scientifically optimal is the power possessed by specific individuals involved in the technical committee's working groups. Each ISO national standards body party to a particular committee can nominate individuals to represent it in working groups for that committee.[81] Ostensibly, individual representatives are chosen to work on a specific task and reflect their individual expert knowledge on that area.[82] Accordingly, the ISO refers to those individuals as "experts".[83] On the other hand, these experts are encouraged to have "close contact" with their member

---

75 Murphy, above n 3, 30.
76 Ibid 10.
77 Hallstrom, above n 27, 173.
78 Ibid 174.
79 ISO, "Reaching Milestones in Standards Innovation" (Annual Report, International Standards Organisation, 2015).
80 Ibid.
81 Murphy, above n 3, 30
82 ISO, *Economic benefits of Standards: International Case Studies*, above n 6.
83 ISO, "Navigating the World in Transition", above n 10.

national bodies.[84] An ISO representative from the British national body anonymously commented that "members selected are supposed to be experts in the field, not represent industry viewpoints... However from my experience, I see representatives for their domestic [interests], not necessarily experts. They try to make certain that their national viewpoint is supported".[85] This presents a contradiction in terms for the "independent experts" contributing to the technical processes of the ISO. Those individuals do not need to verify their expertise through any particular authorisation or affiliation.[86] Those individuals are then expected to balance technical expertise with an expectation that they will also represent their national body.[87] This presents obvious difficulties for the way the ISO characterises these processes as the objective pursuit of a technically optimal standard. It helps explain how the process of technical committees so readily devolves into the "battleground" described in the preceding paragraph. In many cases, the individuals relied on for "technical expertise" would appear to instead have a role advocating for their national body.

The other issue with the individuals who sit on the technical committee working groups is that they are also expected to conform to the interests of their corporate employers.[88] This reinforces the nature and extent of contradictory allegiances in the standard-setting process. "Experts" are generally expected to finance their own participation on ISO working groups, following their selection by a national body.[89] In most cases, the individual's employers pay for this participation.[90] The fees can be substantial, given that the "experts" need to attend technical committee meetings across a period of months and years, in each case requiring international flights and hotel accommodation.[91] The consequence of this model is that technical committee experts face competing obligations towards their employer, their national body, and potentially the working group they are on.[92]

The consequences of this model go to the question of *who* standards are being set for. By way of example, Hallstrom references an anonymous interview

---

84   Ibid.
85   Hallstrom, above n 27, 6.
86   Machiko Kanetake, "Transnational standards in the domestic legal order: authority and legitimacy" (2017) 8 *Transnational Legal Theory* 2, 177.
87   Murphy, above n 3, 30.
88   Gadinis, n 21, 1.
89   Hallstrom, above n 27, 6.
90   Ibid 70.
91   Fontanelli, above 41, 903.
92   Ibid 904.

with a Swedish representative to the ISO where the Swedish "expert" studiously took notes during working group meetings, and later indicated that they would be able to sell the material for private gain.[93] This represents a corrupting of process that, if widespread, would quickly erode confidence in the objective standard-setting technical processes of the ISO. Other international standard-setting organisations have considered this issue of individuals with competing loyalties.[94] The International Accounting Standards Committee has explicitly discussed the question of whether experts can contribute to technical committees while holding professional roles that may pose a conflict.[95] The ISO, to date, has not acknowledged any such discussion; nor does it consider that it has a problem in terms of its directives to experts more widely.[96] While writers addressing the ISO universally conclude that the technical processes are exposed to several confused ethical entanglements like the one above, it is difficult to draw broad conclusions without any real data.[97] Even the experts who have spoken about issues in the process, like the British and Swedish individuals quoted in this section, have only done so anonymously.

Given this construction of ISO technical committees as politicised bodies, if not the "arenas" they have been deemed by some writers, the importance of relative power within those bodies is pronounced. The ISO is designed in such a way that many aspects of the work of technical committees are allocated to a particular national body, who acts as secretariat.[98] This allocation is done by a group of the most active national bodies; who decide amongst themselves who should lead a given committee.[99] This leadership involves a significant amount of control within each technical committee in terms of organising the process and even setting the committee's rules in terms of the technical process.[100] It can also involve extensive costs: the national bodies acting as secretariats organise and pay for all of the management and record keeping required in a committee or subcommittee.[101] This means that national bodies tend to focus their resources on the committees most important to them. A good example of this is Switzerland, whose national standards body provides the secretariat

---

93   Hallstrom, above n 27, 70.
94   Ibid 71.
95   Rhodes, above n 28, 422.
96   Ibid.
97   Buthe, above n 15, 10.
98   Murphy, above n 3, 30.
99   ISO, *Economic benefits of Standards: International Case Studies*, above n 6.
100   Murphy, above n 3, 30.
101   Ibid 31.

for Technical Committee 114 Horology.[102] This reflects Switzerland's economic interest in preserving the industry dominance of Swiss clock and watchmakers, but also reflects the economic capacity of the Swiss national body to take on those costs.[103] This is one of the ways in which richer national bodies play a disproportionate role within the organisation. According to ISO documents, "ISO members actively encourage the participation of developing countries and work with them on capacity building".[104] While collegial "encouragement" may exist, it certainly has done little to shift the way economic inequality is built into ISO processes: developing states very rarely have lead roles in technical processes.[105]

The distribution of power in ISO technical committees is complex, but this section's exploration sheds light both on which actors are the most powerful and how the design and structure of the technical committees creates the power dynamic. As an important starting point, *national standards bodies* are the actors with power in the ISO, to the exclusion of states and NGOs. As those national standards bodies are composed of industry interests, the power in standard-setting broadly lies with the representatives of corporations and industries. The distribution of that power *between* national standards bodies, however, is unequal. Domination of leadership positions, and greater resources to lobby, mean that national standards bodies from richer, developed economies possess much more power in standard-setting processes than other national standards bodies. This inequality is particularly important given that the evidence of ISO technical committees points towards adversarial, politicised contests between different national bodies looking to advance their particular domestic aims. That technical committees are instead heavily politicised is also evidenced by the role of individual "experts" representing national bodies on technical committee working groups. Further, these individuals are expected to offer an independent expert opinion in working groups as well as reflect the position of a national standards body undermines the "scientific" integrity of technical committees, especially given some reports of corruption on the part of certain individuals. Overall, power in ISO technical committees is held by national bodies composed of industry interests, most of all by those representing developed economies.

---

102   Ibid.
103   Ibid 30.
104   ISO, *Economic benefits of Standards: International Case Studies*, above n 6.
105   Murphy, above n 3, 30.

5 Implications for International Law

5.1 *The Dispersal of Power*

This article has shown how the ISO in global standard-setting represents a large-scale "dispersal" of power. As discussed in previous sections, the ISO is a fragmented organisation, devolving significant authority to about three hundred technical committees, and in this way effectively disseminates the power to decide what specific standards should be.[106] This section argues that this dispersal undermines the evolution of a more democratic and egalitarian international system for regulation. This dispersal also makes the status quo more resistant to reform, by obscuring the role of intentionality in the standard-setting process.[107] These trends reinforce and entrench the existing power of developed states to shape international law.

One impact of this dispersal is to severely constrain the opportunities for weaker national bodies to build coalitions to increase their bargaining power and influence. The ISO is similar to other large international organisations, in that weaker members – generally those national standards bodies belonging to developing economies – are far more numerous, but are also economically more diverse.[108] Evidence at a domestic level is that weak actors are usually able to overcome this issue of diversity by "trading" votes across issues, or agreeing to informal coalitions to achieve separate aims.[109] To illustrate what this could look like in the ISO context, take the example of the national standards bodies of Zambia and Ecuador. Both standards bodies represent developing economies, but the Zambian economy is heavily dependent on mining, while the Ecuadorian economy is reliant on commodities and petroleum in particular.[110] The two national standards bodies could agree to "trade" support: the body representing Zambian industries would support the Ecuadorian preference for petroleum standards in return for Ecuadorian support for the Zambian mining preference. However, this requires a central venue, like a legislature, that makes decisions on a wide range of issues. Instead, the Zambian standards body is unlikely to be represented on the ISO technical committee for petroleum, and the Ecuadorian body is similarly unlikely to be represented

---

106 Eyal Benvenisti and George W Downs, "The Empire's New Clothes: Political Economy and the Fragmentation of International Law" (2007) 60 *Stanford Law Review* 2, 596.
107 Ibid 597.
108 Ibid.
109 Ibid.
110 *The World Bank in Ecuador* (2017) World Bank <https://www.worldbank.org/en/country/ecuador>.

on the committee for mining, due to the country's respective economic priorities. In this way, the dispersal of power across functionalist technical committees strips weaker actors of the ability to collectivise, making the whole process less democratic and egalitarian as a whole.

The second implication of this dispersal of power is by obscuring the role of intentionality in standard-setting, through emphasising the lack of over-arching decision-making. Precisely because of the reliance on technical committees, the standards produced by the ISO are perceived as coming from a technical process rather than a political one.[111] This narrative is assisted both by the way states are excluded from the process, with national standards bodies instead the key actors, and by the secretive and private way the organisation operates. This narrative obscures the fact that different national bodies have very different levels of power in the process. Consider, for instance, if the ISO *did* have a central legislature with representatives from every state, vested with at least some of the key decision-making power that currently resides with technical committees. It would be much clearer over time which national bodies were exerting power and dominating discussion, both because it would be easier to track votes and process; and because lobbying would need to scale up to achieve consensus across a much larger group of members. Even more importantly, it would be comparatively simple to look to that legislature as the lead institution for global standard-setting, and ensure it was held accountable. By contrast, the present-day ISO instead ensures that decision-making power is dissipated in hundreds of mostly secret committees. This dispersal both means that any dominance by stronger actors is harder to assess, gaining the support of smaller parties is easier as the committees only include a fraction of the ISO's full member base, and that there is not any central committee to look to for leadership.

The significance of the way ISO disperses power in this way is illustrated by the way scholars characterise and describe the trend of fragmentation more broadly in international law. For instance, Eyal Benvenisti and George Downs in the *Stanford Law Review* make the argument that powerful states like the United States (in particular) purposefully maintain and even promote fragmentation in international law, using four strategies.[112] These include avoiding broad, integrative agreements in favour of a large number of functional agreements; formulating one-time agreements rather than multilateral negotiations where possible; avoiding the creation of an independent bureaucracy

---

111   Adrian Henriques, "What are standards for? The case of ISO 2600" *The Guardian* (online), 5 January 2012 <https://www.theguardian.com/sustainable-business/blog/iso-26000 -social-impact-sustainability>.

112   Benvenisti, above n 106, 598.

and lastly shifting to an alternative institution when the original becomes too responsive to the interests of weaker states.[113] The dispersal of power by the ISO suggested in this section is remarkably reflective of these strategies.[114] This article has shown how the ISO can be thought of as made up of a large number of autonomous and functionally defined technical committees. Further, the ISO has a particularly weak bureaucracy, with a comparatively small central secretariat whose role is limited to administrative work.[115] Indeed, the evidence points towards the continued power of stronger national bodies, invariably representing the more powerful developed economies.[116] In this way, the ISO's dispersal of power reflects both the broader fragmentation of international law and the strategies pursued by powerful actors.[117]

Some academic international legal scholars have claimed that the fragmentation of international law does not pose major issues. There is speculation that despite the appearance of fragmentation, regulatory coordination among institutions is now better than before, or at least if fragmentation exists it is a harmless side effect of the institutional expression of international pluralism.[118] This article's exploration of how the ISO disperses power helps refute these arguments by scholars by highlighting some of the problematic impacts of dispersed power. The way the ISO dissipates power through a veritable archipelago of functionally-defined technical committees significantly increases transaction costs and logistical barriers. This makes it difficult for weaker actors to engage in the process, let alone engage in the political coordination necessary to form a coalition to set standards in their national interest. The beneficiaries are the more powerful actors at the ISO, whose power is entrenched. Given the importance of these technical committees, and the massive economic consequences of the standards they set, the argument that the dispersal – or fragmentation – of power is "harmless" does not bear much scrutiny.

5.2 The Disempowerment of Citizens

The shift of regulating authority from states to the ISO represents both the empowerment of a new kind of entity, a global private institution, and new challenges stemming from that shift. Chief among these are serious barriers of access for citizens who want to engage with standard-setting processes, and no longer have a forum for doing so. Domestic legislatures, ministries, judges, leading

---

113 Ibid 599–601.
114 Ibid 601.
115 ISO, *Economic benefits of Standards: International Case Studies*, above n 7.
116 Benvenisti, above n 106, 600.
117 Ibid 610.
118 Ibid 595.

corporate entities and lawyers now actively invoke global standards in official statutory instruments, judicial processes and legal practices.[119] Even more strikingly, some states legislate so that new ISO standards are treated as binding domestic laws once they are passed by the international organisation.[120] This blurring of domestic and international contexts risks the critical loss of input from domestic constituencies as to new standards that affect their work and life. While most citizens undoubtedly have little interest in the technical standards of the products they use, this is a poor excuse for denying citizens a voice altogether. At minimum, the disempowerment of citizens in practical terms means a significant decrease in accountability for standard-setting processes, and in legal terms reflects a shift from public to private law-making.

To cast light on this global shift and the repercussions for citizens, this article adopts Kanetake's study of authority and legitimacy as twin concepts in the regulatory sense.[121] Authority in this context means the capacity of an entity to induce deference from others, which rests on the recognition the entity is given by others.[122] Legitimacy is the normative evaluation of authority. For the most part, the concept of authority has developed by situating a sovereign state as representative of the domestic body.[123] Authority is ascribed to the decision-maker in this way, rather than the content of the decisions they make.[124] This traditional view of authority has the benefit of relatively clear roles for who rules and the ruled, with both acting within the confines of the same legal and political orders.[125] However, the way in which authority is transferred to an international body can be seen to blur these basic distinctions between the rulers and the ruled, at least in terms of the way in which authority has traditionally been conceived. The authority of the ISO, as discussed throughout this article, emanates from their technical committees' technical expertise and the industry consensus ostensibly reflected through the committees' process.

This can be contrasted with the authority emanating from a state, which is characterised by a formal capacity to make binding decisions backed up with

119   ISO, "Information Transfer: Handbook on International Standards Governing Informa-
        tion Transfer" (ISO Standards Handbook No 1, International Standards Organisation In-
        formation Centre).
120   Marc Levinson, *The Box: How the Shipping Container Made the World Smaller and the
        World Economy Bigger* (Princeton University Press, 2006).
121   Kanetake, above n 86, 176.
122   Ibid.
123   Ibid.
124   Ibid 177.
125   Ibid 178.

coercive means of enforcement.[126] Of course, the ISO does not have that co-ercive power, and takes pains to articulate that its standards are voluntary.[127] The regulatory significance of the global standards they adopt rely on the ac-ceptance and agreement of states to invoke the standards in their own law. As outlined earlier, international trade law like the *TBT Agreement* may represent some pressure on states to adopt standards as the basis for their own technical regulation; but this is not within the ISO's direct authority. Instead, the organ-isation would appear to ground its authority in a much looser idea of scientific standard-setting that is hard to characterise clearly.[128] Nico Krisch explains this difference as authority taking a "liquid" form in terms of the international body as opposed to the fixed shape of a standard state, making it more difficult to grasp, assess, and control.[129]

Further, consider the ISO process on this point: states are not formally rep-resented and do not participate in technical committees. Those committees are made up of different national standards bodies, invariably amalgamations of different industry interests without representatives from the government or public sector.[130] This can be contrasted with the creation of treaties and other instruments in international law, negotiated by states.[131] On top of this, state adoption of global standards is very rarely a process subject to normal parliamentary or executive approval requirements.[132] Executive bodies often simply defer to global standards to avoid domestic deliberation altogether.[133] Consequently there are no clear processes where citizens can have their voice heard in the standards process either at the international or domestic level. This problem is not helped by the technicality and scientific language of the ISO's standards, which makes it difficult for the wider public to review. This complexity is a feature of technical standards inherently, rather than a fault of the ISOs, but does compound the difficulties facing an average lay citizen. Particularly given the context of ISO's technical committees representing in-dustry interests, this lack of recourse for the general public to review new stan-dards before adoption in the domestic sphere is problematic. This process is even more problematic for a citizen group or interest group that did not want a

---

126 Kanetake, above n 86, 176.
127 Ibid 178.
128 Benvenisti, above n 106, 598.
129 Nico Krisch, "Liquid Authority in Global Governance" (2017) 9 *International Theory* 2.
130 ISO, *Economic benefits of Standards: International Case Studies*, above n 6.
131 Carl Cargill and Sherrie Bolin, "Standardization: A Failing Paradigm" in Shane Greenstein and Victor Stango (eds), *Standards and Public Policy* (Cambridge University Press, 2007).
132 Benvenisti, above n 106, 598.
133 Ibid.

particular ISO standard – depending on their government's process, they may have no recourse whatsoever.

This problem of citizen access is complicated by the fact that a solution is not easy to envisage, let alone implement. On the domestic level, states could allow for participation and input from their constituencies through a "select committee" process or something similar; where citizens wanting to have their voices heard about any particular new standard could have an avenue to do so before the state adopts the standard. States may be unwilling to allow even the possibility that the ISO standard is not adopted, however: states who do *not* adopt global standards like the ISO's risk breaching trade law. On the international level at the ISO, technical committees could more expressly allow for submissions and lobbying by groups of engaged citizens. This is also is unlikely to happen. Because the authority of the ISO emanates from the ostensible technical and scientific focus of the technical committees – allowing submissions from citizens who are *not* technical experts risks undermining the organisation's reputation for scientific and technical optimisation. As a global private organisation, without representatives from states, the ISO is essentially immune to accountability by citizens. Given these difficulties in envisaging a solution to these barriers of access, a loss of input from domestic constituencies seems an inevitable consequence of the global shift of regulatory power from states to the ISO.

5.3   *The Empowerment of Industry*

An important consequence of ISO's internal processes is the structural empowerment of industry interests in the process of creating international law. The way ISO technical committees operate, and in particular which actors have power in those contexts, suggests ISO standards are created by consensus of different representatives of *industry*, rather than representatives of states. Further, this empowerment of industry is uneven: industry representatives from developed economies have a much greater share of power than the representatives from developing economies. This phenomenon is difficult to diagnose due to the lack of accountability and transparency of ISO processes, meaning the lobbying of powerful industry interests is difficult to track. However, the evidence available suggests that certain powerful national bodies, like the British and American national standards bodies, are much more successful than other bodies at having their preferences codified in ISO standards.[134] The fact that certain industry interests wield disproportionate power in a process of international law is deserving of some reflection.

---

134   Kanetake, above n 86, 178.

Certain national bodies, invariably from developed economies, dominate the design and process of technical committees, and have more resources to lobby other members of the committee for consensus. Studying this distribution more closely, it is clear that this process is also apparent in the organisational structure of each individual *national* body.[135] Remember that the ISO is better described as an "organisation of organisations": each national body is itself a large group of corporations and industry interests, who seek to control the agenda and power of the national body.[136] The very same dynamics that favour developed and wealthy national bodies at the ISO level mean that more powerful corporations and industry representations are likely to control national bodies. Given that those more developed national bodies are then allocated disproportionate power by ISO processes by virtue of their resources, it follows that industry interests from developed states have an outsized influence on the process and development of those standards.

Firm conclusions as to the process of lobbying by richer national bodies are complicated by the lack of transparency and accountability procedures in ISO processes. Because the technical committees operate autonomously and privately, powerful national bodies are able to lobby intensively but then present the final standard as an industry consensus. Consider the example of common corporate donations laws in many democracies, as a contrast. If corporations donate over more than a certain limit of money to a political party, they usually have to publicly declare the amount and recipient.[137] These laws are justified as providing transparency as to which companies are supporting which politicians. Appropriate scrutiny can be applied to those politicians to be sure they do not legislate in a way that rewards their donors.[138] On the other hand, national bodies in the ISO can actively pour as much money and resources they like into direct advocacy for the standard that best advances their interests.[139]

These risks of corporate capture in the ISO present a set of issues that are difficult to resolve. While the ISO continues to maintain that its standards are strictly voluntary and non-coercive, their integration into international trade law means that ISO standards are forming part of the patchwork of international law.[140] In that context, the fact that to some large degree those standards are created without input from non-industry groups is seriously concerning.

---

135   Ibid 40.
136   Ibid 30.
137   "Party Secretary Handbook General Election 2017" (2017) Electoral Commission, <https://www.elections.org.nz/party-secretary-handbook>.
138   Buthe, above n 15, 11.
139   Kanetake, above n 86, 179.
140   Benvenisti, above n 106, 600.

ISO standards already risk undermining the democratic ideals of international law, made as they are in private committees and adopt secretive processes. There are ways to resolve some of these problems posed by the empowerment of industry. The ISO could make it easier for states and NGOs to take part in ISO processes, for example by giving them permanent observer status and more opportunities to give input in the technical committee process. At minimum, the ISO could allow journalists to attend technical committee meetings. Other problems posed by the empowerment of industry interests, like the influence of interests from developed economies, are more difficult to solve. This is in no small part because the disproportionate power of richer national bodies in technical committees echoes the way those bodies occupy leadership positions in the organisation.[141] The democratic consequences of these issues are profound: given the way the ISO processes favour standards set in a way that advances the interests of industries from developed states, those from developing economies are likely to face higher transaction costs.[142] This concentrates the economic power of developed states in a very real way, and risks distorting the economic effects of international trade law more broadly. It also highlights some of the ways in which industry influences might make use of lobbying in international law processes in order to advance their interests.

6   Conclusion

This article has analysed the role of the ISO in the process of global standard-setting, drawing three important implications with respect to power in international law. In short, ISO processes *disperse* power in a unique way, *disempower* citizens, and *empower* industry interests. These points carry important implications for international law. The ISO's dispersal of power to technical committees undermines the evolution of a more democratic and egalitarian international system for regulation, and obscures the role of intentionality in the standard-setting process. Both consequences entrench existing power dynamics which favour richer industry influences from developed economies. The disempowerment of citizens is significant in itself, breaching the basic principle of the production of public standards that citizens should have a voice in the rules that govern their lives. The disempowerment of citizens also contributes to the erosion of sovereignty suffered by states as regulatory authority transfers to the ISO and other global private organisations.

---

141   Ibid 601.
142   Gadinis, above n 21, 3.

Lastly, the empowerment of industry risks the production of standards that do not adequately reflect non-corporate concerns, like those that might be held by states or NGOs. This empowerment is also uneven, entrenching the power of rich industries and distorting the economics of trade in a way particularly harmful to less wealthy industry interests. Taken as a whole, the implications of the ISO's standard-setting for international law are profound.

Importantly, these arguments should be weighed against the merits of standardisation and the problems of ensuring democratic and egalitarian production of standards. This article has emphasised the merits of standardisation, in particular those relating to economic growth. Similarly, this article has noted that solutions to the problems posed by the ISO and global standard-setting more broadly are not straightforward. To begin with, it is not clear who the actors would be in improving matters. The ISO council could propose changes to the standard-setting process, like allowing states and NGOs to take part in technical committees, but it may then be up to individual technical committees to decide on a change to process. The ISO has no mechanism for such sweeping changes to process. That said, this article has noted some ideas for process and accountability that may make some improvements. For instance, enabling journalists or interested citizens to attend technical committee meetings as observers would help transparency and allow some form of citizen participation. Ultimately, it is likely that some kind of trade-off must be found between a private system for standard-setting and public accountability. On balance, this trade-off currently seems dangerously tilted in favour of industries and national standards bodies of developed economies.

In any case, this article's analysis of power dynamics in the ISO underscore the need for further research into the nature of the contemporary shift in regulatory authority. The ISO, while the largest, is just one of the standardisation bodies forming part of the shift from state regulators to international organisations. Just as important for further research is how the shift in regulatory authority changes the relationship between the "ruling" and the "ruled". The interplay of citizen engagement and international organisations is relatively new and more work is vital on ways in which citizens can still be involved in shaping rules that impact on them; even where those rules are being produced not by their state but by an international organisation. Aligned to this need is the importance of accountability for these organisations. Standardisation bodies like the ISO play far too important a role in the global economy, and the everyday lives of you and me, to avoid scrutiny of their processes. All of these aspects for future research carry further implications for international law. At minimum, this article's analysis has underscored how organisational design and process can carry weighty consequences for international law.

The South Pacific

∵

Pacific Islands Forum 2017

*Tony Angelo**

1   Forum 2017

The 48th Pacific Islands Forum was held in Samoa from 5–8 September 2017.[1] Eighteen states were represented and there was also attendance by Tokelau as an associate member, and representation from other Pacific and Caribbean states, the United Nations ("UN"), and various international agencies. Fiji, New Zealand and Niue were represented by key Ministers and not by their respective head of state or head of government.

The theme for the Forum was "The Blue Pacific: Our Sea of Islands, Our Security through Sustainable Development, Management and Conservation". This followed the earlier commitments by the Pacific countries to the importance, in the climate change context, for the emphasis be not only on "green", but also on "blue" as representing the dominant feature of the Pacific region and Pacific life. The Forum continued its concern to advance its vision in respect of the Pacific Ocean.

The Post-Forum Dialogue was attended by 18 Partners: present was a French Minister of State in relation to the implementation of the *Paris Agreement*; a delegation from The People's Republic of China ("PRC") addressed matters of marine economy and climate change; and a United States ("US") delegation led by an assistant Secretary of State was concerned with sustainable growth, regional stability and climate change matters.

The European Union ("EU") was represented at the Forum by the Commissioner of International Cooperation and Development and senior EU officials. An important aspect of that delegation's visit was in relation to Pacific-EU relations after 2020 and the expiry of the *Cotonou Agreement*.

The Forum was also addressed by the President of the International Criminal Court ("ICC") whose goal in the region was to urge Forum members to join the ICC's treaty: eight Forum members are parties to the *Rome Statute*; eight are yet to join.

---

*   Professor of Law, Victoria University of Wellington, New Zealand.
1   For the official record of the meeting see *48th Pacific Islands Forum Communique* (5–8 September 2017) Pacific Island Forum Seritariat <https://cropict.usp.ac.fj/images/papers/ForumCommunique/2017-48th-Pacific-Islands-Forum-Communique.pdf>.

2   Sustainable Funding Strategy

Following the Funding Review initiated in 2013, a Sustainable Funding Strategy
for the Secretariat was established. The goal was to ensure the continued operation of the Secretariat as an independent advisory body in relation to Pacific
regionalism. It was agreed at this Forum meeting to delay the implementation
of that funding strategy so that further work could be done on the strategy and
in particular so that account could be taken of the position of the small island
states. In this context it was noted that French Polynesia had formalised its
membership status and that New Caledonia was soon to deposit its instrument
of ratification. In the meantime therefore, the contributions of members remain as established in the 2000 *Agreement* which established the Pacific Islands
Forum Secretariat.[2] The contributions to budget are set out in the annex to that
Agreement. The major contributions to the Regular Budget are made by Australia and New Zealand. In terms of total funding, the bulk is from Australia with
the EU and New Zealand being almost equal contributors at that level.

3   Pacific Regionalism

Pacific regionalism continues to be a matter of Forum interest, building on the
"Framework for Pacific Regionalism".[3] Much clearly remains to be done. The
most obvious development in the context of the Forum meeting was in relation to a "Biketawa Plus"[4] which the Secretary General indicated in a pre-Forum
statement would ideally be a framework "with best practices from RAMSI
incorporated".[5] The Regional Assistance Mission to Solomon Islands ("RAMSI")
was paraded as "a shining example of regional cooperation and diplomacy".[6]
The Forum Secretariat was asked to initiate work on a "Biketawa Plus" Declaration. As noted by the Deputy Secretary General in a pre-Forum statement,[7]
a significant challenge to developing Pacific regionalism and solidarity is the

---

2   *Agreement Establishing the Pacific Islands Forum Secretariat* <http://www.forumsec.org>.
3   "The Framework for Pacific Regionalism" <http://www.forumsec.org>.
4   *Biketawa Declaration of 2000* <http://www.forumsec.org/biketawa-declaration/>.
5   Meg Taylor, "State of Pacific Regionalism – Protecting out peaceful sea of islands" *48th Forum
    in Samoa eSupplement*, 15 <http://www.forumsec.org>.
6   *48th Pacific Islands Forum Communique* (5–8 September 2017) Pacific Island Forum Seritariat
    <https://cropict.usp.ac.fj/images/papers/ForumCommunique/2017-48th-Pacific-Islands-Fo-
    rum-Communique.pdf>.
7   Cristelle Pratt, "State of Pacific Regionalism – Challenges to Pacific Solidarity", *48th Forum in
    Samoa eSupplement,* 10 <http://www.forumsec.org>.

linkages that Pacific countries have with international organisations. That produces both opportunities but also challenges the development of a unique Pacific voice. Currently less than 5% of donor funds target Pacific regionalism.

Fisheries remain a key topic for Forum members. The Communique noted some differences of approach by members to the negotiations relating to the tropical tuna stock and exhorted members to adopt a common approach.

4 General

The Forum agreed to support Fiji's bid for the presidency of Cop 23.

Support for Australia's seat on the UN Human Rights Council for 2018–2020 was confirmed.

Of particular interest in relation to personalia was the renewal of the appointment of Meg Taylor as Secretary General for a further 3 year term.

The venue for the next Pacific Islands Forum is Nauru.

The Year in Review

∴

International Human Rights Law

Shea Elizabeth Esterling*

1 Introduction

This note reviews New Zealand practice concerning international human rights law in 2017. New Zealand continued its engagement with United Nations ("UN") treaty-based bodies for the promotion and protection of human rights as a result of its commitments under various human rights treaties. Engaging in the process of "constructive dialogue" which characterizes the UN efforts to secure compliance with treaty obligations, this year New Zealand submitted its periodic report under the *International Covenant on Economic, Social and Cultural Rights*[1] while the UN issued its concluding observations on New Zealand's human rights practises under the *International Covenant on Civil and Political Rights*[2] and the *International Covenant on the Elimination of All forms of Racial Discrimination*.[3] This year also saw the UN Committee against Torture delivered a list of issues for New Zealand to consider in advance of its state report due in 2019, while the Subcommittee on Prevention of Torture and Other Cruel, Inhuman or Degrading Treatment or Punishment issued it observations and recommendations based upon its visit to New Zealand from 29 April to 8 May 2013. In addition, during 2017 the Human Rights Committee, which oversees the *International Covenant on Civil and Political Rights*, heard a number of individual communications involving New Zealand while the Committee Against Torture, which oversees the implementation of the *Convention against Torture and Other Cruel, Inhuman or Degrading Treatment or Punishment*,[4] also heard a complaint against New Zealand. On the domestic side, the New Zealand Human Rights Commission continued its work, supporting the UN and the reporting process as well as engaging in numerous campaigns to promote and protect the human rights of individuals living in Aotearoa New Zealand.

---

* University of Canterbury.

1 *International Covenant on Economic, Social and Cultural Rights*, opened for signature 16 December 1966, 993 UNTS 3 (entered into force 3 January 1976).

2 *International Covenant on Civil and Political Rights*, opened for signature 16 December 1966, 999 UNTS 171 (entered into force March 1976).

3 *International Covenant on the Elimination of All forms of Racial Discrimination,* opened for signature 21 December 1965, 660 UNTS 195 (entered into force 4 January 1969).

4 *Convention against Torture and Other Cruel, Inhuman or Degrading Treatment or Punishment*, opened for signature 10 December 1984, 1465 UNTS 85 (entered into force 26 June 1987).

© KONINKLIJKE BRILL NV, LEIDEN, 2019 | DOI:10.1163/9789004387935_011

2 New Zealand and UN Human Rights Treaty Bodies

2.1 *Convention against Torture and Other Cruel, Inhuman or Degrading Treatment or Punishment*

In anticipation of New Zealand's seventh periodic state report in 2019 under the *Convention against Torture and Other Cruel, Inhuman or Degrading Treatment or Punishment ("CAT Convention")*, the Committee against Torture ("CAT Committee") delivered its *List of Issues Prior to Reporting*.[5] This list tasks New Zealand with a series of follow-up questions from its last periodic report under the treaty in 2013. It focuses on issues in relation to the substantive provisions of the treaty at articles 1–16 and principally notes that it considers that New Zealand has still not properly addressed issues relating to the Independent Police Conduct Authority and seclusion, solitary confinement and historic claims of abuse.[6] In addition, in 2017 a number of civil society organizations provided information to the CAT Committee in advance of New Zealand's next state report in 2019 including: Intersex Trust Aotearoa New Zealand, StopIGM.org and Zwischengeschlecht.org. The information provided by these organizations focuses on issues relating to premature surgery and other medical treatment to which intersex children are subjected.

Further, in 2017 in accordance with its mandate under the *Optional Protocol to the Convention against Torture and Other Cruel, Inhuman or Degrading Treatment or Punishment ("OpCAT")*,[7] the Subcommittee on Prevention of Torture and Other Cruel, Inhuman or Degrading Treatment or Punishment ("Subcommittee") issued its observations and recommendations[8] based upon its visit to New Zealand from 29 April to 8 May 2013. During this time, the Subcommittee visited 35 places of deprivation of liberty, including police stations, district court cells, prisons, Defence Force facilities, youth justice residences and immigration facilities in Wellington, Auckland, Christchurch, Nelson, Blenheim, Rotorua, Hastings and a number of rural locations.[9] The report deals with a

---

5   Committee Against Torture, *List of issues prior to submission of the seventh periodic report of New Zealand,* UN Doc CAT/C/NZL/QPR/7.

6   Ibid [1].

7   *Optional Protocol to the Convention against Torture and Other Cruel, Inhuman or Degrading Treatment or Punishment,* opened for signature 9 January 2003, A/RES/57/199 (entered into force 22 June 2006).

8   Subcommittee on Prevention of Torture and Other Cruel, Inhuman or Degrading Treatment or Punishment, *Visit to New Zealand undertaken from 29 April to 8 May 2013: observations and recommendations addressed to the State party, Report of the Subcommittee,* UN Doc CAT/OP/NZL/1.

9   Ibid [4].

broad range of overarching and cross-cutting issues, including those related to fundamental safeguards as well as issues facing Māori, youth and those with mental health issues. More broadly, it considers the situation of persons deprived of their liberty and offers recommendations centred on the following themes: police detention, court cells, penitentiary issues, institutions for children and adolescents, military institution, centre for the accommodation of refugees and asylum seekers, border facilities and the transportation of detainees. Of note, regarding penitentiary issues, the Subcommittee recommends that the authorities improve the detention regime, in particular regarding out-of-cell time, offering that New Zealand should ensure the consistent application of rules on exercise and outdoor activities and allow adequate time for such activities for all prisoners.[10] Regarding institutions for the detention of children and adolescents, the Subcommittee recommends that New Zealand consider developing specific Māori literacy programmes in youth justice residences, in addition to the mandatory general curriculum[11] and that authorities ensure that children and young people are made aware of the disciplinary regulations and that proportionate, tailored measures be applied rather than collective responses.[12]

Responding to the Subcommittee's request, New Zealand offered a comprehensive reply[13] in relation to each of the cross-cutting and thematic issues raised in the report. For instance, as regarding recommendations concerning outdoor time in relation to penitentiary issues, New Zealand responded that *The Corrections Act 2004* (NZ) provides that every prisoner may, on a daily basis, take at least one hour of physical exercise, which may be taken in the open air if the weather permits. However, corrections accept that the amount of exercise time that prisoners receive above this minimum entitlement can vary according to a prisoner's risk profile.[14] Further, New Zealand responded that the quality of exercise facilities and extent of natural light inevitably varies across New Zealand's prison system, reflecting the age and design of individual prisons and that at present there is a comprehensive programme of capital improvement across the entire prison estate and improvements being made to

---

10   Ibid [84].

11   Ibid [95].

12   Ibid [97].

13   Subcommittee on Prevention of Torture and Other Cruel, Inhuman or Degrading Treatment or Punishment, *Visit to New Zealand undertaken from 29 April to 8 May 2013: observations and recommendations addressed to the State party, Report of the Subcommittee, Addendum, Replies of New Zealand*, UN Doc CAT/OP/NZL/1/Add.1.

14   Ibid [102].

older facilities.[15] In response to the Subcommittee's recommendations regarding institutions for the detention of children and adolescents, New Zealand reported back that it has addressed concerns related to Māori literacy programmes in youth justice residences. Specifically, New Zealand reported that the youth justice residential schools adhere to Te reo Māori, which has a special place in the New Zealand curriculum. Eight curriculum principles underpin curriculum decision-making in New Zealand, and one of these principles is headed "Treaty of Waitangi". Te reo Māori is included in learning languages, which is one of the eight learning areas in the curriculum.[16]

2.2   *International Covenant on Economic, Social and Cultural Rights*

Further, New Zealand submitted its periodic report as per its commitments under the *International Covenant on Economic, Social and Cultural Rights* (*"ICESCR"*).[17] This is the fourth periodic report that New Zealand has supplied to the Committee on Economic, Social and Cultural rights ("ESCR Committee") and for the first time it was prepared under the simplified reporting procedures responding in sequential order to the ESCR Committee's list of issues prepared prior to the submission of the report.[18] The report covered the period from January 2011 to May 2017. It took a thematic approach in its response to the list of issues focusing on implementation in eleven treaty areas including: the right to freely dispose of natural wealth and resources, the obligation to take steps to the maximum of available resources, non-discrimination, equal rights of men and women, the right to work, the right to just and favorable conditions of work, trade union rights, the right to social security, the right to an adequate standard of living, the right to physical and mental health and the right to education.

However, of specific note in the report are a number issues deemed of "particular relevance".[19] These issues broadly range from constitutional issues to issues concerning health, education and social services. With regards to the former, New Zealand noted that the *ICESCR* has not been directly incorporated into domestic law. However, statutory powers have to be interpreted consistently with international obligations where possible[20] and furthermore that

---

15   Ibid [104].
16   Ibid [116].
17   Committee on Economic, Social and Cultural Rights, *Fourth periodic report submitted by New Zealand under articles 16 and 17 of the Covenant due in 2017*, UN Doc E/C.12/NZL/4 (2017).
18   Ibid [2].
19   See ibid [4]–[85].
20   Ibid [36].

there is a new mechanism in place to ensure the compatibility of laws with international standards which is to append disclosure statements to all Government Bills.[21] Notably, New Zealand's report to the ESCR Committee detailed the work of the independent Constitutional Advisory Panel ("Panel") which was appointed in 2010 to consider constitutional issues, including the status of the *New Zealand Bill of Rights Act 1990* (NZ) ("*NZBORA*"). This report to the ESCR Committee highlights the Panel's report to New Zealand in December 2013 including some of its key findings.[22] A common theme throughout the Panel's report was that people need more information and need to be more involved in discussions about constitutional issues. Its key recommendation was for the Government (of New Zealand) to actively support a continuing conversation about the constitution.[23] As regards the *NZBORA*, the Panel found broad support for exploring changes to the *NZBORA* and enhancing mechanisms for ensuring compliance with the standards set in the Act, including adding economic, social and cultural rights, improving compliance by the executive and Parliament with the standards in the Act, and giving the judiciary powers to assess legislation for consistency with the Act.[24] However, New Zealand noted in its report here to the ESCR Committee that it has no plans to review the *NZBORA* at this stage but that the Panel's recommendations will be a useful starting point if such a review takes place in the future. As regards the Treaty of Waitangi, the Panel stressed the need to continue the conversation about the place of the Treaty in the constitution. It recommended a Treaty education strategy be developed that includes the current role and status of the Treaty and the Treaty settlement process, so people can inform themselves about the rights and obligations under the Treaty. New Zealand noted for the ESCR Committee that education about the Treaty is a formal part of the New Zealand curriculum and the national conversation about its place in our constitutional arrangements is ongoing.[25] As regards the latter issues of "particular relevance", those of health, education and social services, New Zealand's report to the ESCR Committee focused on disparities in outcomes across these sectors for Māori, Pasifika and low-income families and focuses on developments in each of these areas to combat these inequalities.

---

21   Ibid [14].
22   The report is available at: <http://www.ourconstitution.org.nz/The-Report>.
23   Ibid [4]–[5].
24   Ibid [6]–[7].
25   Ibid [9]–[10].

2.3 *International Covenant on Civil and Political Rights*

In 2016, the Human Rights Committee ("HRC") issued its *Concluding Observations on the Sixth Periodic Report of New Zealand*[26] which New Zealand supplied as per its commitments under the *International Covenant on Civil and Political Rights ("ICCPR")*. Continuing its engagement in this process of constructive dialogue, in 2017 New Zealand issued further information in response to these observations. Responding to the HRC's principal areas of concern in its *Concluding Observations*, the follow-up report issued by New Zealand in 2017 centered on issues related to domestic and gender-based violence and child abuse.[27] As regards the latter, New Zealand noted that, as response to the Child Youth and Family ("CYF") review, the Government agreed in 2016 to develop and implement a new operating model for care and protection in youth justice systems. The Ministry for Children, Oranga Tamariki, was established as a new child-centered, stand-alone ministry and has been operational since 1 April 2017.[28] Concerning gender-based violence, New Zealand noted that it had "established the Ministerial Group on Family Violence and Sexual Violence with the objective of establishing a comprehensive response to family violence and sexual violence to stop perpetrators hurting their families, protect victims, and break the cycle of re-victimisation and re-offending".[29] The result of this creation has been that the group has identified and developed critical projects to strengthen the foundations of the system to improve practice across all agencies and service types while building data and evidence to guide future investment over the medium-to-long term.[30] Where there was a clear need for immediate action and a solid evidence base, the Government has already put in place better services, pilots and other improvements. These include:

(a) National Home Safety Service (to keep victims safe in their own home without having to rely on alternative, safe accommodation);

(b) Developing the Risk Assessment and Management Framework (ramf), which aims to develop a common approach to consistently and effectively identify, assess and manage the risks of family violence;

---

26   Human Rights Committee, *Concluding Observations on the Sixth Periodic Report of New Zealand*, UN Doc CCPR/C/NZL/CO/6 (2016).

27   Human Rights Committee, *Concluding observations on the sixth periodic report of New Zealand: Addendum Information received from New Zealand on follow-up to the concluding observations*, UN Doc CCPR/C/NZL/CO/6/Add.1(2017).

28   Ibid [23].

29   Ibid [1].

30   Ibid [4].

(c)   Developing the Workforce Capability Framework, co-designed with a sector-led Expert Design Group, which identifies the knowledge, skills and behaviours needed for a safe and competent workforce;

(d)   Four community pilots that work with gang-connected populations and their communities to build safer communities, support adult victims, address perpetrator behaviour and reduce the effects of multi-generational gang involvement;

(e)   Expanding the Family Start intensive home visiting service for high-risk families with children;

(f)   Launching the "Danger Signs" public awareness campaign in late 2016 as part of the "It's Not OK" campaign. This highlights the signs that a woman is in danger from a partner and where to get help;

(g)   Extending E Tū Whānau (a community based violence prevention programme) into hard to reach communities, particularly those belonging to gangs and refugee and migrant communities;

(h)   Expanding the bail information pilot from two to eight locations to give judges making bail decisions more information about a defendant's previous family violence history to help support informed bail decision;

(i)   The $503 million Safer Communities package to substantially increase police staff and resources across the country, and which includes new capability particularly relevant to family and sexual violence, such as:
  –   140 additional specialist investigators for child protection, sexual assault, family violence and other serious crimes;
  –   20 additional ethnic liaison officers to support Chinese, Indian and other ethnic communities.[31]

2.4   *International Covenant on the Elimination of All Forms of Racial Discrimination*

Following New Zealand's 2016 submissions of its periodic reports as per its commitments under the *International Convention on the Elimination of All Forms of Racial Discrimination ("ICERD"),*[32] in 2017 numerous civil society organizations took the opportunity to file Shadow Reports to be considered in conjunction with New Zealand's state report. A Shadow Report is a report from a source other than the government in an effort to fill in the gaps of the "not so good" which might be minimized or overlooked by the government in its

---

31   Ibid.
32   Committee on the Elimination of Racial Discrimination, *Consideration of Reports submitted by States Parties under Article 9 of the Convention. Twenty-first and twenty-second Periodic Reports of States parties due in 2015: New Zealand,* UN Doc CERD/C/NZL/21-22 (2016).

report.[33] Considering all of this information, the Committee on the Elimination of Racial Discrimination ("CERD Committee") issued its concluding observations in September 2017.[34] The CERD Committee opened with praise for
New Zealand on a number of different matters:

The Committee commends the State party for:

(a) Acknowledging that social inequities exist today between racial groups
     and the acceptance by the State party of responsibility to correct them;

(b) Adopting the Te Awa Tupua (Whanganui River Claims Settlement) Act
     2017.

The Committee also welcomes the State party's recent efforts to establish policies, programmes and administrative measures to further ensure the protection of human rights and the implementation of the Convention, including:

(a) The second national plan of action on human rights, for the period
     2015–2019;

(b) Various educational and linguistic strategies and measures targeting
     Maori and Pasifika, including the Maori Language Act of 2016;

(c) He Kai Kei Aku Ringa (the Maori economic development strategy and
     action plan);

(d) English as a second language support for students of migrant and refugee
     backgrounds in schools;

(e) 'Ala Mo'ui: Pathways to Pacific Health and Wellbeing 2014–2018;

(f) The Whenua Maori Fund to improve the productivity of Maori land;

(g) The Whanau Ora development strategy;

(h) The Youth Crime Action Plan 2013–2023;

(i) He Korowai Oranga (the Maori health strategy) and the Healthy Families
     NZ initiative;

(j) The Pacific Economic Strategy 2015–2021;

(k) The $10 million fund to address Maori overrepresentation in the criminal
     justice system.

     The Committee notes with appreciation the active role of a vibrant civil
     society and of the national human rights institution, the Human Rights
     Commission, which was again assigned "A" status by the Global Alliance
     of National Human Rights Institutions in May 2016.[35]

---

33   See Tony Ellis, *In the Matter of New Zealand's 6th Periodic Report: Alternative Shadow Re-
      port Filed by Dr. Tony Ellis*, (2016) <http://tbinternet.ohchr.org/Treaties/CCPR/Shared%20
      Documents/NZL/INT_CCPR_CSS_NZL_23261_E.pdf>.

34   Committee on the Elimination of Racial Discrimination, *Concluding observations on the
      combined twenty-first and twenty-second periodic reports of New Zealand*, UN Doc CERD/
      C/NZL/CO/21-22 (2017).

35   Ibid [3]–[5].

However, a number of concerns remain: general concerns related to racist hate speech, hate crimes and acts of racial discrimination and specific concerns regarding the treatment of Māori. For instance, the CERD Committee is concerned by the apparent lack of progress in the implementation of the 2013 recommendations of the Constitutional Advisory Panel concerning the Treaty of Waitangi. It notes that an independent, Māori-led initiative, Matike Mai Aotearoa, has also undertaken wide-ranging consultation and issued its own report, in which it put forward other proposals for discussion on a range of constitutional models that also have not been taken up by New Zealand.[36] In particular, the observations note that the CERD Committee sees that little progress had been made during the reporting period in securing Indigenous rights to self-determination under the Treaty or the power-sharing arrangement between hapu and New Zealand as required by the Treaty.[37] Similarly, the CERD Committee remains concerned about the lack of progress in implementing the recommendations contained in the Waitangi Tribunal's 2011 Wai 262 report regarding, among other issues, Māori intellectual and cultural property rights and Māori treasured possessions, including language, culture and knowledge.[38] Further, the CERD Committee remains concerned about the application of the *Marine and Coastal Area (Takutai Moana) Act 2011* (NZ) on Māori land and resource rights, and by reports that the State party has not attempted to review the Act in accordance with the relevant recommendation contained in the previous concluding observations.[39] The CERD Committee also noted with concern that there continue to be poorer outcomes for Māori and Pasifika in health, employment and education with Māori and Pasifika children remaining the most vulnerable.[40]

3 International Human Rights Law Jurisprudence: UN Cases Concerning New Zealand

2017 saw consideration of a number of communications concerning New Zealand before UN treaty committees the HRC and the *CAT Committee*.

In March 2017, the HRC issued its decision concerning the communication of *MB v New Zealand*.[41] MB, a national of New Zealand, claimed that the State

---

36   Ibid [12].
37   Ibid.
38   Ibid [16].
39   Ibid [20].
40   Ibid [24]–[38].
41   Human Rights Committee, *Decision adopted by the Committee under article 5 (4) of the Optional Protocol, concerning communication No. 2934/2017*, UN Doc CCPR/C/119/D/2934/2017.

violated his rights under articles 14 (1)–(3), (5) and 17 of the *ICCPR* which relate to the fairness of criminal proceedings arising from his conviction for accessing a computer system without claim of right and for dishonest purpose in order to obtain a pecuniary advantage contrary to Section 249(1)(a) of the *Crimes Act 1961* (NZ). Specifically, the author argued his rights under article 14(1) and (3) of the Covenant were violated as his trial counsel was permitted to disregard his defence instructions. Further, the author claimed that his rights under article 14(3) of the Covenant were also violated as there was an undue delay in the proceedings against him. Moreover, the author also claims that his rights under article 14(2) were violated as the appellate courts did not adequately review the safety of the conviction. In addition, the author also claims that his rights under article 14(5) were violated because of a systemic defect in the laws of New Zealand regarding the right to appeal in criminal cases, as the appellate courts attached inadequate importance as to whether the instructions of the defendant had been followed by trial counsel. Finally, the author claimed that his rights under article 17 were violated as the failure by the trial counsel to follow his instructions breached his right of autonomy. Ultimately, the HRC found the entire matter inadmissible on grounds resulting from articles 2 and 5(2)(b) of the *Optional Protocol to the International Covenant on Civil and Political Rights.*[42] As regards the latter, the HRC noted that the author did not provide any arguments to justify why he considers that no effective remedies are available in New Zealand for violation of Article 14(3) concerning the delay in proceedings. In these circumstances, and in the absence of any further information on file, the Committee declared this part of the communication inadmissible pursuant to article 5(2)(b) of the Optional Protocol. As regards the former, the HRC noted in relation to the remaining claims that the author failed to substantiate, for purposes of admissibility, that the conduct of the national courts amounted to arbitrariness or a denial of justice and so found these claims inadmissible under article 2 of the Optional Protocol.

The HRC also issued its views concerning *Communication No. 2502/2014* in November 2017.[43] The authors of the communication were Allan Brian Miller and Michael John Carroll, nationals of New Zealand. They claimed violations of their rights under articles 2, 9, 10 and 14(1) of the *ICCPR* which pertain to arbitrary detention, conditions of imprisonment, the social rehabilitation aim of imprisonment and limited scope of judicial review arising from their

---

42   *Optional Protocol to the International Covenant on Civil and Political Rights*, opened for signature 16 December 1966, 999 UNTS 171 (entered into force 23 March 1976).

43   Human Rights Committee, *Views adopted by the Committee under article 5 (4) of the Optional Protocol, concerning communication No. 2502/2014*, UN Doc. CCPR/C/121/D/2502/2014.

imprisonment for sexual offences. The HRC found the authors' claims admissible concerning issues under articles 9(1) and (4), 10(1) and (3), and 14(1) of the *ICCPR*. Moving to the merits, the HRC found that the information before it disclosed violations by New Zealand of articles 9(1) and (4) and article 10(3) of the Covenant with respect to each author. Specifically, the HRC found that the length of the authors' preventive detention, together with the State party's failure to appropriately alter the punitive nature of the detention conditions after the expiration of their period of non-eligibility for parole, constituted a violation of articles 9(1) and 10(3) of the *ICCPR*. Further, concerning the independence and impartiality of the parole board, the HRC also found that the State party failed to show that judicial review over the lawfulness of detention was available to the authors in order to challenge their continued detention pursuant to article 9(4) of the *ICCPR*.

Aside from the HRC, in December 2017, the *CAT Committee* also issued a decision under article 22 of the *CAT Convention* concerning *Communication No 672/2015*.[44] The decision concerned a complaint put forward by John Alfred Vogel, a national of New Zealand, who claims that the prolonged solitary confinement to which he was subjected and the denial of his right to adequate compensation constituted a violation by New Zealand of articles 14 and 16 of the *CAT Convention*, which respectively pertain to the right to fair and adequate compensation and cruel, inhuman or degrading treatment or punishment. Finding the communication admissible, the *CAT Committee* found a violation by the State of article 16. Specifically, the confinement imposed on the complainant for 21 days amounted to cruel, inhuman or degrading treatment or punishment in violation of article 16 of the Convention. However, the *CAT Committee* did not find a violation of article 14 in relation to compensation rights from the State's requirement that the complainant exhaust the avenues for complaint provided for in the *Prisoners' and Victims' Claims Act* (NZ).

4   Human Rights in the Domestic Context: The Activities of the New Zealand Humans Rights Commission

Deriving its statutory mandate from the *Human Rights Act 1993* (NZ) ("*HRA*") as set out in ss 5(1)–(2), the New Zealand Human Rights Commission ("Commission") is Aotearoa New Zealand's National Human Rights Institution ("NHRI"). It is an independent Crown entity responsible for promoting and encouraging

---

44   Committee against Torture, *Decision adopted by the Committee under article 22 of the Convention, concerning communication No. 672/2015*, UN Doc CAT/C/62/D/672/2015.

the protection of human rights and harmonious relations between all people in New Zealand.[45] During 2017 the Commission prepared over 30 submissions for select committees, government departments and other agencies in relation to key human rights issues. These submissions included:

- a submission to the Law Commission on its review of the *Search and Surveillance Act 2012*;
- a submission to the Foreign Affairs and Trade Select Committee on the *Security Intelligence Bill*;
- a submission to the Māori Affairs Select Committee on the Te Ture Whenua Bill;
- a submission to the *Education and Science Committee on the Education (Update) Amendment Bill 2016*;
- input and guidance to the Ministry of Business, Innovation and Employment ("MBIE") on embedding human rights into procurement processes;
- a submission on the Children, Young Persons and their families, *Oranga Tamariki Bill*;
- various submissions in relation to proposed pieces of legislation relating to family violence.[46]

Furthermore, the Commission received 5453 new human rights enquiries and complaints in 2016/17, an increase of 117 over the previous year. This total is made up of:

- 3716 complaints about a human rights issue of which 1211 were complaints about unlawful discrimination;
- 1501 requests for other assistance including enquiries about human rights training, advice or resources, legal intervention or advocacy (there were 224 enquiries for the Commission's publications);
- 236 registrations of concern (this does not include concern expressed over the Commission's social media sites, but concerns specifically sent to the Commission).[47]

Aside from these domestic activities, the Commission remained involved in New Zealand and abroad with the UN as it is accredited as an "A" status NHRI with the Global Alliance of National Human Rights Institutions ("GANHRI"). Operating in accordance with the *Principles Relating to the Status of National Institutions ("Paris Principles")*, this status is the highest recognition of independence that a national human rights institution can achieve and

---

45   New Zealand Human Rights Commission, "New Zealand Human Rights Commission Annual Report" (HRC, Wellington, 2017).

46   Ibid 20.

47   Ibid 23.

provides the Commission with speaking rights at relevant UN Human Rights Council (the principal UN Charter-based mechanism for the protection of human rights) and human rights treaty committee sessions. In 2017, the Commission submitted several comprehensive shadow reports[48] including reports to the *CAT Committee*, the *CERD Committee* and the *Committee on the Elimination of Discrimination against Women* to help with the development of the list of issues prior to New Zealand's next state report under each of these treaties. Moreover, in 2017 the Commission continued to work with the Treasury and the Ministry of Foreign Affairs and Trade to progress and publicise the UN's Sustainable Development Goals in the state sector.[49] In addition, the Commission, along with IHC,[50] hosted and supported the visit of Ms Catalina Devandas, UN Special Rapporteur on the Rights of Persons with Disabilities, with key stakeholders, including government agencies and the recently elected member of the *UN Convention on the Rights of Persons with Disabilities*, and held a community event at Te Papa.[51] With the funding from the UN, in 2017 the Commission released *Thinking outside the box? A Review of New Zealand's seclusion and restraint practices* which examined these practices across different detention contexts in New Zealand.[52] Furthermore, the Commission continued with its mission to support the *UN Declaration on the Rights of Indigenous Peoples ("UNDRIP")* holding eight Indigenous Rights Information forums across Aotearoa New Zealand to promote awareness about the *UNDRIP* and to highlight its relevance and application to a range of issues, including the right to language, health, environment, indigenous women's leadership, equality and non-discrimination, and indigenous rights.[53]

In 2017, the Commission also engaged in a number of different domestic campaigns. For instance, the Commission's *That's Us* campaign was New Zealand's first anti-racism campaign to ask New Zealanders to share personal stories about racism, intolerance and hatred, as well as their hopes for the future. It garnered a lot traction on social media in New Zealand and reached over 3 million people online via video and website content. A second campaign, *Give Nothing to Racism*, was launched which challenged New Zealanders to confront and eliminate casual racism. Of particular note the campaign featured "40 high-profile and influential Kiwis who generously gave their time,

---

48   See Tony Ellis, above n 33, and accompanying text (discussing shadow reports).
49   New Zealand Human Rights Commission, above n 45, 16.
50   See <https://ihc.org.nz/>.
51   New Zealand Human Rights Commission, above n 45, 19.
52   Ibid 13.
53   Ibid 18.

reputation and support".[54] The Commission notes that its core object with these campaigns is to create a culture in which racist, discriminatory attitudes and behaviours are considered unacceptable by most New Zealanders, and in which diversity is accepted and welcomed.[55] In addition, the Commission launched the *Never Again E Kore Ano* campaign in February which called for (i) an independent inquiry into the abuse of people held in state care, (ii) a public apology to those who were affected, (iii) appropriate steps to be taken to acknowledge the harm that has been caused to the victims and to provide appropriate redress and rehabilitation, and (iv) action to be taken to ensure this never happens again. This campaign also garnered extensive media coverage.[56] Finally, the Commission continued its work in addressing and raising awareness of bullying in schools through participation on the Bullying Prevention Advisory Group. The Commission continues to advocate for the Ministry of Education to develop a comprehensive, evidence-based anti-bullying programme for New Zealand schools, which includes all the identifications used by bullies in school: race, disability, gender, economic status, family status and GLBTI.[57]

---

54   Ibid 12.
55   Ibid.
56   Ibid.
57   Ibid 19.

Indigenous 'Peoples'' Rights under International Law

*Fleur Te Aho**

1 Introduction

This note reviews New Zealand's state practice regarding Indigenous peoples' rights under international law in 2017 and traces key international developments concerning those rights. New Zealand remained active in discussions in international fora regarding Indigenous peoples and their rights, including concerning protection of their traditional cultural expressions ("TCES"). Negotiations on a new process for Indigenous participation at the United Nations ("UN") stalled, but Indigenous peoples were referenced in texts advancing the UN General Assembly's ("GA") Sustainable Development Goals ("SDGs"), the UN Framework Convention on Climate Change ("UNFCCC"),[1] and the Convention on Biological Diversity ("CBD").[2] National developments of significance included the ground-breaking decision in *Wakatū v Attorney General*.[3] The UN Committee on the Elimination of Racial Discrimination ("CERD") devoted considerable attention to the human rights situation of Māori in its periodic review of New Zealand.[4] Other international bodies continued to devote attention to Indigenous peoples' rights in carrying out their mandates.

2 Developments in Relation to International Resolutions, Recommendations and Other Forms of Non-binding or Soft Law Instruments

2.1 *Indigenous Peoples' Participation in the UN*
Formal consultations, through the advisors to the President of the GA, on measures to enable the participation of Indigenous peoples in UN meetings

---

* University of Auckland. Ngāti Mutunga and English.
1 *United Nations Framework Convention on Climate Change*, opened for signature 4 June 1992, 1771 UNTS 107 (entered into force 21 March 1994).
2 *Convention on Biological Diversity*, opened for signature 5 June 1992, 1760 UNTS 79 (entered into force 29 December 1993).
3 [2017] NZSC 17.
4 Committee on the Elimination of Racial Discrimination, *Concluding observations on the combined twenty-first and twenty-second periodic reports of New Zealand*, UN Doc CERD/C/NZL/CO/21-22 (22 September 2017).

affecting them concluded in 2017 without consensus agreement on a new process, after an impasse in inter-governmental negotiations.[5] New Zealand had supported these efforts. Attention to the issue will continue, however. In September, the GA adopted a compromise resolution encouraging "further efforts to facilitate" Indigenous participation in UN meetings, requesting the UN Secretary-General to report to the GA, by the end of its 75th session, "on achievements, analysis and concrete recommendations on the possible further measures necessary" for Indigenous participation at UN meetings,[6] and, with state support, to seek input from Indigenous peoples in preparing that report (encouraging regional consultations).[7] The UN GA will consider the issue again at its 75th session and will hold informal interactive hearings in the lead-up.[8]

2.2   *2030 Agenda for Sustainable Development*

The Ministerial Declaration of the High Level Political Forum ("HLPF") 2017, connected to the 2030 Agenda for the SDGs, references Indigenous peoples.[9] It identifies the need to empower vulnerable peoples, including Indigenous peoples;[10] stresses the importance of "implementing nationally appropriate social protection systems and measures for all, including social protection floors", with particular attention to Indigenous peoples;[11] notes that "[c]limate change and land degradation are increasing the vulnerability to extreme weather events of small-scale food producers" particularly Indigenous peoples and others;[12] and emphasises that "[e]fforts should be made to reach

---

5   Claire Charters, *Briefing to the UN Expert Mechanism on the Rights of Indigenous Peoples: Agenda Item 7* (12 July 2017) United Nations Web TV <http://webtv.un.org/search/item-7-indigenous-peoples%E2%80%99-participation-5th-meeting-10th-session-expert-mechanism-on-rights-of-indigenous-peoples/5502629199001/?term=10th%20Expert%20 Mechanism%20on%20Rights%20of%20Indigenous%20Peoples&sort=date&page=2>; *Letter from the advisors of the President of the UN General Assembly* (11 September 2017) United Nations <https://www.un.org/development/desa/indigenouspeoples/participa-tion-of-indigenous-peoples-at-the-united-nations.html>.
6   UN General Assembly, *Enhancing the participation of indigenous peoples' representatives and institutions in meetings of relevant United Nations bodies on issues affecting them*, UN Doc UN GA 71/321 (8 September 2017) [5].
7   Ibid [6].
8   Ibid [7], [8].
9   UN Economic and Social Council, *Ministerial declaration of the 2017 high-level political forum on sustainable development, convened under the auspices of the Economic and Social Council, on the theme "Eradicating poverty and promoting prosperity in a changing world"*, UN Doc E/HLS/2017/1 (20 July 2017).
10   Ibid [2].
11   Ibid [14].
12   Ibid [15].

out to all stakeholders", including Indigenous peoples, in order to localise and communicate the SDGs.[13] Indigenous peoples unsuccessfully advocated for an acknowledgement in the text that their land rights needed to be secure to eradicate poverty.[14] And only a small proportion of the Voluntary National Reviews, which outline state progress on implementation of the SDGs, referred to Indigenous peoples.[15]

3   Developments in Relation to International Treaties

3.1   *UN Framework Convention on Climate Change*
Several 2017 developments associated with the UNFCCC are of relevance to Indigenous peoples. First, the Local Communities and Indigenous Peoples' Platform ("LCIP Platform") was finalised at the UNFCCC's 23nd Conference of the Parties ("COP"), which New Zealand participated in. It is concerned with enhancing the engagement of Indigenous peoples in the UNFCCC process and facilitating the sharing of their mitigation and adaptation practices.[16] Positively, the LCIP Platform refers to the *UN Declaration on the Rights of Indigenous Peoples ("UNDRIP")*[17] in its preamble,[18] and four of the five principles Indigenous peoples put forward for inclusion are reflected in the text.[19] However, the structure of the LCIP Platform (the subject of the excluded principle) remains contentious. Indigenous peoples required that the LCIP Platform be

---

13   Ibid [28]. Indigenous peoples were also referenced in the President of the Economic and Social Council's summary of the HLPF 2017 discussions, see *President's Summary of the 2017 High-level political forum on sustainable development* (2017) United Nations Sustainable Development Knowledge Platform <https://sustainabledevelopment.un.org/content/documents/16673HLPF_2017_Presidents_summary.pdf>. For discussion see Joan Carling, "Indigenous Peoples' Engagement in the SDGs" in Pamela Jacquelin-Andersen (ed), *The Indigenous World 2018* (International Work Group for Indigenous Affairs, 2018) 570.

14   Carling, above n 13, 569–70.

15   Division for Sustainable Development, UN Department of Economic and Social Affairs *2017 Voluntary National Reviews: Synthesis Report* (2018). For discussion see Carling, above n 13.

16   UNFCCC Subsidiary Body for Scientific and Technological Advice, *Local communities and indigenous peoples platform*, FCCC/SBSTA/2017/L.29 (15 November 2017).

17   *United Nations Declaration on the Rights of Indigenous Peoples*, GA Res 61/295, UN GAOR, 61st sess, 107th plen mtg, Supp No 49, UN Doc A/RES/61/295 (13 September 2007).

18   UNFCC, above n 16, 1.

19   Hindou Oumarou Ibrahim et al., "UN Framework Convention on Climate Change (UNFCC)" in Pamela Jacquelin-Andersen (ed), *The Indigenous World 2018* (International Work Group for Indigenous Affairs, 2018) 599.

established "within the UNFCCC framework, allowing it to inform decision-making and actions at national, regional, and international levels".[20] But the UNFCCC rules of procedure only allow parties to the UNFCCC (not Indigenous peoples) to speak and participate in UNFCCC negotiating bodies.[21] Secondly, the Gender Action Plan, which aims to improve women's participation in UNFCCC processes, was finalised at the 23rd COP.[22] It references the need to financially support Indigenous women to participate in national delegations and calls for information on the differentiated impacts of climate change on Indigenous women and men.[23] Thirdly, the Green Climate Fund ("GCF") continued to work on its draft Indigenous Peoples' Policy.[24] In its decision on the UN Program for Reducing Emissions from Deforestation and Forest Degradation-Plus' ("REDD+") request for proposals for results-based payments, the GCF requires all proposals to meet the requirements of the draft policy.[25]

4   Overseas Developments of International Significance

4.1   *African Court of Human and Peoples' Rights' Rules on Indigenous Rights*

The African Court of Human and Peoples' Rights issued its first judgment on Indigenous peoples' rights in *African Commission of Human and Peoples' Rights v The Republic of Kenya* (the Ogiek case).[26] The case concerned the eviction of the Ogiek people from the Mau Forest by the Kenyan Forest Service. The Court found numerous violations of the Ogiek's rights under the African Charter of Human and Peoples' Rights, including of their right to property (Article 14), to their culture (Article 17(2) and (3)) and to free disposal of their wealth and natural resources (Article 21).[27]

---

20   Ibid.

21   Ibid.

22   UNFCCC, *Gender and Climate Change*, FCCC/SBI/2017/L.29 (13 November 2017).

23   Ibid 4, 6. For discussion see Ibrahim et al., above n 19, 600–1.

24   Ibrahim et al., above n 19, 602.

25   Green Climate Fund, *Decisions of the Board – eighteenth meeting of the Board, 30 September – 2 October 2017*, GCF/B.18/23 (2 November 2017) 89. For discussion see Ibrahim et al., above n 19, 602–3.

26   *African Commission on Human and Peoples' Rights v Kenya (Judgment)* No. 006/2012, African Court on Human and Peoples' Rights 6 (26 May 2017) African Court <http://www.african-court.org/en/index.php/56-pending-cases-details/864-app-no-006-2012-african-commission-on-human-and-peoples-rights-v-republic-of-kenya-details>.

27   *African Charter on Human and Peoples' Rights*, 21 ILM 58 (entered into force 27 June 1981).

5   National Developments of International Significance

5.1   *Supreme Court Decision on Crown Fiduciary Duties to Māori*
In a landmark decision in *Wakatū v Attorney General*[28] the New Zealand Supreme Court held that the Crown had a legally enforceable fiduciary duty to the customary owners of Nelson land sold to the Crown in the late 1830s and early 1840s to reserve one tenth of the land purchased for their benefit and to exclude their living areas, burial grounds and cultivations from the sale. The UNDRIP was cited in the judgment.[29] The High Court will now consider the extent of the breach and the remedies to be granted.

5.2   *Mount Taranaki to have Legal Personality*
Eight iwi (nations) of Taranaki signed a record of understanding with the Crown, which provides for Mount Taranaki to become its own legal personality. Local iwi and the government will share joint responsibility for its governance.[30]

5.3   *Waitangi Tribunal Finds Crown Breaches Regarding Reoffending Rates of Māori*
The Waitangi Tribunal found that the Crown, through the Department of Corrections, had breached the principles of the Treaty in failing to make the reduction of Māori reoffending rates a priority.[31] Its recommendations included that the Department, in partnership with Māori, design and implement a Māori-specific strategy to reduce reoffending rates.[32] At the Permanent Forum on Indigenous Issues ("PFII") New Zealand described the recommendations as "fair and an indication that there is still much work" ahead.[33]

---

28   [2017] NZSC 17 (28 February 2017).
29   Ibid [491], [657], [679].
30   Hon Andrew Little, *Landmark day for Taranaki Maunga* (20 December 2017) Beehive <https://www.beehive.govt.nz/release/landmark-day-taranaki-maunga>.
31   Waitangi Tribunal, *Tū Mai te Rangi! Report on the Crown and Disproportionate Reoffending Rates* (2017).
32   Ibid 87–90.
33   Jaclyn Williams, New Zealand representative, *Item 4: Implementation of the six mandated areas of the Permanent Forum with reference to the Declaration* (2017) Indigenous Peoples' Centre for Documentation, Research and Information <http://cendoc.docip.org/collect/cendocdo/index/assoc/HASHf02a/9eb78dda.dir/PF17JaclynNZ.pdf>.

6   International Oversight of New Zealand's Compliance with
          Indigenous Peoples' Rights

6.1   *UN Committee on the Elimination of Racial Discrimination*
The CERD, in its 2017 concluding observations on New Zealand, raised a collection of concerns regarding the situation of Māori. Notably, it criticised New
Zealand's slow progress in securing Māori self-determination as required by the
Treaty of Waitangi: "[t]he Committee sees that little progress has been made
during the reporting period in securing indigenous rights to self-determination
under the Treaty or the power-sharing arrangement between hapu and the
State party required by the Treaty".[34] It also raised concerns regarding, inter
alia, the protection of Māori rights to their lands and resources;[35] application
of the principle of free, prior and informed consent ("FPIC");[36] the overrepresentation of Māori in the criminal justice system;[37] barriers to Māori access to
health care, employment and their language;[38] and the removal of Māori children into state care.[39] Its recommendations included that New Zealand issue a
timetable for debating, in partnership with Māori, the role of the Treaty within
New Zealand's constitutional arrangements;[40] ensure that the "free and informed consent of Maori" is obtained "before approving any project affecting
the use and development of their traditional land and resources";[41] review the
Marine and Coastal Area (Takutai Moana) Act 2011;[42] and "ensure full respect
for the rights of Maori communities to freshwater and geothermal resources".[43]

7   Discussion of International Issues Related to Indigenous Peoples in
          International Fora

7.1   *UN Expert Mechanism on the Rights of Indigenous Peoples*
          ("EMRIP")
During EMRIP's 10th session EMRIP presented its draft study and advice on
good practices and challenges in business and access to financial services by

---

34   Committee on the Elimination of Racial Discrimination, *Concluding observations on the*
      combined twenty-first and twenty-second periodic reports of New Zealand, UN Doc CERD/
      C/NZL/CO/21-22 (22 September 2017) [12].
35   Ibid [16], [20], [22].
36   Ibid [18], [20].
37   Ibid [24].
38   Ibid [26], [29], [35].
39   Ibid [33].
40   Ibid [13(a)].
41   Ibid.
42   Ibid [21].
43   Ibid [23].

Indigenous peoples.[44] In response, New Zealand emphasised its efforts at supporting Māori economic development, focusing on its work to drive employment opportunities for Māori.[45]

7.2 Permanent Forum on Indigenous Issues ("PFII")

At the PFII's 16th session on the special theme of the 10th anniversary of the UNDRIP, New Zealand reiterated its commitment to the UNDRIP (albeit with its usual qualifying language). New Zealand stated that it "remains committed to the common objectives of the Declaration and the Treaty of Waitangi alongside New Zealand's existing legal and constitutional frameworks" and is "identifying priorities for enhancing our commitment to indigenous peoples [sic] rights".[46]

New Zealand also identified steps it was taking to advance the PFII's areas of work, including the legislative recognition of the legal personality of the Whanganui River, the enactment of Te Ture mō Te Reo Māori 2016, Whānau Ora, and progress in Māori educational achievement.[47]

7.3 Convention on Biological Diversity Conference of the Parties

Indigenous peoples were referenced in the CBD's Subsidiary Body on Scientific, Technical and Technological Advice's ("SBSTTA") 2017 recommendations on scenarios for the 2050 vision for biodiversity. It emphasised the importance of Indigenous peoples' participation and called for the following issues, inter alia, to be taken into account: Indigenous peoples' contributions to "the conservation of biological diversity and the sustainable use of its components", "[t]he consequences of alternative scenarios for the customary sustainable use of biodiversity by indigenous peoples and local communities", and "[t]echnology developments that may have positive or negative impacts on the achievement

---

44 Expert Mechanism on the Rights of Indigenous Peoples, *Good Practices and challenges, including discrimination, in business and in access to financial services by indigenous peoples, in particular indigenous women and indigenous persons with disabilities. Draft study of the Expert Mechanism on the Rights of Indigenous Peoples*, UN Doc A/HRC/EMRIP/2017/CRP.1 (July 2017).

45 Jillian Dempster, New Zealand Permanent Representative, *Expert Mechanism on the Rights of Indigenous Peoples 10th session 10 - 14 July 2017 Item 4: Study and advice on good practices and challenges in business and in access to financial services by indigenous peoples* (2017) Indigenous Peoples' Centre for Documentation, Research and Information <http://cendoc.docip.org/collect/cendocdo/index/assoc/HASH411b/8e13db7b.dir/EM17NewZealand40711.pdf>.

46 Te Puni Kokiri, *Item 8: Discussion on the theme "Tenth Anniversary of the United Nations Declaration on the Rights of Indigenous Peoples: Measures taken to implement the Declaration"* (2017) Indigenous Peoples' Centre for Documentation, Research and Information <http://cendoc.docip.org/collect/cendocdo/index/assoc/HASH01b5/2e83c29e.dir/PF17new-zealand82504.pdf>.

47 Williams, above n 33.

of the three objectives of the Conventions as well as on the lifestyles and traditional knowledge of indigenous peoples and local communities".[48] Reference to Indigenous peoples also featured in a raft of other decisions of the SBSTTA, including regarding a sustainable wild meat sector; health and biodiversity; the mainstreaming of biodiversity in energy and mining, infrastructure, manufacturing and processing, and health; and tools to evaluate the effectiveness of policy instruments for the implementation of the Strategic Plan for Biodiversity 2011–2020.[49]

7.4   World Intellectual Property Office

The World Intellectual Property Office's Intergovernmental Committee on Intellectual Property and Genetic Resources, Traditional Knowledge and Folklore ("IGC") held its 33rd and 34th sessions in 2017, where the drafting of an international legal instrument on TCEs continued.[50] New Zealand participated in both sessions and was a co-facilitator of the TCEs agenda item at the 34th session. At the 34th session New Zealand, in discussion on Articles 2 and 3 of the draft text, put forward suggestions to narrow the differences in the text regarding eligibility.[51] New Zealand also suggested revisions to Article 10 concerning the scope of protection provided.[52]

7.5   Commission on the Status of Women

The emerging focus area for the UN Commission on the Status of Women's 61st session was the empowerment of Indigenous women. During the session New Zealand stated that it was "committed to the aspirations" of the UNDRIP and that "[w]ith Māori, Government has developed unique approaches to support Māori development" where "the principle of 'partnership' is central".[53]

---

48   Subsidiary Body on Scientific, Technical and Technological Advice, *Report of the Subsidiary Body on Scientific, Technical and Technological Advice on its Twenty-first meeting Montreal, Canada, 11–14 December 2017*, CBD/COP/14/4, CBD/SBSTTA/21/10 (14 December 2017) 3, 4.

49   Ibid 8–18, 24, 27–31, 34–5.

50   World Intellectual Property Office Intergovernmental Committee on Intellectual Property and Genetic Resources, Traditional Knowledge and Folklore, *Thirty-Third Session Geneva, February 27 to March 3, 2017: Report Adopted by the Committee*, WIPO/GRTKF/IC/33/7 (12 June 2017); World Intellectual Property Office Intergovernmental Committee on Intellectual Property and Genetic Resources, Traditional Knowledge and Folklore, *Thirty-Fourth Session Geneva, June 12 to 16, 2017: Report Adopted by the Committee*, WIPO/GRTKF/IC/34/14 (19 March 2018) ["WIPO IGC 34th Session"].

51   WIPO IGC 34th Session, above n 50, [68].

52   Ibid [200].

53   Ministry of Foreign Affairs and Trade *Commission on the Status of Women 61* (15 March 2017) MFAT <https://www.mfat.govt.nz/en/media-and-resources/ministry-statements-and-speeches/commission-on-the-status-of-women-61/>.

Examples it identified were "initiatives to get more Māori women into trades training and the Māori Women Development Incorporated", a business loan and leadership programme for Māori women.[54]

8 Developments Contributing to Customary International Law or of Particular Relevance to New Zealand

8.1 Committee on the Elimination of Racial Discrimination

CERD's recommendations included that states: recognise Indigenous peoples' right to self-determination (Australia and Finland);[55] implement the UND-RIP (Canada);[56] ensure access to healthcare services (Ecuador),[57] education (Canada and Ecuador),[58] and Indigenous languages (Australia, Finland);[59] address the overrepresentation of Indigenous peoples in prisons (Australia and Canada)[60] and improve access to justice, including by building the capacity of alternative justice systems (Kenya);[61] revise its law on Indigenous peoples' land rights (Finland and Australia);[62] incorporate the principle of FPIC into law (Australia and Canada)[63] and obtain it from Indigenous peoples before the approval of any project affecting their lands (Australia, Canada, Ecuador, Finland, Kenya and the Russian Federation).[64]

---

54   Ibid.
55   Committee on the Elimination of Racial Discrimination, *Concluding observations on the eighteenth to twentieth periodic reports of Australia*, UN Doc CERD/C/AUS/CO/18-20 (26 December 2017) [20] (*"CERD on Australia"*); Committee on the Elimination of Racial Discrimination, *Concluding observations on the twenty-third periodic report of Finland*, UN Doc CERD/C/FIN/CO/23 (8 June 2017) [15] (*"CERD on Finland"*).
56   Committee on the Elimination of Racial Discrimination, *Concluding observations on the combined twenty-first to twenty-third periodic reports of Canada*, UN Doc CERD/C/CAN/CO/21-23 (13 September 2017) [18] (*"CERD on Canada"*).
57   Committee on the Elimination of Racial Discrimination, *Concluding observations on the combined twenty-third and twenty-fourth periodic reports of Ecuador*, UN Doc CERD/C/ECU/CO/23-24 (15 September 2017) [7] (*"CERD on Ecuador"*).
58   *CERD on Canada*, above n 56, [30]; *CERD on Ecuador*, above n 57, [7], [27], [29].
59   *CERD on Australia*, above n 55, [37]; *CERD on Finland*, above n 55 [19].
60   *CERD on Australia*, above n 55, [26], [28]; *CERD on Canada*, above n 56, [16].
61   Committee on the Elimination of Racial Discrimination, *Concluding observations on the fifth to seventh periodic reports of Kenya*, UN Doc CERD/C/KEN/CO/5-7 (8 June 2017) [16] (*"CERD on Kenya"*).
62   *CERD on Finland,* above n 55, [17]; *CERD on Australia,* above n 55, [22].
63   *CERD on Australia,* above n 55, [22]; *CERD on Canada,* above n 56, [20].
64   Committee on the Elimination of Racial Discrimination, *Concluding observations on the twenty-third and twenty-fourth periodic reports of the Russian Federation,* UN Doc CERD/C/RUS/CO/23-24 (20 September 2017) [24]; *CERD on Ecuador,* above n 57, [19]; *CERD on*

8.2   Committee on Economic, Social and Cultural Rights

The Committee on Economic, Social and Cultural Rights ("CESCR") recommended, inter alia, that Australia constitutionally recognise its Indigenous peoples;[65] the Russian Federation establish federally protected Indigenous territories;[66] Australia reform the Native Title Act 1993;[67] the Russian Federation conduct impact assessments prior to land exploitation and provide adequate remedies and reparation;[68] the Netherlands remove obstacles to holding companies domiciled within the state accountable for rights violations abroad;[69] Australia, Colombia and the Russian Federation obtain the FPIC of affected Indigenous peoples before implementing development projects;[70] Australia and Colombia ensure access to healthcare and bilingual education;[71] and Colombia and the Russian Federation investigate acts of violence and threats faced by indigenous rights defenders.[72]

Additionally, the CESCR adopted *General Comment No. 24 (2017) on State obligations under the International Covenant on Economic, Social and Cultural Rights in the context of business activities*, which devotes especial attention to the position of Indigenous peoples.[73]

8.3   Committee on the Elimination of Discrimination against Women

The Committee on the Elimination of Discrimination against Women's ("CEDAW") recommendations included that Guatemala and Thailand ensure

---

        Canada, above n 56, [20]; *CERD on Finland,* above n 55, [17]; *CERD on Kenya,* above n 61, [20]; *CERD on Australia,* above n 55, [22].

65   Committee on Economic, Social and Cultural Rights, *Concluding observations on the fifth periodic report of Australia,* UN Doc E/C.12/AUS/CO/5 (11 July 2017) [16] ("*CESCR on Australia*").

66   Committee on Economic, Social and Cultural Rights, *Concluding observations on the sixth periodic report of the Russian Federation,* UN Doc E/C.12/RUS/CO/6 (16 October 2017) [15] ("*CESCR on Russian Federation*").

67   *CESCR on Australia,* above n 65, [16].

68   *CESCR on Russian Federation,* above n 66, [15].

69   Committee on Economic, Social and Cultural Rights, *Concluding observations on the sixth periodic report of the Netherlands,* UN Doc E/C.12/NLD/CO/6 (6 July 2017) [12].

70   *CESCR on Australia,* above n 65, [16]; Committee on Economic, Social and Cultural Rights, *Concluding observations on the sixth periodic report of Colombia,* UN Doc E/C.12/COL/CO/6 (19 October 2017) [18] ("*CESCR on Colombia*"); *CESCR on Russian Federation,* above n 66, [15].

71   *CESCR on Australia,* above n 65, [44], [52].

72   *CESCR on Colombia,* above n 70, [10]; *CESCR on Russian Federation,* above n 66, [8].

73   Committee on Economic, Social and Cultural Rights, *General comment No. 24 (2017) on State obligations under the International Covenant on Economic, Social and Cultural Rights in the context of business activities,* UN Doc E/C.12/GC/24 (10 August 2017).

the representation of Indigenous women in political life and decision-making positions;[74] Guatemala ensure Indigenous women's access to land ownership;[75] Kenya immediately "implement the ruling of the African Commission on Human and Peoples" Rights regarding the rights of the Endorois people to their ancestral land, and ensure consultation with Endorois women during this process';[76] and Costa Rica, Guatemala and Thailand secure the FPIC of affected Indigenous women to major projects on their lands as well as provide compensation or benefit-sharing.[77]

The rights of Indigenous women were also referred to in two CEDAW General Recommendations: No. 35 on gender-based violence against women[78] and No. 36 on girls' and women's right to education.[79]

8.4   Committee on the Rights of the Child

The Committee on the Rights of the Child's recommendations included that Ecuador and the Democratic Republic of the Congo address the impact of extractive industries on children's rights, including ensuring the implementation of international standards,[80] and Ecuador seek the FPIC of Indigenous peoples and children in relation to measures impacting their lives.[81]

---

74   Committee on the Elimination of Discrimination against Women, *Concluding observations on the combined eighth and ninth periodic reports of Guatemala*, UN Doc CEDAW/C/GTM/CO/8-9 (22 November 2017) [27] ("*CEDAW on Guatemala*"); Committee on the Elimination of Discrimination against Women, *Concluding observations on the combined sixth and seventh periodic reports of Thailand*, UN Doc CEDAW/C/THA/CO/6-7 (24 July 2017) [17] ("*CEDAW on Thailand*").

75   *CEDAW on Guatemala*, above n 74, [41].

76   Committee on the Elimination of Discrimination against Women, *Concluding observations on the eighth periodic report of Kenya*, UN Doc CEDAW/C/KEN/CO/8 (22 November 2017) [45].

77   Committee on the Elimination of Discrimination against Women, *Concluding observations on the seventh periodic report of Costa Rica*, UN Doc CEDAW/C/CRI/CO/7 (24 July 2017) [37]; *CEDAW on Guatemala*, above n 75, [41]; *CEDAW on Thailand*, above n 74, [43].

78   Committee on the Elimination of Discrimination against Women, *General recommendation No. 35 on gender-based violence against women, updating general recommendation No. 19*, UN Doc CEDAW/C/GC/35 (26 July 2017).

79   Committee on the Elimination of Discrimination against Women, *General recommendation No. 36 (2017) on the right of girls and women to education*, UN Doc CEDAW/C/GC/36 (27 November 2017).

80   Committee on the Rights of the Child, *Concluding observations on the combined fifth and sixth periodic reports of Ecuador*, UN Doc CRC/C/ECU/CO/5-6 (26 October 2017) [41] ("*CRC on Ecuador*"); Committee on the Rights of the Child, *Concluding observations on the combined third to fifth periodic reports of the Democratic Republic of the Congo*, UN Doc CRC/C/COD/CO/3-5 (28 February 2017) [14].

81   *CRC on Ecuador*, above n 80, [41].

8.5   *Human Rights Committee*
The Human Rights Committee recommended, inter alia, that Australia revise its Constitution to fully protect the rights of Indigenous peoples and amend the Native Title Act 1993 to take into account relevant international standards,[82] and Bangladesh resolve the land disputes in the Chittagong Hill Tracts.[83]

8.6   *Human Rights Council Universal Periodic Review ("HRC")*
During the HRC's Universal Periodic Review states' recommendations regarding Indigenous peoples included that Peru "[g]uarantee the Indigenous Peoples' right to free, prior and informed consent and ensure they receive land titles"[84] and Japan "[r]atify the ILO Indigenous and Tribal Peoples Convention, 1989 (No. 169)".[85]

---

82   Human Rights Committee, *Concluding observations on the sixth periodic report of Australia,* UN Doc CCPR/C/AUS/CO/6 (1 December 2017) [50], [52].

83   Human Rights Committee, *Concluding observations on the initial report of Bangladesh,* UN Doc CCPR/C/BGD/CO/1 (27 April 2017) [12].

84   Human Rights Council, *Report of the Working Group on the Universal Periodic Review: Peru,* UN Doc A/HRC/37/8 (27 December 2017) [111.169] (Germany).

85   Human Rights Council, *Report of the Working Group on the Universal Periodic Review: Japan,* UN Doc A/HRC/37/15 (4 January 2018) [161.30] (Guatemala).

International Economic Law

*An Hertogen**

1   Introduction

In 2017, the 2016 election of President Trump in the United States continued to reverberate in the international trade law arena. The challenges posed to the rules-based multilateral trading system by his "America First" policy and his preference for a power-based system were met by a renewed energy to negotiate new rules to strengthen the trading law system.[1] However, these efforts – particularly at the global level – have not always been successful. This review gives an overview of New Zealand's participation in negotiations for new preferential and multilateral agreements as well as in World Trade Organisation ("WTO") trade disputes to enforce existing trade agreements in the course of 2017.

2   Preferential Trade Negotiations

The saga of the *Trans-Pacific Partnership Agreement* ("*TPP*")[2] bookended the year in trade. On 30 January 2017, merely days into the Trump administration, the United States notified New Zealand, as TPP depository, of its intention not to become a party. To the surprise of many, the remaining 11 parties[3] renegotiated the agreement, and, on 11 November 2017, reached an agreement on the core elements of a *Comprehensive and Progressive Agreement for Trans-Pacific*

---

*   University of Auckland.
1   See, for example, the affirmation of support for the multilateral trading system, delivered at the 11th Session of the Ministerial Conference of the WTO, *Joint Ministerial Declaration by Albania; Argentina; Australia; Benin; Canada; Chile; Colombia; Costa Rica; Côte d'Ivoire; Dominican Republic; El Salvador; Guatemala; Hong Kong, China; Iceland; Israel; Kazakhstan; The State of Kuwait; Republic Of Korea; Kyrgyz Republic; Lao People's Democratic Republic; Liberia; Liechtenstein; Mauritania; Mexico; Montenegro; Myanmar; Republic of Moldova; New Zealand; Nigeria; Norway; Pakistan; Panama; Paraguay; Peru; Qatar; Russian Federation; Senegal; Singapore; Switzerland; Chinese Taipei; Thailand; The Former Yugoslav Republic of Macedonia; Turkey; Ukraine; Uruguay and Viet Nam*, WTO Doc WT/MIN(17)/55/Rev.1 (19 December 2017) (Declaration of 11 December 2017).
2   Ministry of Foreign Affairs and Trade, *Trans-Pacific Partnership* <http://www.tpp.mfat.govt.nz/>.
3   Australia, Brunei-Darussalam, Canada, Chile, Japan, Malaysia, Mexico, Peru, Singapore, Viet Nam, and New Zealand.

Partnership ("*CPTPP*").[4] At the same time, the parties also released an outline of the *CPTPP*,[5] including a list of suspended provisions and of four issues that required further negotiations.[6] The most important of the suspended provisions relate to investor-state dispute settlement ("ISDS"), which is now significantly curtailed compared to the TPP, as well as to intellectual property standards. The negotiations on the remaining issues concluded on 23 January 2018, and the *CPTPP* was signed in Santiago, Chile, on 8 March 2018.[7] Although New Zealand completed the steps for entry into force of the *TPP* on 11 May 2017,[8] it did not ratify the agreement until late 2018.

New Zealand's 2017 activities in terms of negotiating preferential trade agreements were however not limited to the *TPP* and its *CPTPP* successor. It also concluded negotiations on the *Pacific Agreement on Closer Economic Relations Plus* ("*PACER-Plus*"),[9] continued negotiating the *Regional Comprehensive Economic Partnership* ("*RCEP*") as well as the update to its free trade agreement ("*FTA*") with China, and started talks for a trade deal with the Pacific Alliance and with the European Union ("EU"). In contrast, nothing happened in the FTA negotiations with India,[10] and the negotiations for a FTA with the Russia-Belarus-Kazakhstan Customs Union remain suspended following the 2014 Crimea crisis.

PACER-Plus was signed in Nuku'alofa on 14 June 2017, between Australia, New Zealand and eight Pacific Island Forum members.[11] The agreement is intended

---

4   *Trans-Pacific Partnership Ministerial Statement* (11 November 2017) Ministry of Foreign Affairs and Trade <https://www.mfat.govt.nz/assets/FTAs-in-negotiations/TPP/2017.11.10-Ministerial-Statement-FINAL.pdf>.

5   *Annex I – Outline of the TPP 11 Agreement* (11 November 2017) Ministry of Foreign Affairs and Trade <https://www.mfat.govt.nz/assets/FTAs-in-negotiations/TPP/Annex-I_Outline -of-Agreement.pdf>.

6   *Annex II – List of Suspended Provisions* (11 November 2017) Ministry of Foreign Affairs and Trade <https://www.mfat.govt.nz/assets/FTAs-in-negotiations/TPP/ANNEX-II_LIst -of-suspended-Provisions.pdf>.

7   The text of the CPTPP can be found at Ministry of Foreign Affairs and Trade <https:// www.mfat.govt.nz/en/about-us/who-we-are/treaties/cptpp>. As the agreement was concluded after the cut-off date for the current review, a more detailed analysis of the provisions has not been included.

8   *Text of the Trans-Pacific Partnership* (2016) Ministry of Foreign Affairs and Trade <https://www.mfat.govt.nz/en/about-us/who-we-are/treaties/trans-pacific-partnership-agreement-tpp/text-of-the-trans-pacific-partnership/>.

9   *Pacific Agreement on Closer Economic Relations Plus,* signed 14 June 2017 (not yet in force) <https://www.mfat.govt.nz/assets/Uploads/PACER-Plus-consolidated-legal-text.pdf>.

10   Ministry of Foreign Affairs and Trade, *New Zealand – India FTA* <https://www.mfat.govt .nz/en/trade/free-trade-agreements/agreements-under-negotiation/india/>.

11   The eight members are the Cook Islands, Kiribati, Nauru, Niue, Samoa, the Solomon Islands, Tonga and Tuvalu. Vanuatu signed up in September 2017. The Federated States

to be more than just a trade agreement, but also includes a development package. However, the two largest Pacific economies, Fiji and Papua New Guinea, are notably absent. The agreement has been criticized for favouring Australia and New Zealand, who are the main beneficiaries of the tariff reductions that will lower revenues for Pacific Island governments. Moreover, there are the traditional concerns about regulatory autonomy and the power of private investors to challenge domestic regulation. At the time of writing, *PACER Plus* has not yet entered into force. When it enters into force, side letters between Australia and New Zealand[12] will govern potential conflicts between *PACER Plus* and the mutual rights and obligations of these parties under the *Australia–New Zealand Closer Economic Relations Trade Agreement* ("*NZCERTA*"),[13] the *ASEAN-Australia-New Zealand Free Trade Area* ("*AANZFTA*")[14] or the *TPP*.[15]

Australia and New Zealand, alongside a few of the other *CPTPP* members, continue to negotiate the *RCEP*. This partnership, between the Association of Southeast Asian Nations ("*ASEAN*")[16] and the six states that have FTAs with ASEAN,[17] intends to consolidate these FTAs with the goal of establishing a comprehensive free trade area. In 2017, four more negotiation rounds took place, bringing the total to 20.[18] No new chapters were concluded in 2017, but a working group on government procurement and a sub-working group on trade remedies were agreed to in round 18 and met for the first time in round 19. For

---

of Micronesia, Palau and the Republic of Marshall Islands have concluded the negotiations, but have not yet signed the agreement, see Ministry of Foreign Affairs and Trade, *Briefing to Foreign Affairs, Defence and Trade Committee* (February 2018) New Zealand Parliament <https://www.parliament.nz/en/pb/sc/submissions-and-advice/document/52SCFD_EVI_75555_299/ministry-of-foreign-affairs-briefing-on-pacer-plus>.

12   Letter from the Hon Todd McClay to the Hon Keith Pitt MP, 14 June 2017 <https://www.mfat.govt.nz/assets/FTA-Publications/PACER-Plus/New-Zealand-Australia-Side-Letter-PACER-Plus.pdf>; Letter from the Hon Keith Pitt MP to the Hon Todd McClay, 14 June 2017 <https://www.mfat.govt.nz/assets/FTA-Publications/PACER-Plus/Australia-New-Zealand-Side-Letter-PACER-Plus.pdf>.

13   *Australia–New Zealand Closer Economic Relations Trade Agreement*, signed 28 March 1983, [1983] ATS 2 (entered into force 1 January 1983).

14   *Agreement Establishing the ASEAN–Australia–New Zealand Free Trade Area*, signed 27 February 2009, [2010] ATS 1 (entered into force 1 January 2010).

15   As the side letters predate the conclusion of the CPTPP, there is no reference to the CPTPP.

16   The ASEAN members are Brunei-Darussalam, Cambodia, Indonesia, Laos, Malaysia, Myanmar, the Philippines, Singapore, Thailand and Viet Nam.

17   These FTA parties are Australia, China, India, Japan, Korea and New Zealand.

18   Ministry of Foreign Affairs and Trade, *Regional Comprehensive Economic Partnership negotiating rounds* <https://www.mfat.govt.nz/en/trade/free-trade-agreements/agreements-under-negotiation/regional-comprehensive-economic-partnership-rcep/regional-comprehensive-economic-partnership-negotiating-rounds/>.

the first time since 2012, a Leaders' Summit took place in 2017, after which an outline of the RCEP was released.[19] The negotiations on the chapters however remain shrouded in mystery, although 2016 draft texts were leaked.[20]

In addition to RCEP, New Zealand and China are also negotiating bilaterally on an upgrade to their existing FTA that entered into force in 2008. Three negotiation rounds took place in 2017, with progress being reported on trade facilitation, technical barriers to trade, and competition policy.[21] No specific timeframe is set for the conclusion of these upgrade negotiations, although the goal is to achieve $30 billion of bilateral trade by 2020.[22]

Continuing the focus on the Pacific, but venturing outside of the Asia-Pacific region, was a call for public submissions and a first round of negotiations for an FTA with the Pacific Alliance, which comprises Columbia, Mexico, Chile and Peru,[23] with the goal of concluding an agreement in 2018.[24] While this is an ambitious timeframe, the negotiations aim to reduce tariffs on imports which is much more contained than other modern trade agreements.

In 2017, New Zealand also ventured outside of the Pacific in its trade negotiations when early forays were made for an FTA between the EU and New Zealand. New Zealand is one of only six WTO Members who do not have preferential access to European markets,[25] despite the EU being one of New Zealand's largest trading partners. Scoping discussions for this FTA were completed in March 2017[26] with discussions dealing with issues such as animal welfare, consumer protection, and energy policy. Agriculture and geographical

---

19   Association of Southeast Asian Nations, *Joint Leaders' Statement on the Negotiations for the Regional Comprehensive Economic Partnership (RCEP)* (November 2017) <http://asean.org/storage/2017/11/RCEP-Summit_Leaders-Joint-Statement-FINAL1.pdf>.

20   Bilaterals.org, *RCEP Leaks* <https://www.bilaterals.org/rcep-leaks>.

21   See Ministry of Foreign Affairs and Trade, *NZ-China FTA Upgrade* <https://www.mfat.govt.nz/en/trade/free-trade-agreements/agreements-under-negotiation/nz-china-fta-upgrade/>. See, for a Chinese news report, Zhang Hongpei, "China, New Zealand set to upgrade FTA", *Global Times* (online), 4 December 2017 <http://www.globaltimes.cn/content/1078666.shtml>.

22   Bill English, "China FTA upgrade talks to begin next month" (Press Release, 28 March 2017) <https://www.beehive.govt.nz/release/china-fta-upgrade-talks-begin-next-month>.

23   The latter three are also part of CPTPP.

24   Ministry of Foreign Affairs and Trade, *Pacific Alliance FTA* <https://www.mfat.govt.nz/en/trade/free-trade-agreements/agreements-under-negotiation/pacific-alliance-fta/>.

25   European Commission, *Countries and Regions – New Zealand* (16 April 2018) <http://ec.europa.eu/trade/policy/countries-and-regions/countries/new-zealand/>.

26   Ministry of Foreign Affairs and Trade, *Outline of ambition and scope of future negotiations* (May 2017) <https://www.mfat.govt.nz/assets/FTA-Publications/EU-FTA/EU-NZ-FTA-Scoping-Summary-and-Q-A-May-2017.pdf>.

indications are expected to be the most sensitive issues for the EU in these negotiations.

Formal negotiations did not yet start in 2017, but were awaiting the European Council's approval of the European Commission's proposal of September 2017,[27] which the European Parliament approved in October 2017.[28] The Council's approval was granted in the first half of 2018.[29] The Ministry of Foreign Affairs and Trade sets out a timeframe of two to three years for these negotiations,[30] although the European Commission has a more ambitious target of the end of 2019.[31]

Any agreement reached is said to only cover matters within the EU's exclusive competences. However, this is incompatible with statements that the FTA will include an ISDS mechanism, which was found not to be an area of exclusive competence in Opinion 2/15 of the European Court of Justice.[32] Restricting the agreement to the EU's exclusive competences means that the domestic legislatures of the EU member states, and relevant regional parliaments where competences have been devolved, will not need to ratify any FTA that results from these negotiations. This avoids issues such as when the Parliament of Belgium's Walloon Region refused to ratify the *Comprehensive Economic and Trade Agreement* (*"CETA"*) between the EU and Canada.[33]

---

27   European Commission, *Recommendation for a Council Decision authorising the opening of negotiations for a Free Trade Agreement with New Zealand,* COM (2017) 469 final (13 September 2017) <https://eur-lex.europa.eu/legal-content/EN/TXT/?uri=COM%3A2017%3A 469%3AFIN>.

28   European Parliament, *Resolution of 26 October 2017 containing Parliament's recommendation to the Council on the proposed negotiating mandate for trade negotiations with New Zealand,* 2017/2193(INI) (26 October 2017) <http://www.europarl.europa.eu/sides/getDoc .do?type=TA&language=EN&reference=P8-TA-2017-0420>.

29   European Council, *Negotiating directives for a Free Trade Agreement with New Zealand,* ST7661 2018 ADD 1 DCL 1 (25 June 2018) <https://data.consilium.europa.eu/doc/ document/ST-7661-2018-ADD-1-DCL-1/en/pdf>.

30   Ministry of Foreign Affairs and Trade, *New Zealand-European Union free trade agreement* <https://www.mfat.govt.nz/en/trade/free-trade-agreements/agreements-under-negotiation/eu-fta/>.

31   European Parliament, *International Agreements in Progress: EU-New Zealand free trade agreement – All set for the launch of negotiations,* European Parliament Think Thank (11 October 2017)<http://www.europarl.europa.eu/thinktank/en/document.html?reference= EPRS_BRI(2017)608755>.

32   *Opinion 2/15 of the Court* (Court of Justice of the European Union, 16 May 2017).

33   *Comprehensive and Economic Trade Agreement between Canada, of the one part, and the European Union and its Member States, of the other part,* signed 30 October 2016 (partially and provisionally entered into force 21 September 2017) [2017] OJ L 11/23. Belgium has requested the Court of Justice of the European Union for an Opinion on the compatibility of CETA with the European Treaties, in particularly in relation to the creation of an

3   World Trade

The WTO is undeniably the most important international organisation when it comes to the negotiation and enforcement of the rules-based international trading system. In 2017, New Zealand was involved in both aspects of the WTO's work.

3.1   *New Zealand and the WTO Negotiations*
The main 2017 event in the World Trade Organization was the 11th Ministerial Conference, which took place in Buenos Aires in December. The Ministerial Conference is the highest official body of the WTO that brings together ministerial representatives from all members.[34] Although no new substantive agreements were concluded, the Conference resulted in four formal decisions, two of which dealt with issues described by the Hon David Parker in his opening speech as important to New Zealand.[35]

A first decision relates to fisheries subsidies;[36] WTO Members decided on a work programme towards reaching an agreement by the next Ministerial Conference in 2019. This agreement would remove fisheries subsidies that lead to overfishing as well as subsidies that contribute to illegal, unreported and unregulated fishing. In addition, the Members agreed to improve transparency on fisheries subsidies by re-committing to the implementation of notification obligations under the *Subsidies and Countervailing Measures Agreement*.[37] Basing itself on the precedent of fisheries subsidies, New Zealand also launched an initiative to outlaw fossil fuel subsidies, which in 2015 amounted to USD 245 billion globally.[38] This initiative resulted in a Ministerial Statement, supported

---

Investment Court System, see Government of Belgium, *CETA Belgian Request for an Opinion from the European Court of Justice* (9 September 2017) <https://diplomatie.belgium.be/sites/default/files/downloads/ceta_summary.pdf>. For background on Wallonia's refusal, Jennifer Rankin "Belgian politicians drop opposition to EU-Canada trade deal", *The Guardian* (online), 27 October 2016 <https://www.theguardian.com/world/2016/oct/27/belgium-reaches-deal-with-wallonia-over-eu-canada-trade-agreement>.

34   *Marrakesh Agreement Establishing the World Trade Organization*, opened for signature 15 April 1994, 1867 UNTS 3 (entered into force 1 January 1995) art IV:1.

35   *Statement by Hon David Parker, Minister for Trade and Export Growth* (11 December 2017) World Trade Organization <https://www.wto.org/english/thewto_e/minist_e/mc11_e/webcasting_plenary_e.htm#nzl>.

36   *Fisheries Subsidies*, WTO Doc WT/MIN(17)/64 WT/L/1031 (18 December 2017) (Ministerial Decision of 13 December 2017) [1].

37   Ibid [2].

38   Ministry of Foreign Affairs and Trade, *Fossil Fuel Subsidies Reform* <https://www.mfat.govt.nz/en/environment/clean-energy-and-fossil-fuels/>

by 11 other WTO Members, to start discussions on the reform of fossil fuel subsidies.[39]

A second Ministerial Decision of interest to New Zealand relates to e-commerce. Again, the parties did not reach a substantive agreement but agreed not to impose duties on electronic transmissions until the next Ministerial Conference.[40] New Zealand also signed up to a statement proposing exploratory work for a WTO agreement on trade related aspects of electronic commerce.[41]

No progress was made in negotiations on disciplines on domestic services regulation, although New Zealand reaffirmed its commitment to such negotiations under Article VI: 4 of the *General Agreement on Trade in Services* (*"GATS"*).[42] New Zealand also joined a statement calling for "structured discussions with the aim of developing a multilateral framework on investment facilitation", which would aim to reduce administrative barriers to investment, but would exclude issues such as market access, investment protection, and ISDS.[43] As part of its efforts to gain public support for trade agreements,[44] New Zealand also supported the *Buenos Aires Declaration on Women and Trade*[45] which endorses initiatives to increase women's participation in trade.

Importantly, and of particular interest to New Zealand, no agreement was reached on agriculture, for which New Zealand and other members of the Cairns Group had called prior to the conference.[46]

2017 also marked the entry into force of the *Agreement on Trade Facilitation*,[47] a new multilateral trade agreement under the WTO umbrella, after it met the ratification threshold of two-thirds of WTO members. The Agreement had been

---

39   *Fossil Fuel Subsidies Reform*, WTO Doc WT/MIN(17)/54, (12 December 2017) (Ministerial Statement of 11 December 2017).

40   *Work Programme on Electronic Commerce*, WTO Doc WT/MIN(17)/65 WT/L/1032 (18 December 2017) (Ministerial Decision of 13 December 2017).

41   *Joint Statement on Electronic Commerce*, WTO Doc WT/MIN(17)/60 (13 December 2017).

42   *Marrakesh Agreement Establishing the World Trade Organization*, opened for signature 15 April 1994, 1867 UNTS 3 (entered into force 1 January 1995) Annex 1B; *Joint Ministerial Statement on Services Domestic Regulation*, WTO Doc WT/MIN(17)/61 (13 December 2017).

43   *Joint Ministerial Statement on Investment Facilitation For Development*, WTO Doc WT/MIN(17)/59 (13 December 2017).

44   As mentioned by the Hon David Parker in his speech, above n 35.

45   *Joint Declaration on Trade and Women's Economic Empowerment on the Occasion of the WTO Ministerial Conference in Buenos Aires in December 2017* World Trade Organisation <https://www.wto.org/english/thewto_e/minist_e/mc11_e/genderdeclarationmc11_e .pdf>

46   *The Cairns Group's Objectives for MC11 and Beyond*, WTO Doc JOB/AG/91 (19 May 2017) (Communication by the Cairns Group).

47   *Protocol Amending The Marrakesh Agreement Establishing the World Trade Organization*, WTO Doc WT/L/940 (28 November 2014) (Decision of 27 November 2014) Annex.

agreed to at the 2013 Bali Ministerial Conference, and New Zealand had ratified in 2015. With the entry into force on 22 February 2017, New Zealand exporters can now reap the benefits of the agreement's standardized and simplified customs procedures that aim to reduce the costs of importing and exporting, and to speed up the process.

In addition to the negotiations for multilateral agreements, a few negotiations at the WTO are for plurilateral agreements. The latter agreements do not involve all WTO members, although can become multilateralised when more members sign up. However, in 2017, both negotiations for plurilateral agreements that New Zealand is involved in reached a standstill.

A first proposed plurilateral agreement is for an *Environmental Goods Agreement*, which would reduce barriers to trade, such as tariffs and local content requirements, in "environmental goods", i.e. goods that contribute to environmental protection, such as solar panels and recycling machinery. However, negotiations came to a halt in 2016 when parties could not agree on a list of products that would benefit from the elimination of tariffs because of their environmental nature. No new initiatives were taken in 2017 to revive the negotiations.

A second plurilateral agreement under negotiation is the *Trade in Services Agreement ("TiSA")*. This agreement is intended to further liberalize trade in services between the 23 participating WTO members, by expanding on the *GATS*. Between 2013 and 2016, 21 negotiating rounds took place, but these have come to a halt with the incoming Trump administration. It is unclear whether the United States will continue with these negotiations or whether the other states will continue if the United States drops out.[48]

3.2   *New Zealand and WTO Disputes*

In 2017, New Zealand requested to join as a third-party in the United States' request for consultations with Canada about measures governing the sale of wine in grocery stores in British Columbia which are alleged to breach Article III: 4 of the *General Agreement on Tariffs and Trade ("GATT")*.[49]

---

48   *Answer given by Ms Malmström on behalf of the Commission* (10 November 2017) European Parliament <http://www.europarl.europa.eu/sides/getAllAnswers.do?reference=E-2017 -006013&language=EN>.

49   *Marrakesh Agreement Establishing the World Trade Organization*, opened for signature 15 April 1994, 1867 UNTS 3 (entered into force 1 January 1995) Annex 1A; *Canada – Measures Governing the Sale of Wine in Grocery Stores – Request to Join Consultations*, WTO Doc WT/DS520/2 (30 January 2017) (Communication from New Zealand). This request was accepted by Canada, *Canada – Measures Governing the Sale of Wine in Grocery*

New Zealand was also still involved in a number of ongoing cases, including one as the complainant. As discussed in last year's review, in late 2016 New Zealand was successful at the Panel level in its claims that Indonesian import restrictions on beef were inconsistent with WTO law. This was however not the end of this dispute. On 17 February 2017, Indonesia notified the WTO's Dispute Settlement Body ("DSB") of its decision to appeal. Workload issues[50] meant that the Appellate Body only released its report on 9 November 2017,[51] but it ultimately upheld the Panel's findings that Indonesia's measures were inconsistent with its WTO obligations.[52] On 22 November 2017, the DSB adopted the report, together with the Panel Report.[53] The report in another case involving Indonesia, and New Zealand as a third party, *Indonesia – Chicken Meat and Products*, was on the agenda for the same DSB meeting. In this case, the Panel found that Indonesia's import regime, which excluded certain chicken products, amounted to a legal ban of these products and was therefore inconsistent with Indonesia's obligations under Article XI *GATT*.[54] Other measures were found to be inconsistent with the national treatment obligation of Article III: 4 *GATT*. None of the inconsistent measures were found to be justified under Article XX *GATT*. In both cases, Indonesia signalled its intention to comply with the recommendations, but requested a reasonable period of time to do so. It then cited the WTO's Ministerial Conference and the WTO's year-end closure

---

Stores – Acceptance by Canada of the Requests to Join Consultations, WTO Doc WT/DS520/6 (14 February 2017).

50   One reason for the workload issues at the Appellate Body level is the ongoing impasse caused by the United States' refusal to support new appointments to the Appellate Body, which has increased the vacancies on the Appellate Body and concomitantly increased the workload for the remaining members. See Rosalind Mathieson, "U.S. Block of WTO Appeals Body Compromises System, Director Says", *Bloomberg* (online), 9 November 2017 <https://www.bloomberg.com/news/articles/2017-11-08/u-s-block-of-wto-appeals-body-compromises-system-azevedo-says>. Within the Dispute Settlement Body, New Zealand's has expressed its "grave concern" at the impasse, *Minutes of the Meeting Held in the Centre William Rappard on 31 August 2017,* WTO Doc WT/DSB/M/400 (31 October 2017) [5.16].

51   Rather than within the 90 days prescribed by Article 17:5 of the Dispute Settlement Understanding. *Indonesia – Importation of Horticultural Products, Animals and Animal Products,* WTO Doc WT/DS477/12; WT/DS478/12 (13 April 2017) (Communication from the Appellate Body).

52   Appellate Body Report, *Indonesia – Importation of Horticultural Products, Animals and Animal Products,* WTO Doc WT/DS477/AB/R; WT/DS478/AB/R, AB-2017-2 (9 November 2017).

53   *Indonesia – Importation of Horticultural Products, Animals and Animal Products – Appellate Body Reports and Panel Reports,* WTO Doc WT/DS477/15; WT/DS478/15 (22 November 2017) (Action by the Dispute Settlement Body).

54   Panel Report, *Indonesia – Measures Concerning the Importation of Chicken Meat and Chicken Products,* WTO Doc WT/DS484/R (17 October 2017).

as reasons why the parties may need more than the prescribed 45 days from the date of adoption of the report to mutually agree this reasonable period of time.[55] As a result, neither of the cases were concluded by the end of 2017.

Delays at the Panel and the Appellate Body affected other cases in which New Zealand was involved as a third-party. A first was *Korea – Radionuclides*. The case involved a challenge by Japan against Korea's import ban and additional testing and certification requirements for certain Japanese food products, following the Fukushima nuclear accident. During the 2016 third party hearings in this case, New Zealand had made oral statements as to whether the non-discrimination analysis should be less demanding for provisional measures under Article 5.7 *SPS Agreement*[56] and as to the transparency issues raised by this case. After multiple delays in 2017,[57] a panel report was finally circulated in early 2018[58] and subsequently appealed by Korea.[59]

A second case with significant delays is *Australia – Plain Packaging*. Although the Panel promised its report in the third quarter of 2017,[60] the report was not released until mid-2018 and will be covered in the next edition of this review. Nevertheless, in May 2017, Bloomberg reported, based on anonymous

---

55   *Indonesia – Importation of Horticultural Products, Animals and Animal Products*, WTO
      Doc WT/DS477/16; WT/DS478/16 (15 December 2017) (Communication from Indonesia concerning Article 21.3(B) of the DSU); *Indonesia – Measures Concerning the Importation of Chicken Meat and Chicken Products*, WTO Doc WT/DS484/13 (15 December
      2017) (Communication from Indonesia concerning Article 21.3(B) of the DSU). Indonesia and Brazil have set an expiration date for the reasonable period of time in their
      dispute, see *Indonesia – Measures Concerning the Importation of Chicken Meat and
      Chicken Products – Agreement under article 21.3(b) of the DSU*, WTO Doc WT/DS484/16
      (15 March 2018) (Communication from Brazil and Indonesia). No such agreement has
      yet been reached between Indonesia, New Zealand and its co-complainant the United
      States.

56   *Marrakesh Agreement Establishing the World Trade Organization*, opened for signature 15
      April 1994, 1867 UNTS 3 (entered into force 1 January 1995) Annex 1A.

57   *Korea – Import Bans, and Testing and Certification Requirements For Radionuclides*, WTO
      Doc WT/DS495/6 (29 May 2017) (Communication from the Panel); *Korea – Import Bans,
      and Testing and Certification Requirements For Radionuclides*, WTO Doc WT/DS495/7 (28
      September 2017) (Communication from the Panel).

58   Panel Report, *Korea – Import Bans, and Testing and Certification Requirements For Radionuclides*, WTO Doc WT/DS495/R (22 February 2018, unadopted).

59   *Korea – Import Bans, and Testing and Certification Requirements For Radionuclides*, WTO
      Doc WT/DS495/8 (9 April 2018) (Notification of Appeal by Korea). As this is a 2018 case,
      its discussion will be left to next year's review.

60   *Australia – Certain Measures Concerning Trademarks, Geographical Indications and Other
      Plain Packaging Requirements Applicable to Tobacco Products and Packaging*, WTO Doc
      WT/DS458/21, WT/DS467/22 (21 September 2017) (Communication from the Chairperson
      of the Panel).

sources, that the Panel had decided in favour of Australia.[61] At the same time, the New Zealand government publicly stated its confidence in an Australian win[62] and introduced its own plain packaging regime that has since entered into force on 14 March 2018.[63]

Also still on-going in 2017 was *US – Tuna II*, in which Mexico has challenged certain measures regarding eco-labelling of dolphin-safe tuna products. New Zealand made its first submissions in this case before the panel in 2010,[64] and had reserved its third-party rights in the second round of compliance proceedings, lodged by the United States and Mexico to consider whether the United States' 2016 measures complied with the *TBT Agreement*[65] and the *GATT 1994*.[66] A compliance panel report, affirming compliance, was circulated on 26 October 2017.[67] It has since been appealed by Mexico.[68]

4   Conclusion

In 2017, New Zealand continued to work on the elaboration of the rules-based trading system as well as to avail itself of the mechanisms in place to ensure compliance. Both aspects of the rules-based system – the rules and the

---

61   Bryce Baschuk, "Tobacco Logo Ban Said to Get WTO Backing in Landmark Case", *Bloomberg* (online), 4 May 2017 <https://www.bloomberg.com/news/articles/2017-05-04/wto-said-to-uphold-australia-s-ban-on-cigarette-logos>.

62   New Zealand Government, "NZ confident of plain packaging WTO case" (Release, 7 May 2017) <https://www.beehive.govt.nz/release/nz-confident-plain-packaging-wto-case>.

63   Smoke-free Environments Act 1990 s 31A, as introduced by the Smoke-free Environments (Tobacco Standardised Packaging) Amendment Act 2016 and further elaborated by the Smoke-free Environments Regulations 2017. These regulations entered into force on 14 March 2018, subject to transition provisions that expired on 6 June 2018.

64   Ministry of Foreign Affairs and Trade, *Current WTO Disputes* <https://www.mfat.govt.nz/en/trade/trade-law-and-dispute-settlement/current-disputes/>.

65   *Marrakesh Agreement Establishing the World Trade Organization*, opened for signature 15 April 1994, 1867 UNTS 3 (entered into force 1 January 1995) Annex 1A.

66   New Zealand had not reserved its rights in relation to arbitration proceedings under Article 22:6 DSU to determine the appropriate level of remedies Mexico was entitled to. Therefore, this has not been included in this overview.

67   Panel Reports, *United States – Measures Concerning the Importation, Marketing and Sale of Tuna and Tuna Products – Recourse to Article 21.5 of the DSU by the United States – Second Recourse to Article 21.5 of the DSU by Mexico*, WTO Doc WT/DS381/RW/USA, WT/DS381/RW2 (26 October 2017, unadopted).

68   *United States – Measures Concerning the Importation, Marketing and Sale of Tuna and Tuna Products – Recourse to Article 21.5 of the DSU by the United States – Second Recourse to Article 21.5 of the DSU by Mexico*, WTO Doc WT/DS381/45 (1 December 2017) (Notification of Appeal by Mexico).

compliance mechanisms – are considered important for export-oriented, but small, economies such as New Zealand.

The ongoing negotiations can be seen as a reaction to the pressures that the rules-based system is under, particularly those coming from the Trump administration in the United States. However, we also see an awareness of the issues that have most raised populist ire, such as regulatory autonomy issues and – related to this – the powers of private investors to challenge public measures under ISDS mechanisms.

There is a significant overlap between the parties involved in the different negotiations, and these overlaps may need to be handled carefully and undoubtedly will increase the complexity of international trade law, as traders and states will have to assess carefully the scope of their rights and obligations under the different treaties.

International Environmental Law

*Josephine Toop**

1 Introduction

In October, Aotearoa New Zealand had a change in government. For the last nine years, New Zealand has had a National Party (economically centre-right, somewhat socially conservative) led government. New Zealand now has a Labour Party (centre-left and socially liberal) led government formed by a coalition agreement with the New Zealand First Party (centre-left, socially conservative, and some might say populist and nationalist), along with a confidence and supply agreement with the Green Party of Aotearoa (further left than Labour, more socially liberal, and with an environmental focus). Since this report covers all of 2017, it will include events occurring under the old government (January to October 2017) as well as the new (October to December 2017). Implications for New Zealand's environmental position flow from the change in government. For instance, there has been a shift in the approach to climate change. The current Prime Minister, the Rt Hon Jacinda Ardern, has described climate change as her "generation's nuclear free moment"[1] and has indicated that she intends "to take a lead role on climate change".[2] New Zealand now plans to erase its carbon footprint by 2050, in contrast to the previous government's 50 per cent reduction by 2050 goal. Members of the environmentally focused Green Party also hold ministerial positions for the first time, one under-secretary and three ministers outside cabinet.

New Zealand submitted reports to the *United Nations Framework Convention on Climate Change* ("*UNFCCC*")[3] in 2017; outlined its revised approach to climate change at the 23rd conference of the parties ("COP-23"); took action on fossil fuel subsidy reform at the World Trade Organisation ("WTO"); agreed to cooperate more closely with China on climate change; and committed to establishing a "New Zealand – Africa Geothermal Facility". Other

---

* University of Canterbury.
1 Claire Trevett, "Jacinda Ardern's rallying cry: Climate change the nuclear-free moment of her generation" *New Zealand Herald* (online), 20 August 2017 <https://www.nzherald.co.nz/nz/news/article.cfm?c_id=1&objectid=11907789>.
2 Anna Bracewell-Worrall, "Jacinda Ardern: It's my responsibility to lead on climate change" *Newshub* (10 November 2017) <https://www.newshub.co.nz/home/politics/2017/11/jacinda-ardern-it-s-my-responsibility-to-lead-on-climate-change.html>.
3 Opened for signature 9 May 1992, 1771 UNTS 107 (entered into force 21 March 1994).

developments included the *Comprehensive and Progressive Trans-Pacific Partnership* ("*CPTPP*"),[4] the successor to the controversial *Transpacific Partnership Agreement* ("*TPP*"),[5] which continued to raise environmental concerns. New Zealand attended the 48th Pacific Islands Forum, signed the *Treaty on the Prohibition of Nuclear Weapons*,[6] and was once again told by the Committee of the International Whaling Commission ("IWC SC") that its protection measures for the critically endangered Māui dolphin fell short.

National developments included a court case against the outgoing government over its emission reduction goals and a report from the Parliamentary Commissioner for the Environment ("PCE") which considered the United Kingdom's approach to climate change and recommended New Zealand do something similar. The new government outlined its intentions regarding a Zero Carbon Act and an independent Climate Commission. There was also some legislation relating to supporting emerging energy innovation and electric vehicles. The New Zealand Emissions Trading Scheme ("NZETS") review concluded in 2017 and in-principle proposals for NZETS reform were announced. In addition, reports were released on ways to transition to a low-emissions economy and on ways to adapt to climate change. The OECD reviewed New Zealand's environmental performance, and New Zealand released national reports on fresh water as well as atmosphere and climate. 2017 also saw a report from the PCE on the desperate state of New Zealand's native birds.

There were also 2017 developments connected to fisheries, the marine environment and Antarctica. These are not addressed here because they are covered in the reviews of Joanna Mossop "Law of the Sea and Fisheries" and Alan Hemmings "The Antarctic Treaty System" (this issue).[7] Additional reference to

---

4   Will be opened for signature in 2018 (not yet in force).

5   Signed by all parties 4 February 2016 (will not come into force).

6   Opened for signature 20 September 2017 (not yet in force).

7   Omitted developments include New Zealand's accession to the *1995 International Convention on Standards of Training, Certification and Watchkeeping for Fishing Vessel Personnel* (see Joanna Mossop, "Law of the Sea and Fisheries" (2017) 15 *New Zealand Yearbook of International Law* (this volume)); New Zealand's participation in the Preparatory Committee for a new treaty to protect marine biodiversity, and in negotiations for United Nations General Assembly resolutions on oceans and fishing (see Mossop, cited above); New Zealand assistance patrolling the Fijian EEZ (see Mossop, cited above); New Zealand joining calls for Japan to end its whaling in the Southern Ocean and to respect International Whaling Commission processes (see Mossop, cited above); New Zealand's participation and tabling papers at the 40th Antarctic Treaty Consultative Meeting (see Alan Hemmings, "The Antarctic Treaty System" (2017) 15 *New Zealand Yearbook of International Law* (this volume)); participation and tabling papers at the 36th Meeting of the Commission for the Conservation of Antarctic Marine Living Resources (see Hemmings, cited above); and Resolution 5 (2017) on "Establishment of the Ross Sea Region Marine Protected Area" (New Zealand was joint proponent, along with

those reviews is suggested for a fuller account of New Zealand's international environmental law activities in 2017.

2   International Developments

2.1   *Biodiversity and Conservation*
Māui dolphin (*Cephalorhynchus hectori Māui*) are an IUCN red list critically endangered subspecies of Hector's dolphin. They are the smallest and rarest marine dolphin in the world, found only on the west coast of the North Island of New Zealand. The June IWC SC's report expressed continued grave concern over the status of this small, severely depleted subspecies.[8] The IWC SC once again noted that no new management action regarding the Māui dolphin had been enacted in New Zealand since 2013, and concluded, as it has repeatedly in the past, that existing management measures in relation to bycatch mitigation fall short of what is needed.[9] The SC reiterated its previous recommendation that "highest priority should be assigned to immediate management actions to eliminate bycatch of Māui dolphins including closures of any fisheries within the range of Māui dolphins that are known to pose a risk of bycatch to dolphins (i.e. set net and trawl fisheries)" and "respectfully urges the New Zealand Government to commit to specific population increase targets and timelines for Māui dolphin conservation".[10] Less than 30 per cent of Māui habitat is protected from set nets and only eight per cent is protected from both set net and trawl threats.[11] Investigation of longlines as a potential alternative to reduce risk found favour with the IWC SC.[12]

2.2   *Climate Change*
In May, New Zealand submitted *New Zealand's Greenhouse Gas Inventory 1990–2015* to the *UNFCCC*. This is the official annual report of all anthropogenic

---

the United States, of this marine protected area) (see Hemmings, cited above); as well as the enactment of the *Maritime Crimes Amendment Act 2017* to implement the *2005 Protocol to the 1988 Convention for the Suppression of Unlawful Acts against the Safety of Maritime Navigation*, with the notable inclusion in this domestic legislation of an "avoidance of doubt" provision that peaceful protest at sea activity is not criminalised (see Mossop, cited above).

8   International Whaling Commission, *Report of the Scientific Committee of the IWC*, IWC/67/ Rep01(2017) rev1 (May 2017) 95.

9   Ibid.

10   Ibid 96.

11   Ibid 68.

12   Ibid.

(human-induced) emissions and removals of greenhouse gases ("GHG") in New Zealand. The Inventory shows total (gross) emissions; i.e. emissions from the energy, industrial processes and product use, agriculture and waste sectors, but not including net removals from land use, land-use change and forestry ("LULUCF"). It also shows net emissions, i.e. gross emissions together with emissions and removals from the LULUCF sector. New Zealand's gross GHG emissions in 2015 were 80.2 million tonnes of carbon dioxide equivalent (Mt CO_2-e), meaning that New Zealand's gross emissions have increased by 24.1 per cent since 1990. The two largest contributors to New Zealand's gross emissions in 2015 were agriculture (47.9 per cent) and energy (40.5 per cent). New Zealand's net emissions under the UNFCCC were 56.4 Mt CO_2-e in 2015, meaning net emissions have increased by 63.6 per cent since 1990. The *Inventory* attributes this large increase in net emissions to the increase in gross emissions and the higher harvesting rates in planted forests in 2015 compared with 1990.[13]

In December, New Zealand submitted its Seventh National Communication and its Third Biennial Report to the UNFCCC. The Communication provides a snapshot of New Zealand's progress in implementing its commitments. It includes a section on climate change impacts on New Zealand and vulnerability and adaptation work (Chapter 6), which also serves as New Zealand's first adaptation communication under the *Paris Agreement*.[14] The Communication includes a summary of GHG emissions and removals drawn from the *Inventory* mentioned above. Based on current data and policies, New Zealand's gross emissions by 2020 are projected to be 79.9 Mt CO_2-e (23.8 per cent above 1990 levels or 0.3 per cent below 2015 levels), and net emissions are expected to rise to 64.3 Mt CO_2-e (86.5 per cent above 1990 levels or 13.9 per cent above 2015 levels). By 2030, gross emissions are projected to be 77.2 Mt CO_2-e (19.6 per cent above 1990 or 3.7 per cent below 2015 levels), and net emissions are expected to rise to 73.2 Mt CO_2-e in 2030 (112.5 per cent above 1990 levels or 29.7 per cent above 2015 levels). The impact of New Zealand's policies and measures are estimated to reduce gross emissions by 41.8 Mt CO_2-e from 2016–30

---

13   Ministry for the Environment, *New Zealand's Greenhouse Gas Inventory 1990–2015* (May 2017, ME 1309) <http://www.mfe.govt.nz/publications/climate-change/new-zealands-greenhouse-gas-inventory-1990%E2%80%932015>. See also Ministry for the Environment, *Snapshot: New Zealand's Greenhouse Gas Inventory 1990–2015* (May 2017, INFO 798) <http://www.mfe.govt.nz/publications/climate-change/new-zealands-greenhouse-gas-inventory-1990%E2%80%932015-snapshot>.

14   *Paris Agreement*, opened for signature 22 April 2016, Dec. 1/CP.21, Annex, UN Doc FCCC/CP/2015/10/Add.1 (entered into force 4 November 2016).

and reduce total net emissions by 113.2 Mt CO_2-e from 2016–30.[15] The Biennial Report includes estimates of emissions and removals and information on how the government plans to meet its various targets. It projects New Zealand will meet its 2020 target of reducing GHG emissions to 5 per cent below 1990 levels ('5 by 20') with surplus of 97.7 million units.[16]

In November, New Zealand participated in COP-23 to the *UNFCCC*, MOP-13 to the *Kyoto Protocol*,[17] and the first session, second part, of the COP serving as the MOP to the *Paris Agreement* ("CMA-1.2") in Bonn, Germany. New Zealand welcomed Fiji's leadership of the meeting; the first time a small island developing state has presided over the COP.[18] The New Zealand Climate Change Minister, very recently in the role given the change in government, gave the New Zealand address and told the conference that New Zealand intends to become a leader in the global fight against climate change.[19] The Minister outlined New Zealand's new goals of becoming a net zero emission economy by 2050; achieving 100 per cent renewable electricity by 2035 (currently around 80 per cent); planting one billion trees over the next 10 years; joining with high ambition countries to lead the worldwide fight against climate change; and transitioning to an electric government car fleet by 2025.[20] At the meeting, New Zealand endorsed the *Bonn Communique of the Climate and Clean Air Coalition on Tackling Air Pollution to Save Lives and Protect the Environment*[21] and joined an

---

15   Ministry for the Environment, *New Zealand's Seventh National Communication – Fulfilling reporting requirements under the United Nations Framework Convention on Climate Change and the Kyoto Protocol* (December 2017), 24–5 and 116 <http://unfccc.int/files/national_reports/annex_i_natcom_/application/pdf/091345_new_zealand-nc7-1-21-12-17_web_final_-_seventh_national_communication_2017.pdf>.

16   Ministry for the Environment, *New Zealand's Third Biennial Report Under the United Nations Framework Convention on Climate Change* (December 2017), 43 <http://unfccc.int/files/national_reports/biennial_reports_and_iar/submitted_biennial_reports/application/pdf/148395_new_zealand-br3-1-new_zealand_third_biennial_report.pdf>.

17   *Kyoto Protocol to the United Nations Framework Convention on Climate Change*, opened for signature 16 March 1998, 2303 UNTS 162 (entered into force 16 February 2005).

18   Aupito William Sio and James Shaw, "Ministers welcome Pacific focus at climate meeting" (Press Release, 9 November 2017) <https://www.beehive.govt.nz/release/ministers-welcome-pacific-focus-climate-meeting>.

19   James Shaw, "NZ to become a leader in the fight against climate change" (Press Release, 17 November 2017) <https://www.beehive.govt.nz/release/nz-become-leader-fight-against-climate-change>.

20   James Shaw, "National Statement from New Zealand to 23rd Conference of the Parties to the UNFCCC" (Press Release, 17 November 2017) <https://www.beehive.govt.nz/speech/national-statement-new-zealand-23rd-conference-parties-unfccc>.

21   James Shaw, "NZ endorses international plan to reduce agricultural and waste emissions" (Press Release, 15 November 2017) <https://www.beehive.govt.nz/release/nz-endorses-international-plan-reduce-agricultural-and-waste-emissions>.

international "Powering Past Coal" alliance which is committed to phasing out the use of coal for electricity generation.[22] In addition, New Zealand formally brought Tokelau (a dependent territory) into the UNFCCC. Going forward, New Zealand will need to include information regarding Tokelau in its reporting under the UNFCCC and in any reporting required under the *Paris Agreement*. Whether New Zealand's Nationally Determined Contribution ("NDC") will include Tokelau is yet to be decided.[23] More details about the climate conference can be found on the UNFCCC website.[24]

In December, New Zealand attended the "One Planet" summit in Paris, France. It was held to mark the two-year anniversary of the *Paris Agreement* and was jointly hosted by the French President, the United Nations Secretary General and the President of the World Bank. The theme was climate change financing and the aim was to mobilise funding to advance projects that fight climate change, including clean transport, renewable energies, and sustainable cities.[25] At the summit, New Zealand became a founding member of a newly formed "Towards Carbon Neutrality Coalition".[26] The New Zealand Superannuation Fund also joined other international investors at the summit.[27]

In December, New Zealand co-hosted an event with Finland to deliver a Ministerial statement on Fossil Fuel Subsidy Reform at the 11th Ministerial Conference of the WTO. Endorsed by more than a dozen other WTO Members, the Ministerial statement seeks the phaseout of inefficient fossil fuel subsidies that encourage wasteful consumption, encourages the international community to join in these efforts, and seeks to advance discussion in the WTO, including through reporting, to enable the evaluation of the trade and resource effects of fossil fuel subsidies programmes.[28] New Zealand takes the view that

---

22   Shaw, above n 19.

23   James Shaw, "Global climate change agreement extended to Tokelau" (Press Release, 14 November 2017) <https://www.beehive.govt.nz/release/global-climate-change-agreement -extended-tokelau>.

24   See <http://unfccc.int>.

25   Alice Cuddy, "5 things you need to know about the 'One Planet' summit" *Euronews* (online), 12 December 2017 <http://www.euronews.com/2017/12/12/5-things-you-need-to-know-about-the-one-planet-summit>.

26   James Shaw, "Clear message on clean energy at OnePlanet Summit" (Press Release, 13 December 2017) <https://www.beehive.govt.nz/release/clear-message-clean-energy-oneplanet-summit>.

27   Ibid.

28   *Fossil Fuel Subsidies Ministerial Statement on behalf of Chile; Costa Rica; Iceland; Liechtenstein; Mexico; The Republic of Moldova; New Zealand; Norway; Samoa; Switzerland; The Separate Customs Territory of Taiwan, Penghu, Kinmen and Matsu; and Uruguay* (19 December 2017) Ministry of Foreign Affairs and Trade <https://www.mfat.govt.nz/en/media-and-resources/ministry-statements-and-speeches/wto-11th-ministerial-conference/>.

each year governments are spending at least $425 billion subsidising the pro-
duction and sale of coal, oil, gas and other GHG emitting fuels, and this money
could be better spent pursuing other development goals or investing in the
renewable energy sector.[29]

New Zealand also agreed to cooperate more closely with China on climate
change. 2017 saw a climate change action plan to give practical effect to the
broad approach set out in the *New Zealand-China Climate Change Cooperation Arrangement* signed by the two countries in 2014. The action plan enables
Chinese and New Zealand experts to share technical information and expertise on agricultural GHG mitigation, carbon markets and emission trading
schemes.[30] New Zealand also began joint discussions on developing carbon
markets in the region with Korea in 2017.[31]

Finally, New Zealand signed a Partnership Agreement with the African
Union Commission to establish a "New Zealand – Africa Geothermal Facility".
The Facility, managed by the New Zealand Development Programme, aims to
expand access to affordable, reliable and clean energy. About $10 million will
be provided over the next five years to enhance geothermal development in 11
East African countries, and New Zealand will also share expertise and targeted
technical help.[32]

2.3 *The Pacific*

New Zealand attended the 48th Pacific Islands Forum in September in Apia,
Samoa. The theme was "The Blue Pacific – Our Sea of Islands – Our Security
through Sustainable Development, Management and Conservation". Leaders recognised the Blue Pacific as a new narrative calling for inspired leadership and a long-term Forum foreign policy commitment to act as one Blue

---

See also David Parker, "WTO Ministerial Conference Concludes" (Press Release, 14 December 2017) <https://www.beehive.govt.nz/release/wto-ministerial-conference-concludes>.

29   David Parker, "Minister calls on WTO to support fossil fuel subsidy reform" (Press Release,
     12 December 2017) <https://www.beehive.govt.nz/release/minister-calls-wto-support
     -fossil-fuel-subsidy-reform>.

30   *Implementing Arrangement on Strengthening Cooperation on Climate Change between
     the Ministry of Foreign Affairs and Trade of New Zealand and the National Development
     and Reform Commission of the People's Republic of China* (27 March 2017) Ministry of For-
     eign Affairs and Trade <https://www.mfat.govt.nz/assets/Environment/Climate-change/
     NRA-2017-04-Climate-Change.pdf>. See also Paula Bennett, "Climate action plan
     with China" (Press Release, 28 March 2017) <https://www.beehive.govt.nz/release/
     climate-action-plan-china>.

31   Paula Bennett, "Korea and New Zealand discuss carbon markets" (Press Release, 14 April 2017)
     <https://www.beehive.govt.nz/release/korea-and-new-zealand-discuss-carbon-markets>.

32   Gerry Brownlee, "NZ sharing energy expertise around the globe" (Press Release, 26 July
     2017) <https://www.beehive.govt.nz/release/nz-sharing-energy-expertise-around-globe>.

Continent. Leaders also, inter alia, reaffirmed their commitment to the effective implementation of the *Paris Agreement* and supported calls for continued advocacy in multilateral institutions like the World Bank to ensure that definitions of fragility take into account the specific vulnerabilities faced by Forum Island Countries.[33] The Forum Chair has called for close collaboration with the United Nations to drive the Blue Pacific.[34]

2.4   *Nuclear Treaty*

In September, New Zealand signed the *Treaty on the Prohibition of Nuclear Weapons*. New Zealand has already enacted a national ban on nuclear weapons. This treaty provides the first legal prohibition on nuclear weapons at a global level. Among other things, the treaty highlights the catastrophic consequences of nuclear weapons and grave implications for human survival and the environment and requires environmental remediation of contaminated areas.[35] The New Zealand foreign minister has, however, acknowledged that since none of the states which currently possess nuclear weapons took part in the negotiations, the treaty may realistically not have a large impact in the short term.[36]

2.5   *Free Trade Agreements*

As previously reported, New Zealand signed the large, multi-country regional trade agreement, the TPP, in 2016. Whilst proponents argued that the agreement would benefit New Zealand's environment,[37] others suggested that the environment was a significant casualty under the TPP.[38] Threats to the environment have been tied to investor-state dispute settlement provisions ("ISDS"), since many ISDS cases in the past have challenged environmental and public health legislation. There are also concerns about the chilling effect caused by investors being able to sue governments for enacting legislation to protect the

---

33   *Forum Communiqué*, PIFS(17)10 (September 2017), [6], [20], [21] <https://www.forumsec
      .org/wp-content/uploads/2018/02/Final_48-PIF-Communique_2017_14Sep17.pdf>.

34   *Pacific Islands Forum Chair highlights priorities for the Blue Pacific at the United Nations* (21
      September 2017) Pacific Islands Forum Secretariat <https://www.forumsec.org/pacific-
      islands-forum-chair-highlights-priorities-for-the-blue-pacific-at-the-united-nations/>.

35   Opened for signature 20 September 2017, Preamble and Article 6.

36   Gerry Brownlee, "NZ welcomes success of nuclear treaty talks" (Press Release, 9 July 2017)
      <https://www.beehive.govt.nz/release/nz-welcomes-success-nuclear-treaty-talks>.

37   Nick Smith and Todd McClay, "TPP good for environment and trade" (Press Release, 6
      April 2016) <https://www.beehive.govt.nz/release/tpp-good-environment-and-trade>.

38   Simon Terry, *Expert Paper #4: The Environment under TPPA Governance* (January 2016),
      5–6 <https://tpplegal.files.wordpress.com/2015/12/tpp-environment.pdf>.

environment (meaning governments are put off from doing so).[39] See the 2015 and 2016 reports for more information.[40]

In early 2017, the United States withdrew from the *TPP*. New Zealand subsequently continued to meet with the other members of the *TPP*: Australia, Brunei Darussalam, Canada, Chile, Japan, Malaysia, Mexico, New Zealand, Peru, Singapore, and Vietnam. In November, the core elements of the new agreement, the *Comprehensive and Progressive Trans-Pacific Partnership ("CPTPP")*, were agreed. The text, with similarities to the *TPP*, is set to be finalised and signed in 2018. A small number of provisions (22 out of more than a thousand) from the original *TPP* will be suspended under the *CPTPP*. The New Zealand Ministry of Foreign Affairs and Trade has summarised the differences between the two agreements online.[41] Among other things, there are suspensions in the investment chapter reducing the scope of the ISDS mechanism. Critics remain concerned that suspended provisions can be revived by consensus;[42] that ISDS is still permitted in some contexts[43] including for public regulatory measures;[44] that ISDS is an outmoded mechanism, rejected by the European Union; and that ISDS "is undergoing a crisis in legitimacy due to concerns about structural biases in favour of investors."[45]

3   National Developments

3.1   *Trade*

As noted above, the new iteration of the controversial *TPP*, the *CPTPP*, was negotiated in 2017 amongst the original *TPP* countries minus the United States, with the expectation of finalisation and signature in 2018. Labour's coalition

---

39   Ibid 4, 11–4.

40   Josephine Toop, "International Environmental Law" (2015) 13 *New Zealand Yearbook of International Law* 250–66, 255–7; Josephine Toop, "International Environmental Law" (2016) 14 *New Zealand Yearbook of International Law* 264–81, 272.

41   *CPTPP vs TPP* Ministry of Foreign Affairs and Trade <https://www.mfat.govt.nz/en/trade/free-trade-agreements/free-trade-agreements-concluded-but-not-in-force/cptpp/tpp-and-cptpp-the-differences-explained/>.

42   Oliver Hailes et al., "Editorial: Climate change, human health and the CPTPP" 131 *The New Zealand Medical Journal* 1471 (9 March 2018) 7–12, 8.

43   Barry Coates, "Gains under TPP not worth risks to democracy" *NZ Herald* (online), 15 February 2018 <https://www.nzherald.co.nz/nz/news/article.cfm?c_id=1&objectid=11994205>.

44   Hailes et al., above n 42, 9.

45   Ibid, citing George III Kahale, "Is Investor-State Arbitration Broken?" *Transnational Dispute Management* (2012) 7.

partner New Zealand First has indicated its support is not guaranteed,[46] and its confidence and supply partner the Green Party says it will not support this "outdated form of trade agreement".[47] The Green Party does not consider the reductions in the scope of ISDS sufficient; it does not want ISDS (which it calls "a particular threat to environmental protections")[48] in the agreement at all since that affects the ability of current or future Governments to act on progressive agenda.[49] They voice continued concerns about "transparency issues" and consider that the risk to democracy, the environment, and human rights protections still outweigh the benefits of the agreement.[50] The Labour party will therefore likely have to rely on the opposition (National Party), under whose governance the original *TPP* was negotiated, to pass legislation for it. The *Trans-Pacific Partnership Agreement Amendment Act 2016* (NZ) (which made changes in 2016 to New Zealand legislation to be consistent with the *TPP*) will need amendment to reflect the move to *CPTPP*.

The International Transparent Treaties Bill (255–1) was introduced in 2017 by New Zealand First (prior to being in government) in response to "secret trade deals" like the *TPP* and its successor *CPTPP*. The bill proposes that all international treaties should be approved by Parliament prior to the treaty being signed, since:

> Currently, Parliament or Select Committees do not have the right to examine and review the terms of international treaties before or during negotiation. There is need for a higher level of transparency when recent events show a disproportionately small and non-representative group of individuals negotiate and sign secret trade deals on the country's behalf.[51]

This New Zealand First bill was also supported by Labour (not then governing) and the Green Party (not then in confidence and supply) and was narrowly defeated at the first reading 57 to 62. Although the focus of this latest failed bill

---

46   Anna Bracewell-Worrall, "NZ First support for TPP not guaranteed" *Newshub* (online), 13 November 2017 <https://www.newshub.co.nz/home/politics/2017/11/nz-first-support-for-tpp-not-guaranteed.html>.

47   Stacy Kirk, "Greens won't support new TPP legislation as changes 'don't go far enough'" *Stuff* (online), 13 November 2017 <https://www.stuff.co.nz/national/politics/98830660/greens-wont-support-new-tpp-legislation-as-changes-dont-go-far-enough>.

48   *CPTPP deal threatens to side-line environmental quality* (15 November 2017) Resource Management Law Association <https://www.rmla.org.nz/2017/11/15/cptpp-deal-threatens-to-side-line-environmental-quality/>.

49   Kirk, above n 47.

50   Ibid.

51   International Transparent Treaties Bill (255-1) 2017, Explanatory Note.

is on transparency and examination, it is somewhat reminiscent of another
New Zealand First bill also triggered by *TPP*, the Fighting Foreign Corporate
Control Bill (14–1) 2015, which tried to enact a prohibition against entering into
international agreements that include ISDS. That bill was narrowly defeated
60 for to 61 against. Those who were for the bill at the time included Labour,
the Green Party, and New Zealand First (not then governing). Time will tell
whether there will be any renewed attempts at bills of this nature now that the
political parties previously in support may have the numbers to enact them, or
whether they no longer wish to place such constraints upon themselves now
that they are in power. It will be interesting to see whether there will be continued political will to constrain trade negotiations and agreements in these
kinds of ways, or not, especially given the Labour Party's apparent willingness
to accept limited ISDS in the *CPTPP*.

3.2   *Biodiversity and Conservation*

As mentioned, in June, the New Zealand government came under scrutiny
once again by the IWC SC regarding the critically endangered Māui dolphin.
The IWC SC noted, as repeatedly in the past, that existing management measures by New Zealand in relation to bycatch mitigation fall short of what is
required to protect these dolphins.[52] Fishing is not the only threat to these dolphin; marine tourism, construction, coastal pollution, vessels, oil spills, plastic
bags, sedimentation, marine farming, climate change, and the effects of marine mining, drilling, and construction, including seismic surveys, are all other
threats.[53] Oil and Gas Block Offer 2017 brought new potential hazards to the
Māui dolphin range, since the Offer included a large offshore area in Taranaki
(Māui habitat is thought to include large areas of the Taranaki coastline). The
Green Party has said that the 2017 Block Offer equates to 35 per cent of the dolphins' habitat being opened up to exploration, which is a "reckless move" given
only 63 Māui dolphins remain and "[w]e know that the seismic surveys, the oil
rigs, the risk of oil spills could be catastrophic for the species".[54]

  The schedules that list endangered, threatened, and exploited species in the
Trade in Endangered Species Act 1989 (NZ) were also updated in 2017 to align
the schedules with changes made to the *Convention on International Trade in*

---

52   IWC/67/Rep01(2017)rev1, above n 8, 95.

53   Department of Conservation, "Threats caused by people" <https://www.doc.govt
      .nz/nature/native-animals/marine-mammals/dolphins/maui-dolphin/threats/threats
      -caused-by-people/>.

54   Anna Bracewell-Worrall, "Oil drilling in Maui dolphin habitat threatens species – Green
      Party" *Newshub* (online), 23 March 2017 <https://www.newshub.co.nz/home/new-zea-
      land/2017/03/oil-drilling-in-maui-dolphin-habitat-threatens-species-green-party.html>.

Endangered Species of Wild Fauna and Flora ("CITES").[55] Some changes relating to threatened species of sharks came into force in April and some changes took effect in October.[56]

As previously reported, New Zealand aims to make the country predator-free by 2050 to preserve native species threatened with extinction by predators. The goal is to completely eradicate invasive rats, stoats and possums. In 2017, the PCE released a report looking at the desperate state of New Zealand's native birds. The report notes that four out of every five native birds are in trouble. Many are teetering on the brink of extinction. Millions of feral cats are major killers of wading birds like the wrybill – the only bird in the world with a beak that curves to the side. Other problems include ensuring genetic diversity among small bird populations. The PCE recommends investing a great deal more money in conservation, further research, focusing on a way to tackle feral cats, preventing bird populations getting so low that they resort to inbreeding, early engagement with the public, habitat protection and restoration, increased support for, and coordination of, conservation community groups, and developing a plan for Predator Free 2050 since "all the disparate efforts currently underway will not just magically come together".[57]

Plastic microbeads were a hot issue in New Zealand in 2017, with widespread public approval for a ban "to prevent plastic microbeads, which are non-biodegradable, entering our marine environment" where they can "harm both marine life and life higher on the food chain including humans".[58] New Zealand now joins the list of countries who have banned, or who plan to ban, microbeads with the adoption of 2017 regulations, which will come into effect in June 2018, prohibiting the manufacture and sale of wash-off products (other than medical devices or medicines) that contain plastic microbeads for the purposes of exfoliation, cleaning, abrasive cleaning or visual appearance of the product.[59]

The Crown Minerals (Protection of World Heritage Sites) Amendment Bill (252–1) was put forward in 2017 by a member of the Labour Party (while in opposition). The Explanatory Note to the bill notes that currently UNESCO world

---

55   Opened for signature 3 March 1973, 993 UNTS 243 (entered into force 1 July 1975).
56   Trade in Endangered Species Order 2017, Explanatory Note.
57   Jan Wright, PCE, *Taonga of an Island Mation: Saving New Zealand's birds* (May 2017) Parliamentary Commissioner for the Environment, "Overview" 5–8, quote at 6 <http://www.pce.parliament.nz/media/1695/taonga-of-an-island-nation-web-final-small.pdf>.
58   *Plastic microbeads ban* (7 June 2018) Ministry for the Environment <http://www.mfe.govt.nz/waste/plastic-microbeads>. On the public support point: 16 223 submissions supported or partially supported the ban, with no submissions opposed to the ban.
59   Waste Minimisation (Microbeads) Regulations 2017, Explanatory Note.

heritage sites have no formal legal protection within New Zealand. This became an issue in early 2012 after it was discovered that surveying for minerals in world heritage sites was occurring. The bill proposed adding world heritage sites to Schedule 4 of the *Crown Minerals Act 1991* (NZ), to provide those sites with protection from mining. It also proposed expanding the limited number of New Zealand world heritage sites to include several other special areas. The bill was defeated on June 7 at the first reading (Labour and Green Party for, other parties against).

The (previous) government set a target in 2017 to make 90 per cent of New Zealand's rivers and lakes swimmable by 2040.[60] Changes were made to the *National Policy Statement for Freshwater Management* to support this goal. However, the move came under fire, as containing very confusing standards (even to scientists),[61] with particular criticism of the definition used for "swimmable" being different to what an ordinary person would consider swimmable.[62] Some critics argued that thresholds were in fact being lowered, i.e. the changes now meant more pollution was permitted (though the (then) government argued otherwise).[63]

The *Wildlife (Powers) Amendment Act 2017* (NZ) increased the ability of the New Zealand's Department of Conservation ("DOC") to prevent and prosecute crimes against vulnerable native species such as geckoes and skinks. The enforcement powers had not been updated for 60 years and so they were strengthened and modernised to assist with protecting native wildlife from poaching and smuggling. Four new powers were granted to DOC rangers: the ability to take action to prevent an offence in progress or about to occur; the power to temporarily stop persons suspected of an offence to allow an investigation; the ability to seize a broader range of evidence such as mobile phones, laptops, and cameras; and the power to require suspected offenders to provide their date of birth and proof of identification. DOC's small highly experienced

---

60   Nick Smith, "90% of rivers and lakes swimmable by 2040" (Press Release, 24 February 2017) <https://www.beehive.govt.nz/release/90-rivers-and-lakes-swimmable-2040>.

61   Kate Gudsell, "Swimmable waterways standard 'confusing' – scientist" *Radio New Zealand* (online), 24 April 2017 <https://www.radionz.co.nz/news/national/329349/swimmable-waterways-standard-'confusing'-scientist>.

62   Charlie Mitchell, "The thorny politics of 'swimmable', a word losing its meaning" *Stuff* (online), 24 February 2017 <https://www.stuff.co.nz/environment/89750791/the-thorny-politics-of-swimmable-a-word-losing-its-meaning>.

63   See Kate Gudsell, "Water quality measure 'less stringent'" *Radio New Zealand* (online), 24 February 2017 <https://www.radionz.co.nz/news/national/325214/water-quality-measure-'less-stringent'>. See also Nick Smith, "Claims of lowered water standards wrong" (Press Release, 24 February 2017) <https://www.beehive.govt.nz/release/claims-lowered-water-standards-wrong>.

team of specialist enforcement officers also gained the power to arrest for serious offending (illegal hunting, killing, or export) against absolutely protected wildlife. Fish and Game rangers also got an extension of their powers, as did officers from Crown agencies who work with DOC on joint operations (Police, Fisheries, Customs, and the Defence Force).[64]

3.3   *Climate Change*

3.3.1   New Government's Direction

Labour's government forming agreements with the Green Party and New Zealand First both supported introducing a Zero Carbon Act and an independent Climate Commission.[65] In late 2017, the new government announced that it will start public consultation next year on the framework for a zero emissions economy by 2050, with the aim to pass a Zero Carbon Act by mid-2019. The government also announced that it will establish an independent Climate Change Commission, and an interim Climate Change Committee to do the groundwork while the Commission is being set up.[66] The New Zealand First coalition agreement stated that the Zero Carbon Act and the independent Climate Commission should be based on the recommendations of the PCE (some recommendations had been released earlier in the year). If the PCE recommendations are anything to go by (see 3.3.5.1 below), we may see five-year carbon budgets, and a Commission whose purpose will be to provide independent, expert advice and to hold successive governments to account for progress.[67]

3.3.2   Climate Change Case Law

In mid-2017, a judicial review case of emission reduction goals (a first for New Zealand),[68] was bought against the then Climate Change Minister Paula

---

64   The Wildlife (Powers) Amendment Bill (99-1) 2017, Explanatory Note. See also Maggie Barry, "Wildlife Powers Amendment Bill becomes law" (Press Release, 9 February 2017) <https://www.beehive.govt.nz/release/wildlife-powers-amendment-bill-becomes-law>.

65   *Confidence & Supply Agreement: New Zealand Labour Party & Green Party of Aotearoa New Zealand* (24 October 2017, 52nd Parliament) 3 <https://www.parliament.nz/media/4487/ nzlp__gp_c_s_agreement.pdf>; *Coalition Agreement: New Zealand Labour Party & New Zealand First* (24 October 2017, 52nd Parliament) 5 <https://www.parliament.nz/media/4 486/36242978olabourandnewzealandfirstcoalitionagreement.pdf>.

66   Derek Cheng, "Prime Minister announces formulation of Zero Carbon Act, climate change commission" *NZ Herald* (18 December 2017) <https://www.nzherald.co.nz/nz/ news/article.cfm?c_id=1&objectid=11961862>.

67   Jan Wright, PCE, *Stepping Stones to Paris and Beyond: Climate Change, Progress, and Predictability* (July 2017) Parliamentary Commissioner for the Environment, Ch. 6 <https:// www.pce.parliament.nz/media/1724/stepping-stones-web-oct-2017.pdf>.

68   Ged Cann, "First-of-its-kind case as student takes Government to court over climate change" *Stuff* (online), 23 June 2017 <https://www.stuff.co.nz/environment/climate-news/94015415/ firstofitskind-case-as-student-takes-government-to-court-over-climate-change>.

Bennett (old government) by Thomson (a law student).[69] Thomson alleged the government's response to climate change was inadequate. It is an interesting case, with some arguments from both sides finding favour. The first of the government's climate change targets at issue was that of reducing emissions by 50 per cent by 2050 ('50 by 50'). Thomson argued this target, set under domestic legislation, should have been reviewed after the Intergovernmental Panel on Climate Change published its 2014 scientific assessment. The court agreed, saying the 2050 target should have been reviewed in light of the new 2014 evidence.[70] But since the matter had been overtaken by events, the recent general election and formation of a Labour-led coalition government with its intention to set a new 2050 target of carbon neutrality ('0 by 50'), the court felt it was unnecessary to make any order or to consider the matter further.[71]

The second cause of action related to an international target: New Zealand's NDC of a 30 per cent reduction in GHG by 2030 (compared with 2005 levels) ('30 by 30') (equating to 11 per cent below 1990 levels by 2030). Thomson enjoyed less success here on some fronts, but was pleased with the justiciability finding.[72] As to the latter, the court rejected the government's arguments that international obligations like the Paris 2030 NDC target were a political matter and could not be subject to judicial review, and that the matter was also not reviewable because it involved balancing of many factors best undertaken by elected officials.[73] The court considered case law from other jurisdictions, most of which succeeded to some extent, and which, although different from the present case, helped to "illustrate that it may be appropriate for domestic courts to play a role in Government decision making about climate change policy".[74] Indeed, '[t]he courts have recognised the significance of the issue for the planet and its inhabitants and that those within the court's jurisdiction are necessarily amongst all who are affected by inadequate efforts to respond to climate change.'[75] The court concluded that "[t]he importance of the matter for all and each of us warrants some scrutiny of the public power [by Courts] in addition to accountability through Parliament and the General

---

69   *Thomson v Minister for Climate Change Issues* [2017] NZHC 733.

70   Ibid [94], [178].

71   Ibid [97]–[98], [178].

72   Sarah Thomson, "I took the climate change minister to court and won – kind of. Now I'm looking at you, James Shaw" *The Spinoff* (online), 4 November 2017 <https://thespinoff .co.nz/society/04-11-2017/i-took-the-climate-change-minister-to-court-and-won-kind-of-now-im-looking-at-you-james-shaw/>.

73   *Thomson* [2017] NZHC 733, the Government's arguments are at [102].

74   Ibid [133]. See also [105]–[134].

75   Ibid [133].

Elections",[76] although there are constitutional limits in how far that role may extend.[77] Less successful were Thomson's arguments that when making INDC and NDC decisions the New Zealand government was required to incorporate in its economic modelling the costs to New Zealand of dealing with dangerous climate change,[78] and that the Minister failed to consider (in the step between communicating the INDC and confirming the NDC) the scientific consensus that the Parties' combined INDCs fell short of the extent and speed of reductions needed to stabilise GHG to levels that would prevent dangerous anthropogenic interference with the climate.[79] Thomson also argued that the government failed to properly consider low-lying Tokelau (a New Zealand territory) which is highly exposed to rising seas, consideration of which should have led the Minister to pursue efforts to limit the temperature increase to 1.5°C. While the Court agreed that the impact on Tokelauans is a mandatory relevant consideration for New Zealand in its approach to climate change,[80] and found no evidence that the impact on Tokelauans was factored into what New Zealand's INDC and NDC should be,[81] it was not persuaded this meant New Zealand's NDC needed to be consistent with a 1.5°C target.[82] Thomson may yet see the 2030 target revisited since the new Climate Change Minister has said that the 2030 target looks inconsistent with the 2050 goal of carbon neutrality and is likely to be reviewed in 2018.[83]

3.3.3 New Zealand Emissions Trading Scheme and Its Review

By way of brief background, the NZETS was originally introduced by the previous Labour Party-led government in 2008 and was significantly amended in 2009 and 2012 by the subsequent National Party-led government to slow its implementation and make it more business-friendly. For instance, a transitional "two for one" surrender obligation was introduced which allowed some businesses to pay only one emissions unit for every two tonnes of emissions. This

---

76 Ibid [134].
77 Ibid [133].
78 Ibid: since "neither the Convention nor the Paris Agreement stipulate any specific criteria or process for how a country is to set its INDC and NDC" [139]. See also [137]–[141].
79 Rejected for similar reasons to that mentioned at above n 78. See [158]–[160].
80 Ibid [156].
81 Ibid [149].
82 Ibid [157].
83 James Shaw, "Government considering experimental climate change visa" *Stuff* (online), 1 November 2017 <https://www.stuff.co.nz/national/politics/98429364/Government-considering-experimental-climate-change-visa>. See also James Shaw, "High Court decision on climate change response welcomed" (Press Release, 3 November 2017) <https://www.beehive.govt.nz/release/high-court-decision-climate-change-response-welcomed>.

transitional measure was extended by three years beyond what was initially envisaged. Agriculture was excluded from the NZETS, despite contributing roughly half of New Zealand's emissions. In November 2015, the government began a review of the NZETS focusing on what would come next for the transitional measures, and how the NZETS needs to evolve to meet future targets, as well as operational and technical improvements.

Stage one of the NZETS review ended in May 2016 and the one-for-two surrender obligation/subsidy was subsequently removed (phased out over three years). The initial 50 per cent unit cost increased to 67 per cent from January 2017, and from January 2018 it will rise to 83 per cent. From January 2019 a full surrender obligation will be in place for all sectors in the NZETS, meaning all participants will surrender one unit for every tonne of CO_2-e emissions.

Stage two of the NZETS review focused on broader issues relating to the design and operation of the NZETS into the 2020s. Following completion of stage two, a package of proposed changes to the NZETS was announced in June 2017. Cabinet made an in-principle decision to implement four proposals and asked officials to work on how they will be developed and implemented in the NZETS over the next few years. The proposals are to introduce auctioning of units to align the NZETS to climate change targets, limit participants' use of international units when the NZETS reopens to international carbon markets, develop a different price ceiling to eventually replace the current \$25 fixed price option, and to coordinate decisions on the supply settings in the NZETS over a rolling five-year period. Further consultation and engagement will help determine how to implement these proposals.[84] As these in-principle decisions were taken by the old government, it remains to be seen what impact the change in government will have on the proposed NZETS changes.

The previous government decided not include agriculture in the NZETS review,[85] meaning that the agricultural sector continues to remain outside the NZETS for now. However, under the 2017 Coalition Agreement between Labour and New Zealand First, the decision to include agriculture in the NZETS was agreed to be determined by an independent Climate Change Commission.[86] The current Climate Change Minister has also suggested that the interim

---

84   Paula Bennett, "New tools to help meet climate change targets" (Press Release, 26 July 2017)   <https://www.beehive.govt.nz/release/new-tools-help-meet-climate-change-targets>. Also, for more information on the proposals see *Outcomes from stage two of the NZ ETS Review 2015/16* (12 April 2018) Ministry for the Environment <http://www.mfe.govt.nz/node/23440>.

85   Tim Groser, "Government begins review of ETS" (Press Release, 24 November 2015) <https://www.beehive.govt.nz/release/government-begins-review-ets>.

86   Coalition agreement, above n 65, 5.

climate change committee could start by looking at agriculture.[87] So it is possible that agriculture may yet come to be included in the NZETS.

Various minor 2017 amendments to the NZETS included prescribing requirements for collecting information about, and calculating, removals of GHG owing to the export of natural gasoline or polyol containing hydrofluorocarbons;[88] prescribing allocative baselines;[89] clarifying definitions, adding global warming potential figures, and updating the emissions factor for natural gas;[90] specifying the price of carbon for 2018, prescribing the rates of levy for leviable motor vehicles and goods for the 2018 levy year, and expanding the list of leviable goods;[91] allowing applicants for unique emissions factors for geothermal liquid use to take measurements using venturi flow meters, vortex flow meters, or orifice plates, and requiring applicants for unique emissions factors relating to landfill gas to model emissions from all areas that contribute landfill gas to a disposal facility's destruction equipment irrespective of whether the area is part of that disposal facility.[92]

3.3.4   Renewable Energy

2017 also saw the *Energy Innovation (Electric Vehicles and Other Matters) Amendment Act* (NZ) to encourage emerging energy technologies and innovation such as electric vehicles. The Act encourages the uptake of electric vehicles by extending the road user charge exemptions and makes it possible for electric vehicles to access bus and high-occupancy vehicle lanes. It also clarifies electricity industry legislation and expands the purposes for which the existing electricity efficiency levy, and other levies, can be used.[93]

New Zealand Energy Efficiency and Conservation Strategy 2017–2022 was released in mid-2017 as a companion to the *New Zealand Energy Strategy*

---

87   James Shaw, "First Important Step towards the Zero Carbon Act" (Press Release, 18 December 2017) <https://www.beehive.govt.nz/release/first-important-step-towards-zero-carbon-act>.

88   *Climate Change (Other Removal Activities) Amendment Regulations 2017*, Explanatory Note.

89   *Climate Change (Eligible Industrial Activities) Amendment Regulations 2017*, Explanatory Note.

90   *Climate Change (Stationary Energy and Industrial Processes) Amendment Regulations 2017*, Explanatory Note.

91   *Climate Change (Synthetic Greenhouse Gas Levies) Amendment Regulations 2017*, Explanatory Note.

92   *Climate Change (Unique Emissions Factors) Amendment Regulations 2017*, Explanatory Note.

93   Energy Innovation (Electric Vehicles and Other Matters) Amendment Bill (196-2), Commentary.

2011–2021. The new Strategy sets the overarching direction for Government between 2017–2022, as well as setting out some specific actions for the promotion of energy efficiency and renewable sources of energy. The strategy focuses on three priority areas. The first is efficient and renewable process heat with a target of decreasing industrial emissions intensity by at least 1 per cent per year on average between 2017 and 2022. The second is efficient and low emissions transport, with the goal that the vehicle fleet is at least two per cent electric vehicles by the end of 2021. The third priority is innovative and efficient use of electricity with a target of 90 per cent of electricity generated from renewable sources by 2025.[94] The new government may perhaps be inclined towards something more ambitious, since the Green Party has indicated that promoting electric vehicles is a priority area.[95]

The International Energy Agency ("IEA") also reviewed New Zealand's energy policies in 2017. Member countries have their energy policies reviewed every five years. The report notes that New Zealand ranks second after Norway among IEA member countries for renewable electricity, but that "New Zealand has yet to adopt additional policies required for the investment in decarbonising the economy up to 2030 and beyond, towards 2050. Current energy efficiency targets and carbon price policies are not sufficient".[96]

3.3.5   Climate-Related Reports
3.3.5.1   *Stepping Stones to Paris*
In July, the PCE published *Stepping Stones to Paris and Beyond: Climate Change, Progress, and Predictability*. This report examines the United Kingdom approach to climate change and considers whether New Zealand should do something similar. The PCE notes that, between 1990 and 2015, New Zealand's net emissions have risen by 64 per cent, whereas the United Kingdom's net emissions have fallen by 38 per cent. This disparity may not be entirely attributable to legislative and policy differences; for instance, New Zealand has had considerably faster population growth and has a different emissions profile

---

94   *Unlocking our Energy Productivity and Renewable Potential: New Zealand Energy Efficiency and Conservation Strategy 2017–2022* (June 2017) Ministry of Business, Innovation & Employment, 7 <https://www.mbie.govt.nz/assets/346278aab2/nzeecs-2017-2022.pdf>.

95   "James Shaw: Greens will push electric cars, help farmers to become sustainable" *One News Now* (online), 22 October 2017 <https://www.tvnz.co.nz/one-news/new-zealand/james-shaw-greens-push-electric-cars-help-farmers-become-sustainable>.

96   *Energy Policies of IEA Countries: New Zealand 2017 Review* (2017) International Energy Agency, 15 <https://www.iea.org/publications/freepublications/publication/EnergyPoliciesofIEACountriesNewZealand2017.pdf>.

with a high percentage of emissions from agriculture. Nevertheless, the United Kingdom's GHG curve has bent downward, whereas New Zealand's has not. In the United Kingdom, emissions targets have been enshrined in legislation that sets up a process for reaching them, including through carbon budgets which comprise stepping stones to targets. The Act requires the United Kingdom government to develop proposals and policies that will keep emissions within carbon budgets and help the country move towards its targets. For instance, in 2015, it was announced that all United Kingdom coal-fired power stations are to be closed by 2025, which was a significant move given that about 25 per cent of the electricity in the United Kingdom at that time was generated by burning coal. The United Kingdom also has an independent expert body to provide objective analysis and advice, expert evidence and transparency. The approach is designed to endure through changing governments. In contrast to the United Kingdom, New Zealand has not yet set any carbon budgets, nor does it have any other kind of plan for reaching its emissions targets. The PCE considers that, despite differences in the way the two governments operate, key features of the United Kingdom system could be incorporated into New Zealand legislation (these would be sitting above the NZETS rather than replacing it). She suggests that a Climate Change Commission should be established as an independent Crown entity, with Board members appointed for their relevant expertise and knowledge, and not because they represent certain sectors of the economy. The process should begin with the Commission recommending a carbon budget, with supporting information publicly available. The government should then adopt a carbon budget, explaining why if the adopted budget differed from the Commission's recommendation. The government should then have to develop policies to keep emissions within the budget. Every year, the Commission should report on progress towards meeting both the carbon budgets and the overall targets, and indicate areas where policies need to be developed or strengthened. After each annual report, the government should have to respond to the points raised. Both the reports and responses should be tabled in Parliament, freely available and unredacted.[97]

3.3.5.2 *PCE Submission to the Productivity Commission Inquiry*

The PCE also made a submission to the Productivity Commission in 2017. The Commission is conducting an inquiry on how New Zealand can reduce its GHG emissions through a transition to a low-emissions economy, while at the same time continuing to grow income and wellbeing. The PCE notes that '[d]espite having made a series of international commitments, New Zealand is currently

---

97   PCE, *Stepping Stones to Paris*, above n 67, see especially 4, 20, 24, 26 and 27.

on track to overshoot its Paris target by about 20 million tonnes of carbon dioxide'.[98] She states that while tightening of the NZETS may help, the NZETS by itself will not be enough. The PCE goes on to make the case for New Zealand to enact legislation along the lines of the United Kingdom's *Climate Change Act*. The PCE also covers scope for generating even more low-carbon electricity, highlights major opportunities presented by forestry, and suggests changing the mandate of the Energy Efficiency and Conservation Authority ("EECA") to align with the goal of a low emissions economy. The EECA is the government agency that works to improve the energy efficiency of New Zealand's homes and businesses, and to encourage the uptake of renewable energy. The PCE submits that the EECA mandate should now be changed to that of working to reduce carbon dioxide emissions.[99]

3.3.5.3   *Adapting to Climate Change in New Zealand*

The Climate Change Adaptation Technical Working Group's stocktake report, *Adapting to Climate Change in New Zealand*, was published in December. The report summarizes the expected impacts on New Zealand of climate change over the medium and long term, takes stock of existing adaptation work, and identifies the gaps in knowledge and work programmes. The report discusses various climate-related changes New Zealand can expect, including more hot days, warmer oceans, unprecedented ocean acidification, loss of glaciers, increased drought, sea level rise (most of New Zealand's major urban centres and the majority of the population lives on the coast or floodplains of major rivers); impacts on society and culture; and significant economic impacts, for example, the agricultural, fisheries, forestry and tourism sectors are all dependent on climate-sensitive natural resources. The report notes that there are gaps in our knowledge, including the potential costs to the economy over the medium and long term if no action is taken to adapt. After providing a stocktake of what New Zealand sectors are doing to adapt to climate change, the report notes gaps in the current response, for instance, there is a lack of an overarching strategy or plan for how New Zealand can adapt to climate change, a lack of a coordinating mechanism across and within sectors on climate change adaptation, a lack of enabling tools to help facilitate adaptation, resource scarcity, including lack of expertise and funding across all sectors, and a lack of role clarity within and across sectors. It finds there is limited evidence of proactive

---

98   Jan Wright, PCE, *Low-emissions economy: Issues Paper: Submission to the Productivity Commission* (2 October 2017) Parliamentary Commissioner for the Environment, 3 <https://www.pce.parliament.nz/media/1720/low-emissions-economy-submission-web.pdf>.

99   Ibid 3 and 9.

actions that reduce medium and long-term risks. The report concludes that New Zealand is in the early stages of planning for climate change impacts but currently lacks a coordinated plan on how to adapt to climate change.[100] The Working Group is now drawing on this report to make recommendations for how New Zealand can effectively adapt to the impacts of climate change. This new report is due in March 2018.

3.4 *Environmental Reporting*

In March, an OECD environmental performance review on New Zealand was released. The report notes that while New Zealander's enjoy a very good environmental quality of life, with low air pollution and easy access to nature, New Zealand's growth model has started to show its environmental limits, with increased GHG emissions, freshwater contamination, and threats to biodiversity. Addressing GHG emissions from agriculture, particularly dairy farming, should be a priority if New Zealand wants to meet its 2030 emissions target. The management of diffuse nutrient pollution from pastoral agriculture remains a significant environmental challenge. The report notes that New Zealand has one of the world's highest rates of endemic flora and fauna species. Unfortunately, it also has one of the world's highest shares of threatened species with about a quarter of native mammals, a third of birds, a third of fish, a third of reptiles, and 60 per cent of native amphibians threatened (some sources pointing to even higher risks of extinction). The report contains several recommendations on climate change, including developing a strategic plan for the achievement of the 2030 target and developing vulnerability assessments for all major economic sectors to inform adaptation strategies. For biodiversity, it recommends, inter alia, improving the information base on the state of biodiversity, especially on private lands, and identifying conservation priorities. For waste, it recommends extending the waste disposal levy and improving collection of data on generation disposal and treatment of waste. For air, it recommends strengthening monitoring and reporting of air quality data. The report also contains recommendations on environmental governance and management, green growth, water resources management, and sustainable urban development.[101]

---

100   Climate Change Adaptation Technical Working Group, *Adapting to Climate Change in New Zealand: Stocktake Report from the Climate Change Adaptation Technical Working Group* (December 2017) Ministry for the Environment, 15–6, 94 <http://www.mfe.govt.nz/sites/default/files/media/Climate%20Change/adapting-to-climate-change-stocktake-tag-report.pdf>.

101   OECD, *OECD Environmental Performance Reviews: New Zealand 2017* (OECD Publishing, 2017), 3, 75, 84, 112, 147, 194, 242.

The *Environmental Reporting Act 2015* (NZ) which came into effect in 2016 required a report on one of five environmental domains every six months (air, fresh water, land, marine and climate) and a synthesis report of cross-domain trends and interactions every three years. 2016 brought the first individual domain report on the marine environment. In 2017, the reports on fresh water as well as atmosphere and climate were published. The fresh water report noted, among other things, that 90 per cent of wetlands have been drained since people arrived in New Zealand; that urban rivers are the most polluted; that nitrogen levels, generally from farming runoff, and related to risk of algal bloom, are worsening at more river sites, with a 29 per cent nitrogen leaching increase (though phosphorus levels are improving at some river sites); and that many of our native freshwater fish, invertebrates, and plants are threatened with, or at risk of, extinction.[102] The report on atmosphere and climate noted, inter alia, that since 1990 there has been a 24 per cent rise in New Zealand's gross GHG emissions and a 64 per cent increase in our net GHG emissions; New Zealand has the fifth highest level of emissions per person of the 35 countries in the OECD; 25 per cent of the volume of New Zealand ice glaciers has been lost since 1977; there has been a 14 to 22cm sea-level rise at four main New Zealand ports since 1916; deforestation is outpacing the area of new forest planted; there has been a 0.03 pH decrease of New Zealand's oceans in the last 19 years; and New Zealand has experienced a 1°C temperature increase since 1909.[103] The next national report, which deals with land, is due to be released in 2018.

---

102   Ministry for the Environment and Stats NZ, *New Zealand's Environmental Reporting Series: Our Fresh Water 2017* (April 2017, ME 1305), Executive Summary 8–17 <http://www.mfe .govt.nz/sites/default/files/media/Environmental%20reporting/our-fresh-water-2017_1. pdf>. See also Ministry for the Environment and Stats NZ, *New Zealand's Fresh Water at a Glance* (April 2017, INFO 792) <https://www.mfe.govt.nz/sites/default/files/media/Environmental%20reporting/our-fresh-water-at-a-glance_0.pdf>.

103   Ministry for the Environment and Stats NZ, *New Zealand's Environmental Reporting Series: Our Atmosphere and Climate 2017* (October 2017, ME 1332), 6–8, 17 <https://www.mfe .govt.nz/sites/default/files/media/Environmental%20reporting/our-atmosphere-and-climate-2017.pdf>. See also Ministry for the Environment and Stats NZ, *New Zealand's Atmosphere and Climate at a Glance* (October 2017, INFO 812) <https://www.mfe.govt. nz/sites/default/files/media/Environmental%20reporting/our-atmosphere-and-climate-2017-at-a-glance-poster.pdf>.

Law of the Sea and Fisheries

*Joanna Mossop**

1   Introduction

New Zealand was very active in multilateral initiatives related to the oceans in 2017. In addition to its participation in the Preparatory Committee for a new treaty to protect marine biodiversity (discussed below), it participated in the negotiations for United Nations General Assembly resolutions on oceans and fishing. New Zealand was also represented at the Fourth "Our Ocean" Conference in Malta and the first UN Ocean Conference in New York.[1] Legislation was passed to implement the *2005 Protocol to the 1988 Convention for the Suppression of Unlawful Acts against the Safety of Maritime Navigation* ("*2005 SUA Protocol*"),[2] ten years after New Zealand initially signed the Protocol.

2   Marine Environment

2.1   *Marine Biodiversity beyond National Jurisdiction*

States have been working towards the negotiations for a new treaty on the conservation and sustainable use of biodiversity beyond national jurisdiction during Preparatory Conferences held in 2016 and 2017. In December 2017 New Zealand co-chaired (with Mexico) negotiations that resulted in General Assembly Resolution 69/292.[3] This Resolution authorised the development of an international legally binding instrument under the *United Nations Convention on the Law of the Sea* ("*UNCLOS*").[4] The new instrument is expected to address a "package" of issues including the legal regime for marine genetic resources, area-based management, environmental impact assessment and

---

*   Victoria University, Wellington.

1   See Maggie Barry, "New Zealand's Ocean Conference Commitments" (Press Release, 11 June 2017) <https://www.beehive.govt.nz/release/new-zealands-ocean-conference-commitments>.

2   *Protocol of 2005 to the 1988 Convention for the Suppression of Unlawful Acts against the Safety of Maritime Navigation*, IMO Doc LEG/CONF.15/21 (entered into force 28 July 2010).

3   *International legally binding instrument under the United Nations Convention on the Law of the Sea on the conservation and sustainable use of marine biological diversity of areas beyond national jurisdiction*, GA Res 72/249, UN Doc A/RES/72/249 (24 December 2017).

4   *United Nations Convention on the Law of the Sea*, UNTS 1833 (entered into force 16 November 1994).

capacity-building and the transfer of marine technology. The first meetings of the Intergovernmental Conference will be in 2018.

2.2   Marine Protected Areas

Two developments reported in 2016, the proposed Kermadec Ocean Sanctuary and the revision of the Marine Reserves Act 1971, made no substantial progress in 2017. However, Nick Smith, the former Minister for Conservation, introduced a Members bill, the Kermadec/Rangitāhua Ocean Sanctuary Bill. Members bills are drawn by ballot, and so discussion of this bill in Parliament is not guaranteed.

3   Fisheries

The UN General Assembly adopted its annual sustainable fisheries resolution which focused on the incorporation of the UN Ocean Conference Call for Action outcome document, the forthcoming informal consultation of States Parties to the *Fish Stocks Agreement* and the negotiation of trade-related issues.[5] New Zealand was active in seeking the inclusion of text referencing the 11th Ministerial Conference at the World Trade Organisation ("WTO") in the context of ongoing work to eliminate harmful fisheries subsidies as well as protecting existing language referencing the WTO.[6] New Zealand also put forward a proposal related to the inclusion of relevant Sustainable Development Goal targets in the resolution in the context of encouraging states to maintain their commitment in reporting on their implementation of the Code of Conduct.

3.1   Maritime Surveillance Cooperation

New Zealand regularly uses New Zealand Defence Force vessels and aircraft for surveillance outside New Zealand's exclusive economic zone ("EEZ"). In May, a Royal New Zealand Navy inshore patrol vessel was deployed to Fiji for six months to assist in patrolling the Fijian EEZ.[7]

---

5   *Sustainable Fisheries, including through the 1995 Agreement for the Implementation of the Provisions of the United Nations Convention on the Law of the Sea of 10 December 1982 relating to the Conservation and Management of Straddling Fish Stocks and Highly Migratory Fish Stocks, and related instruments*, GA Res 72/72, UN Doc A/RES/72/72 (5 December 2017).

6   See also David Parker, "WTO Ministerial Conference Concludes" (Press Release, 14 December 2017) <https://www.beehive.govt.nz/release/wto-ministerial-conference-concludes>.

7   Gerry Brownlee, "Fiji and NZ to partner on maritime surveillance press release" (Press Release, 6 April 2017) <https://www.beehive.govt.nz/release/fiji-and-nz-partner-maritime-surveillance>.

4   Maritime Security

A significant development in 2017 was the enactment of the *Maritime Crimes Amendment Act 2017*. This Act implements the *2005 SUA Protocol*. The Protocol was negotiated under the auspices of the International Maritime Organisation to supplement the *1988 Convention for the Suppression of Unlawful Acts against the Safety of Maritime Navigation* ("*SUA Convention*").[8] The *SUA Convention* created a framework for the suppression of unlawful acts that were not covered by piracy, with a specific reference to hijackings (prompted by the hijacking of the *Achille Lauro* in 1985). The Convention created a range of offences and established an obligation on states in whose territory an offender is found to either prosecute or extradite to a country with jurisdiction over the offence. The *2005 SUA Protocol* expands the categories of criminal offences to include using a ship for terrorist purposes or transporting biological, chemical or nuclear weapons and other material that is destined for terrorist purposes. It also establishes a ship boarding process. States are required to obtain permission from the flag state before boarding on the high seas any vessel on which a person suspected of one of the crimes is located. However, states may choose to deposit notification with the Secretary-General that it gives permission for other states to board suspect vessels flying its flag, either after four hours has passed with no reply from the flag state, or immediately.

The 1988 *SUA Convention* was implemented into New Zealand law by the *Maritime Crimes Act 1999*. The 2017 amendments modified the Act to give effect to the 2005 Protocol. One interesting point to note is the addition of Section 3B, which does not reflect the content of the international instruments. Section 3B reads:

3B Protest and Other Activity

To avoid doubt, the fact that a person engages in any protest, advocacy, or dissent, or engages in any strike, lockout, or other industrial action, is not, by itself, a sufficient basis for inferring that the person–

(a) is carrying out an act for a purpose, or with an intention, specified in any offence in this Act; or

(b) intends to cause an outcome specified in any offence in this Act.

---

8   *Convention for the Suppression of Unlawful Acts against the Safety of Maritime Navigation*, 1678 UNTS 201 (entered into force 1 March 1992).

This section of the Act was added at the suggestion of the Foreign Affairs, Defence and Trade Selection Committee. New Zealand has a history of protests at sea, including protests against the visits of nuclear powered ships in the 1980s. More recently, a skipper of a vessel was prosecuted under the *Maritime Transport Act* for navigating his vessel into the path of a seismic survey vessel undertaking a survey.[9] This was part of a protest against deep sea oil exploration. The Tribunal in the *Arctic Sunrise* arbitration noted that protest at sea is an internationally lawful act exercised in conjunction with the freedom of navigation.[10] The intention of the new section is to indicate that the Act is not intended to criminalise peaceful protest activity. The Select Committee considered that the original bill would not have done so, but characterised Section 3B as an "avoidance of doubt" provision.[11]

It remains to be seen how the section will be interpreted by the courts. If a protester against oil exploration undertook an activity notionally prohibited by the Act, such as causing damage to the survey vessel that might endanger navigation, it seems that Section 3B would prevent prosecution under the *Maritime Crimes Act*. However, such activities would still be able to be prosecuted under other criminal and administrative Acts. This seems appropriate given the *1988 SUA Convention* and *2005 SUA Protocol* were aimed at responding to serious acts of terrorism and the highest level of criminal activity.

It is also worth noting that, in the *Maritime Crimes Act 1999*, New Zealand has not asserted all possible grounds for jurisdiction over alleged offenders permitted by the *SUA Convention*. Article 6(1) of the *SUA Convention* requires state parties to establish jurisdiction over offences where it is committed on a ship flying the state's flag, in the territory of the state or by a national of the state. These grounds for jurisdiction are reflected in Section 8 of the *Maritime Crimes Act*. The *SUA Convention* also provides three further possible grounds for a state to establish jurisdiction: when the offence is committed by a stateless person whose habitual residence is in that state; when a national of the state is killed; or when the offence is done in an attempt to compel the state to do or abstain from any act. Section 8 only asserts jurisdiction in the first of these.

---

9   See Joanna Mossop, "Law of the Sea and Fisheries" (2012) 10 New Zealand Yearbook of International Law 232, 235; (2013) 11 New Zealand Yearbook of International Law 262, 267; (2014) 12 New Zealand Yearbook of International Law 227, 233.

10   *Arctic Sunrise (Netherlands v Russia) (Merits)* (2016) 55 ILM 5, [227].

11   Foreign Affairs, Defence and Trade Committee, *Maritime Crimes Amendment Bill* (7 December 2016) New Zealand Parliament <www.parliament.nz/en/pb/sc/reports/document/51DBSCH_SCR72013_1/maritime-crimes-amendment-bill-128-2>.

5   Whaling

New Zealand was a member of a group of states that issued a call in December 2017 for Japan to end its on-going whaling in the Southern Ocean and to respect the International Whaling Commission ("IWC") processes.[12] This follows Japan's resumption of scientific permit whaling in the Southern Ocean despite concern expressed by the Scientific Committee about whether the revised programme meets the criteria set out by the International Court of Justice ("ICJ") in the *Whaling in the Antarctic* case.[13]

The statement contained the following paragraphs:

> Japan has not sufficiently demonstrated that it has given due regard to the guidance found in the International Court of Justice judgment delivered on 31 March 2014 on ensuring that lethal research is consistent with the obligations under the International Convention for the Regulation of Whaling.
>
> Resolution 2014–5, adopted at the 65th meeting of the International Whaling Commission, and as recalled in Resolution 2016–2, requested that proponents not issue further permits for existing or new special permit research until the Commission had the opportunity to consider the Scientific Committee's review of special permit programs and make recommendations as it sees fit.
>
> At the International Whaling Commission meeting in 2016, we joined the majority of member governments present in noting that Japan had issued special permits for its Southern Ocean whaling program, "NEWREP-A", before the Commission's review processes were complete. Based on the material before the Commission, we assessed that NEWREP-A was not "for purposes of scientific research" as required by Article VIII, paragraph 1 of the International Convention for the Regulation of Whaling. We requested that Japan cease the lethal component of NEWREP-A.
>
> Japan's decision to return to the Southern Ocean this year is contrary to the Commission's requests.

---

12   The joint statement was from Argentina, Australia, Brazil, Chile, Costa Rica, the Dominican Republic, Ecuador, the European Union and its Member States, Mexico, New Zealand, Panama, Peru and Uruguay. New Zealand Ministry of Foreign Affairs and Trade, *Joint statement against whaling* (18 December 2017) <https://www.mfat.govt.nz/en/media-and-resources/ministry-statements-and-speeches/joint-statement-on-whaling/>.

13   *Whaling in the Antarctic (Australia v Japan, NZ Intervening) (Judgment)* [2014] ICJ Rep 226.

States such as New Zealand, opposed to whaling, are frustrated by Japan's refusal to work through the IWC in relation to its scientific programme. Because Japan has amended its recognition of the compulsory jurisdiction of the ICJ to exclude disputes connected to marine living resources, there are few options open to those states if Japan ignores or works around IWC processes.

6   Ratification of Labour Instruments

New Zealand has acceded to the *International Convention on Standards of Training, Certification and Watchkeeping for Fishing Vessel Personnel, 1995*. New Zealand deposited an instrument of accession with the International Maritime Organization on 21 November 2017, which will take effect on 4 March 2018. Some consequential amendments were made to the Maritime Rules under the *Maritime Transport Act 1994* to ensure the Rules comply with the Convention.[14]

---

14   Ministry of Transportation, STCW-F-related Amendments 2017 (3 April 2017) <https://www.maritimenz.govt.nz/rules/rule-documents/STCW-F-amendments-2017.pdf>.

The Antarctic Treaty System

*Alan D. Hemmings**

1   Introduction

The key Antarctic Treaty System ("ATS")[1] events of 2017 were, as is usual, its two annual diplomatic meetings: the Antarctic Treaty Consultative Meeting ("ATCM") and the Meeting of the Commission for the Conservation of Antarctic Marine Living Resources ("Commission"). These diplomatic meetings include the main sessions of the advisory bodies, the Committee for Environmental Protection ("CEP") and the Scientific Committee for the Conservation of Antarctic Marine Living Resources ("SC-CAMLR"), established under the relevant international instruments.[2] The ATCM received reports (as Working Papers ("WPs")) from six intersessional contact groups operating through electronic means between the 39th and 40th ATCMs. These comprised four formal groups considering: Criteria for Consultative Status; Education and Outreach; Inspections in Antarctica under Article VII of the Antarctic Treaty and Article 14 of the Environmental Protocol; Developing Guidance Material for Conservation approaches for the Management of Antarctic Heritage Objects; and two informal groups considering: Implementation of the Climate Change Response Work Programme; and the Proposal for a new Antarctic Specially Managed Area at Chinese Antarctic Kunlun Station, Dome A. No Meeting of Experts was held between these ATCMs. In relation to the Commission, and following normal practice, three intersessional meetings of Working Groups of SC-CAMLR (Ecosystem Monitoring and Management; Statistics, Assessments and Modelling; and Fish Stock Assessment) and a meeting of the Subgroup on Acoustic Survey and Analysis Methods were held during 2017. In addition, Italy hosted a Ross Sea Region Marine Protected Area Research and Monitoring Plan development workshop in April 2017. New Zealand was, as usual, an active and

---

* Gateway Antarctica, University of Canterbury.

1   "Antarctic Treaty system" means the Antarctic Treaty, the measures in effect under that Treaty, its associated separate international instruments in force and the measures in effect under those instruments': *Protocol on Environmental Protection to the Antarctic Treaty,* opened for signature 4 October 1991, 30 ILM 1455 (entered into force 14 January 1998) (*"Madrid Protocol"*) art 1.

2   *Madrid Protocol,* arts 11 and 12; *Convention for the Conservation of Antarctic Marine Living Resources,* opened for signature 5 May 1980, 1329 UNTS 48 (entered into force 7 April 1982) (*"CCAMLR"*) arts XIV and XV, respectively.

significant participant across all the major issues before the ATS institutions. In 2017, the most significant facets of ATS activity were the hosting of the ATCM by China for the first time, given the increasing importance of China in Antarctic affairs,[3] and the entry into force on 1 December 2017 of the Ross Sea Region Marine Protected Area (New Zealand was joint proponent, with the United States, of the marine protected area).[4]

2   1959 Antarctic Treaty[5]

The 40th ATCM[6] was convened in Beijing, China, from 22 May to 1 June 2017.[7] This was the first ATCM to be held in China. ATCMs are rotated around the Consultative Parties, in a rough alphabetical sequence (in English).

For the eighth successive year, all eight of the legally-binding Measures adopted related to Protected Areas or Historic Sites and Monuments (indeed, this year, all eight concerned Protected Areas). Only two of these Measures were related to the region of particular interest to New Zealand,[8] the Ross Sea region that New Zealand claims as the Ross Dependency (of course the pole is also "in" other claimed sectors). These were: *Measure 7 (2017) Antarctic Specially Protected Area No 165 (Edmonson Point, Wood Bay, Ross Sea): Revised Management Plan*, tabled by Italy;[9] and *Measure 8 (2017) Antarctic Specially Managed Area No 5 (Amundsen-Scott South Pole Station, South Pole): Revised Management Plan*, tabled by the United States and Norway.[10]

---

3   Amongst a now substantial literature on China in the polar regions, see generally Anne-Marie Brady, *China as a Great Polar Power* (Cambridge University Press, 2017).

4   See Alan D Hemmings, "Year in Review: The Antarctic Treaty System" (2016) 14 *New Zealand Yearbook of International Law* 294–6.

5   *Antarctic Treaty*, opened for signature 1 December 1959, 402 UNTS 71 (entered into force 23 June 1961).

6   ATCMs address the full range of obligations under both the Antarctic Treaty and the Madrid Protocol, and the presently more limited reporting obligations under the *Convention on the Conservation of Antarctic Seals* opened for signature 1 June 1972 (entered into force 11 March 1978).

7   Antarctic Treaty Secretariat, *Final Report of the Fortieth Antarctic Treaty Consultative Meeting* (Beijing, 2017).

8   The other six were in the Antarctic Peninsula, South Shetland and South Orkney Islands.

9   Italy, "Revision of the Management Plan for Antarctic Specially Protected Area (ASPA) No. 165 Edmonson Point, Wood Bay, Ross Sea" (Working Paper No 38, 2017).

10   United States and Norway, "Updated Management Plan and maps for Antarctic Specially Managed Area No. 5 Amundsen-Scott South Pole Station, South Pole" (Working Paper No 14 Rev 1, 2017).

Seven administrative Decisions ("D") were adopted: (D1) *Subsidiary Group of the Committee for Environmental Protection on Climate Change Response* (*SGCCR*); (D2) *Guidelines on the procedure to be followed with respect to Consultative Party status*; (D3) *Measures withdrawn*; (D4) *Procedure for Appointing Antarctic Treaty Consultative Meeting Working Group Chairs*; (D5) *Secretariat Report, Programme and Budget*; (D6) *Appointment of the Executive Secretary*; and (D7) *Multi-Year Strategic Work Plan for the Antarctic Treaty Consultative Meeting.*

Six hortatory Resolutions ("R") were adopted: (R1) *Guidance Material for Antarctic Specially Managed Area (ASMA) designations*; (R2) *SCAR's Code of Conduct for the Exploration and Research of Subglacial Aquatic Environments*; (R3) *Revised Antarctic Conservation Biogeographic Regions*; (R4) *Green Expedition in the Antarctic*; (R5) *Establishment of the Ross Sea Region Marine Protected Area* (see further below); and (R6) *Guidelines on Contingency Planning, Insurance and Other Matters for Tourist and Other Non-Governmental Activities in the Antarctic Treaty Area.*

The listing of Measures, Decisions and Resolutions itemized above is followed at the section of the Antarctic Treaty Secretariat website dealing with outputs from the Beijing ATCM with two further items, termed "Procedures".[11] These are not reproduced in the corresponding parts of the ATCM Final Report. The first is identified as "Procedure upon receiving invitations from the U.N. Secretariat". This relates specifically to the resolution adopted in 2015 by the UN General Assembly: *Development of an international legally binding instrument under the United Nations Convention on the Law of the Sea on the conservation and sustainable use of marine biological diversity of areas beyond national jurisdiction.*[12] The "Procedure" reads in full:

> The Meeting agreed that in the event that the Secretariat received any further invitations from the United Nations Secretariat pertaining to the process referred to in General Assembly Resolution 69/292, the Secretariat would circulate the invitation immediately to all Parties. It was agreed that unless any objection was received within 14 days of the circulation, the Secretariat would respond using the following language:
>
> Dear Sir/Madam,
>
> I have the pleasure of acknowledging receipt of your letter of (X DATE), which has been transmitted to the Antarctic Treaty Consultative

---

11   *Fortieth Antarctic Treaty Consultative Meeting – Twentieth Committee for Environmental Protection Meeting* (2017) Secretariat of the Antarctic Treaty <https://www.ats.aq/devAS/ats_meetings_meeting.aspx?lang=e&id=82>.

12   GA Res 69/292, 69th sess, UN Doc A/Res/69/292 (6 July 2015) <http://www.un.org/ga/search/view_doc.asp?symbol=A/RES/69/292&Lang=E>.

Parties. Thank you for such a kind invitation. I take this opportunity to re-call that the Antarctic Treaty System is the competent framework within which to address the conservation and sustainable use of biodiversity in the Antarctic region.

Executive Secretary
Antarctic Treaty Secretariat[13]

This text reflects both the generic caution that Antarctic Treaty Consultative Parties individually and collectively display when engaging with the UN system in relation to the region over which they see themselves as bearing prime responsibility, and the tradition of crafting a collective formal position in relation to the modalities of any engagement with the UN.[14] The second "Procedure", identified as "Procedures for intersessional CEP consideration of draft CEEs", merely reiterates the operative part of paragraph 86 of the CEP's Final Report and does not warrant further consideration.

The 40th ATCM conducted its work through three forums: the Committee for Environmental Protection, and two Working Groups: Working Group 1 on Policy, Legal and Institutional Issues and Working Group 2 on Operations, Science and Tourism.[15]

New Zealand tabled ten Working Papers, seven Information Papers ("IPs") and two Background Papers ("BPs"). The seven IPs included three tabled by New Zealand alone.[16] Two IPs involved three states or observers: one by Australia, New Zealand and the Scientific Committee for Antarctic Research ("SCAR");[17] the other by New Zealand, Norway and the United Kingdom.[18] Two IPs involved six states, observers or experts: one involving Australia, Japan,

---

13   *Other, adopted by ATCM XL – CEP XX* (2017) Secretariat of the Antarctic Treaty <https://www.ats.aq/devAS/ats_meetings_meeting_measure.aspx?lang=e>.

14   See, generally, Peter J. Beck, "Antarctica and the United Nations" in Klaus Dodds, Alan D Hemmings and Peder Roberts (eds), *Handbook on the Politics of Antarctica* (Edward Elgar, 2017) 255–68.

15   As in 2016, the latter Working Group was co-chaired by the head of the Argentine delegation and the Director of the British Antarctic Survey from the UK delegation.

16   New Zealand, "Procedures for Safe use of Unmanned Aerial Systems in Antarctica" (Information Paper No 27, 2017); New Zealand, "Supporting the analysis of environments and impacts: A tool to enable broader-scale environmental management" (Information Paper No 76, 2017); New Zealand, "Use of UAS for Improved Monitoring and Survey of Antarctic Specially Protected Areas" (Information Paper No 86, 2017).

17   Australia, New Zealand and SCAR, "Antarctic biogeography revisited: updating the Antarctic Conservation Biogeographic Regions" (Information Paper No 15, 2017).

18   New Zealand, Norway and the United Kingdom, "Representation of Important Bird Areas in the network series of Antarctic Specially Protected Areas" (Information Paper No 16, 2017).

New Zealand, Norway, SCAR and the USA;[19] the other Australia, the International Association of Antarctica Tour Operators ("IAATO"), New Zealand, Norway, United Kingdom and USA.[20] The two BPs (for CEP agenda items) were tabled by New Zealand alone.[21]

Two of the ten WPs were tabled by New Zealand alone: one of which was a report on informal intersessional discussions on implementation of the climate change response programme;[22] the other on a strategic approach to environmentally managed tourism.[23] The latter continues a focus on strategic (as opposed to the more routine operational and particular focus of the tourism discussion at recent ATCMs) following an intersessional contact group between the 38th and 39th ATCMs that was reported in a joint New Zealand and India WP in 2016.[24] Three WPs involving New Zealand were tabled by three states or observers: one by Chile, New Zealand and Uruguay;[25] one by Australia, New Zealand and SCAR;[26] and one by France, New Zealand and Norway.[27] Three WPs involving New Zealand were tabled by five states or observers: one by New Zealand, USA, Argentina, Chile and France, proposing the "adoption by the ATCM of a resolution recognising the establishment of the Ross Sea Region Marine Protected Area" and including a draft resolution;[28] one by the United Kingdom, Australia, New Zealand, Norway

---

19   Australia, Japan, New Zealand, Norway, SCAR and USA, "Antarctic Environments Portal: Content Management Plan" (Information Paper No 14, 2017).

20   Australia, IAATO, New Zealand, Norway, United Kingdom and USA, "Update on work to develop a methodology to assess the sensitivity of sites used by visitors" (Information Paper No 83 rev 1, 2017).

21   New Zealand, "Antarctic Historic Resources: Ross Sea Heritage Restoration Project. Conservation of Hillary's Hut, Scott Base, Antarctic HSM 75" (Background Paper No 4, 2017); New Zealand, "Using virtual reality technology for low impact monitoring and communication of protected and historic sites in Antarctica" (Background Paper No 8, 2017).

22   New Zealand, "Informal Intersessional Discussion: Implementation of the Climate Change Response Work Programme" (Working Paper No 2, 2017).

23   New Zealand, "A Strategic Approach to Environmentally Managed Tourism" (Working Paper No 31, 2017).

24   New Zealand and India, "Report of the Intersessional Contact Group 'Developing a Strategic Approach to Environmentally Managed Tourism and non-Governmental Activities'" (Working Paper No 28, 2016).

25   Chile, New Zealand and Uruguay, "Report of the Intersessional Contact Group (ICG) on Criteria for Consultative Status" (Working Paper No 3, 2017).

26   Australia, New Zealand and SCAR, "Proposed update to the Antarctic Conservation Biogeographic Regions" (Working Paper No 29, 2017).

27   France, New Zealand and Norway, "Updating Resolution 4 (2004) on contingency planning, insurance and other matters for tourist and other non-governmental activities, to reflect the IMO Polar Code" (Working Paper No 33, 2017).

28   New Zealand, USA, Argentina, Chile and France, "Establishment of the CCAMLR Ross Sea Region Marine Protected Area" (Working Paper No 32, 2017).

and Spain;[29] and one by the United Kingdom, Australia, Belgium, New Zealand and Norway.[30] New Zealand was also involved in the tabling of one WP by six states or observers (Australia, Japan, New Zealand, Norway, SCAR and USA);[31] and another involving 11 states (Australia, Chile, China, France, Germany, India, Republic of Korea, New Zealand, Norway, United Kingdom and USA).[32] The latter WP's summary noted that it introduced "the Green Expedition concept and presents a resolution proposal reminding Parties of their commitment under the Environmental Protocol to plan and conduct their activities in Antarctica in an efficient and sustainable way".

Working Paper 32 led to the ATCM's adoption by consensus of Resolution 5 (2017) on "Establishment of the Ross Sea Region Marine Protected Area" (below).

Resolution 5 (2017)
Establishment of the Ross Sea Region Marine Protected Area
The Representatives,
Recalling Resolution 1 (2006) in which the Consultative Parties, conscious that the Convention on the Conservation of Antarctic Marine Living Resources is an integral part of the Antarctic Treaty system, encouraged increased cooperation at the practical level between the Antarctic Treaty Consultative Meeting ("ATCM") and the Commission for the Conservation of Antarctic Marine Living Resources ("CCAMLR");

Recognising the contributions of the ATCM in the designation and implementation of Antarctic Specially Protected Areas and Antarctic Specially Managed Areas, and of CCAMLR in the designation and implementation of marine protected areas to conserve important areas of the Antarctic marine environment;

Noting the agreement reached at the 35th meeting of CCAMLR to establish the Ross Sea Region Marine Protected Area ("RSRMPA"), commencing on 1 December 2017;

Recalling freedom of scientific investigation in Antarctica as enshrined in Article II of the Antarctic Treaty and recognising the importance of

---

29 United Kingdom, Australia, New Zealand, Norway and Spain, "Antarctic Specially Protected Areas and Important Bird Areas" (Working Paper No 37, 2017).

30 United Kingdom, Australia, Belgium, New Zealand and Norway, "Environmental Impact Assessments – Update on broader policy discussions" (Working Paper 41, 2017).

31 Australia, Japan, New Zealand, Norway, SCAR and USA, "Antarctic Environments Portal" (Working Paper No 25, 2017).

32 Australia, Chile, China, France, Germany, India, Republic of Korea, New Zealand, Norway, United Kingdom and USA, "Green Expedition in the Antarctic" (Working Paper No 36, 2017).

scientific research and monitoring to support and evaluate progress in achieving the objectives of the RSRMPA, as well as international collaboration in such research and monitoring;

Noting that CCAMLR Conservation Measure 91-05 provides for the regular review of the RSRMPA;

Noting the importance of collaboration between the ATCM and CCAMLR;

Recommend that their Governments:

1. welcome the establishment of the Ross Sea Region Marine Protected Area ("RSRMPA") as an important contribution towards the conservation of Southern Ocean ecosystems and biodiversity;

2. encourage Antarctic Treaty Parties that are not Members of the Commission for the Conservation of Antarctic Marine Living Resources ("CCAMLR") to familiarise themselves with CCAMLR Conservation Measure 91-05, including the Management Plan and the forthcoming Research and Monitoring Plan for the RSRMPA, and to encourage, as appropriate, compliance with relevant RSRMPA management measures;

3. invite the Committee on Environmental Protection to consider any appropriate actions within the Antarctic Treaty Consultative Meeting's competence to contribute to the achievement of the specific objectives set forth in CCAMLR Conservation Measure 91–05, particularly in the designation and implementation of Antarctic Specially Protected Areas and Antarctic Specially Managed Areas in the Ross Sea region and the management of relevant human activities; and

4. identify opportunities to conduct and support relevant research and monitoring activities that support the objectives and the forthcoming Research and Monitoring Plan of the RSRMPA, in particular through international collaborations.[33]

Working Paper 36 also led to the ATCM's adoption by consensus of Resolution 4 (2017) on "Green Expedition in the Antarctic", the operative part of which reads as follows:

Recommend that their Governments:

1. reaffirm their commitment to protect the Antarctic environment and dependent and associated ecosystems and to encourage collaborative efforts to this end;

---

33   New Zealand, USA, Argentina, Chile and France, "Establishment of the CCAMLR Ross Sea Region Marine Protected Area" (Working Paper No 32, 2017).

2. support the concept of Green Expedition by encouraging their National Antarctic Programmes to conduct science in an environmentally-friendly manner in the Antarctic;

3. encourage their National Antarctic Programmes to work more closely with other Parties, including through participation and interaction with organisations such as Scientific Committee for Antarctic Research ("SCAR") and the Council of Managers of National Antarctic Programs ("COMNAP"), to develop more collaborative projects and to promote the sharing of experiences and advanced technology; and

4. produce high-quality Environmental Impact Assessments when new activities are planned that include as far as possible best practices to prevent and minimise environmental impact.[34]

Without, it is hoped, being parochial or chauvinistic, the significance of Resolution 4 is perhaps that it was proposed in a WP tabled by a large and diverse group of states, involving not just the usual Western coterie but significant Antarctic states from Asia (China, India and the Republic of Korea – but interestingly *not* Japan, an original signatory of the Antarctic Treaty), at an ATCM hosted by China. The fact of the Resolution's adoption, which required consensus across all 29 Antarctic Treaty Consultative Parties, is significant, notwithstanding the entirely hortatory nature of a resolution. There has been a contraction of the issues for which it is now possible to adopt a legally binding Measure at an ATCM.[35] Consequently, management of most issues within the purview of the Antarctic Treaty or the Madrid Protocol that arise at ATCMs, and the tone of the implementation of treaty obligations, may now essentially rely on these soft-law approaches.

3   1980 Convention on the Conservation of Antarctic Marine Living Resources ("CCAMLR")

The regular 2017 (36th) Meeting of the Commission for the Conservation of Antarctic Marine Living Resources ("Commission") was held at the CCAMLR

---

34   Australia, Chile, China, France, Germany, India, Republic of Korea, New Zealand, Norway, United Kingdom and USA, "Green Expedition in the Antarctic" (Working Paper No 36, 2017).

35   To Protected Areas designations and the periodic updating of their Management Plans. See Alan D Hemmings. "Year in Review: The Antarctic Treaty System" (2015) 13 *New Zealand Yearbook of International Law* 273–5.

Secretariat in Hobart, Tasmania, Australia from 16 to 27 October 2017.[36] Commission decisions are adopted as "Conservation Measures".[37]

The Ministry of Foreign Affairs and Trade describes New Zealand as having "a particular interest in the exploratory toothfish fisheries in the Ross Sea",[38] and this is the primary area of fisheries activity by New Zealand operators. The Ross Sea is divided between CCAMLR Statistical Subareas 88.1 and 88.2.[39] For the 2017/18 season, New Zealand vessel activity was, again, confined to these two subareas.

In Subarea 88.1 the precautionary catch limit ("PCL") for the 2017/18 season was set at 3,157 tonnes (up from 2,870 tonnes in the previous season and spread across 24 rather than the 18 vessels of that season) across a maximum of three New Zealand, two Australian, one Japanese, five South Korean, one Norwegian, four Russian, one Spanish, five Ukrainian, one United Kingdom and one Uruguayan flagged vessels. Of the total PCL, 2,645 tonnes was set in two areas outside the Ross Sea Region marine protected area ("MPA"); 467 tonnes in the Special Research Zone of the MPA;[40] with a further 45 tonnes assigned to New Zealand for the Ross Sea Shelf Survey.[41]

For Subarea 88.2, whilst an overall PCL figure is not provided in the Conservation Measure itself, it appears that it may be 619 tonnes, which is identical to the figure last year. The Conservation Measure identifies the component allowances for the Small Scale Research Units ("SSRUs") within the Subarea (below).

The total catch of *Dissostichus mawsoni* in Statistical Subarea 88.2 in the 2017/18 season shall not exceed a precautionary catch limit applied as follows:

(i)   SSRUs A and B outside the Ross Sea region marine protected area and north of 70°S – included in the catch limit in Conservation Measure 41-09, paragraph 2(i)

(ii)   SSRUs A and B outside the Ross Sea region marine protected area and south of 70°S – included in the catch limit in Conservation Measure 41-09, paragraph 2(ii)

---

36   CCAMLR Secretariat, *Report of the Thirty-sixth Meeting of the Commission*, CCAMLR-XXXVI (Hobart, 2017).

37   CCAMLR Secretariat, *Schedule of Conservation Measures in Force 2017/18* (Hobart, 2017).

38   Ministry of Foreign Affairs and Trade, *The Antarctic Treaty System* <https://www.mfat. govt.nz/en/environment/antarctica/the-antarctic-treaty-system>.

39   CCAMLR Secretariat, *Convention Area* <https://www.ccamlr.org/en/organisation/ convention-area>.

40   See Figure 1 in Alan D Hemmings, "Year in Review: The Antarctic Treaty System" (2016) 14 *New Zealand Yearbook of International Law* 295.

41   *CCAMLR Conservation Measure 41-09 (2017): Limits on the exploratory fishery for Dissostichus mawsoni in Statistical Subarea 88.1 in the 2017/18 season.*

(iii) The part of SSRU A within the Special Research Zone of the Ross Sea region marine protected area – included in the catch limit in Conservation Measure 41-09, paragraph 2(iii)

(iv) SSRUs C, D, E, F and G – 419 tonnes total only in the research blocks as defined in Annex 41-10/A

(v) SSRU H – 200 tonnes

(vi) SSRU I – 0 tonnes.

Within SSRUs C, D, E, F and G no more than 200 tonnes shall be taken in any one research block (defined in Annex 41-10/A).

The catch limit for SSRUs A and B, which prior to the 2017/18 season was set at zero, shall be reviewed by the Scientific Committee and its working groups with a view to providing advice to the Commission at its 2018 meeting.[42]

This PCL is spread across 21 vessels (compared to 16 in 2016/17) comprising a maximum of three New Zealand, one Australian, four South Korean, one Norwegian, four Russian, five Ukrainian, one United Kingdom and two Uruguayan flagged vessels.[43]

New Zealand tabled six papers in the Commission and two in the Scientific Committee. The Commission papers included a joint New Zealand and United States paper on consequential changes to other Conservation Measures in light of the entry into force of the Ross Sea Region MPA;[44] a paper on improvements to the CCAMLR inspection reporting system, jointly with the United Kingdom and Australia;[45] and a joint paper with Australia on establishment of an exploratory fishery in Subarea 88.3 (to the east of the Ross Sea),[46] which was also tabled in the Scientific Committee. Three Background Papers were tabled in the Commission, each by New Zealand alone: one examining reports into late removal of fishing gear following fishery closure notification;[47] a report on CCAMLR Inspections conducted from HMNZS *Wellington*;[48] and its report as

---

42　*CCAMLR Conservation Measure 41-10 (2017): Limits on the exploratory fishery for Dissostichus mawsoni in Statistical Subarea 88.2 in the 2017/18 season.*

43　Ibid.

44　New Zealand and United States, "Ross Sea region marine protected area: consequential changes to other conservation measures" CCAMLR-XXXVI/16.

45　United Kingdom, Australia and New Zealand, "Improvements to the CCAMLR inspection reporting system" CCAMLR-XXXVI/14.

46　Australia and New Zealand, "Establishment of an exploratory fishery for *Dissostichus mawsoni* in Statistical Subarea 88.3" CCAMLR-XXXVI/29.

47　New Zealand, "New Zealand investigation reports into late removal of fishing gear following fishery closure notification" CCAMLR-XXXVI/BG/23.

48　New Zealand, "CCAMLR inspections undertaken by New Zealand from HMNZS *Wellington* during 2016/17" CCAMLR-XXXVI/BG/24.

the CCAMLR Observer to an Advisory Committee Meeting of the Agreement for the Conservation of Albatrosses and Petrels.[49]

In the Scientific Committee, in addition to the joint paper with Australia already referred to,[50] New Zealand tabled a preliminary assessment of the potential for proposed bottom fishing activities to have significant adverse impacts on vulnerable marine ecosystems.[51]

The most problematical issue for the Commission at its 36th Meeting, in the assessment of many of its Members, was (as New Zealand expressed it) "that [the Standing Committee on Implementation and Compliance] was prevented from adopting a Preliminary Compliance Report this year, and that the Commission was unable to assign a status to all items in the final Compliance Report".[52] The issue concerned the assertion that China was non-compliant, which China strongly objected to. Interestingly, China was merely one among a number of states identified in the CCAMLR Compliance Report, which is appended to the Commission Final Report,[53] but it alone appears to have taken exception to its inclusion. The outcome was a terse exchange of statements recorded in the Commission Final Report.[54]

4   New Zealand Legislative Activity

No substantive legislative activity relating to Antarctica occurred during 2017. The *Antarctica (Environmental Protection: Liability Annex) Amendment Act 2012* (NZ) has not yet entered into force.[55]

---

49   New Zealand, "Report from the CCAMLR Observer (New Zealand) on the 10th Advisory Committee Meeting of the Agreement for the Conservation of Albatrosses and Petrels (ACAP) (Wellington, New Zealand, 11 to 15 September 2017)" CCAMLR-XXXVI/BG/35.
50   Australia and New Zealand, above n 46.
51   New Zealand, "Preliminary assessment of the potential for proposed bottom fishing activities to have significant adverse impacts on vulnerable marine ecosystems" SC-CAMLR-XXXVI/BG/07 Rev. 1.
52   CCAMLR Secretariat, *Report of the Thirty-sixth Meeting of the Commission*, CCAMLR-XXXV (Hobart, 2017) [3.36].
53   Ibid; Annex 8, CCAMLR Compliance Report.
54   CCAMLR Secretariat, *Report of the Thirty-sixth Meeting of the Commission*, CCAMLR-XXXV (Hobart, 2017) [3.22]–[3.48].
55   See Alan D Hemmings, "Year in Review: The Antarctic Treaty System" (2016) 14 *New Zealand Yearbook of International Law* 296–7.

International Criminal Law and International Humanitarian Law

*Treasa Dunworth**

1   Introduction

2017 saw the culmination of the Humanitarian Initiative on Nuclear Weapons with the adoption of the *Treaty on the Prohibition of Nuclear Weapons* on 7 July 2017. That development is discussed in Part 2. Less encouraging was the continued lack of progress in New Zealand with ratification of the Crime of Aggression Amendment of the *Rome Statute*. This was in spite of significant developments at the international level: in December, States Parties to the *Rome Statute* re-affirmed the Amendment paving the way for jurisdiction over the Crime to activate from mid-July 2018. The dynamics behind that development, and in particular New Zealand's position, are discussed in Part 3. Finally, with the publication of *Hit & Run: The New Zealand SAS in Afghanistan and the Meaning of Honour* momentum picked up again in calls for an independent inquiry to be established to examine allegations of wrongdoing by New Zealand Defence Force forces in Afghanistan. This is discussed in Part 4.

2   The Humanitarian Initiative Realised: The Treaty on the Prohibition of Nuclear Weapons

For several years now this subject matter update has been reporting on what came to be known as the "Humanitarian Initiative on Nuclear Weapons" which had as its aim to reframe the debate on nuclear weapons.[1] That is, the aim was to turn away from a state-centred security lens and more squarely focus on the humanitarian consequences of nuclear weapons. Those efforts came to

---

*   University of Auckland.
1   Treasa Dunworth, "International Criminal Law and International Humanitarian Law" (2015) 13 *New Zealand Yearbook of International Law* 282, 282–4; Treasa Dunworth, "International Criminal Law and International Humanitarian Law" (2016) 14 *New Zealand Yearbook of International Law* 298, 298–301.

fruition with the adoption by states of the *Treaty on the Prohibition of Nuclear Weapons* ("*TPNW*") on 7 July 2017.[2]

The *TPNW* is, of course, a disarmament treaty in the sense that it requires states to declare any possession of nuclear weapons within 30 days of the treaty entering into force for them,[3] and then provides a roadmap (which includes the possible involvement of the International Atomic Energy Agency) for any nuclear possessor states that do join the treaty.[4] As with other multilateral disarmament treaties, the *TPNW* contains prohibitions on use and possession. In Article 1, states parties undertake never to use, threaten to use, produce, manufacture, test, possess, stockpile, allow any stationing or installation, or engage in the transfer of nuclear weapons.[5]

However, the *TPNW* also squarely fits within the understanding of a "humanitarian disarmament" instrument. Much of the motivation behind the treaty were the humanitarian concerns of its founding states, and an active, engaged civil society.[6] Reflecting that, the treaty has a number of cooperation and assistance provisions, including on victim assistance and environmental remediation measures. Article 6 requires states to provide assistance such as medical care, rehabilitation and psychological support to individuals under their jurisdiction who are affected by the use or testing of nuclear weapons. Article 7 requires states to take "necessary and appropriate" measures towards environmental remediation of areas under their jurisdiction and control that have been contaminated as a result of nuclear weapons use and testing. It also acknowledges the rights of states to seek and receive assistance in that regard and obliges all states to cooperate in implementation.

Consistent with its longstanding support for a ban on nuclear weapons, New Zealand attended and actively participated in the negotiations of the Treaty,

---

2   *Treaty on the Prohibition of Nuclear Weapons*, opened for signature 20 September 2017, UN Doc A/CONF.229/2017/L.3/Rev.1 (not yet in force) ("TPNW").

3   Ibid Art 2(1).

4   Ibid Art 4. Although such an eventuality seems unlikely in the current climate. None of the nine states thought or known to possess nuclear weapons (China, Democratic People's Republic of Korea, France, India, Israel, Pakistan, Russian Federation, United Kingdom, and United States) participated in the negotiations – indeed, all voted against the negotiations convening. See also *Joint Press Statement from the Permanent Representatives to the United Nations of the United States, United Kingdom, and France Following the Adoption of a Treaty Banning Nuclear Weapons* (7 July 2017) United States Mission to the United Nations <https:// usun.state.gov/remarks/7892>.

5   TPNW Art 1.

6   Indeed, the International Campaign to Abolish Nuclear Weapons ("ICAN"), was awarded the 2017 Nobel Peace Prize for "its work to draw attention to the catastrophic humanitarian consequences of any use of nuclear weapons and for its ground-breaking efforts to achieve a treaty-based prohibition of such weapons." *Prize Announcement* (2017) The Nobel Prize <https://www.nobelprize.org/prizes/peace/2017/prize-announcement/>.

both in the organisational meetings which took place earlier in the year from 27 to 31 March 2017 and then in the substantive negotiations which took place from 15 June to 7 July 2017. New Zealand was also one of the Vice Presidents of the Conference assisting the President. It was one of 122 states to vote in favour of adopting the Treaty on 7 July,[7] and it signed the Treaty on 20 September, on the first day it was open for signature.[8]

The Treaty needs 50 ratifications to enter into force. As the year ended, only three states had taken that step,[9] although already 56 states had signed the Treaty, the vast majority of them at the Opening Ceremony. It is generally anticipated that New Zealand will ratify the Treaty in the course of 2018.

3   Crime of Aggression

On 14 December 2017, the States Parties to the *Statute of the International Criminal Court*[10] adopted a resolution activating the jurisdiction of the International Criminal Court ("the Court") over the crime of aggression.[11] That vote was the final step in a long and often tortuous process of including aggression as the fourth crime in the Statute. While the crime of aggression had been included in the original Statute, unlike the other three crimes (war crimes, crimes against humanity and genocide) it did not take immediate effect.[12] The *Kampala Amendment*, agreed to by States Parties in 2010, provided that jurisdiction of the Court over the crime of aggression would only activate with 30 ratifications of the Amendment by States Parties as well as a further vote by States Parties to trigger the jurisdiction – a vote that could not take place earlier than 1 January 2017.[13] The 30 ratification threshold was reached in 2016.[14] This paved

---

7   Only The Netherlands voting against adoption. Singapore abstained.

8   Gerry Brownlee, "NZ to sign prohibition of nuclear weapons treaty" (Press Release, 18 September 2017) <https://www.beehive.govt.nz/release/nz-sign-prohibition-nuclear-weapons-treaty>.

9   Guyana, Holy See and Thailand.

10   *Rome Statute of the International Criminal Court*, opened for signature 14 July 1998, 2187 UNTS 90 (entered into force 1 July 2002) ("*Rome Statute*").

11   "Activation of the jurisdiction of the Court over the crime of aggression" (ICC-ASP/16/ Res.5, Assembly of State Parties to the Rome Statute, 14 December 2017).

12   *Rome Statute* Art 5(2).

13   *Resolution RC/Res.6 of the Review Conference of the Rome Statute: The crime of aggression*, RC/Res.6, 13th plen mtg, UN Doc RC/11 (11 June 2010) Annex I, Art 15bis(3).

14   Treasa Dunworth, "International Criminal Law and International Humanitarian Law" (2016) 14 *New Zealand Yearbook of International Law* 298, 301.

the way for the December vote which finally activated the Court's jurisdiction over the crime of aggression – which will start to operate from 17 July 2018.[15]

New Zealand was not among those first 30 states, nor indeed among the 35 states that had ratified the Amendment when the states parties met in December to discuss the activation. Further, despite the recent change in government at home, there were no indications that ratification was being treated as a priority (legislative action is required before ratification can proceed). This may well simply reflect a busy legislative schedule of an incoming government with domestic concerns taking priority.

In contrast, at the international level, New Zealand was clearly engaged and supportive of the crime becoming operational within the Court's jurisdiction. At the Assembly of States Parties in December, New Zealand addressed the issue in its statement during the General Debate, noting that the decision about activating the crime of aggression was an "important milestone", and expressing the view that it was important for states parties to be united on the issue so as to send "a clear message to the international community regarding the Court's ability to fulfil its mandate".[16] This level of engagement was in marked contrast to its statement the previous year, when the statement ignored the issue completely.[17] Following late night negotiations on the last day of the meeting, the Assembly did adopt the triggering resolution and managed to do that by consensus, but it was by no means an easy feat and New Zealand was among those states that worked hard to broker a compromise that was acceptable enough to allow for agreement.[18]

The problem was the division between states as to whether a "restrictive position" or a "permissive position" should be adopted as to the scope of jurisdiction of the Court in respect of the crime of aggression.[19] The restrictive position was that the Court would only be able to exercise jurisdiction over the crime of aggression where the alleged crime has taken place on the territory of

---

15   "Draft resolution proposed by the Vice-Presidents of the Assembly Activation of the jurisdiction of the Court over the crime of aggression" (ICC-ASP/16/L.1014, Assembly of State Parties to the Rome Statute, December 2017) [1].

16   Victoria Hallum, *New Zealand Statement: 16th Session of the Assembly of States Parties to the Rome Statute of the International Criminal Court* (7 December 2017) Ministry of Foreign Affairs and Trade <https://asp.icc-cpi.int/iccdocs/asp_docs/ASP16/ASP-16-NZL.pdf>.

17   Treasa Dunworth, "International Criminal Law and International Humanitarian Law" (2016) 14 *New Zealand Yearbook of International Law* 298, 301.

18   Claus Kreß, "On the Activation of ICC Jurisdiction over the Crime of Aggression" (2018) 16 *Journal of International Criminal Justice* 1, 9–13.

19   See *Report on the Facilitation on the Activation of the Jurisdiction of the International Criminal Court over the Crime of Aggression*, ICC-ASP/16/24, Assembly of State Parties to the Rome Statute, 27 November 2017, Section IV.

a state which has ratified the *Kampala Amendment*, or if the alleged crime was committed by a national of such a state. This position relies on Article 121(5) of the Statute, which provides that when a State Party has not accepted an amendment to Articles 5, 6, 7 or 8 of the Statute (and the *Kampala Amendment* addressed Article 5), the Court shall not exercise jurisdiction when committed by that State Party's nationals or on its territory. The permissive position in contrast was that as soon as jurisdiction over the crime is activated, the normal rules of jurisdiction apply, meaning that the Court might well have jurisdiction even where a State Party has not ratified the amendment.[20] In between, there were several states – New Zealand among them – attempting to bridge the differences and suggesting varying mechanisms whereby non ratifying states parties objecting to the Court's jurisdiction over their nationals or on their territory could be identified in an annex to the resolution such that the Court would be prohibited from exercising jurisdiction over them.

In the final analysis, the "pure" restrictive approach won the day. From accounts of the negotiations, it seems that this was not because that was the most favoured or broadly supported position among the States Parties, but rather because of the unwillingness of a few states supporting the restrictive position to compromise to any degree. Although New Zealand started on the restrictive side of the debate, it did show willingness to compromise in order to reach some agreement, so activating the Court's jurisdiction over the crime of aggression was clearly important.[21] Interestingly, due to the adoption of the restrictive position, New Zealand being a non-ratifying state will not find its nationals before the Court facing a charge of aggression.

4   The NZ sas in Afghanistan

In March 2017, Nicky Hager and Jon Stephenson published *Hit & Run: The New Zealand sas in Afghanistan and the Meaning of Honour.*[22] Among other things, the book gave an account of a raid of two villages in Afghanistan in 2010 undertaken by the New Zealand Special Air Service ("nzsas"). The authors claimed that the raid had been targeting insurgents and that it resulted in the death of six people, with a further 15 being injured, all civilians. The book was building

---

20   *Rome Statute* Art 12(2), together with Art 15*bis*(4) of the Kampala Amendment.
21   Claus Kreß, "On the Activation of icc Jurisdiction over the Crime of Aggression" (2018) 16 *Journal of International Criminal Justice* 1, 10.
22   Nicky Hager and Jon Stephenson, *Hit & Run: The New Zealand sas in Afghanistan and the Meaning of Honour* (Potton and Burton, 2017).

on earlier work by Jon Stephenson in 2010 raising questions about the handling of persons captured by the NZSAS and their subsequent detention by Afghan or other authorities in Afghanistan.[23] The publication re-ignited public concerns about New Zealand's involvement in the Afghan conflict and triggered calls for an independent inquiry from a number of quarters.[24]

Response from the New Zealand Defence Force ("NZDF") was swift. On 26 March, the Chief of Defence Force, Lieutenant General Tim Keating, stated that there were some "major inaccuracies" in the book, in particular the location and names of the villages in question and suggested that the authors may have confused interviews, stories and anecdotes from locals with accounts of so-called Operation Burnham, which was an operation carried out with the Afghan Crisis Response Unit and the United States Armed Force in Tirgiran Valley in Baghlan Province.[25] There had been an enquiry into Operation Burnham at the time, Keating asserted – an investigation by the International Security Assistance Force which found no evidence of civilian casualties. The then Prime Minister, Bill English, also dismissed the calls for an independent inquiry. In a press conference following a "detailed briefing" from Tim Keating, he decided that there was "no basis for launching an inquiry".[26] Wayne Mapp, on the other hand, who had been the Minister of Defence at the relevant time, suggested that the NZSAS raid was a "fiasco".[27]

In August, with no further progress and with *Official Information Act* requests made by journalists continuing to be stalled, lawyers representing Afghan villagers caught up in the raids, filed proceedings in the High Court

---

23   Treasa Dunworth, "International Criminal Law and International Humanitarian Law" (2011) 9 *New Zealand Yearbook of International Law* 308, 310.

24   See, e.g., Bryce Edwards, "Is something rotten in the New Zealand government and military?", *New Zealand Herald* (online), 24 March 2017 <https://www.nzherald.co.nz/nz/news/article.cfm?c_id=1&objectid=11824932>; Editorial, "The public deserves to know what happened in SAS raid", *Dominion Post* (online), 23 March 2017 <https://www.stuff.co.nz/dominion-post/comment/editorials/90732380/Editorial-The-public-deserves-to-know-what-happened-in-SAS-raid>; "NZ lawyers demand independent inquiry over deadly raid in Afghanistan" *New Zealand Herald* (online), 24 March 2017 <https://www.nzherald.co.nz/nz/news/article.cfm?c_id=1&objectid=11824691>.

25   "NZDF Statement on Hager/Stephenson book" (Media Release, 26 March 2017) <http://www.nzdf.mil.nz/news/media-releases/2017/20170326-nzdf-statement-on-hager-stephenson-book.htm>.

26   Toby Manhire, "Bill English says no inquiry into Hit & Run claims – his reasons, and Hager's response", *The Spinoff* (online), 3 April 2017 < https://thespinoff.co.nz/politics/03-04-2017/bill-english-says-no-inquiry-into-hit-run-claims-his-reasons-and-hagers-response/>.

27   Patrick Gower, "Wayne Mapp's openness shames Government's stonewalling", *Newshub* (online), 22 March 2017 <https://www.newshub.co.nz/home/politics/2017/03/patrick-gower-wayne-mapp-s-openness-shames-government-s-stonewalling.html>.

seeking judicial review of the "decision by the Government to decline to hold an independent inquiry into the Operation Burnham events and subsequent cover-up".[28] Rodney Harrison QC stated that the Chief of the Defence Force was "the wrong person to make that decision [not to hold an independent inquiry]" as he had already "taken the position that the allegations were unfounded" and as such, he was biased.[29]

In November 2017, the Prosecutor of the International Criminal Court filed a "Request for authorisation of an investigation pursuant to Article 15" in the Situation in the Islamic Republic of Afghanistan, triggering the first step in a possible investigation and prosecution of alleged crimes committed in Afghanistan or in the context of that conflict taking place elsewhere.[30] Although there is no mention of New Zealand anywhere in the document, and noting that, as yet, this is only a request by the Prosecutor to open an investigation, this move towards seeking criminal accountability for alleged crimes in Afghanistan may well add to the impetus to calls at home for greater transparency and accountability of the NZDF.

As the year ended, the matter was before the Ombudsman due to a complaint by journalist Sam Warburton about the earlier refusal of the NZDF to release their own photos to prove the "major inaccuracies" in *Hit & Run*.[31] The High Court judicial review proceedings were also pending. It was hoped with the incoming government that the dynamic would change and that the persistent calls for a public independent inquiry would be heeded.

---

28   Anna Leask, "Government faces legal action over Afghan civilian deaths", *New Zealand Herald* (online), 18 August 2017 <https://www.nzherald.co.nz/nz/news/article.cfm?c_id=1&objectid=11906565>.

29   Ibid.

30   *Public redacted version of "Request for authorisation of an investigation pursuant to article 15"* (International Criminal Court, Pre-Trial Chamber III, Doc No ICC-02/17-7-Conf-Exp, 20 November 2017) [1].

31   Sam Warburton, *How we found the NZDF was wrong on Hit & Run* (16 March 2018) Pundit <https://www.pundit.co.nz/content/how-we-found-the-nzdf-was-wrong-on-hit-run>.

International Law and Security 2017

Anna Hood*

1   International Security

In 2015 and 2016, the international law and security issues that were documented in the *New Zealand Yearbook of International Law* report concerned New Zealand's role on and contributions to the United Nations Security Council, matters relating to the Security Treaty between Australia, New Zealand and the United States of America ("ANZUS"), New Zealand's efforts with the Proliferation Security Initiative, and our contributions to foreign conflicts. In 2017, these issues seemed to fade from the spotlight: the prominence of the United Nations Security Council in New Zealand's actions dimmed with New Zealand's time as an elected member coming to a close at the end of 2016; ANZUS did not make the headlines and appeared only once in Hansard (in Murray McCully's valedictory speech to Parliament);[1] and New Zealand did not take a lead role in the Proliferation Security Initiative. New Zealand's involvement with foreign conflicts did land squarely on the front pages in March 2017 with the publication of Nicky Hager and John Stephenson's book *Hit and Run*,[2] which detailed a New Zealand SAS raid on two Afghani villages in 2010 which left 21 civilians dead or wounded. However, as the substance of *Hit and Run* concerns international humanitarian law matters more than security matters,[3] this event is dealt with in Treasa Dunworth's report on International Humanitarian Law and International Criminal Law.

In the place of the above matters, issues concerning New Zealand's approach to refugees and a New Zealand company's failure to comply with United Nations sanctions on North Korea emerged in the international security space. These two matters are detailed below. There were some other domestic security issues such as the passage of the *Intelligence and Security Act 2017* (NZ).

---

*   University of Auckland.

1   New Zealand, *Parliamentary Debates,* 9 August 2017, Valedictory Speech (Murray McCully).

2   Nicky Hager and Jon Stephenson, *Hit and Run: The New Zealand SAS in Afghanistan and the meaning of honour* (Potton and Burton, 2017).

3   Admittedly, the distinction between international security matters and other areas of international law such as international humanitarian law is sometimes blurry and the ways we categorise issues is far from an exact science. This issue arises again later in this report with respect to the discussion about New Zealand's approach to refugees on Manus Island in Papua New Guinea.

© KONINKLIJKE BRILL NV, LEIDEN, 2019 | DOI:10.1163/9789004387935_018

However, as they did not directly raise international legal issues, they will not be discussed in this piece.

2   Attempts to Construe Asylum Seekers/Refugees as Security Threats

I am reluctant to include an item concerning asylum seekers or refugees under the banner of "International Security". The idea that people fleeing persecution should be understood as a security threat in any context is deeply problematic; in the New Zealand context it is simply absurd. Nonetheless, asylum seeker/refugee issues reared their heads in New Zealand at the end of 2017 and were cast by some as security issues.

The genesis of this issue was the closing of the Manus Island refugee detention centre in October 2017. The Supreme Court of Papua New Guinea had declared the detention centre unconstitutional in April 2016[4] and steps were put in place to shut down the centre by 31 October 2017. The problem with this was that the arrangements that had been put in place for the refugees in the detention centre were far from ideal: new detention facilities were still under construction; inadequate security measures were in place; and there were concerns about the extent to which the refugees would be able to access food and medicine.[5] Consequently, when the detention centre was closed and the power and water turned off, 600 refugees chose to remain in the facility.[6] Many of the refugees remained in the centre without food, water or medical supplies for weeks sparking concerns around the world for their well-being.[7]

In response to the situation, the newly-elected Labour-led government in New Zealand reiterated the offer that the previous National government had made to accept 150 of the refugees on Manus Island and/or Nauru as part of New Zealand's annual refugee quota.[8] The offer was repeatedly rejected by Australia on the basis that it would provide the refugees with a backdoor to

---

4   *Namah v Pato* [2016] PGSC 13; SC1497 (26 April 2016).
5   Helen Davidson and Calla Wahlquist, "Power shut off to, final Manus compounds as 600 men refuse to leave" *The Guardian* (online) 1 November 2017 <https://www.theguardian. com/australia-news/2017/nov/01/power-shut-off-to-final-manus-compounds-as-600-men-refuse-to-leave>.
6   Ibid.
7   Kelsey Munro, "Smuggled footage reveals conditions inside closed Manus detention centre" *SBS News* (online) 10 November 2017 <https://www.sbs.com.au/news/smuggled -footage-reveals-conditions-inside-closed-manus-detention-centre>.
8   Laura Walters, "Jacinda Ardern reconfirms offer to take 150 refugees from Australian detention centres" *Stuff* (online) 3 November 2017 <https://www.stuff.co.nz/national/politics/98537618/ jacinda-ardern-reconfirms-offer-to-take-150-refugees-from-australian-detention-centres>.

Australia.[9] Then in mid-November 2017, two weeks into the crisis, Australian media reported that the Australian government initiative "Operation Sovereign Borders" had turned back four boats holding 164 asylum seekers heading to New Zealand.[10] This unverified report generated a wave of concerns that New Zealand's offer to take refugees from Manus Island and Nauru was encouraging people smugglers to target New Zealand, a scenario that was seen as troubling both because it might lead to the people smugglers' cargo (asylum seekers) drowning at sea and because it may lead to New Zealand being inundated with asylum seekers.[11] The Prime Minister's response was to downplay concerns about the prospect of boats arriving in New Zealand, to reiterate New Zealand's offer to take 150 refugees and to denounce the people smuggler trade.[12]

On one level the Prime Minister's response to reports of boats headed to New Zealand was admirable because she refused to bow to pressure to withdraw the offer to take 150 refugees. On another level, however, she failed to counter either ideas about boats of asylum seekers posing a threat to New Zealand or the demonisation of people smugglers. The idea that asylum seekers pose a threat to New Zealand is hard to stomach: there is little to no prospect of vast numbers of asylum seekers reaching our shores by boat (or any other means); if they were able to navigate the perilous terrain of the Tasman Sea, it is difficult to see how they would pose a security threat to New Zealand; and in the event that some individuals did pose such a threat, both international and national laws ensure that anyone posing a security risk will be denied refugee status and deported.[13] With respect to the demonisation of people smugglers,

9   Alice Workman, "Thanks but no thanks" *Buzzfeed* (online) 5 November 2017 <https://www.buzzfeed.com/aliceworkman/thanks-but-no-thanks?utm_term=.yn567VOPb#.egWgaWwzy>.

10   Renee Viellaris, "People smuggler boats turned back on their way to New Zealand", *Courier Mail* (online) 14 November 2017 <https://www.couriermail.com.au/news/queensland/queensland-government/manus-island-people-smuggler-boats-turned-back-on-their-way-to-nz/news-story/1b40d426f6f8eb7002db2021d384f26f>.

11   Indeed, Malcolm Turnbull declared that "I mean the people smugglers, the only reason New Zealand does not have thousands of people arriving in an unauthorised way on their shores is because of our border protection policies": Sam Sachdeva, "Ardern rebuffs talk of people smuggled to New Zealand", *Newsroom* (online) 14 November 2017 <https://www.newsroom.co.nz/2017/11/14/60240/ardern-rebuffs-talk-of-people-smuggled-to-nz>.   On Prime Minister Jacinda Ardern's response to reports of boats coming to New Zealand see also, Jane Patterson, "PM denies New Zealand becoming a soft target for people smuggling" *Radio New Zealand* (online) 14 November 2017 <https://www.radionz.co.nz/news/political/343787/pm-denies-nz-becoming-a-soft-target-for-people-smuggling>.

12   Sachdeva, above n 11; Patterson, above n 11.

13   Article 33(2) of the *Refugee Convention 1951* denies refugee status to individuals who pose a danger to a nation's security.

the international system we have created provides only the slimmest of pathways for those facing persecution to reach safe havens. People smugglers provide an additional avenue for people who fear severe human rights abuses to reach safety. That avenue is frequently dangerous and, at times, the people smugglers involved may engage in problematic activity. But we need to be careful about casting all people smugglers as the world's villains. In World War II, we saw those who smuggled Jews out of Germany as heroes.[14] It is time that we took note of this history and thought about its relevance for the world today.

3   New Zealand Company Breaches United Nations Sanctions

In February 2017, a United Nations Panel of Experts[15] determined that the New Zealand company, Pacific Aerospace Limited, had breached the sanctions measures imposed on North Korea in Security Council Resolution 1718 (2006).[16] Eight months later in the New Zealand District Court, Pacific Aerospace pleaded guilty to three charges related to the breach of the sanctions in Security Council Resolution 1718 and one charge of making an erroneous export entry under the *Customs and Excise Act 1996*.[17]

The background to these incidents is the sanctions regime set up under Security Council Resolution 1718. Security Council Resolution 1718 was adopted in 2006 to impose far-reaching sanctions on North Korea in a bid to temper its nuclear programme. One aspect of the sanctions' regime in the resolution forbid states from sending "luxury goods"[18] to the dictatorship. Exactly what constitutes "luxury goods" varies from state to state in the United Nations. In

---

14   Daniel Johnson, "Wartime 'people smugglers' finally feted as heroes", *Swiss Info* (online) 8 October 2014 <https://www.swissinfo.ch/eng/politics/wwii-resistance_wartime--people-smugglers--finally-feted-as-heroes/40929358>; Joe Sommerland, "Holocaust Memorial Day 2018: Meet three unsung heroes who helped Europe's Jews escape the Nazis", *The Independent* (online) 26 January 2018 <https://www.independent.co.uk/news/world/holocaust-memorial-day-2018-unsung-war-heroes-saved-jews-nazis-irena-sendler-frank-foley-raoul-a8179146.html>.

15   The United Nations Panel of Experts was established under Security Council Resolution 1874 (2009) to investigate the implementation of Security Council Resolution 1718.

16   *Resolution 1718 (2006) Non-proliferation/Democratic People's Republic of Korea*, SC Res 1718 (14 October 2006).

17   *Customs and Excise Act 1996* (NZ) ss 203(1)(b), (3)(b).

18   *Resolution 1718 (2006)*, above n 16, operative paragraph 8(a)(iii). See also Thomas Manch, "Pacific Aerospace guilty of unlawful exports to North Korea", *Stuff* (online) 11 October 2017 <https://www.stuff.co.nz/business/96724372/pacific-aerospace-guilty-of-unlawful-exports-to-north-korea>.

New Zealand, we have determined that the term includes aircraft or aircraft parts.

Pacific Aerospace did not send aircraft or aircraft parts directly to North Korea at any stage. It did, however, indirectly send aircraft parts there in 2016. The events leading up to this were that in 2015 Pacific Aerospace sold a P-750 XSTOL aircraft to a company in China. That company sold the aircraft onto another Chinese company and this second Chinese company sent the aircraft to North Korea in December 2015. In January 2016, Pacific Aerospace was informed that the aircraft was in North Korea. Later that year, they were asked on three separate occasions to supply replacement parts for the aircraft. Pacific Aerospace complied with these requests, sending the parts to the company in China which then passed them onto people on the ground in North Korea. It was these actions that gave rise to the sanctions breaches.[19]

These breaches may never have come to light were it not for the Wonsan air show in North Korea in September 2016. Pictures of the Wonsan air show – North Korea's first air show – were beamed around the globe. One of the photos featured the P-750 SXTOL and raised the suspicions of both the United Nations Panel of Experts and the New Zealand Customs Service and lead to their investigations.[20] While no consequences have flowed for New Zealand or Pacific Aerospace from the United Nations Panel of Experts' report, it is highly likely that Pacific Aerospace will face fines. The District Court is due to sentence the company in 2018.

---

19   *Report of the Panel of Experts established pursuant to resolution 1874 (2009)* UN Doc S/2017/150 (27 February 2017); *New Zealand Customs Service Prosecutor v Pacific Aerospace Limited* [2018] NZDC 5034 (29 May 2018).

20   Dan Satherley and Jenna Lynch, "What's a Hamilton-made plane doing in North Korea?" *Newshub* (online) 3 October 2016 <https://www.newshub.co.nz/home/money/2016/10/whats-a-hamilton-made-plane-doing-in-north-korea.html>; Anna Fifield, "How did North Korea get its hands on a New Zealand plane made with American parts?" *Washington Post* (online) 3 October 2016 <https://www.washingtonpost.com/world/how-did-north-korea-get-its-hands-on-a-new-zealand-plane-made-with-american-parts/2016/10/03/105591d2-892e-11e6-8a68-b4ce96c78e04_story.html?noredirect=on&utm_term=.3c7f14951f9f>.

New Zealand State Conduct

∴

Treaty Action and Implementation

Mark Gobbi*

1 Overview

This article documents governmental activity undertaken to implement New Zealand's international obligations during the current interval.[1] It concludes that the level of activity in the current interval, relative to the previous interval,[2] decreased for the parliamentary branch but has increased for the executive and judicial branch branches. This overview summarises that activity and compares it with the activity undertaken during the previous interval.

1.1 *Parliamentary Activity*
1.1.1 Acts of Parliament
During the current interval, Parliament enacted 43 Bills with implications for New Zealand's international obligations. Thirty-five simply amended Acts that had implemented treaties, six improved compliance with treaties that had already been implemented, and two implemented new treaties. Thirty-nine of these bills involved multilateral agreements, three involved bilateral agreements, and one involved a code.

In terms of Acts, this level of activity is less than the previous interval. During the previous interval, Parliament enacted 45 bills with implications for New Zealand's international obligations. Thirty-nine simply amended Acts that had implemented treaties, four improved compliance with treaties that had already been implemented, and two implemented new treaties. Thirty-two of these bills involved multilateral agreements, nine involved bilateral agreements, three concerned recommendations, and one involved a code.[3]

---

* The author is currently serving as Parliamentary Counsel in New Zealand's Parliamentary Counsel Office. However, the views expressed herein are the author's own and may not be attributed to the Parliamentary Counsel Office or the Attorney-General. The splendid research work of Emma Pairman and Victoria Squires, who gathered the material found in Parts 3.1 and 4, is gratefully acknowledged.

1 The current interval began on 1 July 2016 and ended on 30 June 2017.
2 The previous interval began on 1 July 2015 and ended on 30 June 2016.
3 Mark Gobbi, "Treaty Action and Implementation" (2016) 14 *New Zealand Yearbook of International Law* 311, 322–33.

1.1.2   Treaty Examination Reports

During the current interval, the House of Representatives considered 8 select committee reports on treaties (10 agreements in all). Five reports brought matters to the attention of the House. Public submissions featured in three of these reports, and none warranted a Government response.[4]

In terms of reports, this level of activity is less than during the previous interval (four less reports). In terms of agreements examined, this level of activity is also less than during the previous interval (two less agreements). During the previous interval, the House of Representatives considered 12 select committee reports on treaties (12 agreements in all). Eleven reports brought matters to the attention of the House. Public submissions featured in six of these reports, and none warranted a Government response.[5]

1.2   *Executive Activity*

1.2.1   Regulations

During the current interval, the Executive made 43 regulations relevant to New Zealand's international obligations. Three of these regulations implemented a bilateral agreement, three implemented recommendations, three implemented standards, and 34 implemented multilateral agreements. Twenty concerned environmental agreements, eight dealt with civil aviation, six concerned trade, three involved land transport, two dealt with money laundering, one dealt with social welfare, one dealt with food, one dealt with intellectual property, and one adopted resolutions of the United Nations Security Council.

This level of activity is more than the level of activity that took place during the previous interval. During the previous interval, the Executive made 33 regulations relevant to New Zealand's international obligations. Three of these regulations implemented a bilateral agreement, two implemented recommendations, one implemented standards, and 27 implemented multilateral agreements. Fourteen concerned environmental agreements, six dealt with civil aviation, four adopted resolutions of the United Nations Security Council, three concerned trade, two dealt with money laundering, two dealt with labour, one dealt with taxes, and one dealt with drugs.[6]

1.2.2   Treaty Actions

During the current interval, the Executive was involved in 44 treaty actions with respect to seven multilateral agreements and 28 bilateral agreements.

---

4   See Standing Order 252 (2017).
5   Gobbi (2016), above n 3, 312, 318–22.
6   Ibid 312, 333–45.

Of the seven multilateral agreements (11 actions), the Executive ratified one, accepted two, and acceded to one. Seven came into force. Of the 28 bilateral agreements (32 actions), the Executive signed 12. Twenty came into force.

This level of activity is more than the level of activity that took place during the previous interval. During the previous interval, the Executive was involved in 38 treaty actions with respect to five multilateral agreements and 22 bilateral agreements. Of the five multilateral agreements (seven actions), the Executive signed three, ratified one, accepted one, and acceded to one. One came into force. Of the 22 bilateral agreements (31 actions), the Executive signed 22. Nine came into force.[7]

1.2.3 Periodic Reports

New Zealand is required to provide periodic reports to the United Nations regarding its compliance with the following human rights treaties: the International Covenant on Civil and Political Rights (1966), the International Covenant on Economic, Social and Cultural Rights (1966), the International Convention on the Elimination of All Forms of Racial Discrimination (1966), the Convention on the Elimination of All Forms of Discrimination against Women (1979), the Convention against Torture and Other Cruel, Inhuman or Degrading Treatment or Punishment (1984), the Convention on the Rights of the Child (1989), and the Convention on the Rights of Persons with Disabilities (2006).[8]

During the current interval, the Executive submitted New Zealand's eighth periodic report in respect of the Convention on the Elimination of All Forms of Discrimination against Women (1979).[9]

In terms of periodic reports, this level of activity is less than the level of activity that took place during the previous interval. During the previous interval, the Executive submitted New Zealand's twenty-first and twenty-second periodic reports in respect of the International Convention on the Elimination of All Forms of Racial Discrimination (1966) and New Zealand's fifth periodic report in respect of the Convention on the Rights of the Child (1989). It also

---

7   Ibid 312–13, 316–18.
8   For an online record of New Zealand's periodic reporting under these agreements, see <http://tbinternet.ohchr.org/_layouts/TreatyBodyExternal/Countries.aspx?CountryCode= NZL&Lang=EN; http://tbinternet.ohchr.org/_layouts/TreatyBodyExternal/Countries.aspx? CountryCode=NZL&Lang=EN>; see also <https://www.justice.govt.nz/justice-sector-policy/ constitutional-issues-and-human-rights/human-rights/international-human-rights/>.
9   For a copy of this report, see Committee on the Elimination of Discrimination against Women, *Consideration of reports submitted by States parties under article 18 of the Convention: Eighth periodic report of States parties due in 2016: New Zealand*, UN Doc CEDAW/C/NZL/8 (15 July 2016).

submitted further information following a review of New Zealand's sixth periodic report under the Convention against Torture and Other Cruel, Inhuman or Degrading Treatment or Punishment (1984).[10]

1.3   *Judicial Activity*

During the current interval, the judiciary delivered 106 judgments that referenced New Zealand's international obligations. Twenty of these judgments were reported in the New Zealand Law Report series; the Supreme Court delivered four, the Court of Appeal delivered 10, and the High Court delivered six. Eighty-six were reported in other series; the Supreme Court delivered one, the Court of Appeal delivered seven, the High Court delivered 52, the Family Court delivered 12, the Employment Court delivered five, the District Court delivered three, the Youth Court delivered two, the Human Rights Review Tribunal delivered three, and the Privy Council delivered one. None were unreported.

Of these 106 judgments, 20 dealt with family law, 15 with criminal law, 13 with deportation, eight with refugee law, seven with employment law, five with immigration law, four with prisoners' rights, four with civil procedure, three with extradition, three with taxation, three with accident compensation, two with Māori land, two with aviation law, two with evidence law, two with social security, two with the Bill of Rights, two with judicial review, two with discrimination law, two with copyright law, one with insolvency, one with equity, one with local government, one with defamation, and one with constitutional law.

These 106 judgments referred to 36 different international instruments (one of which does not have New Zealand as a party), of which 34 are multilateral agreements and two are model laws. In total, these judgments have 154 references.

In these cases, the most frequently cited international agreements are the International Covenant on Civil and Political Rights (1966) (37 references), the United Nations Convention on the Rights of the Child (1989) (23 references), the Hague Convention on the Civil Aspects of International Child Abduction (1980) (11 references), the United Nations Convention Relating to the Status of Refugees (1951) (eight references), the European Convention for the Protection of Human Rights and Fundamental Freedoms (1950) (eight references), the International Covenant on Economic, Social and Cultural Rights (1966) (eight references), the United Nations Convention Against Torture and Other Cruel, Inhuman or Degrading Treatment or Punishment (1984) (six references), the Vienna Convention on the Law of Treaties (1969) (four references), the Berne Convention for the Protection of Literary and Artistic Works (1886 as amended 1971) (three references), the United Nations Convention on the Rights of

---

10   Gobbi (2016), above n 3, 313–14.

Persons with Disabilities (2006) (three references), the United Nations Declaration on the Rights of Indigenous Peoples (2007) (three references), and the Universal Declaration of Human Rights (1948) (six references); three other instruments are referenced twice and 17 others are referenced once.

In terms of the number of judgments delivered, the level of activity is more than the activity that took place during the previous interval. During the previous interval, the judiciary delivered 63 judgments that referenced New Zealand's international obligations. Seven of these judgments were reported in the New Zealand Law Report series; the Supreme Court delivered two, the Court of Appeal delivered three, and the High Court delivered two. Fifty-six were reported in other series; the Supreme Court delivered three, the Court of Appeal delivered 12, the High Court delivered 30, the District Court delivered one, the Family Court delivered eight, the Youth Court delivered one, and the Human Rights Review Tribunal delivered one. None were unreported.

Of these 63 judgments, 17 dealt with family law, nine with immigration, seven with judicial review, five with criminal law, four with civil procedure, two with evidence law, two with extradition, two with human rights law, two with social security, one with arbitration, one with criminal procedure, one with legal aid, one with constitutional law, one with criminal justice, one with contract law, one with sentencing, one with privacy, one with social welfare, one with employment law, one with youth justice, one with environmental law, and one with cross-border insolvency.

These 63 judgments referred to 27 different international instruments (one of which does not have New Zealand as a party), of which 24 are multilateral agreements, one is a bilateral agreement, one is a declaration, and one is a set of principles and guidelines. In total, these judgments have 101 references. In these cases, the most frequently cited international agreements are the United Nations Convention on the Rights of the Child (1989) (26 references), the International Covenant on Civil and Political Rights (1966) (18 references), the United Nations Convention Relating to the Status of Refugees (1951) (10 references), the European Convention for the Protection of Human Rights and Fundamental Freedoms (1950) (nine references), the Hague Convention on the Civil Aspects of International Child Abduction (1980) (six references), the Protocol Relating to the Status of Refugees (1967) (four references), the United Nations Convention on the Rights of Persons with Disabilities (2006) (three references), and the Convention against Torture and Other Cruel, Inhuman or Degrading Treatment or Punishment (1984) (three references). Three other instruments are referenced twice and 16 others are referenced once.[11]

---

11   Gobbi (2016), above n 3, 314–16, 345–54.

1.4   *Conclusion*

During the current interval, each of the three branches of government contributed to the implementation of New Zealand's international obligations. The level of activity for the current interval decreased relative to the previous interval for Parliament, but increased for the Executive and Parliament. International agreements continue to be a significant source of law in New Zealand.

2   Treaty Action

This Part sets out the treaty actions taken by the Executive during the current interval. It lists the agreements that New Zealand has signed, ratified, accepted, approved, or acceded to, or that entered into force for New Zealand. It also sets out the reports on treaties that the Executive tabled in the House during the current interval.

2.1   *Executive Treaty Action*[12]
2.1.1   Multilateral Treaties

Seventh Additional Protocol to the Constitution of the Universal Postal Union done at Bucharest on 5 October 2004 (entered into force on 8 September 2016)

Eighth Additional Protocol to the Constitution of the Universal Postal Union done at Geneva on 12 August 2008 (entered into force on 8 September 2016)

Optional Protocol to the Convention on the Rights of Persons with Disabilities done at New York on 13 December 2006 (acceded to and entered into force on 3 November 2016)

Paris Agreement on Climate Change done at Paris on 12 December 2015 (entered into force on 4 November 2016)

Protocol Amending the TRIPS Agreement done at Geneva on 6 December 2005 (accepted and entered into force on 23 January 2017)

World Trade Organisation: Trade Facilitation Agreement done at Geneva on 29 September 2015 (accepted and entered into force on 22 February 2017)

---

12   See New Zealand Ministry of Foreign Affairs and Trade, *Annual Report 2016–17*, A.1 AR (2017) 101–2. See also New Zealand Treaties online at <www.treaties.mfat.govt.nz/>.

Maritime Labour Convention done at Geneva on 23 September 2006 (ratified and entered into force on 9 March 2017)

2.1.2 Bilateral Treaties

Air Services Agreement between the Government of the Republic of Mauritius and the Government of New Zealand (signed 27 July 2016)

Air Services Agreement between the Government of the State of Kuwait and the Government of New Zealand (entered into force 1 August 2016)

Air Services Agreement between the Government of the Republic of Finland and the Government of New Zealand (entered into force 1 September 2016)

Agreement between the Government of New Zealand and the Government of the French Republic regarding the Status of Visiting Forces and Defence Cooperation (entered into force 1 September 2016)

Air Services Agreement between the Government of New Zealand and the Government of the Lao People's Democratic Republic (signed 8 September 2016 and entered into force 5 May 2017)

Audiovisual Co-production Treaty between the Government of New Zealand and the Government of Canada (signed 11 September 2016 and entered into force 1 May 2017)

Air Services Agreement between the Government of the Kingdom of Cambodia and the Government of New Zealand (entered into force 22 September 2016)

Partnership Agreement on Relations and Cooperation between New Zealand and the European Union (signed 5 October 2016)

Agreement between the Government of New Zealand and the Government of St Vincent and the Grenadines on the Exchange of Information with respect to Taxes (entered into force 17 October 2016)

Side Letters on the treatment of items covered by HS headings 2203, 2204, 2205, 2206, 2207, and 2208 of the Malaysia New Zealand Free Trade Agreement (signed 20 October 2016 and entered into force 2 November 2016)

Third Protocol to the Convention between the Government of the Republic of India and the Government of New Zealand for the Avoidance of Double Taxation and the Prevention of Fiscal Evasion with Respect to Taxes on Income (signed 26 October 2016)

Agreement between the Government of New Zealand and the Government of the Republic of Vanuatu on the Exchange of Information with respect to Taxes (entered into force 27 October 2016)

Exchange of letters which comprise the Resolute Support Mission Financial and Participation Agreement between NATO and New Zealand (signed and entered into force 28 October 2016)

Agreement between the Government of the State of Qatar and the Government of New Zealand for Air Services (entered into force 4 December 2016)

Agreement on Film Co-Production Between the Government of New Zealand and the Government of the State of Israel (entered into force 7 December 2016)

Agreement on Social Security between the Government of New Zealand and Government of Australia (signed 8 December 2016)

Agreement between the Government of New Zealand and the Government of the United States of America on Technology Safeguards Associated with United States Participation in Space Launches from New Zealand (entered into force 12 December 2016)

Agreement between the Government of New Zealand and the Government of the British Virgin Islands for the Exchange of Information Relating to Taxes (entered into force 23 December 2016)

Agreement between the Government of New Zealand and the Government of the British Virgin Islands for the Allocation of Taxing Rights with Respect to Certain Income of Individuals (entered into force 23 December 2016)

Agreement between the Government of New Zealand and the Government of the Turks and Caicos Islands on the Exchange of Information with Respect to Taxes (entered into force 23 December 2016)

Agreement on a Working Holiday Scheme Between the Government of the Republic of Lithuania and the Government of New Zealand (entered into force 1 January 2017)

Agreement between the Government of New Zealand and the Government of Anguilla on the Exchange of Information with Respect to Taxes (entered into force 6 January 2017)

Air Services Agreement between the Government of the Republic of Mauritius and the Government of New Zealand (entered into force 3 February 2017)

Agreement Relating to Science, Research and Innovation Cooperation Between the Government of Australia and the Government of New Zealand (signed 17 February 2017)

Exchange of Letters amending the existing Agreement on a Working Holiday Scheme between the Government of New Zealand and the Government of the French Republic (entered into force 10 March 2017)

Exchange of Letters between the Government of New Zealand and the Government of the United States of America implementing the Asia Pacific Economic Cooperation Mutual Recognition Arrangement for Conformity Assessment of Telecommunications Equipment (signed and entered into force 22 March 2017)

New Zealand-Australia Side Letter: Application of PACER Plus between Australia and New Zealand (signed 14 June 2017)

Second Protocol to amend the Agreement between the Government of Hong Kong Special Administrative Region of the People's Republic of China and the Government of New Zealand for the Avoidance of Double Taxation and the Prevention of Fiscal Evasion with respect to taxes on income (signed 28 June 2017)

2.2   *Reports on Treaties Tabled in the House of Representatives*
2.2.1   Reports Where No Substantive Matters were Drawn to the
             Attention of the House
International treaty examination of the 1999 Amendments to the Plant Protection Agreement for the Asia and Pacific Region; Primary Production Committee (23 June 2017)

International treaty examination of the Agreed Record of the Amendments to the Treaty on Fisheries between the Governments of Certain Pacific Island States and the Government of the United States of America; Primary Production Committee (23 June 2017)

International treaty examination of the Agreement between the Government of New Zealand and the Government of the Republic of San Marino on the Exchange of Information with Respect to Taxes; Finance and Expenditure Committee (16 February 2017)

2.2.2   Reports Where Substantive Matters were Drawn to the Attention of the House

International treaty examination of the Partnership Agreement on Relations and Cooperation between New Zealand, of the one part, and the European Union and its Member States, of the other part; Foreign Affairs, Defence and Trade Committee [2 submissions] (21 November 2016)

> The Committee noted that New Zealand's strategic objective with the European Union is to develop a comprehensive partnership that includes a free trade agreement, and that the Agreement is a co-requisite and a pre-requisite to a free trade agreement. The Committee also noted that, owing to European Union's ratification process, the Agreement is likely to take some time to come into force.

International treaty examination of the Paris Agreement; Foreign Affairs, Defence and Trade Committee [14 submissions, 10 heard] (4 October 2016)

> The Committee supported becoming a party to the Agreement. In doing so, the majority noted that the Agreement is to come into force when at least 55 parties have ratified it, set out the reasons for ratification, discussed New Zealand's target, canvassed New Zealand's key obligations, and outlined the possible economic effects of the Agreement. The minority endorsed the majority's support for the Agreement while critiquing the majority's report to give the public full knowledge of where New Zealand stands in the United Nations negotiations on climate change.

International treaty examination of the Optional Protocol to the Convention on the Rights of Persons with Disabilities; Justice and Electoral Committee [24 submissions] (22 August 2016)

The Committee supported ratification of the Optional Protocol. It canvassed the implications of doing so.

International treaty examination of the Universal Postal Convention Final Protocol, General Regulations, Seventh Additional Protocol to the Constitution, and Eighth Additional Protocol to the Constitution; Commerce Committee (22 August 2016)

> The Committee supported adoption of the various amendments to the Acts of the Universal Postal Union. In doing so, it noted that none of the amendments require legislative change and that the advantages of ratifying the amendments significantly outweigh the disadvantages.

International treaty examination of the Convention on Registration of Objects Launched into Outer Space; Foreign Affairs, Defence and Trade Committee (19 August 2016)

> The Committee noted that, while unnecessary to launch space objects from New Zealand, accession to the Convention would help to develop and maintain an internationally credible space industry in New Zealand. It also noted that it would also be consistent with New Zealand's position of promoting a rules-based approach to the responsible use of space.

3 Legislation Related to New Zealand's International Obligations

This Part sets out the legislation dealt with during the current interval that concerns New Zealand's international obligations. It is divided into two sections, the first listing the Acts that were enacted and the second listing the regulations that were made.

3.1 *Acts of Parliament*

Acts of Parliament relating to New Zealand's international obligations are identified as: (3.1.1) Acts simply amending legislation that has implemented treaties; (3.1.2) Acts improving compliance with treaties that have already been implemented; or (3.1.3) Acts implementing new treaty obligations.

3.1.1 Acts Simply Amending Legislation that Implemented Treaties
Accident Compensation Amendment Act 2016

This Act amends the Accident Compensation Act 2001. The Accident Compensation Act 2001 repealed and replaced the Accident Insurance Act 1998. The

Accident Insurance Act 1988 continues to apply with respects to Parts 10 and 11 of the Accident Compensation Act 2001. The Accident Insurance Act 1998 implemented the ILO Convention 12 (1921): Workmen's Compensation (Agriculture), the ILO Convention 17 (1925): Workmen's Compensation (Accidents), and the ILO Convention 42 (1934): Workmen's Compensation (Occupational Diseases).

Agricultural Compounds and Veterinary Medicines Amendment Act 2016

This Act amends the Agricultural Compounds and Veterinary Medicines Act 1997, which implements the Convention on Persistent Organic Pollutants (2001).

Arbitration Amendment Act 2016

This Act amends the Arbitration Act 1996, which implements the Protocol on Arbitration Clauses (1923), the Convention on the Execution of Foreign Arbitral Awards (1927), the Convention on the Recognition and Enforcement of Foreign Arbitral Awards (1958), and the Model Law on International Commercial Arbitration adopted by the United Nations Commission on International Trade Law (1985).

Bills of Exchange Amendment Act 2016

This Act amends the Bills of Exchange Act 1908, which implements the Convention on the Stamp Laws in Connection with Bills of Exchange and Promissory Notes (1930), the Convention on the Stamp Laws in Connection with Cheques (1931), and the Convention Providing a Uniform Law for Cheques (1931).

Broadcasting (Election Programmes and Election Advertising) Amendment Act 2017

This Act amends the Broadcasting Act 1989, which implements International Chamber of Commerce International Code of Advertising Practice (1987).

Children, Young Persons, and Their Families (Advocacy, Workforce, and Age Settings) Amendment Act 2016

This Act amends the Children, Young Persons, and Their Families Act 1989 (since renamed the Oranga Tamariki Act 1989), which implements the Arrangement between New Zealand and Australian States and Territories regarding the transfer of children subject to child protection orders (2000).

Children, Young Persons, and Their Families Amendment Act 2016

This Act amends the Children, Young Persons, and Their Families Act 1989 (since renamed the Oranga Tamariki Act 1989), which implements the Arrangement between New Zealand and Australian States and Territories regarding the transfer of children subject to child protection orders (2000).

Children, Young Persons, and Their Families Amendment Act (No 2) 2016

This Act amends the Oranga Tamariki Act 1989, which implements the Arrangement between New Zealand and Australian States and Territories regarding the transfer of children subject to child protection orders (2000).

Climate Change Response (Removal of Transitional Measure) Amendment Act 2016

This Act amends the Climate Change Response Act 2002, which implements the United Nations Framework Convention on Climate Change (1992) and the Kyoto Protocol to the United Nations Framework Convention on Climate Change (1997).

Copyright Amendment Act 2016

This Act amends the Copyright Act 1994, which implements the Berne Convention for the Protection of Literary and Artistic Works (1896 as amended 1971), the Universal Copyright Convention (1952), the GATT Agreement on Trade-Related Aspects of Intellectual Property Rights (1994), the Madrid Agreement Concerning the International Registration of Marks (1989), the Nice Agreement Concerning the International Classification of Goods and Services for the Purposes of the Registration of Marks (1957 as amended 1979), and the Singapore Treaty on the Law of Trademarks (2006).

Corrections (Electronic Monitoring of Offenders) Amendment Act 2016

This Act amends the Corrections Act 2004, which implements the United Nations Standard Minimum Rules for the Treatment of Prisoners (1955, amended 1977) and the Convention on the Rights of the Child (1989).

Customs and Excise (Tobacco Products – Budget Measures) Amendment Act 2016

This Act amends the Customs and Excise Act 1996, which implements the Customs Convention on the Temporary Importation of Private Road Vehicles

(1954), the Customs Convention on Containers (1972), the Recommendations of Financial Action Task Force (Task Force established 1989), the Protocol of Amendment to the International Convention on the Simplification and Harmonization of Customs Procedures (1999), the Free Trade Agreement between the Government of New Zealand and the Government of the People's Republic of China (2008), and the Agreement Establishing the ASEAN–Australia–New Zealand Free Trade Area (2009). The Act also implements a standard for motor fuel testing established by the American Society for Testing and Materials International (ASTM D2699:79).

Education Legislation Act 2016
This Act amends the Education Act 1989, which implements the ILO Convention 10 (1921): Minimum Age (Agriculture), the ILO Convention 58 (1936): Minimum Age (Sea), the ILO Convention 59 (1937): Minimum Age (Industry), the Convention against Discrimination in Education (1960), and the ILO Convention 122 (1964): Employment Policy.

Education (Update) Amendment Act 2017
This Act amends the Education Act 1989, which implements the ILO Convention 10 (1921): Minimum Age (Agriculture), the ILO Convention 58 (1936): Minimum Age (Sea), the ILO Convention 59 (1937): Minimum Age (Industry), the Convention against Discrimination in Education (1960), and the ILO Convention 122 (1964): Employment Policy.

Electoral Amendment Act 2017
This Act amends the Electoral Act 1993, which implements aspects of the International Covenant on Civil and Political Rights (1966) and the Convention on the Elimination of All Forms of Discrimination against Women (1979).

Employment Relations Amendment Act 2016
This Act amends the Employment Relations Act 2000, which implements the ILO Convention 11 (1921): Right of Association (Agriculture), the ILO Convention 14 (1921): Weekly Rest (Industry), the ILO Convention 22 (1926): Seamen's Articles of Agreement, the ILO Convention 32 (1932): Protection against Accidents (Dockers), and the ILO Convention 122 (1964): Employment Policy. The Act also incorporates the principles underlying ILO Convention 87 (1948): Freedom of Association and ILO Convention 98 (1949): Right to Organise and Bargain Collectively.

Employment Relations Amendment Act (No 2) 2016

This Act amends the Employment Relations Act 2000, which implements the ILO Convention 11 (1921): Right of Association (Agriculture), the ILO Convention 14 (1921): Weekly Rest (Industry), the ILO Convention 22 (1926): Seamen's Articles of Agreement, the ILO Convention 32 (1932): Protection against Accidents (Dockers), and the ILO Convention 122 (1964): Employment Policy. The Act also incorporates the principles underlying ILO Convention 87 (1948): Freedom of Association and ILO Convention 98 (1949): Right to Organise and Bargain Collectively.

Evidence Amendment Act 2016

This Act amends the Evidence Act 2006, which implements the Hague Convention Abolishing the Requirement of Legalisation for Foreign Public Documents (1961), the International Covenant on Civil and Political Rights (1966), the Convention on the Taking of Evidence Abroad in Civil or Commercial Matters (1970), the Convention on the Civil Aspects of International Child Abduction (1980), and the Convention against Torture and Other Cruel, Inhuman or Degrading Treatment or Punishment (1984).

Family Courts Act 1980

This Act amends the Family Courts Act 1980, which implements aspects of the Convention on the Elimination of All Forms of Discrimination against Women (1979).

Health (Protection) Amendment Act 2016

This Act amends the Health Act 1956, which implements aspects of the Convention for the Constitution of the World Health Organisation (1946) and the Protocol concerning the Office International d'Hygiène Publique (1946).

Holidays Amendment Act (No 2) 2016

This Act amends the Holidays Act 2003, which implements the ILO Convention 52 (1936): Holidays with Pay and the ILO Convention 101 (1952): Holidays with Pay (Agriculture).

Land Transport Amendment Act 2016

This Act amends the Land Transport Act 1998, which implements the Convention on Road Traffic (1949).

Medicines Amendment Act 2016

This Act amends the Medicines Act 1981, which implements the Single Convention on Narcotic Drugs (1961), Article 14 of the International Covenant on Civil and Political Rights (1966), the Convention on Psychotropic Substances (1971), the Protocol to the Single Convention on Narcotic Drugs (1972), and the Convention against Illicit Traffic in Narcotic Drugs and Psychotropic Substances (1988).

Mental Health (Compulsory Assessment and Treatment)
Amendment Act 2016

This Act amends the Mental Health (Compulsory Assessment and Treatment) Act 1992, which implements the Universal Declaration of Human Rights (1948).

Misuse of Drugs Amendment Act 2016

This Act amends the Misuse of Drugs Act 1975, which implements the Single Convention on Narcotic Drugs (1961), the Convention on Psychotropic Substances (1971), the Protocol to the Single Convention on Narcotic Drugs (1972), the Convention on the Physical Protection of Nuclear Material and Nuclear Facilities (1980), the Convention against Illicit Traffic in Narcotic Drugs and Psychotropic Substances (1988), the Recommendations of Financial Action Task Force (Task Force established 1989), and the Convention on the Marking of Plastic Explosives for the Purpose of Detection (1991).

Official Information (Parliamentary Under-Secretaries) Amendment
Act 2016

This Act amends the Official Information Act 1982, which implements aspects of the Universal Declaration of Human Rights (1948), the Convention relating to the Status of Refugees (1951), and the International Covenant on Civil and Political Rights (1966).

Policing (Cost Recovery) Amendment Act 2016

This Act implements the Policing Act 2008, which implements Article 43 of the Charter of the United Nations (1945).

Resource Management Amendment Act 2016

This Act amends the Resource Management Act 1991, which implements aspects of the Convention on Wetlands of International Importance especially as Waterfowl Habitat (1971), the United Nations Framework Convention on

Climate Change (1992), and the Kyoto Protocol to the United Nations Framework Convention on Climate Change (1997).

Sale and Supply of Alcohol (Display of Low-alcohol Beverages and Other Remedial Matters) Amendment Act 2016

This Act amends the Sale and Supply of Alcohol Act 2012, which implements
aspects of the International Covenant on Civil and Political Rights (1966) and
the ILO Convention 59 (1937): Minimum Age (Industry).

Sentencing (Drug and Alcohol Testing) Amendment Act 2016

This Act amends the Sentencing Act 2002, which implements the Convention
on the Physical Protection of Nuclear Material and Nuclear Facilities (1980)
and the Convention on the Marking of Plastic Explosives for the Purpose of
Detection (1991).

Sentencing (Electronic Monitoring of Offenders) Amendment Act 2016

This Act amends the Sentencing Act 2002, which implements the Convention
on the Physical Protection of Nuclear Material and Nuclear Facilities (1980)
and the Convention on the Marking of Plastic Explosives for the Purpose of
Detection (1991).

Telecommunications (Property Access and Other Matters) Amendment Act 2017

This Act amends the Telecommunications Act 2001, which implements aspects
of the International Telecommunication Convention with Annexes, Final Protocol, and Additional Protocols I to VII, and Annexed Radio Regulations (1932)
and the Constitution of the Asia–Pacific Telecommunity (1979).

Smoke-free Environments (Tobacco Standardised Packaging) Amendment Act 2016

This Act amends the Smoke-free Environments Act 1990, which implements
the Convention for the Suppression of Unlawful Acts against the Safety of Civil
Aviation (1973), and the Convention on the Rights of the Child (1989).

Social Security (Extension of Young Persons Services and Remedial Matters) Amendment Act 2016

This Act amends the Social Security Act 1964, which implements the ILO Convention 44 (1934): Unemployment Provision, the ILO Convention 122 (1964):
Employment Policy, and the Convention on Social Security between the

Government of the United Kingdom of Great Britain and Northern Ireland and the Government of New Zealand (1969).

Trans-Pacific Partnership Agreement Amendment Act 2016

Part 1 of the Act amends the Copyright Act 1994, which implements the Berne Convention for the Protection of Literary and Artistic Works (1896 as amended 1971), the Universal Copyright Convention (1952), the GATT Agreement on Trade-Related Aspects of Intellectual Property Rights (1994), the Madrid Agreement Concerning the International Registration of Marks (1989), the Nice Agreement Concerning the International Classification of Goods and Services for the Purposes of the Registration of Marks (1957 as amended 1979), and the Singapore Treaty on the Law of Trademarks (2006).

Part 2 of the Act amends the Customs and Excise Act 1996, which implements the Customs Convention on the Temporary Importation of Private Road Vehicles (1954), the Customs Convention on Containers (1972), the Recommendations of Financial Action Task Force (Task Force established 1989), the Protocol of Amendment to the International Convention on the Simplification and Harmonization of Customs Procedures (1999), the Free Trade Agreement between the Government of New Zealand and the Government of the People's Republic of China (2008), the Agreement Establishing the ASEAN–Australia–New Zealand Free Trade Area (2009), and the Customs and Excise Act 1996 also implements a standard for motor fuel testing established by the American Society for Testing and Materials International (ASTM D2699:79).

Part 4 of the Act amends the Hazardous Substances and New Organisms Act 1996, which implements the Convention on Persistent Organic Pollutants (2001).

Part 7 of the Act amends the Patents Act 2013, which implements the Budapest Treaty on the International Recognition of the Deposit of Microorganisms for the Purposes of Patent Procedure (1977), and the Patent Cooperation Treaty (1970). The amendments are designed to give better effect to the joint registration regime in accordance with the Arrangement between the Government of Australia and the Government of New Zealand Relating to Trans-Tasman Regulation of Patent Attorneys (2013).

Part 8 of the Act amends the Tariff Act 1988, which implements the General Agreement on Tariffs and Trade (1947 and 1997), the Agreement between New Zealand and Singapore on Closer Economic Partnership (2001), the New Zealand–Thailand Closer Economic Partnership Agreement (2005), Trans-Pacific Strategic Partnership Agreement among Brunei Darussalam, Chile, New Zealand, and Singapore (2005), the Free Trade Agreement between the Government of New Zealand and the Government of the People's Republic of

China (2008), the Malaysia–New Zealand Free Trade Agreement (2009), the Agreement Establishing the ASEAN–Australia–New Zealand Free Trade Area (2009), the New Zealand–Hong Kong, China Closer Economic Partnership Agreement (2010), and the Free Trade Agreement between New Zealand and the Republic of Korea (2015).

Part 10 of the Act amends the Trade Marks Act 2002, which implements the Convention for the Protection of Industrial Property (1883), the GATT Agreement on Trade-Related Aspects of Intellectual Property Rights (1994), the Madrid Agreement Concerning the International Registration of Marks (1989), the Nice Agreement Concerning the International Classification of Goods and Services for the Purposes of the Registration of Marks (1957 as amended 1979), and the Singapore Treaty on the Law of Trademarks (2006).

3.1.2   Acts Improving Compliance with Treaties Already Implemented
          Contract and Commercial Law Act 2017
This Act is a revision Act intended to consolidate older Acts in an accessible form. The Contract and Commercial Act imports the obligations from the following Acts:

–   the Carriage of Goods Act 1979, which implements the International Convention for the Unification of Certain Rules of Law relating to Bills of Lading ("Hague Rules") (1924), and Protocol of Signature (1924), the Convention for the Unification of Certain Rules Relating to International Carriage by Air (1929), the Guadalajara Convention, supplementary to the Warsaw Convention, for the Unification of Certain Rules relating to International Carriage by Air Performed by a Person other than the Contracting Carrier (1961), and the Protocol to Amend the International Convention for the Unification of Certain Rules of Law Relating to Bills of Lading ("Visby Rules") (1979)

–   the Electronic Transactions Act 2002, which implements the Model Law on Electronic Commerce Law Adopted by the United Nations Commission on International Trade Law (1996), and the Model Law on International Trade Law issued by the United Nations Commission on International Trade Law (1996)

–   the Minor's Contract Act 1969 which implements the Convention relating to the Status of Refugees (1951), and the International Covenant on Civil and Political Rights (1966)

–   the Sale of Good (United Nations Convention) Act 1994, which implements the United Nations Convention on Contracts for the International Sale of Goods (1980)

Geographical Indications (Wine and Spirits) Registration
Amendment Act 2016

This Act amends the Geographical Indications (Wine and Spirits) Registration Act 2006, which implements aspects of the GATT Agreement on Trade-Related Aspects of Intellectual Property Rights (1994).

Intelligence and Security Act 2017

This Act repeals and replaces several old Acts. The International and Security Act 2017 imports the obligations from the following Acts:
- the New Zealand Security Intelligence Service Act 1969, which implements the Convention on the physical protection of nuclear material and nuclear facilities (1980), and the Convention on the Marking of Plastic Explosives for the purpose of Detection (1991)
- the Government Communications Security Bureau Act 2003, which implements the International Convention on Civil and Political Rights (1966)

Senior Courts Act 2016

This Act repealed and replaced the Judicature Act 1908, which implemented the Trans-Tasman Court Proceedings and Regulatory Enforcement (ongoing agreement between New Zealand and Australia). The following rules continue in force under the Act:
- the Evidence (Trans-Tasman Service of, and Compliance with, New Zealand Subpoenas and Australian Subpoenas Issued in Criminal Proceedings) Rules 2013
- the Trans-Tasman Proceedings Regulations and Rules 2013

Trade (Anti-dumping and Countervailing Duties) Amendment
Act 2017

This Act amends the Dumping and Countervailing Duties Act 1988 (and renames it the "Trade (Anti-dumping and Countervailing Duties) Act 1988"), which implements the Agreement on Implementation of Article VI of the GATT (anti-dumping code) (1979), the Agreement establishing the World Trade Organization (1994), and the Agreement between New Zealand and Singapore on Closer Economic Partnership (2001).

Trans-Tasman Proceedings Amendment Act 2016

This Act amends the Trans-Tasman Proceedings Act 2010, which implements the Trans-Tasman Agreement (2008).

3.1.3   Acts Implementing New Treaties
             Patents (Trans-Tasman Patent Attorneys and Other Matters)
             Amendment Act 2016
This Act amends the Patents Act 2013, which implements the International
Recognition of the Deposit of Microorganisms for the Purposes of Patent Pro-
cedure (1977), the Patent Cooperation Treaty (1984), the Regulations under the
Patent Cooperation Treaty (1992), and the GATT Agreement on Trade-Related
Aspects of Intellectual Property Rights (1994). The amendments, among other
things, implements the Arrangement between the Government of Australia
and the Government of New Zealand Relating to Trans-Tasman Regulation of
Patent Attorneys (2013).

             Resource Legislation Amendment Act 2017
This Act amends the Resource Management Act 1991, which implements aspects of the Convention on Wetlands of International Importance especially
as Waterfowl Habitat (1971), the United Nations Framework Convention on
Climate Change (1992), and the Kyoto Protocol to the United Nations Framework Convention on Climate Change (1997). It also amends the Exclusive Economic Zone and Continental Shelf (Environmental Effects) Act 2012, which
implements the Convention on the Prevention of Marine Pollution by Dumping Wastes and Other Matter (1972), the International Convention for the
Prevention of Pollution from Ships (1973), the United Nations Convention on
the Law of the Sea (1982), and the Convention on Biological Diversity (1993).
The latter amendments implement the Protocol to the Convention on the Prevention of Marine Pollution by Dumping Wastes and Other Matter (1996).

3.2   *Regulations*[13]
This section sets out the regulations made during the current interval that
relate to New Zealand's international obligations.[14]

---

13   The regulations listed under this heading supplement the list of regulations known to
      have implications for New Zealand's international obligations set out in Part V of Mark
      Gobbi, "In Search of International Standards and Obligations relevant to New Zealand
      Regulations" (2007–2008) 5 *New Zealand Yearbook of International Law* 327, 343–72.
14   This list of regulations does not include commencement orders for Acts that implement
      international obligations. See, e.g., Biosecurity Law Reform Act 2012 Commencement
      Order 2017, Crimes Amendment Act 2005 Commencement Order 2017, Geographical Indi-
      cations (Wine and Spirits) Registration Act Commencement Order 2017, Misuse of Drugs
      (Classification and Presumption of Supply – 25B-NBOMe, 25C-NBOMe, and 25I-NBOMe)
      Order Commencement Order 2016, Patents (Trans-Tasman Patent Attorneys and Other
      Matters Amendment Act 2016) Commencement Order 2017, and Telecommunications
      (Property Access and Other Matters) Amendment Act 2017 Commencement Order 2017.

3.2.1   Agricultural Compounds and Veterinary Medicines (Exemptions
          and Prohibited Substances) Amendment Regulations 2016
These regulations are made under Section 75 of the Agricultural Compounds
and Veterinary Medicines Act 1997. They amend the Agricultural Compounds
and Veterinary Medicines (Exemptions and Prohibited Substances) Regulations 2011, which implement aspects of the Convention on Persistent Organic
Pollutants (2001). The amendment augments the list of substances that are
prohibited from use as agricultural compounds or as ingredients in agricultural compounds. It also complements amendments made by the Hazardous
Substances and New Organisms (Schedules 1AA and 2A) Order 2016 and the
Imports and Exports (Restrictions) Prohibition Order (No 2) 2004 Amendment
Order 2016.

3.2.2   Anti-Money Laundering and Countering Financing of Terrorism
          (Exemptions) Amendment Regulations 2016
These regulations are made under sections 153 and 154 of the Anti-Money
Laundering and Countering Financing of Terrorism Act 2009 and Section
56(1)(e) and (2) of the Financial Transactions Reporting Act 1996. They amend
the Anti-Money Laundering and Countering Financing of Terrorism (Exemptions) Regulations 2011, which provide for certain exemptions to the rules set
out in the Anti-Money Laundering and Countering Financing of Terrorism Act
2009, which implements the Recommendations issued by the Financial Action
Task Force on Money Laundering (established 1989). The amendment exempts
a reporting agency that is an intermediary institution from making a prescribed transaction report under Section 48A of the Anti-Money Laundering
and Countering Financing of Terrorism Act 2009 in respect of any wire transfer.

3.2.3   Anti-Money Laundering and Countering Financing of Terrorism
          (Prescribed Transactions Reporting) Regulations 2016
These regulations are made under Sections 48A, 48B, 153, and 154 of the Anti-
Money Laundering and Countering Financing of Terrorism Act 2009 and Sec-
tion 56(1)(e) and (2) of the Financial Transactions Reporting Act 1996. They
prescribe details to be provided by reporting entities in reports under Section
48A of the Anti-Money Laundering and Countering Financing of Terrorism
Act 2009, which implements the Recommendations issued by the Financial
Action Task Force on Money Laundering (established 1989).

3.2.4   Climate Change (Eligible Industrial Activities) Amendment
          Regulations (No 2) 2016
These regulations are made under Section 161A of the Climate Change Response
Act 2002. The Act implements the United Nations Framework Convention

on Climate Change (1992) and the Kyoto Protocol to the United Nations Framework Convention on Climate Change (1997). These regulations amend the Climate Change (Eligible Industrial Activities) Regulations 2010. The amendments relate to the allocation of New Zealand units for the eligible industrial activity of manufacturing iron and steel from iron sand, adding steel billet and long products of hot-rolled steel as products of that manufacturing that must be used as the basis of allocation.

3.2.5   Climate Change (Eligible Industrial Activities) Amendment
           Regulations 2017
These regulations are made under Section 161A of the Climate Change Response Act 2002. The Act implements the United Nations Framework Convention on Climate Change (1992) and the Kyoto Protocol to the United Nations Framework Convention on Climate Change (1997). These regulations amend the Climate Change (Eligible Industrial Activities) Regulations 2010 to refine the allocative baseline figures for the product produced by aluminium smelting.

3.2.6   Climate Change (Forestry Sector) Amendment Regulations 2016
These regulations are made under sections 163 and 168 of the Climate Change Response Act 2002. The Act implements the United Nations Framework Convention on Climate Change (1992) and the Kyoto Protocol to the United Nations Framework Convention on Climate Change (1997). These regulations amend the Climate Change (Forestry Sector) Regulations 2008 to clarify the definition of sub-area, how to calculate the age of trees, and how to calculate carbon stocks, and to remove an unnecessary restriction relating to applications for the allocation of new permanent sample plots.

3.2.7   Climate Change (Stationary Energy and Industrial Processes)
           Amendment Regulations 2016
These regulations are made under Section 163 of the Climate Change Response Act 2002. The Act implements the United Nations Framework Convention on Climate Change (1992) and the Kyoto Protocol to the United Nations Framework Convention on Climate Change (1997). These regulations amend the Climate Change (Stationary Energy and Industrial Processes) Regulations 2009 to update the emissions factor for natural gas from certain fields and to update the national average emissions factor.

3.2.8   Climate Change (Synthetic Greenhouse Gas Levies) Amendment
           Regulations 2016
These regulations are made under sections 233(4)(b) and 245(1) of the Climate Change Response Act 2002. The Act implements the United Nations

Framework Convention on Climate Change (1992) and the Kyoto Protocol to the United Nations Framework Convention on Climate Change (1997). These regulations amend the Climate Change (Synthetic Greenhouse Gas Levies) Regulations 2013 to specify the price of carbon for the 2017 levy year and pre-scribe the rates of levy for leviable motor vehicles and goods for the 2017 levy year.

3.2.9   Copyright (Application to Other Countries) Amendment Order 2016

This order is made under sections 204 and 232 of the Copyright Act 1994, which implements the Berne Convention for the Protection of Literary and Artistic Works (1896 as amended 1971), the Universal Copyright Convention (1952), and the GATT Agreement on Trade-Related Aspects of Intellectual Property Rights (1994). It amends the Copyright (Application to Other Countries) Order 1995 by updating its terminology and adjusting the list of countries specified in the schedules to reflect changes in the membership of the relevant international organisations and treaties.

3.2.10   Customs and Excise Amendment Regulations 2016

These regulations are made under sections 71 and 286 of the Customs and Excise Act 1996. The Act implements the Australia and New Zealand Closer Economic Relations Trade Agreement (1983), the International Conven-tion on the Harmonised Commodity Description and Coding System (1983), the New Zealand–Thailand Closer Economic Partnership Agreement (2005), the Trans-Pacific Strategic Economic Partnership Agreement among Brunei Darussalam, Chile, New Zealand and Singapore (2005), the Agreement Estab-lishing the ASEAN–Australia–New Zealand Free Trade Area (2009), the New Zealand-Hong Kong, China Closer Economic Partnership Agreement (2010), the Agreement between New Zealand and the Separate Customs Territory of Taiwan, Penghu, Kinmen, and Matsu on Economic Cooperation (2013), and the Free Trade Agreement between New Zealand and the Republic of Korea (2015). These regulations amend the Customs and Excise Regulations 1996 to adjust the rules relating to the payment of duty for alcoholic products and the refund of duty for certain alcoholic and tobacco goods.

3.2.11   Customs and Excise Amendment Regulations 2016

These regulations are made under Section 71 of the Customs and Excise Act 1996. The Act implements the Australia and New Zealand Closer Economic Relations Trade Agreement (1983), the International Convention on the Har-monised Commodity Description and Coding System (1983), the New Zealand-Thailand Closer Economic Partnership Agreement (2005), the Trans-Pacific

Strategic Economic Partnership Agreement among Brunei Darussalam, Chile, New Zealand and Singapore (2005), the Agreement Establishing the ASEAN–Australia–New Zealand Free Trade Area (2009), the New Zealand-Hong Kong, China Closer Economic Partnership Agreement (2010), the Agreement between New Zealand and the Separate Customs Territory of Taiwan, Penghu, Kinmen, and Matsu on Economic Cooperation (2013), and the Free Trade Agreement between New Zealand and the Republic of Korea (2015). These regulations amend the Customs and Excise Regulations 1996 to make provision for electronic entries of excisable goods to be made and passed via the Joint Border Management System.

3.2.12   Customs and Excise (Rules of Origin – Harmonised System)
          Amendment Regulations 2016
These regulations are made under Sections 65 and 287A of the Customs and Excise Act 1996. The Act implements the Australia and New Zealand Closer Economic Relations Trade Agreement (1983), the International Convention on the Harmonised Commodity Description and Coding System (1983), the New Zealand–Thailand Closer Economic Partnership Agreement (2005), the Trans-Pacific Strategic Economic Partnership Agreement among Brunei Darussalam, Chile, New Zealand and Singapore (2005), the Agreement Establishing the ASEAN–Australia–New Zealand Free Trade Area (2009), the New Zealand–Hong Kong, China Closer Economic Partnership Agreement (2010), the Agreement between New Zealand and the Separate Customs Territory of Taiwan, Penghu, Kinmen, and Matsu on Economic Cooperation (2013), and the Free Trade Agreement between New Zealand and the Republic of Korea (2015). These regulations amend the Customs and Excise Regulations 1996 to update product-specific rules of origin relating to certain parties with which New Zealand has free trade agreements.

3.2.13   Customs Import Prohibition (Southern Bluefin Tuna) Order 2016
This order is made under Section 54 of the Customs and Excise Act 1996. The order prohibits the importation of southern Bluefin tuna so as to give effect to New Zealand's obligations under the Convention for the Conservation of Southern Bluefin Tuna (1993).

3.2.14   Exclusive Economic Zone and Continental Shelf (Environmental
          Effects – Permitted Activities) Amendment Regulations 2016
These regulations are made under sections 27(1), 30(1) and 35 of the Exclusive Economic Zone and Continental Shelf (Environmental Effects) Act 2012. The Act implements aspects of the Convention on the Prevention of Marine Pollution by Dumping Wastes and Other Matter (1972), the International Convention

for the Prevention of Pollution from Ships (1973), the United Nations Convention on the Law of the Sea (1982), the Convention on Biological Diversity (1993), and the Protocol to the Convention on the Prevention of Marine Pollution by Dumping Wastes and Other Matter (1996). These regulations amend the Exclusive Economic Zone and Continental Shelf (Environmental Effects – Permitted Activities) Regulations 2013 to provide that the deposit on the seabed of material from a space vehicle launched from New Zealand is a permitted activity for the purpose of the Exclusive Economic Zone and Continental Shelf (Environmental Effects) Act 2012 so long as stated conditions are met.

3.2.15   Fisheries (High Seas Fishing Notifications – Commission for the
           Conservation of Antarctic Marine Living Resources) Amendment
           Notice 2017
This notice is made under Section 113C of the Fisheries Act 1996. It amends the Fisheries (High Seas Fishing Notifications – Commission for the Conservation of Antarctic Marine Living Resources) Notice 2009, which gives notice of a list of international conservation and management measures that the Commission for the Conservation of Antarctic Marine Living Resources has adopted. These measures apply to ships that are on the high seas in an area that the Commission covers and that are registered under the Ship Registration Act 1992 or fly the New Zealand flag. The amendment updates the list of international conservation and management measures that the Commission has adopted.

3.2.16   Fisheries (High Seas Fishing Notifications – Commission for the
           Conservation of Southern Bluefin Tuna) Amendment Notice 2016
This notice is made under Section 113C of the Fisheries Act 1996. It amends the Fisheries (High Seas Fishing Notifications – Commission for the Conservation of Southern Bluefin Tuna) Notice 2009, which gives notice of a number of international conservation and management measures that the Commission for the Conservation of Southern Bluefin Tuna has adopted. These measures apply to ships that are on the high seas in an area that the Commission covers and that are registered under the Ship Registration Act 1992 or fly the New Zealand flag. The amendment updates the list of international conservation and management measures that the Commission has adopted.

3.2.17   Fisheries (High Seas Fishing Notifications – South Pacific Regional
           Fisheries Management Organisation) Amendment Notice 2017
This notice is made under Section 113C of the Fisheries Act 1996. It amends the Fisheries (High Seas Fishing Notifications – South Pacific Regional Fisheries

Management Organisation) Notice 2013, which gives notice of a host of international conservation and management measures that the Organisation has adopted. These measures apply to ships that are on the high seas in an area that the Commission covers and that are registered under the Ship Registration Act 1992 or fly the New Zealand flag. The amendment updates the list of international conservation and management measures that the Organisation has adopted.

3.2.18   Fisheries (High Seas Fishing Notifications: Western and Central
            Pacific Fisheries Commission) Amendment Notice 2017
This notice is made under Section 113C of the Fisheries Act 1996. It amends the Fisheries (High Seas Fishing Notifications: Western and Central Pacific Fisheries Commission) Notice 2009, which gives notice of a host of international conservation and management measures that the Commission has adopted. These measures apply to ships that are on the high seas in an area that the Commission covers and that are registered under the Ship Registration Act 1992 or fly the New Zealand flag. The amendment updates the list of international conservation and management measures that the Commission has adopted.

3.2.19   Fisheries (Southern Bluefin Tuna Catch Documentation Scheme)
            Regulations 2017
These regulations are made under Section 297(1) of the Fisheries Act 1996. They establish a catch tagging and documentation scheme for commercial fishing against New Zealand's national allocation of southern bluefin tuna by New Zealand nationals and New Zealand ships, whether within or outside New Zealand fisheries waters. In doing so, they give effect to the Resolution on the Implementation of a CCSBT Catch Documentation Scheme adopted by the Commission for the Conservation of Southern Bluefin Tuna (2009).

3.2.20   Food Amendment Regulations 2017
These regulations are made under sections 43, 76, 343, 383, 387 and 395 of the Food Act 2014. They amend the Food Regulations 2015, which implement aspects of the Agreement between the Government of Australia and the Government of New Zealand concerning a Joint Food Standards System (1995). The amendments adjust a range of regulatory requirements, including those relating to sanitising facilities, record keeping, verification reporting, and standards for water and the labelling of imported wine. They also exempt hemp seed oil from certain standards of the Australia New Zealand Food Standards Code.

3.2.21   Geographical Indications (Wine and Spirits) Registration
           Regulations 2017
These regulations are made under Section 57 of the Geographical Indications
(Wine and Spirits) Registration Act 2006, which implements aspects of the
GATT Agreement on Trade-Related Aspects of Intellectual Property Rights
(1994). The regulations contain the operational and technical provisions that
enable the various steps and procedures set out in the Act to operate in practice.

3.2.22   Hazardous Substances and New Organisms (Schedules 1AA and
           2A) Order 2016
This order is made under Sections 140A(1) and 140B(a) of the Hazardous Substances and New Organisms Act 1996. It makes changes to Schedules 1AA and
2A of the Act to implement the 2013 and 2015 amendments to the Stockholm
Convention on Persistent Organic Pollutants (2004).

3.2.23   Health and Safety at Work (Hazardous Substances) Regulations
           2017
These regulations are made under sections 211, 212, 213 and 218 of the Health
and Safety at Work Act 2015. They implement a slew of Australian/New Zealand standards, and a number of American, Australian, British, British/Euro-
pean, and New Zealand ones.

3.2.24   Imports and Exports (Restrictions) Prohibition Order (No 2) 2004
           Amendment Order 2016
This order is made under Sections 3(1) and 3A(1) of the Imports and Exports
(Restrictions) Act 1988. It amends the Imports and Exports (Restrictions) Prohibition Order (No 2) 2004, which prohibits the importation into or exporta-
tion from New Zealand of certain goods for various reasons, including to ensure
that New Zealand complies with its obligations under the Stockholm Convention on Persistent Organic Pollutants (2004) and the Rotterdam Convention on
the Prior Informed Consent Procedure for Certain Hazardous Chemicals and
Pesticides in International Trade (1998). The amendments account for 2013 and
2015 changes to the Stock Convention and 2011, 2013 and 2015 changes to the
Rotterdam Convention.

3.2.25   Minimum Wage Order 2017
This order is made under Sections 4, 4A and 4B of the Minimum Wage Act
1983. The Act implements ILO Convention 14 (1921): Weekly Rest (Industry)
and ILO Convention 26 (1928): Minimum Wage-Fixing Machinery. This order

increases the minimum rates of pay for adult workers, starting-out workers, and trainees.

3.2.26   Overseas Investment Amendment Regulations (No 2) 2016
These regulations are made under Section 61 of the Overseas Investment Act 2005. They amend the Overseas Investment Regulations 2005, which implement aspects of the Protocol on Investment to the New Zealand–Australia Closer Economic Relations Trade Agreement (2011). The amendments provide for new class exemptions.

3.2.27   Ozone Layer Protection Amendment Regulations 2016
These regulations are made under Section 16 of the Ozone Layer Protection Act 1996. They amend the Ozone Layer Protection Regulations 1996, which implement aspects of the Montreal Protocol on Substances that Deplete the Ozone Layer (1999). The amendments revoke the HCFC wholesaler permit category and clarify that exemptions do not apply to HCFC imports from member States that are not party to or compliant with the Montreal Protocol.

3.2.28   Social Welfare (Reciprocity with Australia) Order 2017
This order is made under Section 19 of the Social Welfare (Reciprocity Agreements, and New Zealand Artificial Limb Service) Act 1990. This order gives effect to the Agreement on Social Security between the Government of Australia and the Government of New Zealand, entered into on 8 December 2016 as corrected by a subsequent exchange of diplomatic notes between the Government of New Zealand and the Government of Australia.

3.2.29   Trade in Endangered Species Order 2017
This order is made under Section 53 of the Trade in Endangered Species Act 1989. This order amends the Trade in Endangered Species Act 1989, which implements the Convention on International Trade in Endangered Species of Wild Fauna and Flora (1973). This amendment aligns the schedules with changes that have been made to the Convention on International Trade in Endangered Species of Wild Fauna and Flora (1973).

3.2.30   United Nations Sanctions (Democratic People's Republic of Korea)
              Regulations 2017
These regulations are made under Section 2 of the United Nations Act 1946. These regulations give effect to resolution 1718 (2006), resolution 1874 (2009), resolution 2087 (2013), resolution 2094 (2013), resolution 2270 (2016), and

resolution 2321 (2016), which are resolutions of the Security Council of the United Nations that relate to the Democratic People's Republic of Korea.

3.2.31   Various Civil Aviation Rules

Section 30 of the Civil Aviation Act 1990 empowers the Minister to make rules for the designation, classification and certification of aircraft, pilots, crew members and other services, for the setting of standards, specifications, restrictions and licensing requirements, the conditions of operation of foreign aircraft and international flights to, from, or within NZ, and for a number of other purposes. Many of these rules incorporate international standards or implement international obligations. The following amendment rules were made during the current interval:

> *Part 1: Definitions and Abbreviations Amendment 2016 (Amendment 51)*
> This rule amends Part 1 of the Civil Aviation Rules, which sets out the definitions and abbreviations contained in the rules. This rule adjusts the definitions and abbreviations into the Civil Aviation Rules to align the rules with current definitions and abbreviations in use by the International Civil Aviation Organization ("ICAO").

> *Part 19: Transition Amendment 2016 (Amendment 19)*
> This rule amends Part 19 of the Civil Aviation Rules, which set out various transition arrangements with respect to the implementation of the Convention on International Civil Aviation (1944) and the Agreement between the Australian and New Zealand Governments on Mutual Recognition of Aviation-Related Certification (2007). The amendments adjust some cross references.

> *Part 91: General Operating and Flight Amendment 2016 (Amendment 27)*
> The rule amends Part 91 of the Civil Aviation Rules, which sets out general operating and flight requirements, some of which stem from the Convention on International Civil Aviation (1944) and the Agreement between the Australian and New Zealand Governments on Mutual Recognition of Aviation-Related Certification (2007). The amendments remove unnecessary references, update document references, revoke an expired transitional provision, clarify the aircraft right of way rule, and update and correct a rule regarding maintenance programmes and schedules.

> *Part 119: Air Operator – Certification Amendment 2016 (Amendment 16)*
> This rule amends Part 119 of the Civil Aviation Rules, which concerns the certification of air operators, and implements aspects of the

Agreement between the Australian and New Zealand Governments on Mutual Recognition of Aviation-Related Certification (2007). The amendments correct data erroneously omitted from appendices A and B, and adjust aspects of the transitional arrangements for safety management.

Part 121: Air Operations – Large Aeroplanes Amendment 2016 (Amendment 28)
This rule amends Part 121 of the Civil Aviation Rules, which concerns the operation of large aeroplanes, and implements aspects of the Agreement between the Australian and New Zealand Governments on Mutual Recognition of Aviation-Related Certification (2007) and the ICAO Technical Instructions for the Safe Transport of Dangerous Goods by Air. The amendments correct an outdated reference to ICAO first aid training.

Part 125: Air Operations – Medium Aeroplanes Amendment 2016 (Amendment 21)
This rule amends Part 125 of the Civil Aviation Rules, which concerns the operation of medium aeroplanes, which are aligned to various ICAO standards and recommended practices. The amendments correct an outdated reference to ICAO first aid training.

Part 139: Aerodromes – Certification, Operation and Use Amendment 2016 (Amendment 13)
This rule amends Part 139 of the Civil Aviation Rules, which provides the regulatory requirements relating to the certification and operation of aerodromes, the security measures applicable to aerodromes and the use of aerodromes by aircraft operators that comply with Annex 14 of the Convention on International Civil Aviation (1944). The amendments correct a paragraph reference, and adjust aspects of the transitional arrangements for safety management.

Part 172: Air Traffic Service Organisations – Certification Amendment 2016 (Amendment 12)
This rule amends Part 172 of the Civil Aviation Rules, which prescribes the certification requirements, for the issue of an aviation document, for organizations currently providing, or intending to provide, any air traffic service. It implements aspects of the Convention on International Civil Aviation (1944). The amendment adjusts aspects of the transitional arrangements for safety management.

3.2.32   Various Land Transport Rules
Part 11 of the Land Transport Act 1998 provides for the making of rules with
respect to various aspects of land transport. Many of these rules incorporate
international standards or implement international obligations. The following
rules were made during the current interval:

> *Land Transport Rule 45001: Dangerous Goods Amendment 2016*
> This rule amends the Land Transport Rule 45001: Dangerous Goods 2005,
> which permits manufacturers of dangerous goods packaging in New Zea-
> land to use the packaging performance standards of the United Nations
> Recommendations on the Transport of Dangerous Goods. The amend-
> ments require a driver or operator of a vehicle carrying dangerous goods
> that is required to display placards to comply with signs which indicate a
> prohibition or restriction on the transport of dangerous goods imposed
> by a road controlling authority on a specified road by bylaw and require
> road controlling authorities to install signs indicating the existence of
> this restriction.

> *Land Transport Rule 33001: Vehicle Exhaust Emissions Amendment 2016*
> This rule amends the Land Transport Rule 45001: Dangerous Goods 2005,
> which is designed to take into account international best practice and is
> based on a slew of specified American, Australian, Californian, European,
> Japanese, and United Nations standards. The Australian standards are
> particularly relevant because of the Trans-Tasman Mutual Recognition
> Arrangement (1998). The amendment adds a Japanese vehicle emissions
> standard.

> *Land Transport Rule 32005: Vehicle Lighting Amendment 2016*
> This rule amends the Land Transport Rule 32005: Vehicle Lighting 2004,
> which implements a host of UN/ECE, Australian, and Japanese safety
> requirements and standards for lighting fitted to vehicles. The amend-
> ments adjust the requirements for cyclist visibility.

3.2.33   Various Marine Protection Rules
Section 386(1) of the Maritime Transport Act 1994 provides for the making of
rules for the purposes of implementing New Zealand's obligations under any
marine protection convention, to enable New Zealand to become a party to
a convention, protocol or agreement relating to the protection of the marine
environment and to implement international practices and standards relating

to the protection of the marine environment that the International Maritime Organisation recommends. The following rules were made during the current interval:

> *Marine Protection Amendment Rules 2016*
> These rules amend Parts 100, 102, 103, 121A and 150 of the Marine Protection Rules to adjust rules for preventing pollution of the sea by oil, noxious liquid substance, and garbage to better align New Zealand with Annex I (oil) and Annex V (garbage) of the International Convention for the Prevention of Pollution from Ships (1973) as modified by the Protocol of 1978 relating thereto (MARPOL), and recommendations from the International Maritime Organisation.

3.2.34   Various Maritime Rules

Maritime Transport Act 1994 s 36(1) provides for the making of rules for the purposes of the implementation of technical standards, codes of practice, performance standards and other requirements of certain conventions. Section 36(1)(u) of the Act provides for the making of rules for prescribing or providing for such matters as may be necessary to enable New Zealand to become a party to any international convention, protocol, or agreement relating to maritime transport as may be recommended by the International Maritime Organization. The following rule was made during the current interval:

> *Maritime Rules Various Amendments 2016*
> These rules amend Parts 23, 24C, 31, 32, 40A, 40B, 40C, 40D, 40E, 40F, 40G, 41, 42B, 45, 46, 47, 50, 51, 53, 90 and 91 of the Maritime Rules to correct minor errors. Some of these Parts implement aspects of various international obligations.

4   Judicial Decisions Related to New Zealand's International Obligations

This Part sets out the reported and unreported judicial decisions rendered during the current interval that concern New Zealand's international obligations. It divides the reported cases into those cases reported in the New Zealand Law Reports ("NZLR") and those cases reported in other series. It also identifies the international agreements that were referenced and sets out the distribution of these references among the various courts.

4.1   *Reported Cases*

4.1.1   NZLR Cases

Attorney-General v Taylor [2017] NZCA 215, [2017] 3 NZLR 24 (Court of Appeal, Kós P, Randerson, Wild, French and Miller JJ), Bill of Rights case that cites the International Covenant on Civil and Political Rights (1966).

B v Waitemata District Health Board [2017] NZSC 88, [2017] 1 NZLR 823 (Supreme Court, William Young, Glazebrook, Arnold, O'Regan and Ellen France JJ), Bill of Rights case that cites the International Covenant on Civil and Political Rights (1966) and the European Convention for the Protection of Human Rights and Fundamental Freedoms (1950).

Director-General of Health v Lowe [2016] NZCA 369, [2016] 3 NZLR 799, (2016) 10 NZELC 79-063 (Court of Appeal, Harrison, Wild and French JJ), employment law case that cites the Convention Concerning Decent Work for Domestic Workers (2011).

Fang v Ministry of Business, Innovation and Employment [2017] NZCA 190, [2017] 3 NZLR 316 (Court of Appeal, Kós P, Winkelmann and Brown JJ), deportation case that cites the United Nations Convention on the Rights of the Child (1989), the Universal Declaration of Human Rights (1948), the International Covenant on Civil and Political Rights (1966), and the International Covenant on Economic, Social and Cultural Rights (1966).

K v Attorney-General [2016] NZCA 416, [2017] 2 NZLR 167 (Court of Appeal, Ellen France P, Wild and Miller JJ), refugee law (judicial review) case that cites the United Nations Convention Relating to the Status of Refugees (1951), the United Nations Convention Against Torture and Other Cruel, Inhuman or Degrading Treatment or Punishment (1984), and the International Covenant on Civil and Political Rights (1966).

Kim v Minister of Justice [2016] NZHC 1490, [2016] 3 NZLR 425 (High Court, Wellington, Mallon J), extradition case that cites the International Covenant on Civil and Political Rights (1966), the United Nations Convention against Torture, the United Nations Convention of the Rights of the Child (1989), and the European Convention for the Protection of Human Rights and Fundamental Freedoms (1950).

Marwood v Commissioner of Police [2016] NZSC 139, [2017] 1 NZLR 260 (Supreme Court, Elias CJ, William Young, Glazebrook, Arnold and O'Regan JJ), evidence law case that cites the International Covenant on Civil and Political Rights (1966).

McDougan v DePuy International Ltd [2016] NZHC 2511, [2017] 2 NZLR 119 (High Court, Wellington, Collins J), accident compensation case that cites the Convention for the Unification of Certain Rules relating to International Carriage by Air (1929).

New Health New Zealand Inc v South Taranaki District Council [2016] NZCA 462, [2017] 2 NZLR 13 (Court of Appeal, Randerson, Wild and French JJ), local government (judicial review) case that cites the International Covenant on Civil and Political Rights (1966) and the International Covenant on Economic, Social and Cultural Rights (1966).

New Zealand Air Line Pilots' Association Industrial Union of Workers Inc v Director of Civil Aviation [2017] NZCA 27, [2017] 3 NZLR 1 (Court of Appeal, Harrison, Wild and Brown JJ), aviation law case that cites the Convention on International Civil Aviation (1947).

New Zealand Basing Ltd v Brown [2016] NZCA 525, [2017] 2 NZLR 93, (2016) 11 HRNZ 133 (Court of Appeal, Harrison, Miller and Winkelmann JJ), civil procedure case that cites the Convention on International Civil Aviation (1947) and the Convention on the Law Applicable to Contractual Obligations (1980).

Ngāti Whātua Orākei Trust v Attorney-General [2017] NZHC 389, [2017] 3 NZLR 516 (High Court, Auckland, Paul Davison J), Māori land case that cites the United Nations Declaration on the Rights of Indigenous Peoples (2007).

Ngāti Hurungaterangi v Ngāti Wahiao [2016] NZHC 1486, [2016] 3 NZLR 378 (High Court, Rotorua, Moore J), Māori land case that cites the United Nations Declaration on the Rights of Indigenous Peoples (2007).

Proprietors of Wakatu v Attorney-General [2017] NZSC 17, [2017] 1 NZLR 423 (Supreme Court, Elias CJ, William Young, Glazebrook, Arnold and O'Regan JJ), equity case that cites the United Nations Declaration on the Rights of Indigenous Peoples (2007).

Queenstown Airport Corporation Ltd v Commissioner of Inland Revenue [2017] NZCA 20, [2017] 2 NZLR 811 (Court of Appeal, Randerson, Miller and Asher JJ), taxation case that cites the Convention on International Civil Aviation (1947).

R v Alsford [2017] NZSC 42, [2017] 1 NZLR 710 (Supreme Court, Elias CJ, William Young, Glazebrook, Arnold and O'Regan JJ), evidence law case that cites the Universal Declaration of Human Rights (1948) and the International Covenant on Civil and Political Rights (1966).

R v Harrison; R v Turner [2016] NZCA 381, [2016] 3 NZLR 602 (Court of Appeal, Ellen France P, Randerson, Harrison, Stevens and Miller JJ), criminal law case that cites the International Covenant on Civil and Political Rights (1966) and the European Convention for the Protection of Human Rights and Fundamental Freedoms (1950).

Refugee and Protection Officer v CV and CW [2016] NZCA 250, [2017] 2 NZLR 585 (Court of Appeal, Ellen France P, Harrison and Winkelmann JJ), refugee law (judicial review) case that cites the United Nations Convention Relating to the Status of Refugees (1951) and the International Covenant on Civil and Political Rights (1966).

Sky Network Television Ltd v Fairfax New Zealand Ltd [2016] NZHC 1883, [2016] 3 NZLR 854 (High Court, Auckland, Fogarty J), copyright law case that cites the Berne Convention for the Protection of Literary and Artistic Works (1886 as amended 1971).

X v Attorney-General [2017] NZHC 768, [2017] 3 NZLR 115 (High Court, Wellington, Simon France J), civil procedure case that cites the United Nations Convention against Torture and Other Cruel, Inhuman or Degrading Treatment or Punishment (1987).

4.1.2   Cases Reported in Other Series that Reference International
           Obligations

AB v Refugee and Protection Officer [2017] NZHC 1424 (High Court, Auckland, Wylie J), refugee law (leave) case that cites the United Nations Convention Relating to the Status of Refugees (1951), the International Covenant on Civil and Political Rights (1966), and the Convention Against Torture and Other Cruel, Inhuman and Degrading Treatment or Punishment (1984).

AI (Somalia) v Immigration and Protection Tribunal [2016] NZHC 2227, [2016] NZAR 1471 (High Court, Auckland, Palmer J), refugee law (judicial review) case that cites the United Nations Convention Relating to the Status of Refugees (1951), the United Nations Convention Against Torture and Other Cruel, Inhuman or Degrading Treatment or Punishment (1984), and the International Covenant on Civil and Political Rights (1966).

Albert v R [2017] NZHC 102 (High Court, Rotorua, Toogood J), criminal law case that cites the United Nations Convention on the Rights of the Child (1989).

Anderson v Hawke [2016] NZHC 2280 (High Court, Auckland, Heath J), criminal law case that cites the European Convention for the Protection of Human Rights and Fundamental Freedoms (1950).

AR v Immigration and Protection Officer [2017] NZHC 132 (High Court, Auckland, Duffy J), refugee law (leave) case that cites the United Nations Convention Relating to the Status of Refugees (1951) and the Protocol Relating to the Status of Refugees (1967).

BLK v FK [2017] NZHC 302 (High Court, Wellington, Thomas J), family law case that cites the United Nations Convention on the Rights of the Child (1989) and the United Nations Convention on the Rights of Persons with Disabilities (2006).

Arorangi Timberland Ltd v Minister of the Cook Islands Superannuation Fund [2016] UKPC 32, [2017] NZAR 226 (Privy Council, Lords Neuberger, Mance, Clarke, Sumption, and Toulson), constitutional law case that cites the International Covenant on Economic, Social and Cultural Rights (1966).

Brown v Police [2016] NZHC 2359 (High Court, Wellington, Clark J), criminal law case that cites the International Covenant on Civil and Political Rights (1996).

Borsboom v Preet PVT Limited [2016] NZEmpC 143 (Employment Court, Colgan CJ, Corkill and Smith JJ), employment law case that cites the Convention concerning Forced or Compulsory Labour (1932), the Convention concerning the Protection of Wages (1952), and the Convention concerning Labour Inspection in Industry and Commerce (1950).

Brown v Police [2016] NZHC 2884 (High Court, Dunedin, Mander J), criminal law case that cites the International Covenant on Civil and Political Rights (1966).

Burden & Ors v ESR Group & Ors [2016] NZHC 1542 (High Court, Auckland, Duffy J), copyright law case that cites the Vienna Convention on the Law of Treaties (1969), the Berne Convention for the Protection of Literary and Artistic Works (1886 as amended 1971), and the Universal Copyright Convention (1952).

BY (China) v The Immigration and Protection Tribunal [2016] NZHC 2244 (High Court, Auckland, Muir J), refugee law (judicial review) case that cites the United Nations Convention Relating to the Status of Refugees (1951), the International Covenant on Civil and Political Rights (1966), and the Convention on the Elimination of All Forms of Discrimination against Women (1979).

Cameron v R [2017] NZSC 89 (Supreme Court, William Young, Glazebrook, Arnold, O'Regan and McGrath JJ), criminal law case that cites the European Convention for the Protection of Human Rights and Fundamental Freedoms (1950).

Chatfield & Co Ltd v Commissioner of Inland Revenue [2017] NZHC 3289 (High Court, Auckland, Wylie J), taxation case that cites the Vienna Convention on the Law of Treaties (1969).

Chief Executive of the Ministry of Social Development v TP (Review of Plan) [2016] NZFC 8909, [2017] NZFLR 135 (Family Court, Levin, Moss J), family law case that cites the United Nations Convention on the Rights of the Child (1989).

Chief Executive of the Ministry for Vulnerable Children, Oranga Tamariki v C [2017] NZFC 4052 (Family Court, Palmerston North, Smith J), family law case that cites the Hague Convention on the Civil Aspects of International Child Abduction (1980).

CF v Attorney-General (No 2) [2016] NZHC 3159 (High Court, Auckland, Moore J), immigration law (judicial review) case that cites the United Nations Convention Relating to the Status of Refugees (1951), the International Covenant on Civil and Political Rights (1966), and the United Nations Convention on the Rights of the Child (1989).

D v N [2017] NZHC 1211, [2017] NZFLR 426 (High Court, Auckland, Downs J), family law case that cites the United Nations Convention on the Rights of the Child (1989).

DA v Immigration and Protection Tribunal [2016] NZHC 1545 (High Court, Auckland, Moore J) refugee law (leave) case that cites the International Covenant on Civil and Political Rights (1966) and the Convention against Torture and Other Cruel, Inhuman or Degrading Treatment or Punishment (1984).

Davies v Chief Executive of the Ministry of Business, Innovation and Employment [2017] NZHC 503 (High Court, Christchurch, Mander J), deportation case that cites the United Nations Convention on the Rights of the Child (1989).

Devi v Minister of Immigration [2017] NZHC 728 (High Court, Auckland, Courtney J), immigration law case that cites the International Covenant on Civil and Political Rights (1966) and the International Covenant on Economic, Social and Cultural Rights (1966).

Dodd v Marsh [2017] NZFC 638 (Family Court, Gisborne, Courtney J), family law case that cites the Hague Convention on the Civil Aspects of International Child Abduction (1980).

Eilenberg v Gutierrez [2017] NZCA 270, [2017] NZFLR 471 (Court of Appeal, Kós P, Harrison and Miller J), family law case that cites the United Nations Convention for the Recovery Abroad of Maintenance (1956).

Emajor v Emajor [2016] NZHC 2022 (High Court, Auckland, Gilbert J), family law case that cites the United Nations Convention for the Recovery Abroad of Maintenance (1956).

Fagauta v Minister of Immigration [2017] NZHC 162 (High Court, Auckland, Venning J), deportation (leave) case that cites the United Nations Convention on the Rights of the Child (1989).

Fang v Ministry of Business Innovation and Employment [2016] NZHC 1630 (High Court, Auckland, Duffy J), deportation (judicial review) case that cites the United Nations Convention on the Rights of the Child (1989), the Universal Declaration of Human Rights (1948), the International Covenant on Civil and Political Rights (1966), and the International Covenant on Economic, Social and Cultural Rights (1966).

Fazley v Minister of Immigration [2017] NZHC 89 (High Court, Auckland, Palmer J), deportation (leave) case that cite the United Nations Convention on the Rights of the Child (1989).

Greeve v Jenkins [2016] NZFC 7265 (Family Court, North Shore, Hunt J), family law case that cites the Hague Convention on the Civil Aspects of International Child Abduction (1980).

Go Bus Transport Ltd v Hellyer [2016] NZEmpC 177 (Employment Court, Christ-church, Colgan CJ), employment law case that cites the Right to Organise and Collective Bargaining Convention (1949) [ILO Convention 98] and the Free-dom of Association and Protection of the Right to Organise Convention (1948) [ILO Convention 87].

Hall v Slate [2016] NZFC 6882 (Family Court, Papakura, Skellern J), family law case that cites the Hague Convention on the Civil Aspects of International Child Abduction (1980).

Hudson v Attorney-General [2017] NZHC 1441, [2017] NZAR 1293 (High Court, Whanganui, Ellis J), prisoners' rights case that cites the United Nations Stan-dard Minimum Rules for the Treatment of Prisoners (1955).

Huynh v Ministry of Business, Innovation, and Employment [2017] NZHC 730 (High Court, Auckland, Katz J), deportation case that cites the International Covenant on Civil and Political Rights (1966) and the International Covenant on Economic, Social and Cultural Rights (1966).

IA v RRN [2017] NZHC 1268 (High Court, Auckland, Muir J), family law case that cites the Hague Convention on the Civil Aspects of International Child Abduction (1980).

K v Accident Compensation Corporation [2016] NZACC 243 (District Court, Dunedin, Powell J), accident compensation case that cites the United Nations Convention on the Rights of Persons with Disabilities (2006).

Kaur v Minister of Immigration [2016] NZHC 3110 (High Court, Auckland, Court-ney J), deportation case that cites the United Nations Convention Against Tor-ture and Other Cruel, Inhuman or Degrading Treatment or Punishment (1984) and the International Covenant on Civil and Political Rights (1966).

Khan v Immigration and Protection Tribunal [2016] NZHC 2365 (High Court, Auckland, Davison J), deportation (judicial review) case that cites the Interna-tional Covenant on Civil and Political Rights (1996).

KN v CN [2016] NZHC 2049 (High Court, Auckland, Muir J), family law case that cites the Hague Convention on the Civil Aspects of International Child Abduc-tion (1980), the International Covenant on Civil and Political Rights (1966), and the International Covenant on Economic, Social and Cultural Rights (1966).

Kuwait Finance House (Bahrain) BSC v Teece [2017] NZHC 1308 (High Court, Christchurch, Mander J), civil procedure case that cites the UNCITRAL Model Law on International Commercial Arbitration (1985).

Labrooy v Chief Executive of the Ministry of Social Development [2016] NZHC 3025 (High Court, Auckland, Edwards J), social security case that cites the International Covenant on Civil and Political Rights (1966).

Lawson v Chief Executive of the Ministry of Social Development [2017] NZHC 967 (High Court, Wellington, Collins J), social security case that cites the United Nations Convention on the Rights of Persons with Disabilities (2006).

Li v Ministry of Business, Innovation and Employment [2016] NZHC 1788 (High Court, Auckland, Paul Davison J), deportation case that cites the International Covenant on Civil and Political Rights (1966) and the United Nations Convention on the Rights of the Child (1989).

Lin v Commissioner of Inland Revenue [2017] NZHC 969, (2017) 28 NZTC 23-016, [2017] NZCCLR 24 (High Court, Auckland, Thomas J), taxation case that cites the Vienna Convention on the Law of Treaties (1969).

MacGregor v Craig (Limited Extension of Confidentiality Orders) [2016] NZHRRT 30 (Human Rights Review Tribunal, Haines QC (Chairperson), Anderson and Goodwin (Members)), civil procedure case that cites the International Covenant on Civil and Political Rights (1966).

Maritime Union of New Zealand Inc v The China Navigation Company Pte. Limited [2016] NZEmpC 111 (Employment Court, Auckland, Colgan CJ), employment law case that cites the Right to Organise and Collective Bargaining Convention (1949) [ILO Convention 98] and the Freedom of Association and Protection of the Right to Organise Convention (1948) [ILO Convention 87].

McKelvey v Minister of Immigration [2017] NZHC 659 (High Court, Christchurch, Dunningham J), immigration law (leave) case that cites the International Covenant on Civil and Political Rights (1966).

Mikova v Tova [2016] NZHC 1983 (High Court, Auckland, Palmer J), family law case that cites the Hague Convention on the Civil Aspects of International Child Abduction (1980).

Milton v Milton [2016] NZFC 10308 (Family Court, Christchurch, Smith J), family law case that cites the Hague Convention on the Civil Aspects of International Child Abduction (1980).

Ministry of Social Development v BK [2016] NZFC 10716, [2017] NZFLR 105 (Family Court, Palmerston North, Moss J), family law case that cites the United Nations Convention on the Rights of the Child (1989).

Mitchell v Ketut [2016] NZFC 6175 (Family Court, Dunedin, Turner J), family law case that cites the Hague Convention on the Civil Aspects of International Child Abduction (1980).

Nacis v Minister of Immigration [2016] NZHC 2627 (High Court, Wellington, Ellis J), deportation (leave) case that cites the International Covenant on Civil and Political Rights (1966).

Nathan v Broadspectrum (New Zealand) Ltd [2016] NZEmpC 135 (Employment Court, Wellington, Smith J), employment law case that cites the Termination of Employment Convention (1982).

New Zealand Airline Pilots' Association Industrial Union of Workers Inc v Director of Civil Aviation [2016] NZHC 1528 (High Court, Wellington, Clark J), aviation law case that cites the Convention on International Civil Aviation (1944).

Nonu v R [2017] NZCA 170 (Court of Appeal, Winkelmann, Woodhouse and Collins JJ), criminal law case that cites the European Convention for the Protection of Human Rights and Fundamental Freedoms (1950).

Olsson v Culpan [2017] NZHC 217, [2017] NZAR 304 (High Court, Christchurch, Nation J), family law case that cites the United Nations Convention on the Rights of the Child (1989).

Opai v Culpan [2017] NZHC 1036 (High Court, Auckland, Katz J), defamation case that cites the European Convention for the Protection of Human Rights and Fundamental Freedoms (1950).

Orlov v New Zealand Lawyers and Conveyancers Disciplinary Tribunal [2016] NZCA 633 (Court of Appeal, French, Miller and Winkelmann JJ), judicial review case that cites the International Covenant on Civil and Political Rights (1966).

Ortmann v United States of America [2017] NZHC 189 (High Court, Auckland, Gilbert J), extradition case that cites the United Nations Convention against Transnational Organised Crime (2000), the Vienna Convention on the Law of Treaties (1969), and the Berne Convention for the Protection of Literary and Artistic Works (1886 as amended 1971).

Perugia v Tobin [2016] NZFC 7068 (Family Court, Hastings, Lendrum J), family law case that cites the Hague Convention on the Civil Aspects of International Child Abduction (1980).

Police v Albert [2017] NZDC 4724 (District Court, Christchurch, Saunders J), criminal law case that cites the Universal Declaration of Human Rights (1948), the Supplementary Convention of the Abolition of Slavery (1956), and the International Covenant on Civil and Political Rights (1966).

Police v CF [2017] NZYC 302 (Youth Court, Manukau, Recordon J), criminal law case that cites the United Nations Convention on the Rights of the Child (1989).

Police v RK [2017] NZYC 172 (Youth Court, Waitakere, Fitzgerald J), criminal law case that cites the United Nations Convention on the Rights of the Child (1989).

Rahal (adoption), Re [2017] NZFC 2152 (Family Court, Waitakere, Pidwell J), family law case that cites the United Nations Convention on the Rights of the Child (1989).

R v Hines [2017] NZHC 437 (High Court, Auckland, Downs J), criminal law case that cites the United Nations Convention against Illicit Traffic in Narcotic Drugs and Psychotropic Substances (1988).

R v Ali [2016] NZHC 2223 (High Court, Auckland, Heath J), criminal law case that cites the United Nations Convention Against Transnational Organised Crime (2001).

R v Ali [2016] NZHC 3077 (High Court, Auckland, Heath J), criminal law case that cites the United Nations Convention Against Transnational Organised Crime (2001), the Protocol to Prevent, Suppress and Punish Trafficking in Persons, Especially Women and Children (2000), and the Protocol Against the Smuggling of Migrants by Land, Sea and Air (2000).

R v Nelson [2016] NZHC 2163 (High Court, New Plymouth, Wylie J), criminal law case that cites that Optional Protocol to the United Nations Convention on the Rights of the Child on the Sale of Children, Child Prostitution and Child Pornography (2000).

Radhi v District Court (Manukau) [2017] NZCA 157, [2017] NZAR 692 (Court of Appeal, Miller, Cooper and Asher JJ), extradition case that cites the United Nations Convention on the Rights of the Child (1989), the International Covenant on Civil and Political Rights (1966), and the International Covenant on Economic, Social and Cultural Rights (1966).

Re Application by Teaupa [2016] NZFC 6920, [2017] NZFLR 89 (Family Court, Hutt Valley, Strettell J), family law case that cites the Hague Convention on Protection of Children and Co-operation in respect of Intercountry Adoption (1993).

Refugee Protection Officer v YL [2016] NZHC 1548 (High Court, Auckland, Brewer J), refugee law case that cites the United Nations Convention Relating to the Status of Refugees (1951).

Runge v Levine [2017] NZFC 1017 (Family Court, North Shore, Maude J), family law case that cites the Hague Convention on the Civil Aspects of International Child Abduction (1980).

S v R [2017] NZCA 83 (Court of Appeal, Randerson, Cooper and Brown JJ), criminal law case that cites the United Nations Convention on the Rights of the Child (1989).

Singh v An Immigration Officer [2016] NZHC 1778 (High Court, Auckland, Lang J), deportation case that cites the International Covenant on Civil and Political Rights (1966) and the United Nations Convention on the Rights of the Child (1989).

Singh (Harpal) v Chief Executive of the Ministry of Business, Innovation and Employment [2016] NZHC 2337, [2017] NZAR 722 (High Court, Auckland, Hinton J), immigration law (judicial review) case that cites the International Covenant on Civil and Political Rights (1996).

Singh (Kulbir) v An Immigration Officer [2016] NZCA 435, [2016] NZAR 1419 (Court of Appeal, Kos P, Winkelmann and Brown JJ), deportation case that cites the International Covenant on Civil and Political Rights (1966).

Singh v Singh [2016] NZHRRT 38 (Human Rights Review Tribunal, Hastings J (Deputy Chairperson)), discrimination law case that cites the International Covenant on the Elimination of All Forms of Racial Discrimination (1966).

Smith v Attorney-General [2016] NZHC 2103 (High Court, Auckland, Edwards J), prisoners' rights case that cites the United Nations Standard Minimum Rules for the Treatment of Prisoners (1955).

Smith v Attorney-General [2017] NZHC 463 (High Court, Auckland, Wylie J), judicial review case that cites the European Convention for the Protection of Human Rights and Fundamental Freedoms (1950).

Sparks v Immigration Advisers Complaints and Disciplinary Tribunal [2017] NZHC 376 (High Court, Wellington, Dobson J), immigration law case that cites the International Covenant on Civil and Political Rights (1966).

Taylor v The Chief Executive of the Department of Corrections [2016] NZHC 1805 (High Court, Auckland, Ellis J), prisoners' rights case that cites the United Nations Standard Minimum Rules for the Treatment of Prisoners (1955).

W v Accident Compensation Corporation [2016] NZACC 287 (District Court, Wellington, Henare J), accident compensation case that cites the United Nations Convention on Rights of the Child (1989).

Waikaira v Chief Executive of the Department of Corrections [2016] NZEmpC 175, (2016) 10 NZELC 79-03 (Employment Court, Auckland, Colgan CJ), employment law case that cites the Universal Declaration of Human Rights (1948).

Waikato District Health Board v New Zealand Nurses [2017] NZCA 247, (2017) NZELR 386 (Court of Appeal, Miller, Winkelmann and Clifford JJ), employment law case that cites the Right to Organise and Collective Bargaining Convention (1949) [ILO Convention 98] and the Freedom of Association and Protection of the Right to Organise Convention (1948) [ILO Convention 87].

Wall v Fairfax New Zealand Ltd [2017] NZHRRT 17 (Human Rights Review Tribunal, Haines QC (Chairperson)), discrimination law case that cites the United Nations Convention on the Rights of the Child (1989), the Universal Declaration of Human Rights (1948), the International Covenant on Civil and Political Rights (1966), and the International Convention on the Elimination of All Forms of Racial Discrimination (1965).

Watson v Chief Executive of the Department of Corrections (No 2) [2016] NZHC 1996, [2016] NZAR 1264 (High Court, Christchurch, Mallon J), prisoners' rights case that cites the International Covenant on Civil and Political Rights (1966).

Whitmann v UCI Holdings Ltd [2016] NZHC 1754 (High Court, Auckland, Duffy J), insolvency case that cites the United Nations Model Law on Cross-Border Insolvency (1997).

Wu v Minister of Immigration (No 2) [2016] NZHC 3194 (High Court, Auckland, Palmer J), deportation (judicial review) case that cites the United Nations Convention on the Rights of the Child (1989).

4.2   Unreported Cases
Owing to the advent of various electronic case law services and the timing of this publication, unreported judicial decisions rendered during the current interval that concern New Zealand's international obligations are rare. This interval has none.

4.3   Distribution of References to International Agreements among Various Courts, NZLR Cases, Other Reported Cases, and Unreported Cases[15]

International obligations	NZLR	Other	Unrep	All	Total
Covenant on Civil and Political Rights (1966)	SC: 3 CA: 6 HC: 1	CA: 3 HC: 21 DC: 1 HT: 1		SC: 3 CA: 9 HC: 22 DC: 1 HT: 1	36

---

15   Key: SC = Supreme Court, CA = Court of Appeal, HC = High Court, FC = Family Court, YC = Youth Court; EC = Employment Court, HT = Human Rights Review Tribunal, PC = Privy Council, * = New Zealand is not a party to this Convention.

International obligations	NZLR	Other	Unrep	All	Total
Convention on the Rights of the Child (1989)	CA: 1 HC: 1	CA: 2 HC: 12 FC: 3 DC: 1 YC: 2 HT: 1		CA: 3 HC: 13 FC: 3 DC: 1 YC: 2 HT: 1	23
Hague Convention on the Civil Aspects of International Child Abduction (1980)		HC: 3 FC: 8		HC: 3 FC: 8	11
Convention Relating to the Status of Refugees (1951)	CA: 2	HC: 6		CA: 2 HC: 6	8
European Convention for the Protection of Human Rights and Fundamental Freedoms (1950)*	SC: 1 CA: 1 HC: 1	SC: 1 CA: 1 HC: 3		SC: 2 CA: 2 HC: 4	8
International Covenant on Economic, Social and Cultural Rights (1976)	CA: 2	PC: 1 CA: 1 HC: 3		PC: 1 CA: 3 HC: 3	7
Convention against Torture and Other Cruel, Inhuman or Degrading Treatment or Punishment (1984)	CA: 1 HC: 1	HC: 4		CA: 1 HC: 5	6
Universal Declaration of Human Rights (1948)	SC: 1 CA: 1	HC: 1 DC: 1 EC: 1 HT: 1		SC: 1 CA: 1 HC: 1 DC: 1 EC: 1 HT: 1	6
Vienna Convention on the Law of Treaties (1969)		HC: 4		HC: 4	4

Distribution of Agreements among Various Courts (cont.)

International obligations	NZLR	Other	Unrep	All	Total
Convention on International Civil Aviation (1947)	CA: 3	HC: 1		CA: 3 HC: 1	4
Berne Convention for the Protection of Literary and Artistic Works (1886 as amended 1971)	HC: 1	HC: 2		HC: 3	3
United Nations Standard Minimum Rules for the Treatment of Prisoners (1955)		HC: 3		HC: 3	3
Convention on the Rights of Persons with Disabilities (2006)		HC: 2 DC: 1		HC: 2 DC: 1	3
Right to Organise and Collective Bargaining Convention (1949) [ILO Convention 98]		EC: 2 CA: 1		EC: 2 CA: 1	3
Freedom of Association and Protection of the Right to Organise Convention (1948) [ILO Convention 87]		EC: 2 CA: 1		EC: 2 CA: 1	3
United Nations Declaration on the Rights of Indigenous Peoples (2007)	SC: 1 HC: 2			SC: 1 HC: 2	3
International Convention on the Elimination of All Forms of Racial Discrimination (1965)		HT: 2		HT: 2	2

International obligations	NZLR	Other	Unrep	All	Total
United Nations Convention against Transnational Organized Crime (2000)		HC: 2		HC: 2	2
Hague Convention on Protection of Children and Co-operation in respect of Intercountry Adoption (1993)		FC: 2		FC: 2	2
Convention for the Unification of Certain Rules for International Carriage by Air (1999) [Montreal Convention]	HC: 1			HC: 1	1
Convention Concerning Decent Work for Domestic Workers (2011)	CA: 1			CA: 1	1
Convention on the Law Applicable to Contractual Obligations (1980)	CA: 1			CA: 1	1
Convention concerning Forced or Compulsory Labour (1932)		EC: 1		EC: 1	1
Convention concerning the Protection of Wages (1952)		EC: 1		EC: 1	1
Convention concerning Labour Inspection in Industry and Commerce (1950)		EC: 1		EC: 1	1

Distribution of Agreements among Various Courts (cont.)

International obligations	NZLR	Other	Unrep	All	Total
Convention on the Elimination of All Forms of Discrimination against Women (1979)		HC: 1		HC: 1	1
United Nations Convention against Illicit Traffic in Narcotic Drugs and Psychotropic Substances (1988)		HC: 1		HC: 1	1
Universal Copyright Convention (1952)		HC: 1		HC: 1	1
Termination of Employment Convention (1982)		EC: 1		EC: 1	1
Optional Protocol to the United Nations Convention on the Rights of the Child on the Sale of Children, Child Prostitution and Child Pornography (2000)		HC: 1		HC: 1	1
Protocol to Prevent, Suppress and Punish Trafficking in Persons, Especially Women and Children, Protocol Against the Smuggling of Migrants by Land, Sea and Air (2000)		HC: 1		HC: 1	1

International obligations	NZLR	Other	Unrep	All	Total
Supplementary Convention of the Abolition of Slavery (1956)		DC: 1		DC: 1	1
Protocol Relating to the Status of Refugees (1967)		HC: 1		HC: 1	1
UNCITRAL Model Law on International Commercial Arbitration (1985)		HC: 1		HC: 1	1
UNCITRAL Model Law on Cross-Border Insolvency (1997)		HC: 1		HC: 1	1
Convention as to the Recovery Abroad of Maintenance (1956)		CA: 1		CA: 1	1
Totals	33	121	0	154	154

5 Update of Master List of Implementing Acts

This Part updates the master list of implementing Acts set out in Part 5 of "In Search of International Standards and Obligations Relevant to New Zealand Acts" (2007) 4 *New Zealand Yearbook of International Law* 366–93 (as amended).[16] The master list entries should be amended as follows:

---

16 For previous amendments to the master list, see Gobbi (2016), above n 3, 355; Mark Gobbi, "Treaty Action and Implementation" (2015) 13 *New Zealand Yearbook of International Law* 295, 335–6; Mark Gobbi, "Treaty Action and Implementation" (2014) 12 *New Zealand Yearbook of International Law* 247, 286; Mark Gobbi, "Treaty Action and Implementation" (2013) 11 *New Zealand Yearbook of International Law* 285, 326–8; Mark Gobbi, "Treaty Action and Implementation" (2012) 10 *New Zealand Yearbook of International Law* 261, 302–3; Mark Gobbi, "Treaty Action and Implementation" (2011) 9 *New Zealand Yearbook of International Law* 351, 386; Mark Gobbi, "Treaty Action and Implementation" (2010) 8 *New Zealand Yearbook of International Law* 283, 328–9; Mark Gobbi, "Treaty Action and Implementation" (2009) 7 *New Zealand Yearbook of International Law* 381, 424–31; Mark Gobbi, "Treaty Action and Implementation" (2008) 6 *New Zealand Yearbook of International Law* 379, 418–20; Mark Gobbi, "Treaty Action and Implementation" (2007–2008) 5 *New Zealand Yearbook of International Law* 279, 326.

5.1   *New Entries*
Add the following entries in their appropriate alphabetical order:

Contract and Commercial Law Act 2017

International Convention for the Unification of Certain Rules of Law relating to Bills of Lading [Hague Rules] (1924), and Protocol of Signature (1924)

Convention for the Unification of Certain Rules relating to International Carriage by Air (1929)

Convention relating to the Status of Refugees (1951) article 12

Guadalajara Convention, supplementary to the Warsaw Convention, for the Unification of Certain Rules relating to International Carriage by Air Performed by a Person other than the Contracting Carrier (1961)

Protocol to Amend the International Convention for the Unification of Certain Rules of Law relating to Bills of Lading [Visby Rules] (1968)

Further Protocol to Amend the International Convention for the Unification of Certain Rules of Law relating to Bills of Lading [Hague–Visby Rules] (1979)

United Nations Convention on Contracts for the International Sale of Goods (1980)

Model Law on Electronic Commerce Law adopted by the United Nations Commission on International Trade Law (1996)

Model Law on International Trade Law issued by the United Nations Commission on International Trade Law (1996)

Intelligence and Security Act 2017

Convention on the Physical Protection of Nuclear Material and Nuclear Facilities (1980)

Convention on the Marking of Plastic Explosives for the Purpose of Detection (1991)

Oranga Tamariki Act 1989

Arrangement between New Zealand and Australian States and Territories regarding the transfer of children subject to child protection orders (2000)

Senior Courts Act 2016

Trans-Tasman Court Proceedings and Regulatory Enforcement (ongoing agreement between New Zealand and Australia)

Trade (Anti-dumping and Countervailing Duties) Act 1988

Agreement on Implementation of Article VI of the GATT (anti-dumping code) (1979)

Agreement establishing the World Trade Organization (1994)

Agreement between New Zealand and Singapore on Closer Economic Partnership (2001)

Delete the following entries:

Carriage of Goods Act 1979
Children, Young Persons, and Their Families Act 1989
Dumping and Countervailing Duties Act 1988
Electronic Transactions Act 2002
Government Communications Security Bureau Act 2003
Judicature Act 1908
Minors Contracts Act 1969
New Zealand Security Intelligence Service Act 1969
Sale of Goods (United Nations Convention) Act 1994

5.2   *Changes to Entries*
Exclusive Economic Zone and Continental Shelf (Environmental Effects) Act 2012
Add the following item:

Protocol to the Convention on the Prevention of Marine Pollution by Dumping Wastes and Other Matter (1996)

Patents Act 2013

Add the following item:

Arrangement between the Government of Australia and the Government of New Zealand Relating to Trans-Tasman Regulation of Patent Attorneys (2013)

Radiation Protection Act 1965
Replace with the following item:

Radiation Safety Act 2016

Agreement between New Zealand and the International Atomic Energy Agency for the Application of Safeguards in Connection with the Treaty on the Non-Proliferation of Nuclear Weapons (1972) [and related protocols]

Convention on the Physical Protection of Nuclear Material (1980)

Convention for the Suppression of Acts of Nuclear Terrorism (2005)

6   Update of Master List of Implementing Regulations

This Part updates the master list of implementing regulations set out in Part v of "In Search of International Standards and Obligations relevant to New Zealand Regulations" (2007–2008) 5 *New Zealand Yearbook of International Law* 327–72 (as amended).[17] The master list should be amended as follows:

---

17   For previous amendments to the master list, see Gobbi (2016), above n 3, 355–8; Mark Gobbi, "Treaty Action and Implementation" (2015) 13 New Zealand Yearbook of International Law 295, 336–9; Mark Gobbi, "Treaty Action and Implementation" (2014) 12 *New Zealand Yearbook of International Law* 247, 287–90; Mark Gobbi, "Treaty Action and Implementation" (2013) 11 *New Zealand Yearbook of International Law* 285, 328–32; Mark Gobbi, "Treaty Action and Implementation" (2012) 10 *New Zealand Yearbook of International Law* 261, 303–6; Mark Gobbi, "Treaty Action and Implementation" (2011) 9 *New*

6.1   *New Entries*

Add the following entries in their appropriate alphabetical order:

Anti-Money Laundering and Countering Financing of Terrorism (Exemptions) Regulations 2011

Anti-Money Laundering and Countering Financing of Terrorism Act 2009, ss 153 and 154; Financial Transactions Reporting Act 1996, s 56

Recommendations issued by the Financial Action Task Force on Money Laundering (established 1989)

Anti-Money Laundering and Countering Financing of Terrorism (Prescribed Transactions Reporting) Regulations 2016

Anti-Money Laundering and Countering Financing of Terrorism Act 2009, ss 48A, 48B, 153, and 154; Financial Transactions Reporting Act 1996, s 56(1) (e) and (2)

Recommendations issued by the Financial Action Task Force on Money Laundering (established 1989)

Fisheries (High Seas Fishing Notifications – South Pacific Regional Fisheries Management Organisation) Notice 2013

Fisheries Act 1996, s 113C

This notice gives notice that the South Pacific Regional Fisheries Management Organisation is an organisation or arrangement within the definition of a global, regional, or subregional fisheries organisation or arrangement in Part 6A of the Fisheries Act 1996. The regulations also give notice of a host of international conservation and management measures that the Organisation has adopted. These measures apply to ships that are on the high seas in an area that the Organisation covers and that are registered under the Ship Registration Act 1992 or fly the New Zealand flag.

Zealand Yearbook of International Law 351, 386–9; Mark Gobbi, "Treaty Action and Implementation" (2010) 8 New Zealand Yearbook of International Law 283, 330–5; Mark Gobbi, "Treaty Action and Implementation" (2009) 7 New Zealand Yearbook of International Law 381, 425–31; Mark Gobbi, "Treaty Action and Implementation" (2008) 6 New Zealand Yearbook of International Law 379, 421–3.

Fisheries (Southern Bluefin Tuna Catch Documentation Scheme) Regulations 2017
Fisheries Act 1996, s 297(1)
Resolution on the Implementation of a CCSBT Catch Documentation Scheme adopted by the Commission for the Conservation of Southern Bluefin Tuna (2009)

Geographical Indications (Wine and Spirits) Registration Regulations 2017
Geographical Indications (Wine and Spirits) Registration Act 2006, s 57
GATT Agreement on Trade-Related Aspects of Intellectual Property Rights (1994)

Hazardous Substances and New Organisms (Schedules 1AA and 2A) Order 2016
Hazardous Substances and New Organisms Act 1996, ss 140A(1) and 140B(a)
Stockholm Convention on Persistent Organic Pollutants (2004 as amended in 2013 and 2015)

Health and Safety at Work (Hazardous Substances) Regulations 2017
Health and Safety at Work Act 2015, ss 211, 212, 213, and 218

Various Australian/New Zealand standards (among others)

Marine Protection Amendment Rules 2016
Maritime Transport Act 1994, ss 386, 387, 388, 389 and 390
These rules amend Parts 100, 102, 103, 121A and 150 of the Marine Protection Rules to adjust rules for preventing pollution of the sea by oil, noxious liquid substance, and garbage to better align New Zealand with Annex I (oil) and Annex V (garbage) of the International Convention for the Prevention of Pollution from Ships (1973), as modified by the Protocol of 1978 relating thereto (MARPOL), and recommendations from International Maritime Organisation.

6.2   *Changes to Entries*
Customs Import Prohibition (Southern Bluefin Tuna) Order 2013
Replace with the following item:

Customs Import Prohibition (Southern Bluefin Tuna) Order 2016
Customs and Excise Act 1996, s 54

Convention for the Conservation of Southern Bluefin Tuna (1993)

Food Regulations 2015
Add the following item:

Australia New Zealand Food Standards Code

Imports and Exports (Restrictions) Prohibition Order (No 2) 2004
Add the following item:

Convention on Persistent Organic Pollutants (2004)

Minimum Wage Order 2016
Replace with the following item:

Minimum Wage Order 2017
Minimum Wage Act 1983, ss 4, 4A and 4B
ILO Convention 14 (1921): Weekly Rest (Industry)
ILO Convention 26 (1928): Minimum Wage-Fixing Machinery

Social Welfare (Reciprocity with Australia) Order 2002
Replace with the following item:

Social Welfare (Reciprocity with Australia) Order 2017
*Social Welfare (Reciprocity Agreements, and New Zealand Artificial Limb
Service) Act 1990, s 19*
Agreement on Social Security between the Government of Australia and
the Government of New Zealand (2016)
Exchange of Diplomatic Notes re Agreement (2017)

**United Nations Sanctions (Democratic Republic of the Congo) Regulations
20XX**
Replace with the following item:

**United Nations Sanctions (Democratic Republic of the Congo) Regula-
tions 2017**
United Nations Act 1946, s 2
Resolution 1718 of the Security Council of the United Nations (2006)
Resolution 1874 of the Security Council of the United Nations (2009)

Resolution 2087 of the Security Council of the United Nations (2013)
Resolution 2094 of the Security Council of the United Nations (2013)
Resolution 2270 of the Security Council of the United Nations (2016)
Resolution 2321 of the Security Council of the United Nations (2016)

Book Reviews

∵

The Rule of Law in Crisis and Conflict Grey Zones: Regulating the Use of Force in a Global Information Environment

by Michael John-Hopkins
[Oxford: Taylor & Francis, 2017, 334 pp. ISBN 978-1-4724-8695-0. £110.00]

Shea Elizabeth Esterling *

Humanitarian law expert Michael John-Hopkins makes an important and much needed contribution to the dialogue concerning armed conflict in the 21st century by responding to continuing calls for clarification and consensus regarding the meaning, scope and interaction of humanitarian law and human rights law in the "grey zones" of unconventional operational environments. He argues that the application of conventional military means and methods of warfare to such situations may be permitted under humanitarian law, but there is the risk that this paradigm is being over-applied to what are essentially situations of crisis rather than conflict. Accordingly this study seeks to clarify at what point violence is so dangerous and intense that it exceeds the capacity of law enforcement methods and thus the regulatory standards set out in international human rights law. Complex by its nature, John-Hopkins presents a nuanced exegesis concerning the use of force in these unconventional and irregular situations of violence such as counterterrorism and counterinsurgency operations. Yet the text remains highly accessible and practical for both a legal and non-legal audience.

Over the course of nine chapters, *The Rule of Law in Crisis and Conflict Grey Zones* offers readers a provocative discussion that attempts to clarify what targeting and weaponry rules apply to the use of force in unconventional and irregular situations of violence, how to coordinate the application of these two very different legal frameworks and argues for the progressive realisation of targeting and weaponry law so that they are fit for purpose in urbanised and civilianised operational environments. Unlike handbooks on humanitarian law, it provides more in-depth accounts of both what the law is as well as what the law should be in relation to targeting and weaponry law and crucially it provides the reader with discussion and proposals about how substantive

* University of Canterbury.

and institutional reform can be achieved in a credible fashion. Whilst having a strong legal approach, John-Hopkins maintains an interdisciplinary appeal in his work (international law, international relations, military and strategic studies, sociology, criminology) by placing international humanitarian law and human rights law in their contemporary political, doctrinal and factual contexts as well as by developing objective frameworks for assessing the intensity of violence and participation in or membership of diffuse organizational structures.

The Rule of Law in Crisis and Conflict Grey Zones can be understood to achieve three main ends: to provide the reader with an empirical study of protection issues in irregular and unconventional conflict situations, to provide the reader with a critical analysis of applicable legal frameworks and mechanisms for these situations and to identify substantive and institutional solutions to fundamental conduct of hostilities rules and issues. These ends are achieved over the course of nine chapters. Chapter 1 *The Contemporary Theatre of Operations* outlines contemporary protection issues and seeks to identify key problems, trends and challenges in relation to the general nature and characteristics of contemporary hostilities which are mostly non-international in character. It takes into account these traditional approaches to the formulation and interpretation of legal standards, as one of the overarching themes of the work is to identify new or nascent interpretations of existing standards through their application to unconventional and irregular conflict situations by states as well as international and regional human rights mechanisms.

Chapter 2 *A General Critique of IHL Targeting And Weaponry Norms and Institutions* discusses whether existing standards for the legal regulation of means and methods of force are fit for purpose and fit for contemporary contexts while exploring the core substantive and procedural weaknesses of the current system of humanitarian protection. In effect, it provides an outline and a critique of mainstream targeting and weaponry law setting the foundation for the discussion of the dynamic ways and shape in which reform may occur.

Chapters 3 through 8 proceed to identify and discuss a range of substantive, procedural and institutional solutions to contemporary protection issues. They identify gaps and obstacles to humanitarian and human rights protection in relation to conduct of hostilities rules and institutions, they identify the transition from the paradigm of human rights law to humanitarian law takes place and where the threshold of status based targeting should apply in non-international armed conflicts before setting out the legal and policy arguments for their progressive development. In turn, these chapters serve as the heart of the analysis of *The Rule of Law in Crisis and Conflict Grey Zones*. They offer important legal and practical insights into classifying situations of violence for the purpose of coordinating the application of human rights law and humanitarian law and in particular, they discuss how humanitarian law and human rights rules on the use of force may be applied in the same operational theatre.

Specifically, Chapter 3 *Reconceptualising the Regulation of the Use Of Force in Situations of Crisis and Unconventional Conflict: Enhanced contextual status determination* sets out improved criteria for categorizing situations of violence and identifies, in practical terms, where a situation is such that it exceeds the capacity of law enforcement methods and regulatory standards set out in human rights law and so enters into the legal paradigm of treaty-based and customary humanitarian law relative to targeting and weaponry. Chapters 4 and 5 seek to put the concepts of direct participation in hostilities and membership of an organised armed group on the most analytical and principled footing to date. They detail improved criteria for assessing whether an individual is directly participating in hostilities or is a member of an organised armed group, and these criteria borrow from international criminal law models of accessorial liability and co-perpetration. Chapter 4 *Reconceptualising the Regulation of the Use Of Force in Situations of Crisis and Unconventional Conflict: Individual Status Determination* argues that due to the "civilianization" of the contemporary battlefield, targeting on the basis of status may only occur at a very high threshold of violence and then only in the context of targeted operations. In relation to this, it is the only book that attempts to identify, in clear and practical terms, where the threshold of status based targeting should apply in non-international armed conflicts as well as setting out legal, doctrinal and policy arguments as to why status based targeting should be confined to a high threshold of applicability and used only in the context of planned and targeted operations. Chapter 5 *Towards a Clearer Framework for Distinguishing those who Participate Directly in Hostilities from those who are to be Protected as Civilians: Extrapolating Models of Accessorial Liability and Coperpetration in the Commission of Harmful Acts* offers the reader a unique analysis of what constitutes direct participation in hostilities as well as de facto membership of an organised armed group. It does this by extrapolating criminal law models of accessorial liability, joint criminal enterprise and indirect perpetration to address important questions surrounding the parameters of civilian immunity from attack. Unlike the existing literature on this topic, this new analysis puts the discussion on a clearer and firmer analytical footing and is likely to provoke further debate and discussion

Chapter 6 *Reconceptualising Targeting and Weaponry Law for the Unconventional Theatre of Operations* and Chapter 7

Weaponry law: Emerging Approaches to the Regulation of Means of Warfare and Law Enforcement discuss how treaty-based and customary targeting and weaponry law and policy have been progressively interpreted and developed to suit the challenges to military operations in a civilianised and urbanised operation theatres. John-Hopkins takes on board a "minimalist" account of the nature and content of the treaty-based and customary targeting and weaponry rules. Yet on the basis of state practice and the authoritative decisions of a range of human rights mechanisms he argues for their progressive interpretation so that there are higher standards of reasonableness in the context of urbanised and civilianised theatres of operations when it comes to targeted killings, proportionality assessments, precautionary measures as well as the use of explosive weaponry and "non-lethal" weapons in civilian populated urban areas. Contrary to what a number of legal and military scholars suggest, it is argued that progressive realisation in these regards need not be considered unrealistic given that it has a firm basis in relevant state practice.

Chapter 8 *Regulating Military Operations Abroad: the Extraterritorial Effect of Human Rights and the Potential Modalities of Parallel Application of the Right to Life under Human Rights Law and International Humanitarian Law* discusses development with regard to extraterritorial effect of human rights restrictions and obligations. This chapter then examines potential modalities for the parallel application of human rights and international humanitarian law in order to ensure that adequate substantive and procedural safeguards are in place in order to regulate the use of force adequately, particularly when it comes to targeted or extrajudicial killing. It provides an alternative and constructive account of how human rights mechanisms may play a more authoritative and credible role in supervising conflict situations and ensuring that existing legal standards are fit for purpose. Chapter 9 *Conclusions: Grey Zones of War and Peace in Our Globally Networked Information Environment* is where John-Hopkins succulently reminds readers that *The Rule of Law in Crisis and Conflict Grey Zones* provides an outline and a critique of mainstream targeting and weaponry law, but unlike existing publications, it proceeds to identify legal, theoretical and policy arguments for a progressive reappraisal of existing standards so that they are fit for contemporary low intensity conflict situations. In particular, it demonstrates that a basic non-international armed conflict has a very high threshold of application and so human rights standards are applicable and appropriate for many situations of low-intensity hostilities.

It is hard to think of an issue more pressing in our current political climate than the maintenance of international peace and security. As history demonstrates, this maintenance often necessitates the use of force in response to international and increasingly non-international crises and conflicts. Uncertainty and controversy not only surrounds the classification of these situations of crisis and conflict but also the meaning, scope and interplay of humanitarian law and human rights law in situations of irregular armed conflict and other situations of violence. Resulting from an increased overlap in jurisdiction between human rights law and humanitarian law, Michael John-Hopkins makes a valuable contribution to this dialogue shedding light on these uncertainties and controversies in a carefully considered, comprehensive and coherent narrative on a range of interrelated fundamental issues concerning the interpretation and ordering of norms of humanitarian and human rights law relating to targeting and weaponry in contemporary conflict situations.

Regulatory Autonomy in International Economic Law: The Evolution of Australian Policy on Trade and Investment

by Andrew D. Mitchell, Elizabeth Sheargold and Tania Voon
[Cheltenham: Edward Elgar Publishing, 2017, 275 pp, ISBN 978-1-78536-816-5, £ 75.00]

*An Hertogen**

Balancing trade and investment liberalisation commitments with other values that states and their constituents hold dear, such as the protection of the environment, public health, financial stability, or national security, is one of the most difficult questions in international economic law. Most trade and investment agreements allow states to regulate for a range of specified purposes subject to certain conditions, such as non-discrimination between domestic and imported products, and fair treatment of foreign investors. However, when interpreting these agreements, international tribunals have at times taken an expansive view of the obligations, or a restrictive view of the exceptions that allow for domestic regulation. As a result, trade and investment agreements have come under closer scrutiny as states, legal scholars, and civil society organisations attempt to better understand the extent to which these agreements curtail states' right to regulate.

The book under review examines how the 21 Bilateral Investment Treaties ("BITs") and the 10 Preferential Trade Agreements ("PTAs") that Australia has entered into in the past three decades have affected its regulatory autonomy. Examining and comparing 31 agreements is a mammoth task, and the authors are to be commended for the ambitious scale of the project. A deep dive into the obligations of a single state reveals the inconsistencies created by the "spaghetti bowl" of BITs and PTAs,[1] with different agreements defining the scope of the obligations differently or providing for different exceptions. Even though the analysis focuses on Australia, its relevance extends to Australia's bilateral

---

* The University of Auckland.
1 The term 'spaghetti bowl' was famously coined in this context by Jagdish Bhagwati, *US Trade Policy: The Infatuation with FTAs* (April 1995) Columbia University Academic Commons, <https://doi.org/10.7916/D8CN7BFM>.

trade partners, who are bound by the same agreements[2] as well as to other states with similar provisions in their BITs and PTAs. Australia's experience is also of broader interest due to its involvement in recent trade law developments, such as the *Trans-Pacific Partnership Agreement* ("*TPP*") and its successor the *Comprehensive and Progressive Agreement for Trans-Pacific Partnership*, the negotiations towards a *Trade in Services Agreement*, and the introduction of – and the subsequent legal challenges to – legislation on the plain packaging of tobacco products.

The book defines regulatory autonomy as "the ability of a State to determine its regulatory goals ... and to adopt and implement policies to pursue those goals" (p. 2). The first Chapter introduces this concept by addressing in general terms why we have international economic law, why it constrains states' regulatory autonomy, and how concerns about regulatory autonomy arose. Given the centrality of the concept of regulatory autonomy to the book's analysis, I found the discussion of its content on the light side. The authors rightly point out that international agreements by their very purpose constrain regulatory autonomy. Indeed, it has long been settled in international law that the conclusion of an international agreement is an exercise of state sovereignty, even if it restricts how that sovereignty can be exercised.[3] Thus, as the authors themselves recognize, "to say that international economic law ... imposes limitations or constraints on regulatory autonomy is neither profound nor necessarily a criticism" (p. 4).

The key question in relation to regulatory autonomy in trade and investment agreements is not to what extent these agreements require states to reduce tariffs, to remove non-tariff barriers to trade, to protect foreign investors within their jurisdiction, or to submit to investor-state dispute settlement ("ISDS"), but to what extent the obligation to liberalize trade or investment restricts a state's autonomy in an area that is not covered by the agreement or for which the agreement provides an exception. As Titi has pointed out in the context of investment law, "the right to regulate ... is a technical term, one that is much narrower in meaning and which should not be confused with the [freedom to engage in political, economic, legislative and other regulatory activity as the state sees fit]".[4] Titi defines the right to regulate as "a legal right that permits a departure from specific investment commitments assumed by a state on the

---

2   Even if they are not necessarily bound to exactly the same obligations as states can modify these through exclusions and non-conforming measures.

3   *SS 'Wimbledon' (United Kingdom, France, Italy & Japan v. Germany)* [1923] PCIJ (Ser A) No 1, 25.

4   Aikaterini Titi, *The Right to Regulate in International Investment Law* (Nomos, 2014) 33.

international plane without incurring a duty to compensate",[5] and her definition can be applied *mutatis mutandis* in the trade context.

In contrast, the authors' definition of regulatory autonomy includes the obligations as well as the exceptions included in international trade and investment agreements. This choice is not without its difficulties. First, it broadens the scope of the study to include not only permitted departures from commitments made, but also the substance of these commitments. It is, however, hard to do justice to all this in only 257 pages. As a result, some chapters of the book are more of a general discussion of the evolution of Australia's policy on trade and investment. While this corresponds to the book's subtitle, it sits in tension with the book's main title and ostensible focus on regulatory autonomy. A second consequence is that key questions in relation to Australia's regulatory autonomy remain unanswered: in particular, there is very little attention paid to how Australia could realistically negotiate amendments to existing obligations. Finally, the broad definition forces the authors to say that regulatory autonomy is "not an absolute good" (pp. 39 and 244). There is an undeniable truth to that statement; if regulatory autonomy were an absolute good, states would not be willing to, nor should they, restrict it by signing up to international obligations. However, if regulatory autonomy is not an absolute good and thus only worthy of protection in some situations, we need criteria to identify when and why regulatory autonomy deserves protection and we need an authority to determine these criteria. The book does not provide either. To illustrate my point, the authors imply (p. 244) that a state should not use its regulatory autonomy to attract investment through lower environmental standards. But who decides what the appropriate level of environmental protection is, if not the state individually (subject to any other international obligations it may have)? Trade and investment agreements do not generally include minimum environmental standards.[6]

After the discussion of regulatory autonomy, Chapter 1 gives a historical overview of the BITs and PTAs included in the book. The agreements of the last three decades are grouped in three "generations", with the first generation spanning two of the three decades studied. With the exception of the 1983 *Australia-New Zealand Closer Economic Relations Trade Agreement*, which is

---

5   Ibid 52.
6   As the authors point out in Chapter 6, change may be afoot in the investment arena if lower environmental standards reduce the value of an investment. However, this is a recent development, and it raises the question whether an investment tribunal is a more legitimate authority than the state to decide on the minimum level of environmental protection, assuming that the state is complying with all its obligations under international environmental law.

the oldest agreement included in the study, all the first generation agreements are BITs that focused solely on investment and left trade issues to be solved multilaterally at the World Trade Organization ("WTO"). A second generation starts with the 2003 *Singapore-Australia Free Trade Agreement*, and runs until the 2009 Free Trade Agreement with New Zealand and the Association of Southeast Asian Nations. This generation is characterised by the shift from multilateral to bilateral or plurilateral PTAs that include "WTO-plus" obligations, i.e. liberalisation commitments that go beyond those agreed to within the WTO, as well as investment obligations that were traditionally dealt with in BITs. The authors point out that civil society concerns about these agreements "varied greatly", depending on the agreement (pp. 29–30). This changed from 2010 onwards, when there was a backlash against these agreements, particularly against the inclusion of ISDS mechanisms and compounded by concerns about treaty-making processes (pp. 32–4). Although Australia continued to sign onto PTAs, the third generation is characterised by an increased wariness that translated into "small but significant changes" in the wording of key provisions (p. 37). This historical overview and the tripartite generational division is interesting, but unfortunately does not feature much in the later chapters.

The next four chapters compare in detail the substantive obligations and their exceptions in four different areas: intellectual property ("IP"), trade in services, investment, and ISDS.

Chapter 2, on IP, is divided in three parts, dealing respectively with copyright, trademarks, and patents. The first part, on copyright, criticizes the extension of the minimum copyright term to 70 years; points out that, for fair use and parallel imports, Australian legislation is more restrictive than what the PTAs require; and adds that domestic law and PTAs are not clear about the legality of circumvention methods. These are not so much questions of regulatory autonomy as questions of the appropriate level of IP protection. What we see here is the impact of the broad definition of regulatory autonomy in Chapter 1 whereby any obligation accepted by a state becomes a limit on its regulatory autonomy. This impact is also visible in the discussion on patents, which reviews how the United States, through the conclusion of the *Australia-United States Free Trade Agreement* and the negotiations of the TPP, have pushed Australia towards more favourable protection of patent holders. In contrast, the debate surrounding Australia's plain packaging legislation, covered in the Chapter's part on trademarks, goes to the heart of regulatory autonomy. The central question in this debate is whether plain packaging, motivated by public health reasons, cuts against the copyright protection offered under trade and investment agreements and against the prohibition to indirectly expropriate investments.

Chapter 3 analyses Australia's commitments in trade in services. Here the book compares PTAs that include services on three different issues: the scope of the respective services chapters, the core obligations, and the general exceptions. A discussion of the agreements' chapters on specific services, such as financial services or telecommunications, is not included. In comparison to the IP chapter, this chapter focuses more on the question of regulatory autonomy but does not address in much depth the evolution of Australia's trade policy.

Attention then turns to investment in Chapter 4. Investment obligations are an important determinant of regulatory autonomy, particularly when services are supplied across the border through the commercial presence of a foreign provider. Such presence requires an investment, and any regulation of the service or its provider could therefore be open to challenge if it interferes with the investment. The investment chapter is structured similarly to Chapter 3, in that it first describes the substantive obligations before moving on to the exceptions. The authors label Australia's efforts to protect its policy space in relation to investment as haphazard: despite being aware of the need to reform overly expansive obligations, Australia has not undertaken a systematic effort to renegotiate international investment agreements ("IIAs"), an umbrella term that refers to BITs and PTAs with an investment chapter. The authors provide some suggestions for change and usefully illustrate their argument with examples from other jurisdictions (pp. 137–8, 161–2). They also critically reflect on proposals to transplant general exceptions from the trade model onto investment obligations. This discussion was illuminating, and adds a dimension that is missing in other chapters.

When discussing investment obligations in IIAs, ISDS is never far away, and it is the subject of Chapter 5. Australia made waves in 2010 when the Productivity Commission took an anti-ISDS stance.[7] However, a change of government has meant a change of heart, with the reintroduction of the previous ad hoc approach. As the authors point out, this approach is not without risks for Australia's regulatory autonomy as it leads to inconsistencies that investors can exploit by structuring their claims to fall within the scope of the most investor-friendly treaty. Although such an attempt failed in the case of Philip Morris' claim against Australia's plain packaging legislation,[8] this may not always be the case. Unlike the other chapters, this chapter explicitly tries to make

---

7   Productivity Commission, 'Bilateral and Regional Trade Agreements' (Research Report, November 2010) 265–77, 285.

8   *Philip Morris Asia Ltd v Australia (Award on Jurisdiction and Admissibility)* (Permanent Court of Arbitration, Case No 2012-12, 17 December 2015).

sense of the inconsistencies regarding the inclusion of ISDS (pp. 171–180) and concludes that ISDS has become a partisan issue as well as a bargaining chip in negotiations. The chapter also includes a discussion of reforms that have been included in PTAs with an investment chapter, and briefly discusses European Union proposals for a standing investment court. Once again the discussion fits better with the book's subtitle, in that its main focus is on the evolution of Australia's policies on ISDS rather than on regulatory autonomy per se.

The book then takes a different turn in Chapter 6 to consider how Australia's PTAs and BITs affect Australia's ability to regulate to protect the environment. This is of course where the impact of trade and investment obligations on regulatory autonomy has been most keenly felt, and this chapter thus provides a case study for the earlier chapters. Indeed, it would have made the earlier chapters more engaging if the example of the environment had been incorporated in those chapters. Chapter 6 sidesteps trade in goods, which the authors justify on the basis that the impact of environmental regulation on trade in goods is most likely to be raised at the WTO's established state-to-state dispute settlement system rather than under the investor-state arbitration mechanisms of PTAs and BITs. With the WTO being outside the scope of this study, the authors have chosen to discuss seven investor-state disputes that arose under the *North-American Free Trade Agreement* ("*NAFTA*") to gain insight about how Australia's PTA and BIT obligations might be interpreted in an environmental context. After a comparison of *NAFTA*'s key provisions with those from Australian PTAs and BITs, the chapter briefly describes the facts and findings in the seven *NAFTA* cases, before outlining lessons for Australia. The general takeaway of these cases, according to the authors, is that "arbitral tribunals are capable of distinguishing between legitimate environmental measures and breaches of investment obligations" (p. 226). Nevertheless, the authors also discuss how a broader use of exceptions could safeguard Australia's regulatory autonomy in relation to the environment. In its last part, the chapter points to a more recent evolution of deploying PTAs and BITs to improve domestic environmental standards through, first, the incorporation of minimum environmental protection standards and, second, the use of ISDS by investors claiming that insufficient environmental regulation reduced their investment's value.

The final chapter concludes that, while Australia has made some efforts to preserve its regulatory autonomy, it still has a way to go. The authors suggest that Australia should reduce inconsistency between agreements, pursue balanced and comprehensive negotiations, and resist further ratcheting up of IP protections (p. 246). The most useful recommendation is the "need to pay greater attention to more mundane matters', such as reviews of existing obligations (internally as well as with treaty partners), joint interpretations, and mutual terminations (p. 251). However, details are lacking. Far more time is spent on recommendations to improve Australia's treaty-making processes (pp. 252–6), but these lessons are the least transferable to other states.

The authors also suggest that more research should be done on the economic and legal impact of existing PTAs on regulatory autonomy. Given that the book set out to provide an "extended legal analysis of how Australia's current framework of PTAs and BITs affects Australia's regulatory autonomy" (p. 2), this was a surprisingly modest conclusion. In my view, the root of the problem is the initial decision to define regulatory autonomy broadly. A narrow definition would have enabled the authors to focus on the scope of the exceptions which is where states will have to do the hard work in justifying their regulation against claims made by investors or trading partners. However, with its detailed description of key provisions of Australia's BITs and PTAs, the book helpfully summarizes the extensive primary texts for legal researchers and those in other disciplines. Moreover, the book is written accessibly in that it does not assume prior knowledge of trade and investment law and its associated jargon. Future researchers will find the book's detailed analysis of the legal texts a useful springboard from which to explore the reasons for the inconsistencies between the different agreements, to evaluate which alternatives are economically superior, and to examine what Australia and similarly situated states could realistically do to protect their regulatory autonomy.

Call for Papers

The *New Zealand Yearbook of International Law* is an annual, international refereed publication.

The Editors call for both short notes and commentaries, and longer in-depth articles, for publication in the 2018 edition (Vol 16) of the *Yearbook*. Notes and commentaries should be between 3,000 to 7,000 words. Articles may be from 8,000 to 15,000 words.

The Editors seek contributions on all current topics in international law. The Editors particularly also encourage submissions that are relevant to the Pacific, the Southern Ocean and Antarctica, and New Zealand.

Submissions will be considered on a rolling basis. However, the closing date for submissions is 1 May 2019.

Submissions should be provided in English, using *MS Word*-compatible word processing software, and delivered by email to the General Editor at janjakob.bornheim@canterbury.ac.nz. Contributions must be original unpublished works and submission of contributions will be held to imply this. Manuscripts must be word-processed and in compliance with the *Australian Guide to Legal Citation*. The Guide is available online at: <http://law.unimelb.edu.au/mulr/aglc/about>.

LLM International Law & Politics

Located in Christchurch, the major city on the magnificent South Island of New Zealand, the School has a long and proud tradition of academic endeavour and boasts a number of dedicated teachers and researchers in the field of international law who have made it possible for the School of Law, together with the School of Language, Social and Political Sciences, to offer a specialist programme in international law and politics.

The Degree

The LLM is a partly taught and partly research-based degree aimed at students with a law background whose main interest is in developing their knowledge of international law, but who also have an interest in examining the political nature of the international order. The degree requires students to successfully

complete a dissertation on a topic of their own choice as well as four courses
from the list set out below. Two of the four courses must be Advanced Principles of Public International Law and Principles and Practice of International
Relations and Diplomacy.

The full list of international law and politics courses is set out below:
- Advanced Principles of Public International Law (*compulsory*)
- Principles and Practice of International Relations and Diplomacy
  (*compulsory*)
- International Criminal Law
- World Trade Law
- International Investment Law
- International Human Rights Law
- Antarctic Legal Studies
- International Environmental Law
- Law of the Sea
- European Union Law
- European Public Law

Not every course will be offered in any one year.

Enrolment Requirements and Start Dates

A candidate for the LLM (International Law and Politics) must, before enrolling
for the degree, *either* qualify for the Degree of Bachelor of Laws, *or* on the basis
of an equivalent qualification be admitted with academic equivalent standing
as entitled to enrol for the degree LLM (International Law and Politics). The
degree may be studied full-time for a year or part-time for two years or more.

For further information contact

Ms Margaret Ricketts
Academic Manager
School of Law
University of Canterbury
Private Bag 4800
Christchurch 8020
New Zealand

Email: margaret.ricketts@canterbury.ac.nz
Web: www.laws.canterbury.ac.nz
Phone: +64 3 369 3662